John Cummins was born in 1937. He has been a teacher of Spanish at the Universities of St Andrews and Birmingham, and he was head of the Department of Spanish at the University of Aberdeen until his retirement in 1995. John Cummins now devotes his time to writing and other interests, which include foreign travel, shooting, fishing, and the restoration and conversion of farm buildings. An expert in Spanish Renaissance manuscripts, his books include *The Spanish Traditional Lyric* (1977), *The Hound and the Hawk: The Art of Medieval Hunting* (1988) and *The Journal of Christopher Columbus* (1992). John Cummins lives in Angus, Scotland.

Also by John Cummins

The Spanish Traditional Lyric
The Hound and the Hawk: The Art of Medieval Hunting
(*editor*) The Journal of Christopher Columbus

FRANCIS DRAKE

The Lives of a Hero

JOHN CUMMINS

A PHOENIX GIANT PAPERBACK

First published in Great Britain by Weidenfeld & Nicolson in 1995
This paperback edition published in 1997 by Phoenix, a division of Orion Books Ltd,
Orion House, 5 Upper St Martin's Lane, London WC2H 9EA

A CIP catalogue record for this book is available
from the British Library

ISBN: 1 85799 881 2

Printed and bound in Great Britain by
Butler & Tanner Ltd, Frome and London

Sir Fraunces Drake, Knight, in commendacion of this Treatise

Who seekes by worthie deedes to gaine renowne for hire,
Whose hart, whose hand, whose purse is prest to pur-
chase his desire;
If anie such there bee that thirsteth after Fame,
Lo! heere a meane to winne himself an everlasting name.

Who seekes by gaine and wealth t'advaunce his house
and blood,
Whose care is great, whose toil no lesse, whose hope is
all for good;
If anie one there be that covets such a trade,
Lo! heere the plot for common wealth and private gain
is made.

He that for vertue's sake will venture farre and neere,
Whose zeal is strong, whose practice trueth, whose faith
is void of feere;
If anie such there bee, inflamed with holie care,
Heere may he finde a readie meane his purpose to declare.

So that for each degree, this Treatise dooth unfolde
The path to fame, the proofe of zeal and way to purchase
gold.

(This sonnet is the only poem attributable to Drake. It was
prefixed to Sir George Peckham's *True Report of the Late
Discoveries of Newfoundland by Sir Humphrey Gilbert*,
1583).

To Susan, Otto and Sarah

CONTENTS

ILLUSTRATIONS

MAPS

ACKNOWLEDGEMENTS

I wish to thank the librarians, of all levels, of the Queen Mother Library of the University of Aberdeen; the National Library of Scotland; the Plymouth City Library; the National Maritime Museum, Greenwich; and the Escuela de Estudios Hispano-Americanos, Seville. My particular thanks are due to the staff of the British Library for their continued good humour towards readers made tetchy by logistical delays, and to the librarians of the Archivo General de Indias, Seville, where computerised efficiency has not usurped the friendly human face.

I acknowledge with gratitude the contributions made towards the cost of my work by the Carnegie Trust for the Universities of Scotland and the Aberdeen University Research Committee. I am also grateful to my Head of Department, Professor Derek Harris, for his encouragement of my continuing research, and to my editor, Benjamin Buchan, for his many perceptive suggestions.

Professor Jorge Urrutia, his wife María Teresa Navarro, and their children Elsa and Sergio contributed enormously to both the pleasure and the productivity of my time in Spain.

Liz Weir, of the Modern Languages Secretariat of the University of Aberdeen, has again demonstrated her unique ability to create peace out of panic.

INTRODUCTION

The island of San Juan de Ulúa, in Mexico, is now a tourist attraction. In the middle of the sixteenth century its attractiveness was minimal except to mariners seeking a haven on a flat and desolate stretch of coast in waters notorious for their unpredictable weather, especially for winds of destructive force blowing down from Florida. The stretch of water between San Juan and the shore provided an anchorage protected against the north winds by the island, and against unlikely intruders by a small battery of cannon. A few miles from the mainland side of the harbour stood the town of Vera Cruz, named by its Catholic founders after the True Cross of Christ. The unprepossessing town and its port, each justifying the other's existence, were backed by a hinterland of wilderness. 'In my time,' wrote an English seafarer,

> many of the marriners and officers of the ships did die with those diseases there accustomed, and especially those that were not used to the Country, nor knew the danger thereof, but would commonly go in the sunne in the heat of the day, and did eat fruite of the Countrey with much disorder, and especially gave themselves to womens company at their first comming; whereupon they were cast into a burning ague, of the which fewe escaped.[1]

Vera Cruz and San Juan de Ulúa were at the end of Mexico City's main route of communication with the Gulf of Mexico, and were therefore an important staging post on one of Spain's most important links with her empire. The harbour was the point of entry for colonial administrators and colonists, and the place in which bullion and goods from New Spain were loaded onto King Philip's ships before their departure in convoy for Andalusia.

On the evening of 22 September 1568 this usually placid haven was a scene of maritime chaos after a day of ferocious and unpremeditated battle. The need for action had been a total surprise to the unwary crews of the Spanish treasure fleet, relieved by their proximity to port, fresh fruit and women's company after their passage from Spain. The Englishmen crewing the ships commanded by John Hawkins had had more reason to be wary, but they must have been almost equally

I

astonished by the day's savagery. They had put in without aggressive intentions to repair their flagship, the *Jesus of Lübeck*, which had been strained by the Caribbean storms.

After the smoking carnage of the day the *Jesus* had been seriously damaged by gunfire and had been abandoned by her crew after losing much of her rigging; other ships had been sunk or captured by the Spanish; vessels on both sides had been sacrificed as fireships, set ablaze by their own crews in an attempt to burn the opposing fleet; a major Spanish ship had been sunk in flames, and another blown apart by the explosion of her powder; and many Englishmen ashore and afloat had been killed. Of the English fleet only the *Minion* and the little 50-ton *Judith*, both overladen with men rescued from the *Jesus*, escaped to face the voyage home in the harsh seas of autumn and winter. To make matters worse, on the following day the wind came into the north and Hawkins, now in the *Minion*, found himself driven towards a lee shore. With only two anchors left, he was lucky to save his ship. The *Judith* sailed away from him, and was seen no more until the two reached England.

Spain and England were at peace at the time.

The voyage by Hawkins which received this bloody setback provides a typical sixteenth-century example of the discrepancy between national policy, stated or understood, and local actualities; of the conflict between obligations imposed by one's country's religion and the day-to-day opportunities of commerce. Neither Spain nor England was able to exert total control over the behaviour of her subjects in matters in which they found it advantageous to make up new rules on the spot. It was an era in which the distinctions between national commitment, doctrinal obligation and private interest were often helpfully vague. From the outset, with Columbus's first voyage, trans-atlantic exploration had been motivated by an ambiguous amalgam of missionary zeal and the pursuit of wealth, and it had been financed by a varying combination of royal and private investment. Spanish power in the Indies was administered by men who were prepared to purchase a job bearing a miserable stipend in order to exploit the opportunities it gave for illicit but hugely remunerative private activities.[2] The fostering of the Catholic faith was in the hands of priests who sometimes became landowners on a large scale, and friars who exploited Indian communities for their own gain.[3]

Dividing lines which it was helpful to blur at a local level were those between the willing sale of goods for money or by barter, the transfer of commodities under varying degrees of threat, and overt pillaging. These optional views of the truth enabled a single incident occurring far from the centres of government to be represented in widely diverging ways, depending on the nationality of the interpreters, their proximity to the events, and their interests and immediate purposes. What for one man was a pillaging raid on a defenceless Caribbean town in gross breach of international agreements could be presented by another as a successful stroke of brave entrepreneurship in which a half-joking allusion to military force had merely speeded the exchange of goods to the advantage of both parties. A Spanish colonial community tempted to trade illicitly with the subjects of a foreign power might welcome, and even suggest, an aggressive posture from the foreign party which would mitigate a profitable breach of the laws of trade in the eyes of King Philip II's agents.

There were seafaring men in England eager and equipped to take advantage of this situation; they found investors to back them, or backed themselves; they were subjects of a nation, and a monarch, willing to place a favourable interpretation on illegalities when it suited; and all these had available if necessary the justification of the defence and propagation of the true, reformed Christian faith and the weakening of its main enemy, the King of Spain. The master of this collusive armed trading was John Hawkins of Plymouth; this was exactly what he had been up to on the voyage which led him to San Juan de Ulúa. Later, when the relations between England and Spain deteriorated into tit-for-tat seizures of vessels and goods, and then into open warfare, Hawkins and men like him knew the winds and weather of the Caribbean; knew where its riches and strengths lay; had found its anchorages, noted its landmarks and sounded its bays.

The activities of Elizabeth's sailors in the ensuing wars were far from consistently successful, but legend and myth are selective. English jingoism and anti-Catholic fervour found richer food for memory in the sacking of Spain's colonial towns, the capture of treasure ships and the largely fortuitous disintegration of the Armada than in the loss of the *Jesus* and the ignominious flight of the *Judith* and the *Minion*. John Hawkins' overall record of success and his subsequent knighthood obliterated national awareness of the expensive fiasco of San Juan de Ulúa. Legend, with history not far behind, has been similarly generous to a kinsman of his who abandoned him that day: the captain of the battered and fleeing *Judith*, Francis Drake.

*

In the four hundred years since his death, and increasingly as time has passed, the overriding image of Drake in the English-speaking world has been of the swashbuckling pirate, the laconic bowls-player, the bearded epitome of the Elizabethan adventurer and sole victor of the Armada. In Hispanic tradition, too, the Drake who is remembered is not the man demoralised by the defeat at San Juan de Ulúa. Among the myths incorporated by Gabriel García Márquez in his novel *One Hundred Years of Solitude*[4] is a Colombian folk-memory of Drake. The fact that its detail has been invented by the novelist himself is neither here nor there; the novel is an explanation of great Latin-American truths in narrative clothing. It appears from García Márquez's story that when Francis Drake attacked Río de la Hacha one local lady was so startled by the rattle of drums and roaring of cannon that she sat down on a hot stove. The results were several, and severe: she was left with a limp which made her unwilling to appear in public, an inability to sit up straight, and a permanent aversion to sexual intercourse. Her social life was ruined by an obsessive conviction that she smelled of singeing. She abandoned sleep, fearful of the dreams in which Englishmen with ferocious dogs clambered in at her bedroom window to apply red-hot instruments of torture to her nether parts. Her husband, having spent a fortune on ineffective remedies for her, eventually sold his business and took her and their children to live far from the sea in a community of peaceful Indians, where he built her a windowless bedroom.

Centuries later, in García Márquez's indeterminate and fluctuating present, this Drakean terror is remembered. The poor victim's descendant, Ursula, incensed by her husband's own lunacies, ignores all the coincidences, meetings and marriages which brought them together, and simply curses Francis Drake for being the motive force which brought her ancestors to the village. The mythical Drake is a threat not only to military security but also to marital confidence.

The aim of my book is not only to recount the facts of Drake's rise from battered ignominy to success and wealth; I hope also to examine the nature of his fame and the processes of his diverging roles in myth and legend; a figure who not only singed the King of Spain's beard, but could also warm the anatomy and fire the dreams of decent Spanish colonial women and haunt their menfolk with a draconian terror.

I

A Man of Meane Calling
1542–58

'The people of quality dislike him for having risen
so high from such a lowly family; the
rest say he is the cause of the wars.'

Gonzalo González del Castillo,
letter to Philip II, 1592

Seventeenth-century accounts say that Drake was born near the small market town of Tavistock, in Devon, 'of mean parents'.[1] This does not imply grinding poverty, though he was certainly from much lowlier origins than many of the people with whom he was to rub shoulders in his life. Drake's paternal grandparents held a lease on the 180-acre farm of Crowndale from Tavistock Abbey. Their son, Edmund Drake, was allocated some land by his father, but it was Edmund's brother John who took over the lease. Edmund's parents had two sons called John, one born after the other had died, and it is not clear which of these became the leaseholder. The younger was still alive in 1587. There was another brother, Robert, whose son, young John Drake, was to have an exciting life, accompanying his cousin Francis on the circumnavigation and later being captured by the Spanish and tried by the Inquisition, after which he was to end his life in Spain as a Catholic. Edmund also had a sister Anne and one, possibly two, other sisters.[2]

Edmund married a daughter of a family called Mylwaye. Their son Francis was probably born in 1542, and they had at least four other sons: Edward, possibly older than Francis, since he died between 1548 and 1566; John, Joseph and Thomas, all younger. Some accounts suggest a total of twelve sons, some of whom died in infancy. The family had good connections; Drake's paternal grandmother was a member of the Hawkins family, who were prosperous Plymouth shipowners and merchants,[3] and Francis was christened after his godfather, Francis Rufford, who later became Earl of Bedford.

Tavistock is in the valley of the River Tavy, to the west of the great bleak uplands of Dartmoor, and Crowndale Farm lies a little way south of the town. In the sixteenth century, as it does today, the town looked to the thriving port of Plymouth, about fifteen miles to the south, as its link with the world beyond. Plymouth's prosperity derived mainly from its splendid location as a trading port and the fine natural haven of the Sound, but these advantages were reinforced by its agricultural hinterland, with which it was linked by the great navigable estuary of the Tamar and its tributary the Tavy. In the mid-sixteenth century Plymouth, clustered on the banks of Sutton Pool and far smaller than it is today, and still separated by open land from Stonehouse and the Hoe, already had a minor grandeur: fortifications on the seaward side, an impressive church, and large, commodious town houses in which its burgesses could live in some style.

The small triangle of England between Tavistock, Plymouth and Torbay produced, within two decades, a succession of men who were to be at the forefront of England's maritime glory in the second half of the century. In 1539 Katherine Gilbert, the wife of Otho Gilbert of Greenway in the valley of the River Dart, gave birth to a son, Humphrey, who was destined to be one of England's greatest seamen and explorers. Humphrey and his brothers had a childhood friend, John Davis, who lived at a farm called Sandridge not far away. Davis, too, became a famous sailor and writer of navigational treatises; he made voyages to the South Seas and in search of the North-West Passage, and the Davis Strait is named after him. Otho Gilbert died eight years after Humphrey's birth, and his widow then married a Walter Raleigh, who lived only a few miles to the east, near Exmouth. In 1552 she gave him a son, also Walter, who was to become the most romanticised of the great West Country seafarers. In 1560 the Plymouth shipowner John Hawkins, whose grandfather had moved to the port from Tavistock, had a son, Richard, who was also to become an ambitious explorer.

This group of South Devon men, some of them bound by ties of blood, were to occupy their lives and enrich their families in the maritime expansion and defence of England. Other West Country men played their part: William and Stephen Borough, of Northam in North Devon, and Raleigh's cousin, the Cornishman Richard Grenville. Of the celebrated English sailors of the period only Thomas Cavendish, from Suffolk, and the Yorkshireman Martin Frobisher were from outside the West Country. Their names were made famous by their extension of English sea-power, and they had much to do.

At the time when these men were born, England's role on the

world's oceans was limited; the great maritime powers were Portugal and Spain. By the end of the previous century the Portuguese had gradually explored the Atlantic coast of Africa until they revealed that it was a way to the Indian Ocean, across which lay the rich trading possibilities of the Far East, the silks and spices which had hitherto been carried to Europe overland. By 1550 the Portuguese were established as the unquestioned masters of this trade. Spain, spurred on by Portuguese achievement but barred by papal decree from exploration east of a line of longitude about 1300 miles west of the Cape Verde Islands, had been quick to exploit Columbus's discovery of the West Indies and the subsequent exploration of the American mainland. The gold artefacts pillaged by the conquistadors had been followed to Europe by shipments of gold and silver from the mines of Mexico and Peru, and native peoples previously engaged in largely communal agriculture or routine but glamorous religious warfare had been transformed into subject populations serving and enriching Spanish colonial entrepreneurs. Portugal, too, had a presence in South America; Spain had been disconcerted to find that the Pope's dividing line ran through what was to become the Portuguese colony of Brazil.

When Drake was growing up, despite the huge wealth flowing into Spain, much remained to be discovered and exploited in South America, and even more in the north of the continent. The Spanish presence in what is now Chile and Argentina was slender; cities such as Arica, Valparaiso and Santiago were little more than clusters of houses, and the native population was not uniformly subjugated. Places named on charts, such as Puerto San Julián between the River Plate and Cape Horn, were in fact unoccupied except by Indians. Magellan had discovered a channel from the Atlantic to the Pacific, but no-one knew that south of the strait named after him lay Cape Horn, and south of that an open ocean; the islands to the south of the strait were thought to be part of a vast antarctic continent.

England, France, and the other countries of northern Europe had been largely onlookers in the period of Iberian expansion. Excluded from the routes of the Spanish and Portuguese, early sixteenth-century English sailors had been comparatively unproductive in their explorations. Their voyages had been directed into northern waters, and had been more concerned with finding new sea routes to the rich markets of the Far East than with the establishment of colonies in the harsh, empty and unwelcoming lands which they found.

Portugal's empire and trade were admired and envied. England's attitude to Spanish power, however, combined envy with fear and distrust, for Spain was not only a great and growing colonial presence; she also had control of large areas of Europe beyond her own frontiers. The marriage of Ferdinand of Aragon to Isabella of Castile in 1469 did much more than simply reunite areas of Spain which had been separated for centuries. It provided the national strength to enable the final overthrow of the Moorish kingdom of Granada, in the aftermath of which Spanish crusading militarism was diverted into the Americas. Moreover, the descendants of the marriage were destined to be not only sovereigns of a united and Catholic Spain, but also the inheritors, through various lines, of large tracts of Europe and of the problems inherent in maintaining the loyalty of their foreign subjects.

Ferdinand brought to the alliance not only his inheritance of the Kingdom of Aragon, but also the Aragonese possessions of Sardinia and Sicily, and the conquest of Naples in 1504 entrenched Spain's presence in the Mediterranean. Ferdinand's diplomatic and military alliances with Venice, the Duke of Milan and the Emperor Maximilian were motivated largely by distrust of France, which also underlay the strategic marriages of his daughters: Joanna to Maximilian's son, the archduke Philip, in 1496; Catherine to Arthur, the eldest son of Henry VII of England, in 1501.

Joanna's son Charles, born in 1500, was to inherit a staggering collection of dominions. When he was only six his father died, leaving him the Low Countries and a claim to the Duchy of Burgundy. He was proclaimed ruler in the Netherlands in 1515, and within a year, on the death of Ferdinand, he was king of Castile, Aragon, Sardinia, Sicily, Naples and Spanish America. In 1519, when his grandfather Maximilian died, he inherited the Habsburg lands in Austria, Tyrol and Southern Germany, and was elected the Emperor Charles V of Germany.[4]

By the second decade of the sixteenth century, which is probably when Drake's father Edmund was born, western Christendom was in a ferment. The Catholic Church, whose medieval grip on the minds and conduct of men and women had been weakened by internal divisions and a generalised dislike of the clergy, was beset in the first half of the century by the rapidly growing challenge of Protestantism. From the preaching of a few pioneers inspired by the teachings of Martin Luther, the Reformation spread within a few decades to affect virtually every country in Western Europe.[5] The new faith's adherents rejected the authority of Church and Pope, the easy obedience to the mediating priests, and replaced them with an older authority: the Scriptures, examined and applied by thinking men.

Such a radical departure from acceptance and complacency led to extremism on both sides. It also brought war, martyrdoms, purges and fear, for the dominant precept of *cuius regio eius religio*, 'he who rules the kingdom decides the religion', could only lead to insecurity of both the ruler and the ruled in an era when dynastic intermarriage dislocated religious continuity at the highest level, the throne.

Only Spain held out virtually untouched by the reformed faith – the heresy, as it was seen from south of the Pyrenees. The Inquisition, set up earlier to examine the sincerity of converted Jews, was available as an instrument against any departure from the orthodox: Judaism; Islam; the survival of paganism in the Americas; or the Protestant heresy. But in the austere climates of Northern Europe, in Sweden, Denmark and Germany, the reformed religion thrived. In France, doctrinal thinking was polarised: the rigorous zeal of Calvinism developed in parallel with the intellectualism of the Society of Jesus. In the Low Countries, resentment of Spanish rule came to acquire a regional sectarian dimension which was to drain Spain of men and money.

In England special factors, some of which had little to do with faith, complicated the situation. One was the long delay in the fathering of a male heir by Henry VIII. In 1527, when his efforts had produced only a daughter, Mary, he decided to divorce the ageing Catherine of Aragon, whom he had married after the death of his brother Arthur had left her a widow. Rome, partly because of pressure from the Emperor Charles V, who was Catherine's nephew and saw the value of the Spanish dynastic presence in England, refused to annul the marriage. This set off a chain of events in which Henry assumed power as Supreme Head of the Church of England. In Henry's eyes this had nothing to do with Protestantism; nor, strictly, did his dissolution of the monasteries, the motives for which were political and financial rather than doctrinal.

The sudden and total rejection of the power of Rome, however, naturally produced emphatic objections from English Catholics which were rigorously suppressed by executions. The conflict took on a regional aspect: in 1536 an unsuccessful revolt in the North demanded the restoration of the monasteries. Hints that Henry, persuaded by Thomas Cromwell, might make concessions to the new faith ended in 1539, when Catholic orthodoxy was newly proclaimed in the Act of the Six Articles, and occasional burnings of Protestants suppressed objections to this brake on progress.

However, in the brief reign (1547–53) of the boy King Edward VI, Henry's son by Jane Seymour, progress came swiftly. Edward's councillors, led by the Duke of Somerset, repealed the Six Articles, Protestant Communion was permitted, and in 1549 a new Prayer Book with a much simplified set of services was produced. These moves were unacceptable to some, and 1549 was a year of unrest. Regional divisions again appeared: there was a rising in Norfolk and another in the West Country, especially Cornwall, where Catholic rebels complained specifically against the imposition of the new Prayer Book and the abandoning of Latin.

According to William Camden, who claims in his *Annales* that Drake himself gave him the details, Drake's father fled from this anti-Protestant turmoil in the West Country and took his family to Kent, where early tradition has it that they lived in a disused hulk on the River Medway. Edmund was evidently literate as well as religious, and 'got a place among the Saylors in the Kings fleet, to reade prayers unto them, and soone after was ordained Deacon, and made Vicar of the Church of Upnore upon the River Medway (where the fleet lyeth at anchor)'.

Some have suggested that Drake's father was not as lily-white as this tale of misery and merit suggests. One Edmund Drake, living in the parish of Tavistock in 1548, and described as a sheep-shearer, was accused of assault and the theft of a horse and money. His partner in the horse-thieving was a tailor, late of Tavistock, called John Hawkyng, possibly a member of the Hawkins family who were kinsmen of the Drakes.[6] This Edmund Drake apparently fled to escape punishment. He was very possibly the man who arrived in Kent with his family, relieved, repentant or both, explaining his sudden arrival with a tale of religious persecution. However, it would not be odd to find two Edmund Drakes in Tavistock at the same time, perhaps cousins, or uncle and nephew.

Another doubt concerns the church where Drake's father became vicar. An Edmund Drake was vicar, not of Upnor, but of Upchurch, south of the Medway estuary, from 1560 until his death soon after Christmas 1566, but this man's will makes no mention of a son Francis, or of John, or of Joseph. It refers, however, to a deceased son Edward, alongside whom Edmund wishes to be buried, and a son Thomas, who is left a feather bed, two pillows, various dishes and clothes, and two chests with all my books, which my son, I would he should make of them above all other goods ... and keep in bosom and feed upon; make much of the Bible that I do here send thee with all the rest of the goodly books.[7]

Since no mention is made in the will of Edmund's wife, she must have died before him.

Whatever the trimmings of the story, we can accept at least the bare bones of the version dating from soon after Drake's death: the young Francis, born near Tavistock, was taken to Kent and brought up near, or even on, the Medway as the son of a fervent hater of Catholics; his father obtained a post connected with the Navy, and subsequently an established charge as a vicar. Whether or not he was a fugitive from justice, Edmund Drake's influence shines through many of his son's later utterances, and especially through his letters, filled with rounded clichés and scriptural echoes imbibed from his father's sermons and prayers. If language and style are anything to go by, parental influence on Francis Drake was definitely that of a preacher rather than of a sheep-shearing horse-thief.

The religious struggle in England was far from over when Edmund Drake found refuge in Kent. The early death of Edward VI brought his half-sister Mary Tudor to the throne, and her devoted Catholicism, repeals of Edward's legislation and zealous burnings of Protestants confirmed the widespread view of Catholicism as a religion of vengeful persecution. Mary's marriage in 1554 to Philip, the heir to Charles V, increased the threat to English Protestantism. Spain was identified as the figurehead of the Catholic Church; the Black Legend of Spanish religious cruelty was widespread in Europe; and the natural consequence of the marriage appeared to be the incorporation of England in the Habsburg empire, control of which was ceded to Philip by Charles in 1556. Charles had lost Germany in 1552, and when his son became King Philip II in 1558 the pillars of his European empire were Spain and the Low Countries.

The people of Plymouth were sometimes made aware of these dynastic affairs more tangibly than most of the country. Catherine of Aragon had landed at Plymouth on her way to her marriage to Arthur, and had given thanks in St Andrew's church after a stormy passage. After her second marriage, to Henry, Plymouth was the assembly point for the force sent to Cadiz to help Spain combat the African Moors. After Henry's marriage to Anne Boleyn a group of Plymouth priests were imprisoned in Launceston Castle for their opposition to the match. Some of the overtures preceding Mary's marriage to Philip were conducted by Spanish noblemen who landed, and were generously entertained, at Plymouth, and Philip himself was to land at the port when he came to visit Mary in 1557.[8]

Meanwhile Drake and his brothers, in their formative years, were living in an atmosphere of domestic prayer and parental resentment of Catholicism. Outside their home they enjoyed the amphibious existence of boys living beside a great estuary, their visual horizons punctuated by the topmasts of the fleet and their mental ones expanded by sailors' tales of far-off places. Drake's early fun must have been on and in the water, and tides, shallows and winds became integral to his instincts. A sixteenth-century Spanish idea that he was employed as a page by the Spanish ambassador in London, with whom he also spent time in Spain, is completely without foundation. He was only a youth when he went to sea on a little cargo bark trading from the Medway across the Channel to France and the Low Countries.

II

The Seafarer's Craft
1558–67

If pylots painfull toyle be lifted then alofte,
For using of his Arte according to his kinde:
What fame is due to them that first this Arte outsought,
And first instructions gave to them that were but blinde!

Robert Norman, *In Commendation of
the painfull Sea-man*, 1587[1]

The kind of small-scale international navigation involved in Drake's
early trading had required little evolution beyond the ancient requirements of coastwise sailing, and its crafts had been passed on not by
theorists and treatises but from father to son or master to apprentice.
It required a vessel not only to enter recognised harbours, but also to
probe tidal estuaries and creeks and even to load and unload cargoes
after being deliberately stranded on a suitable open shore. A ship's
master in the narrow seas needed, constantly, an almost instinctive
awareness of factors which his counterpart in a big transatlantic
trading ship could forget about for long periods: shifting sandbanks;
local currents; changing clouds and tides; fair and foul anchorages;
not only the direction of the wind at breakfast time but also what it
was likely to be doing in the afternoon. If he had charts, they were
crude, and few. The demands and the scale of the trade were still
those which had faced Chaucer's shipman:

> ... of his craft, to reckon well his tides,
> His streams and his dangers him besides,
> His harbour and his moon, his lode-menage,
> There was none such from Hull to Carthage. ...
> He knew well all the havens, as they were,
> From Gotland to the Cape of Finisterre.

Drake's early mastery of these coastwise skills was an ideal preparation for his future activities among the coves, estuaries and islands
of the Spanish Main.

On the higher and broader planes of ocean navigation and cartography, sixteenth-century England had much to learn from Spain and Portugal. The great early treatises on navigation were written by Spaniards and Portuguese, maintaining a tradition of astronomical science which dated back beyond the Middle Ages into Islamic Andalusia and supplementing it with the experience gained in long ocean voyages across the Atlantic, Pacific and Indian Oceans. Early in the fifteenth century it was the Portuguese monarchy which had led the way. Prince Henry the Navigator had brought together and systematised astronomical knowledge, establishing an observatory at Sagres on Cape St Vincent to obtain accurate tables on the declination of the sun. Later in the century King John II's committee on navigation continued Henry's work, compiling more astronomical observations and making minor improvements in instruments. The *Regimento do astrolabio e do quadrante* of 1509 reflects some of the committee's work. The influence of Pero Nunes' two *Tratados* on astronomy, charts and navigation of 1537 was considerable.

In Spain the Council of the Indies prescribed courses in navigation for pilots, including the study of ancient works of cosmography, the use of instruments, cartography and the observation of the heavenly bodies. The *Arte del marear* by a Portuguese, Ruy Faleiro, published in Spain in 1534, was followed by Pedro de Medina's famous *Arte de navegar* (1545) and Martín de Cortés' work of the same title (1556). These were works of immense value in spreading the knowledge of the Iberian experts among practical seafarers. Medina was soon translated into French and Italian, and rather later (1581) into English. Richard Eden's English version of Cortés was published in 1561, and was followed by several later editions. Spanish treatises incorporating new knowledge continued to appear until the end of the sixteenth century, by which time a few original works in English had been published, reflecting the growing English participation in the exploration of the world. The best-known of these was William Bourne's *A Regiment for the Sea* (1574), a practical, down-to-earth work for the seaman.[2]

In chart-making, too, the Iberian Peninsula was pre-eminent. Lisbon had already been a centre of commercial map-making in the fifteenth century; in the sixteenth, international voyaging and the exploitation of new areas of the globe made increasing demands on the cartographers, and Diogo Homem and others were producing charts and atlases of breathtaking quality and beauty, as well as more workaday examples. These included not only charts of oceans and seas, but volumes of detailed plans of colonial harbours, with profile drawings of the coast as it appeared from the sea and indications of leading-marks. Such things were invaluable to any real or potential enemy; in capturing Spanish vessels during the circumnavigation Drake was sometimes as interested in finding charts and knowledgeable pilots as in treasure. Captured Spanish charts and atlases of harbours had high commercial value, and English chart-makers, far from being ashamed of copying them, openly proclaimed the source of their pirated versions as an indication of their reliability. When Drake presented a map showing his discoveries of the islands south of the Magellan Strait to a group considering another voyage, he was to be accused of passing off a Spanish map as his own work, since its detail was so great that it could only have been produced by a Spaniard.

Despite the sixteenth-century advances in astronomical observation and chart-making, startling innovation in the design of navigational instruments was slow to follow. A navigator needed to know where he was, how fast he was travelling, and in which direction. In Drake's time the only way of knowing one's position was by calculating one's movement from a previously known point. A sailor knew his location when he left harbour; once out of sight of land he was dependent on a series of linked calculations. To find his latitude, his distance from the equator, he had a range of instruments with which to read the altitude of the sun or the Pole Star. If it was cloudy, there was nothing he could do about it. One device, antiquated by the sixteenth century, was the quadrant, a simple quarter-circle of wood or brass with a pair of sights along one of the straight edges and a weighted string attached to the right-angle. One had to line up the sights on the sun or star (no easy task on a swaying deck), pinch the plumb-line against the curved edge, and read off the altitude from a scale marked along the arc. The simplest quadrants avoided the need for calculations by having their scale marked with readings for the latitude of the main ports involved in a particular trade; once a reading coincided with that for his destination a master only had to run due east or west, maintaining the same reading.

Another ancient device was the astrolabe, a heavy circle of brass with a rotating arm at its centre bearing two plates with a hole in each. The instrument was hung vertically, the arm was moved until a beam of the sun shone through both holes, and a pointer on the arm indicated a reading on the circle. Both these instruments were used by Columbus on his first great voyage. He was not very reliable with either.

In the sixteenth century these devices were largely supplanted by the cross-staff. This was a square-sectioned rod which was pointed towards the sun or star. It had a set of sliding cross-pieces, one of which was moved along the staff until its two ends coincided with the heavenly body and the horizon, when its position on a scale on the side of the staff gave the altitude. A calculation based on the altitude of a known heavenly body, normally the sun or the Pole Star, gave a sailor his distance from the equator; by the sixteenth century he had books of tables to make the sums easier.

Establishing one's latitude was, at least in theory, scientific. Longitude was a different matter, and was still done by reckoning distance travelled in a known time at an estimated speed. The sailor's clock was the sand-glass, which usually ran out after half an hour and was then turned by a ship's boy. It might be inaccurate, or the boy might be dozing; exact timing was impossible. So was the calculation of speed, for which there was no instrument. A piece of wood might be thrown from the bows and timed as the ship passed it, but experienced seamen often relied on 'feel' to assess their speed. The first work to mention a log-line, with which speed was measured by the amount of line unrolled from a reel by a piece of wood trailed from the stern, was Bourne's *Regiment* of 1574. Direction was more reliable; every ship had a compass by now, though the complications of magnetic variation were still beyond the average mariner.

Between noon one day and noon the next a ship might alter course several times, and run at varying speeds. To cut out the tedious calculations involved, a ship's navigator might have a traverse board. This had thirty-two radial lines of holes indicating the points of the compass; pegs were inserted at regular intervals indicating the time steered along different bearings, and the result was a compounded bearing relative to that twenty-four hours earlier. The new point was marked on the chart using dividers, and the process began again. The danger of cumulative error is obvious, especially in waters where unperceived currents might be slowing or speeding the ship, or moving her sideways.

Calculating longitude, then, was an inexact art. Any master who thought he might be coming anywhere near his landfall after a trans-atlantic passage made sure his forward lookout and his man in the main-top stayed wide awake. In poorly charted waters (which included most coastal waters) the lead-line was an essential tool; it was a rope marked off in fathoms with a lead weight on the end. A skilled seaman swung the line so as to drop the lead slightly ahead of the ship, and read the depth as the weight touched bottom with the line vertical. An idea of the nature of the bottom could be got from the sand or pebbles adhering to tallow in the hollow end of the lead. The use of the lead-line was one of the most basic and essential skills learned by Drake in the Channel trade from his first master, and it was to be one of the most useful in his later activities along the Spanish Main, where small-boat sailing was to be the foundation of his success. His mastery of these coastal skills did not lead him to neglect printed material if it was available; the French book on navigation which he was to take around the world with him was probably an early French edition of Medina's famous *Arte de navegar*.

The owner-master of the bark on which Drake learned his trade was an old man with no heirs. Drake not only became a handy practical seaman; he also got on with his master, and served him well. When the old man died Drake was left the little bark; his own command, in international trade, around the age of twenty.

Having been uprooted in his boyhood by religious conflict, Drake must have been made continually aware of the increasing divisions between Catholic and Protestant by his trading visits to France and, especially, the Low Countries. He may even have made passages to Spain, where there were communities of English merchants who maintained trading links with England despite the religious tensions and their constant awareness of the Inquisition's suspicion of their possible Protestantism. Spain's identification of England with Lutheran heresy was consolidated when Mary Tudor died without an heir in 1558, and was succeeded by her half-sister Elizabeth, whose skilful use of ambivalence never fully concealed her favourable attitude to Protestantism.

How far west in the Channel and south into Biscay Drake took his bark we do not know, but he maintained his parental links with the Hawkins family and with Plymouth. By the early 1560s the Hawkinses had a considerable fleet of merchant vessels, and John Hawkins was well-known in London and was making voyages to Africa and the West Indies. The main commodity involved in these enterprises was African slaves.

By this time, only seventy years after Columbus sighted the islands of the Caribbean, the native populations of some areas of Spain's American possessions had been so reduced by disease, overwork and the forced separation of families that much of the labour force of the colonies' estates and mines was being shipped from Africa. Broadly, the pattern of Hawkins' voyages in the early 1560s was to acquire slaves from Portuguese Guinea, 'partly by the sword and partly by other means', cross the Atlantic, and sell them to the Spanish in the ports of the Caribbean. This involved collusive bartering with local Spanish functionaries in what was an illegal interference in a Spanish monopoly. In Guinea Hawkins acquired his stock-in-trade by whatever means were easiest and cheapest, which often meant simply raiding the coast and rounding up the inhabitants, but at the Caribbean end of the operation he behaved as if he were involved in normal legitimate trading. He acquired documentation of authorisations given him by local officials; he paid Spanish customs dues on his human cargoes; and he even asked for testimonials of his fair dealing.

Without the pragmatic Hawkins, with whose life his own was to be closely, though not always harmoniously, entwined until their deaths, Drake's name would probably never have come to the world's notice. In 1563, having sold his little vessel, Drake went on a Hawkins ship on a voyage to the Guinea coast, and three years after that he sailed out of Plymouth on one of the four ships of an expedition mounted by Hawkins and commanded by John Lovell. Their destination was the West Indies. Off the Cape Verde Islands they captured five Portuguese ships, sent some of the cargo home to England, retained the slaves they found aboard, and made for the Indies. Lovell's negotiating skills were not as good as Hawkins', and he failed to get payment for some of the slaves he put ashore.[3] When he and Drake returned to England, they found a more ambitious venture brewing, with John Hawkins at its centre and Queen Elizabeth herself involved.

III

The Unfortunate Voyage: San Juan de Ulúa 1567–69

'If all the miseries and troublesome affairs of
this sorrowfull voyage should be perfectly and
throughly written, there should neede a
paynfull man with his penne, and as great a
time as hee had that wrote the lives and deathes
of the martirs.'

John Hawkins, *The Third Troublesome Voyage*[1]

Hawkins' star was high as his fleet of six ships weighed anchor in Plymouth on 2 October 1567. A man of his experience probably had some misgivings about the condition of his flagship: the *Jesus of Lübeck*, lent to him by the Queen, was an old vessel, bought from the Hanseatic League by Henry VIII in 1544, but for Hawkins' immediate purposes her large size, at least, was an asset. Though he carried other trade goods, the intention was again to fill his fleet with human cargo on the Guinea coast and sell it in the West Indies. The spacious hold of the old *Jesus*, therefore, would be useful. She was accompanied by the *Minion* (also the Queen's, and also elderly), the *William and John*, the *Judith*, the *Angel* and the *Swallow*. On one or more of the ships fifty bemused and fearful negroes, transhipped in England from an unknown source, resigned themselves to seasickness and squalor.

Hawkins' voyage illustrates well the lack of a clear distinction between ships in the Tudor navy and merchant vessels. Ships built for the monarchy commonly formed part of a fleet organised by a private individual for profit; it was better than letting them lie idle, and it was a way of purchasing shares for the monarch in the proceeds of the voyage. In times of war the reverse happened: merchant ships were commandeered by the Crown, or willingly contributed by their owners, for war, which hindered trade, could replace it as a source of private profit. The distinction between war and peace, even, was blurred. Hawkins was sailing in peacetime, but the *Jesus* carried enough weaponry for any military contingency: twenty-six brass and iron guns, up to culverin size, and another thirty-odd smaller items of ordnance.[2] A culverin was about twelve feet long, and fired an iron shot of seventeen or eighteen pounds. All the other vessels carried some ordnance.

The *Jesus* was quite a large ship for her times, but would have been dwarfed (except in the height of her masts) by a modern warship. An idea of her size can be got from the 600-ton *Mary Rose*, which sank in 1545 and was recently raised; the *Jesus* was a 700-ton ship. The *Minion* was only 300, the *Judith* about 50. The *Jesus*'s heaviest guns were on her lower deck; she had another deck above that with some of her lighter armament, and her already considerable height-to-length ratio was increased by high fore- and sterncastles.

Her sail-plan showed only minor advances from that of late fifteenth-century ships. On her mainmast she set a large square mainsail, and a topsail above it; her foremast also carried two square sails; from her sterncastle rose a mizzenmast with a large, triangular lateen-sail, and being a large ship she carried another mast further aft, also with a triangular lateen-sail. Below her bowsprit was a square spritsail. The *Minion*, being smaller, probably had only three masts, and possibly did without the fore-topsail. The *Angel* and the *Swallow* were later categorised by the Spanish as a *patache* (usually a square-rigged vessel of 80–150 tons) and a *carabela* (similar in size but light and manoeuvrable, with either a fore-and-aft or a square rig).

Off Cape Finisterre a four-day storm scattered the ships, destroying boats and causing such concern about the seaworthiness of the *Jesus* that Hawkins turned for home, but fair weather changed his mind. After watering in the Canaries the fleet fell in with a French ship under a Captain Bland, from La Rochelle, who joined the enterprise. A couple of Portuguese caravels were captured; one was retained, and Francis Drake, who had been no more than a junior officer, at best, when the fleet sailed, was put into her as captain.

On the African coast Hawkins' men began gathering their slaves. They met fierce resistance: many men, including Hawkins, were wounded by poisoned arrows; some men died, and few captives were taken. Hawkins' account does not say how many slaves he hoped to load, but he was very disappointed when, after hunting along the coast as far as Sierra Leone, he had taken only a hundred and fifty by 12 January 1568. The fleet had separated for a while, the *Angel*,

Judith and four pinnaces (smaller vessels, usually with both sails and oars) probing the rivers, and Hawkins sailing ahead with the rest. After they had reassembled Hawkins was invited by a local king to provide men to help him in a civil war, with a promise that any prisoners taken would be handed over to the English. After an initial siege of a town of about 8,000 inhabitants had failed, Hawkins himself led reinforcements, the town fell, and the English found themselves with about 250 prisoners, some of them women and children. Hawkins expected also to have the pick of the king's captives, but the victorious native army decamped in the night, taking the prisoners with them (probably with the intention of bartering them with visiting entrepreneurs). With something over 400 negroes, Hawkins thought it worthwhile to make for the Indies, and after a harder passage than usual (fifty-five days), he made his landfall at Dominica.

It was probably during the Atlantic passage that Drake was made captain of the *Judith*. Job Hortop's account[3] mentions the death during the crossing of a Captain Dudley, who had been injured by a poisoned arrow at Cape Verde. Hortop does not state that Dudley was captain of the *Judith*, but it may well be that his death prompted the transfer of Drake from the captured caravel. Hawkins, with his earlier experience of the connivance of the Spanish colonists and the complicity of local officials in illicit trade, was able once again to coast along in April and May, enjoying 'reasonable trade and traffike, and curteous entertainement in sundry places' on islands such as Margarita and Curaçao, where the inhabitants were away from the beadier eye of Philip's major colonial administrators and were only too pleased to replenish their labour stocks.

At the mainland ports, however, there were problems. In 1565 Hawkins had done a lucrative trade at the port of Borburata, thanks to the laxity, and possibly the corruption, of the Governor of Venezuela, Alonso Bernáldez.[4] Bernáldez had now been replaced by Diego Ponce de León, whose outward attitude was sterner, but who was away on a tour of inspection when Hawkins arrived. The English did a healthy trade while waiting for the governor's reply to a letter from Hawkins which mingled polite requests with overt allusions to force. Even after the governor's official refusal the trade continued; Ponce de León, after all, had the prosperity of his citizens to consider, not to mention his own.

Hawkins' next target was Río de la Hacha, a well-fortified centre of the pearl trade. Here, with the connivance of the treasurer, Miguel

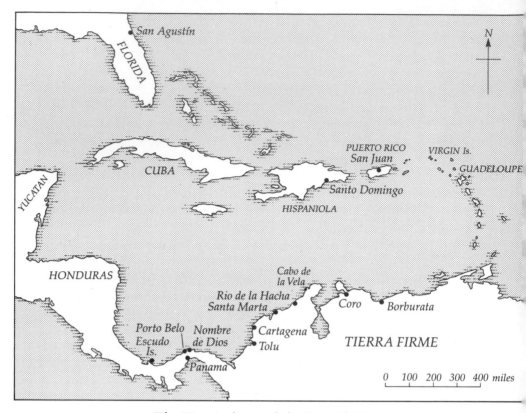

The West Indies and the Spanish Main

de Castellanos, and the town council, he had done lucrative business in 1565. The deal struck then had been on the basis that if Hawkins agreed not to misbehave, but at the same time threatened sufficient misbehaviour to provide the citizens with the excuse of having no alternative, they would grant him a licence to trade.[5] Here too, however, the replacement of the governor had led to a stiffer attitude. In 1567 Lovell's attempt to trade had been so unsuccessful that he had been forced to land ninety-six of his negroes to save water and provisions. Encouraged by this reward for standing fast, Río de la Hacha now took a similar stance against Hawkins.

It is now that we see Francis Drake entrusted with independent command. Hawkins sent him ahead with the *Judith* and *Angel* to sound out Río de la Hacha, which Drake of course knew from his voyage with Lovell. When Drake asked the town for permission to fill his water-casks as a seemly way of opening negotiations, the response was cannon-fire. Drake was happy to return it, targeting the house of the treasurer Castellanos, but shortly anchored out of range of the battery and waited for Hawkins. During his wait he chased a caravel coming from Santo Domingo with despatches, and in spite of musket-fire from a company of Spaniards ashore captured her and re-anchored.

When Hawkins arrived he used his previous ploy of a request to trade backed up by a pointed allusion to armed force. When Castellanos replied in the terms of Philip's prohibition Hawkins saw it as an attempt to force him to dump his negroes ashore for lack of water, like Lovell. His response was to lead 200 men ashore and storm the town, after which 'partly by the Spanyards desire of Negroes, and partly by friendship of the Treasorer, we obtained a secrete trade; whereupon the Spanyards resorted to us by night and bought of us to the number of 200 Negroes'. It was not quite as straightforward as this; according to Castellanos's report to the Crown (which naturally makes no mention of friendship), he gave in only after a stern resistance in which thirty Englishmen were killed (Hawkins reported two deaths), and after the English had burned two-thirds of the town and threatened to kill their prisoners.[6]

Before Hawkins left he put ashore over seventy negroes. A Spanish report says that he left them as recompense for destroying the town, but they were all aged, weak or children, and he probably saw them as an unsaleable burden on the fleet's provisions.[7] In the same report we can see the demoralised state of mind of the mainland authorities, who saw the survival of their whole society threatened by the increasing frequency and insolence of the French and English 'traders':

> We entreat Your Majesty to remedy the grievous conditions prevailing today ... For every two ships that come hither from Spain, twenty corsairs appear ... Unless Your Majesty deign to favour all this coast by remedying the situation, all these settlements must necessarily be abandoned, from which will result grave detriment to Your Majesty's royal patrimony.[8]

It was a plea which Philip was to read again and again in letters from the Indies in the 1570s.

Hawkins' final trading was done at Santa Marta, where the now institutionalised co-operation took the form of a request from the townspeople that he should land a hundred men, fire a token shot, and set fire to an old house.[9] After providing them with this defence against official reprisals and selling them some slaves, Hawkins proceeded to Cartagena, where a written request for permission to sell slaves met with a flat refusal and a demand that he should leave. After further written exchanges Hawkins' patience wore thin; he moved to an anchorage closer to the town and began to encourage it with cannon-fire. A spirited response from the town's batteries brought him down to a more pacific request for provisions of meat, flour and water, but again the response was stony, 'the Governor was so straight'.[10] Hawkins wasted ten or twelve days off Cartagena, and having very few slaves left he decided that his profits were adequate and that it would be as well to make for home before the start of the hurricane season. He weighed anchor from Cartagena on 24 July 1568.

Only now, with the enterprise made, did the aged *Jesus* fail him. On 12 August the fleet was off western Cuba, heading for the Florida coast and the Atlantic westerlies. Hawkins himself tells the tale:

> ... there happened to us ... an extreme storm which continued by the space of 4 daies, which so beat the *Jesus*, that we cut downe all her higher buildings, her rudder also was sore shaken, and withal was in so extreme a leake that we were rather upon the point to leave her than to keepe her any longer; yet hoping to bring all to good passe sought the coast of Florida, where we found no place nor haven; ... thus being in greater dispaire, and taken with a new storme which continued other 3 dayes, we were inforced to take for our succor the port called Saint John de Ullua.[11]

After a month of wrack and misery, with rigging in disarray and the crews weary from pumping ship, they arrived off San Juan; all but the *William and John*, which had lost contact in the storms. She struggled northward and made her lonely way back to England. Off the Mexican coast Hawkins had taken three Spanish ships with a view to using their hundred or so occupants as hostages to ensure a civil reception. On 15 September he not only sailed unmolested into San Juan harbour, joining a dozen Spanish vessels anchored there, but even received a salute from the harbour guns. He had, however, put his head into a noose, and the events which followed were to colour his and Drake's attitudes towards the Spanish for the rest of their lives.

The reason for their easy entry into the harbour was that the port was expecting the arrival of the annual fleet from Spain, and had simply assumed that Hawkins' ships, their numbers augmented by the prize vessels, were Spanish. The consternation of the welcoming party of local officials who came aboard the *Jesus* can be imagined, but Hawkins went to some lengths to reassure them, freeing most of his prisoners, promising to leave the local vessels alone, and asking only to be allowed to repair his ships.

On the following morning it was Hawkins' turn to feel consternation when, one by one, the topsails of the Spanish fleet came over the horizon. The locals sent out a boat to meet the fleet several miles off shore with the news of the English presence. In the emergency Philip's new viceroy, Don Martín Enríquez, on his way to take up his post, took over command of the fleet and the situation. He hove to and called a council. They were lying off a lee shore, and if the north wind strengthened they would be in trouble. When the port captain, Antonio Delgadillo, passed on a message from Hawkins in pacific terms, suggesting a truce and an exchange of twelve men of standing as hostages, Enríquez accepted in the well-buttered phrasing of Spanish diplomacy and a trumpet was blown to indicate a bargain sealed.[12]

After some rather comical self-effacement by potential Spanish hostages, during which Vice-Admiral Juan de Ubilla gave the brave opinion 'that at such junctures it was advisable to give persons of secondary importance as hostages, to do so being for the good of God's and His Majesty's service and for the common welfare', a mixed and reluctant group of minor officers and common sailors and soldiers dressed in gentlemen's clothing was assembled. After a delay of a few days due to unhelpful winds the Spanish fleet entered harbour on Tuesday, 21 September 1568.

In the meantime, Hawkins had been arranging some insurance. The harbour was little more than the area between the mainland and the island of San Juan. The ships were moored with their bow cables on the inner shore of the island for protection from the north wind, and on this shore was a battery of five guns. Hawkins immediately saw the importance of the control of the island to his safety, 'or els the Spaniardes might at their pleasure have but cut our cables, and so with the first Northwinde that blewe we had had our pasport, for our shippes had gone a shore'.[13] He therefore made it one of his conditions that the English should occupy the island, and pre-empted Spanish arguments by landing fifty men and expelling the few occupants who had not fled in panic, mostly negroes kept there for maintenance work. He then landed seven cannon to augment the existing battery.

There was complete distrust on both sides. Hawkins wrote of

his difficulties in coming to a decision, in his knowledge of 'their accustomed treason, which they never faile to execute where they may have oportunitie, ... which by good policy I hoped might be prevented'. Another account, by Miles Phillips, also mentions 'their treasons which we were wel assured they would practise'.

The Spanish were indeed plotting treachery. The viceroy's letter to Hawkins had ended, 'I am confident that, when we meet, friendship between the two fleets will grow, since both are so well-disciplined'. All the accounts of Enríquez's duplicity given by prominent Spaniards who shared in it make it clear that he had no intention of keeping his word, and none expresses dissension, compunction or regret. One says that the pact was 'a just and honest arrangement ... pending such time as they should arrive within the port', and gives 'the good of His Majesty's service' as the excuse for breaking it. The viceroy's own argument was that no arrangement made with a corsair was binding.

Enríquez's plan was that in mid-morning on Thursday 23 a large cargo vessel, presently lying empty close to the English ships, should be quietly filled with men by General Francisco de Luján and Vice-Admiral Ubilla. When they were ready Luján was to make a signal to Enríquez, who would have a trumpet blown on the flagship as a signal to board, and at the same time two storming parties would raid the island, one from either end. The other vessels of the fleet would then send boatloads of reinforcements to the several points of attack.

On the Thursday morning the crew of the *Minion*, which was moored closest to the empty Spanish ship, grew suspicious at the movements of men and weapons. Hawkins was warned, and sent the master of the *Jesus*, Robert Barrett, a Spanish speaker, to ask what was afoot. When Enríquez sent back an emollient reply, 'that he in the faith of a vice Roy would be our defence against all villanies', Hawkins sent Barrett back again to ask why so many men were now in the cargo ship. The viceroy, seeing that surprise was now impossible, put Barrett in irons and threw him below hatches.

Soon afterwards the signal was made to Enríquez (too soon, and by Ubilla, not Luján, which caused enquiries later), the viceroy had the trumpet blown, and the assault began. The *Minion* was stormed from the cargo ship, but under the inspired leadership of Hawkins, who cried 'God and St George upon these traiterous villaines, and rescue the *Minion*, I trust in God the day shal be ours!', the crew of the *Jesus* leaped over into the smaller ship and drove out the Spanish.

Woodcut from an anonymous ballad, The Praise of Sailors

The *Minion*'s guns were brought into play, and a lucky shot hit the magazine of one of the larger Spanish ships and blew her up. Under fire from the Spanish vessel next to her, the *Minion* cut her bow cables and hauled herself away from the shore by her stern moorings, thereby laying the *Jesus* open to the same fire. Hawkins, too, ordered the bow moorings cut, and tried to follow the *Minion*'s example. She was now surrounded by boat parties and under fire from two Spanish ships, and only repelled the boarders with heavy losses. 'Now,' wrote Hawkins, 'when the *Jesus* and the *Minion* weare gotten abroad two shippes length from the Spanish fleete, the fight beganne hott of all sides.'

The English were apparently holding their own on the water; within an hour at least one other large Spanish ship was sinking and another ablaze. The turning point came when the English ships came under heavy fire from the island, where the Spanish landing-parties had met little resistance. All the Englishmen ashore were killed except three,

27

who escaped by swimming to the *Jesus*. From the recaptured battery the Spanish now turned Hawkins' own guns against him, 'which did us so great annoyance, that it cutt all the Mastes and yardes of the *Jesus*, in such sort that there was no hope to carry her away'. She had five cannonballs through her mainmast, her foremast had been cut down by chain-shot, and innumerable shots had gone through her hull. Hawkins, exhorting his gunners to stick to their work, called to his page, Samuel, for a tankard of beer. He emptied it, set it down by the mainmast, and saw it carried away by a shot from a culverin. 'Nothing dismaied ... he ceased not to encourage us', wrote Job Hortop the gunner, 'saying, feare nothing, for God, who hath preserved me from this shot, will also deliver us from these traitours and villaines.'[14]

The Frenchman, Bland, tried to manoeuvre alongside the Spanish ship furthest upwind, meaning to set his own vessel alight as a fireship, but a chain-shot from the island cut down his mainmast. He set her on fire and he and his crew crossed over in their pinnace to the *Jesus*.[15] Hawkins, despairing of the *Jesus*, and with his smaller vessels sunk, had the *Minion* manoeuvred so as to be sheltered from the guns by the larger ship. He ordered Drake in the *Judith* to come in beside the *Minion* and take on board some of the crews and supplies. When Drake had done so a new threat appeared:

> ... suddenly the Spanyardes had fired two great shippes which were comming directly with us, and having no meanes to avoide the fire, it bread among our men a marveilous feare, so that some sayd, let us depart with the *Minion*, other sayde, let us see where the winde will carrie the fyre from us. But to bee short, the *Mynion*'s men, which had always there sayles in a readinesse, thought to make sure worke, and so without eyther consent of the Captayne or Master cutte [i.e. set] their sayle, so that verie hardly I was received into the *Mynion*.

The *Minion* and *Judith*, both greatly overcrowded and pursued by desperate boatloads of men from the other English ships, sailed away from the stricken flagship. Hawkins had had time to transfer much of the proceeds of the voyage to the *Minion*; he left behind his table silver and about fifty uncomprehending negro slaves. The two surviving vessels anchored, some distance apart, out of shot from the Spanish. That night the *Judith* disappeared; in Hawkins' words, she 'forsooke us in our great myserie'.

In the morning the lonely and overcrowded *Minion*, having made only another mile's progress, was forced to anchor by a north wind, in dread of losing her last two anchors and being driven onto a lee shore. 'Wee thought alwayes of death which was ever present.' The accounts of her voyage home are as harrowing as any fiction. Of the 200 men aboard, half were put ashore in Mexico to shift for themselves. One of them, Miles Phillips, eventually returned to England sixteen years later after encounters with hostile Indians, imprisonment by the Spanish, employment as an overseer and interpreter, and a period in Spain. Another, Job Hortop the gunner, spent twenty-three years in the galleys or in Spanish prisons.[16]

The men who remained aboard, some wounded, all desperately hungry and demoralised, increasingly cold in the North Atlantic winter, grew gradually weaker and many died. The crew was so reduced that Hawkins had to put into the Ría de Vigo in Galicia, where he found some English merchantmen who provided him with a dozen seamen to work the ship back to England. She arrived in Mounts Bay in Cornwall on 25 January 1569.

Drake had reached Plymouth just five days earlier. Nothing is known of the *Judith*'s voyage home. No reports mention her as being in the thick of the battle or receiving serious damage, so she may have been in better condition than the *Minion*, but she too was overcrowded. There has been speculation that she arrived home so little in advance of Hawkins because Drake had engaged in some private adventure on his homeward passage, but no-one knows.

Most of the spoil came home in the *Minion*, but on all other accounts the voyage was a catastrophe. Poor Barrett, all the hostages, and many others remained in Spanish hands; less than a quarter of the men came back; over 1,000 tons of shipping had been lost. Hawkins had found, at Cartagena, signs of a sterner resolve to stamp out the illegal trading by which, in recent years, he had been making a fat living.

In the Europe to which they returned, Drake and Hawkins found that there had been striking developments during their absence, for the King of Spain had moved some of his pieces on the chessboard. Philip's territorial wealth and the power it carried with it imposed huge responsibility on the king, who was not only ardent in his faith but obsessively conscientious in his administration; he spent hours every day reading despatches, reports and draft replies, writing his comments and instructions in the margins, and appending his signature, *Yo el Rey*. As the most powerful man in Mediterranean Europe, he was Christendom's standard-bearer against the forces of

Islam, and as ruler of the Netherlands he was the Pope's bulwark against the rising tide of Protestantism in Northern Europe.

In the autumn of 1567 Philip was faced with threats not only on these two fronts, with warlike noises emerging from Turkey and increasing Lutheran disturbances in the Netherlands, but with unrest at home, where almost a century of Inquisition activity had not wiped out the racial divisions inherited from the time of the incorporation of the defeated population of Moorish Andalusia. In the event of a contest between Philip and the Sultan of Turkey the English would have been hard put to cheer whole-heartedly for either side, but Elizabeth's feelings about the Spanish presence in the Netherlands were unequivocal and wary. The Dutch coast was all too near the mouth of the Thames, and when the Duke of Alba brought three of Philip's finest brigades to subdue the Low Countries in the autumn of 1567 the Queen's dismay can be imagined.

Philip, in fact, had no immediate designs on England; he was too occupied with the threats in the Mediterranean, where Turkey's war-galleys were threatening the Venetian island of Cyprus, and in the mountains of southern Spain, where there was a revolt of the *moriscos*, the descendants of the Moorish population defeated in 1492. By sending Alba to the Netherlands he had created new problems for himself. Paying and equipping the armies was a large drain on the national purse, and getting the pay-chests to them was a logistical problem. France, a perpetual thorn in Spain's side, lay in the way, and France too was affected by the Protestant heresy.

Not long before Drake's return French Huguenot privateers had caused an incident which had led to a flurry of correspondence filled with the phrases of understated outrage with which diplomats earn their bread. Philip had raised a loan from Genoese bankers to pay Alba's troops, and the money, in silver coins, was on its way to Antwerp in an unarmed merchantman and a few pinnaces. Storm-wracked in the Channel, and harrassed by French privateers operating out of La Rochelle with commissions from the Prince de Condé, they took refuge in English ports; the ship in Southampton and the pinnaces in Falmouth, Fowey and Plymouth. With the French lurking in wait, they were afraid to sail, and the English authorities had all the silver brought ashore, ostensibly to prevent the wicked French from sailing in and seizing it. Fifty-nine cases were landed in Southampton, and ninety-eight in the West Country ports, including Plymouth, where William Hawkins, John's brother, was mayor.

Elizabeth, being at peace with Spain, could not simply seize the silver as a useful windfall, but any legal pretext for withholding it from the Duke of Alba would be a way of weakening Spain's presence in the Netherlands; unpaid troops tend to become unsupportive. Lord Burghley, the treasurer, scratched his head and came up with the conclusion that the money was the property of the Genoese until it was unloaded in Antwerp. The situation gained a new dimension from William Hawkins, who had heard, possibly via the Spinola banking family in London, of the defeat at San Juan de Ulúa, and now had the news confirmed by Drake's arrival in the *Judith*. He immediately despatched Drake to London to complain to Burghley about the losses and to demand the seizure of the Spanish silver as compensation. William also asked for permission to use four ships of his own in reprisal attacks on Spanish shipping; he already had a commission for one vessel from the French Huguenot Cardinal de Châtillon.* The letter refers to Drake first as 'our kinsman' but later as 'my servant.'[17]

As the situation dragged on and Alba's unpaid troops grew restive, there was a tit-for-tat seizure of English property in the Netherlands and Spanish goods in England, but neither side wanted war, and the brink was not crossed. When John Hawkins arrived home it emerged that his losses on the voyage had been less than William had feared; the major loss, the *Jesus*, was not a Hawkins vessel. Elizabeth retained the silver and took over Philip's debt to the Genoese, the huffing and puffing died down, and Philip began sending his pay-chests, well guarded, overland. However, these preliminary skirmishes over the Netherlands had concentrated the minds of Elizabeth and Philip. The threat to England's south and east coasts, once perceived, did not vanish; the Spanish regiments remained; and Philip knew that Lutheranism was not to be crushed without its defeat in England. Catholic Europe had suffered an additional outrage in the summer of 1568 by Elizabeth's imprisonment of Mary Queen of Scots, and the Pope was urging retribution.

English distrust of Spain was nowhere more bitter than in the minds of Drake and John Hawkins, where the treachery of the viceroy, Martín Enríquez, was indelibly etched. In the years to come this remained an obsession with Drake; he complained repeatedly in conversations with captured Spaniards of the viceroy's duplicity and of the blow dealt to Hawkins' pride and pocket at San Juan de Ulúa.

---

* Châtillon, the brother of the French Huguenot leader the Prince de Condé, was in London distributing commissions empowering seafarers to attack all papists.

How much of this ensuing indignation was caused by Enríquez's actions, and how much by more complex motives within Drake, is hard to know. Perhaps he did consciously abandon Hawkins, and later felt a shame for which he compensated by swearing vengeance on the viceroy. Perhaps, though, the little *Judith* was just as hard pressed on that lee shore as the *Minion* and had to make whatever shift she could, and it was Hawkins' terse comment on what he saw as desertion which prompted Drake's individual campaign to prove his faithfulness to his kinsman and gain him some redress.

IV

RECONNAISSANCE
1569–71

'... finding that no recompence could bee
recovered out of *Spaine*, ... hee used such
helpes as hee might by two severall voiages into
the West Indies, ... to gain such intelligences
as might further him to get some amends for
his losse.'

Anon., *Sir Francis Drake Revived*, 1592[1]

After the débâcle and financial losses of the action at San Juan de
Ulúa, John Hawkins had had enough of the West Indies on a personal
level. His business interest in Caribbean voyages continued, but he
was content to be a provider of ships and finance, and it was a long
time before he saw the waters of the Indies again himself. Drake, in
contrast, was all energy and revenge.

On 4 July 1569, he was married. His bride, Mary Newman, is an
obscure figure. Local tradition claims that she was born in Saltash,
just across the estuary of the Tamar from Plymouth, though Drake's
cousin John later told the Inquisition that he thought she was from
London. Her family was certainly established in the Plymouth area,
for various other women of the same surname, some of them probably
her sisters, were married in the same church as she and Drake, St
Budeaux, in the 1550s and 1560s. One of them, Margaret Newman,
married a John Bodman in 1560; these were probably the parents of
the Jonas Bodenham who became a favourite of Drake's in his later
years. The pattern of Mary's marriage to Drake was soon set: only a
few months after their wedding he was off to sea again.

His first two voyages to the Caribbean in the early 1570s are poorly
documented. There is ample evidence of the presence of English
armed intruders (corsairs, in the eyes of the Spanish) in the West
Indies in these years, especially along the coast of what was called
Tierra Firme. Drake, however, was not yet a celebrity, but one of
many. The task of unravelling his movements is complicated by the

activities of other men, equally anonymous, or bearing pseudonyms such as John Goodweather or John Noble. Another confusing factor is the presence of the French, whose tradition of piracy in the area was older than that of the English. Often two vessels formed brief alliances; French and English, even, teamed up for temporary advantage. Terrified Spanish passengers and crewmen, whose reports provide much of the evidence, were not always good at distinguishing one language from another; there are cases in which the predators were said to be French by one witness, English by another.

The book *Sir Francis Drake Revived*, possibly written and certainly checked by Drake himself, barely mentions his first two individually organised voyages: 'the first with two ships, the one called the *Dragon*, the other the *Swan*, in the yeare 70; the other in the *Swan* alone in the year 71'. Sorting out these voyages one from another is not easy. We shall see that Drake was raiding on the Panama coast in February 1571. To do this he must have sailed from England, almost certainly Plymouth, before Christmas 1570. He was still in the West Indies in May 1571, and returned to England in October of the same year. He could not have got back to England, refitted the *Swan*, and made another voyage between May and October. This, then, must be the voyage ascribed to 1571, though he left England late in 1570.

The previous voyage is hardly documented at all. It must have taken place largely, at least, in 1570, though Drake may have sailed late in 1569. It was probably a relatively innocuous armed trading voyage on the Hawkins pattern, though the *Swan*, which was only 25 tons,[2] was not a large vessel for the purpose, especially for shipping slaves from Guinea. Certainly there were no great explosions of Spanish anger in 1570 because of piratical activities in the Caribbean. The fact that the second voyage involved only the little *Swan* may indicate that the first was no great financial success and the second had to be managed on limited resources. A Spanish list of Drake's depredations[3] includes a voyage to the Indies in a bark of 40 tons with an Exeter merchant called Richard Dennys and others; it ascribes this to 1570, but since only one ship is mentioned this, too, is probably a reference to the second voyage and to a sailing date before the end of 1570. Discrepancies of this scale in the estimated tonnage of ships are nothing out of the ordinary in documents of the period.

Details of the first voyage, then, are almost completely lacking. Our knowledge of the second is fragmentary, but enough to show the germination in Drake's mind of plans for future strategies, incursions and alliances. Its purpose may have been a more financial one than the mere gathering of intelligence, but the knowledge gained in these two voyages was the foundation for later successes which were to shake the Spanish empire to its backbone.

The Spanish fleet arrived in Nombre de Dios, on the Isthmus of Panama, on 21 January 1571. This was a pivotal event in the annual administrative and commercial timetable of Central America. It was also central to the plans of English and French corsairs in the 1570s, not because it was their intention to attack the fleet itself, which was protected by large galleons of war, but because the arrival of the fleet set local maritime society in motion. In the off-season there was a limited coastwise trade in everyday necessities. The things of value which the fleet came to load for shipment to Spain accumulated in warehouses ashore until it arrived: hides, cochineal, sugar, sarsaparilla, copal, cotton.[4] Most of the really valuable cargo, such as the silks and damasks brought across the Pacific from the Far East, and especially the gold and silver shipped up from the West Coast of South America, was stored in the city of Panama, forty miles from Nombre de Dios over difficult terrain.

When the fleet from Spain anchored in Nombre de Dios, warehouse doors in other ports were opened, ships which had lain idle for months emerged from harbour, and the busy two-way traffic began. The cargoes from Spain were unloaded and dispersed, coastwise to other ports, by river and overland to Panama, onward by Pacific traders to Peru and Chile: wine and oil from Andalusia, agricultural implements, powder and shot, French and Flemish linens, mercury from Almadén for the colonial silver mines. The human cargo, too, was dispersed: colonial administrators, priests and friars, soldiers, adventurers, slaves; all the raw material of developing empire. The holds of the ships were swept, aired, and filled with the produce of that empire, partly for the crews' own sustenance, but mainly for shipment to Spain.

Nombre de Dios was a small place in comparison with Panama, whose importance and size had been increased by its position as a funnel for the hugely valuable cargoes arriving from Chile and Peru or by the trans-Pacific trade. Goods travelled between the two cities by two routes, one entirely overland, the other involving the River Chagre, which flows into the Caribbean. Gold and silver were loaded onto mule-trains, called *recuas*, in Panama and were taken overland by tracks through mountain and forest to Nombre de Dios. Bulkier and less valuable cargoes went by road as far as a place called Venta de Cruces on the Chagre, and were then loaded onto small vessels of

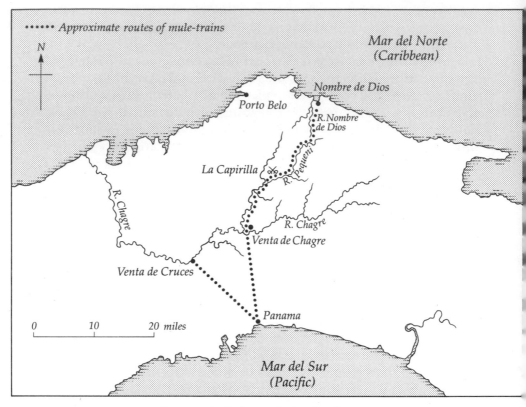

N

Mar del Norte
(Caribbean)

Nombre de Dios

Porto Belo

R.Nombre
de Dios

La Capirilla

R.Pequeni

R. Chagre

R. Chagre

Venta de Chagre

Venta de Cruces

0   10   20 miles

Panama

Mar del Sur
(Pacific)

Panama's links with the Caribbean

about 16 tons which took them down-river with the help of the current and so to Nombre de Dios and into the holds of the Atlantic fleet.[5] Before the corsairs infested the area as they did in the 1570s, precious metals were also taken by the Chagre, but in 1569 the French had discovered the route, attacked and seized two barks in the mouth of the river, and stolen the whole of their cargoes: not only flour and hides, but twelve thousand pesos in gold and silver bars.[6]

Even travelling overland, however, the gold and silver were not invulnerable. The Spaniards' growing difficulties with the corsairs at sea coincided with the aggravation of a problem ashore: the escaped negro slaves or *cimarrones*. The harshness of their owners had driven many of the slaves, especially the men, to abscond into the dense and limitless terrain of the undeveloped land. Many of them had been born and had grown to adulthood in Africa, and still retained the skills which enabled a man to survive without stone walls, wine from

Seville and a regular income. As their numbers grew they banded together, chose or accepted leaders, built villages, and became increasingly bold. García de Paz, the Procurator of Nombre de Dios, wrote for Philip's information in 1571 that 'the *cimarrones* [estimated at 2,000] ... enter daily into the towns, and into this city and Panama, carrying off to the wilds, and to the villages they have established, many negroes and negresses, the servants of the householders'. They had, moreover, begun to intercept the *recuas* between Panama and Nombre de Dios, killing people and making off with the gold and silver.[7]

When García de Paz was writing this, he was faced with two unlinked problems: the corsairs and the *cimarrones*. If he had known that within a few years these two sets of Spain's enemies were to join hands; that an Englishman of whose name he was still ignorant was to forge an alliance with Frenchmen and negroes, using the experience of both to bring a startling new dimension to Spain's colonial defence problems on Paz's very doorstep, his letter to Philip might well have been a request for a transfer to some quieter area. But we are jumping ahead.

The twenty-two vessels of the Atlantic fleet which anchored in Nombre de Dios were under the command of Captain-General Don Diego Flores de Valdés. He was an experienced man, and had been leading Atlantic convoys since 1567. As well as his own large galleon of war, he had another commanded by Admiral Don Gerónimo de Narváez, and the cargo vessels, the *naos*, also carried ordnance. They had had bad weather from the Canaries onwards, but had arrived earlier than expected by the local merchants.[8] Within a month of Flores' arrival French and English corsairs were making a mockery of his protective presence.

Of Drake's Atlantic crossing we know nothing and can speculate about very little. A Spanish list of corsair atrocities compiled in 1575 is devoted largely to incidents involving Drake, some dated, some not.[9] It includes an attack on a caravel carrying powder and shot from Seville to Havana. Drake, it says, seized and carried off the pilot, a man called Ruano, demanded that he act as his guide to Caribbean harbours, and threw him overboard when he refused. Drake often borrowed Spanish pilots from captured ships later in his career, and he was not beyond putting the fear of God into them by one means or another, but there is no record of his deliberately murdering anyone. In any case, if Ruano drowned, who told the tale? This incident, then, may have been a chance encounter in the Atlantic on the 1570–71 voyage. A more substantial incident listed in the 1575 account is an entry into Cartagena harbour at night in which a 180-ton ship was burned and her captain, Bartolomé Farina, abducted, though this may be a reference to a similar incident in a later voyage.[10] It is not mentioned in García de Paz's 1571 letter, which includes a list of recent incidents, but he was concerned mainly with the disturbing situation around Nombre de Dios, and may have left Cartagena to look to its own welfare.

Paz's account mentions corsair outrages committed in 1569 and 1570, and others since the arrival of Flores. French and English raiders, he writes, had arrived without warning and ascended the Chagre in a galliot and a shallop. They had captured two or three river barks, stealing and destroying merchandise – silks, linens, wine, oil, etc. – worth over 20,000 pesos. They had also pillaged a ship belonging to Baltazar de Melo, robbing him and another merchant of clothing, negroes, and the vessel itself, to the value of 15,000 pesos.

It is clear from this that the French and English were acting together. Both Paz and Flores (in a letter to Philip dated 16 March)[11] were in no doubt that the French were a group who had been at the Chagre in 1569, and they were right. A negro called Pedro Mandinga was captured and taken to France in 1569, and returned with his captors in 1571 as a guide. Their ship was called *L'Espérance* and was captained by a Nicolas des Isles (probably a pseudonym). Their aim in 1571 was unprecedented: to ascend the Chagre and attack Venta de Cruces. When they were only a few miles from the Venta Mandinga escaped and warned the Spanish; he later gave evidence to the *Audiencia* in Panama.[12]

Were Nicolas's English allies Drake and his Devonians? On the balance of evidence, probably yes, and the alliance continued. After the partial failure of the incursion into the Chagre, the raiders turned their attention to the coast. On 21 February a frigate owned by Diego Polo of Cartagena was nearing Nombre de Dios. She anchored at El Pontón, between the city and the mouth of the Chagre, possibly to wait for the tide. As she lay at anchor a pinnace drew alongside her, manned by fourteen or fifteen men. They were armed with muskets and bows and arrows, and the pinnace had two small culverins mounted in the bows.

Something of the ferocity and bloodiness of such attacks emerges from the testimonies of Doña Juana de Estrada of Santo Domingo, who was in the ship with her husband, Diego de Azevedo, and another passenger, Luis de Soto.[13] Some of the corsairs (variously described as English; French; English and French; and French and English) had their faces daubed with red or black. A trumpet sounded, and they began clambering aboard with swords drawn and shields on their arms. The crew and passengers of the frigate, with only two swords between them, held them off for a couple of hours, but suffered seriously from a rain of arrows and musket-fire from the pinnace. Doña Juana saw her husband collapse with an arrow in the temple, and watched him die an hour later. De Soto received another arrow through the arm, one of Azevedo's black slaves was killed by a shot from a culverin, and several other men were injured.

At some point the pinnace raised a flag of truce and asked for a parley, but it was either not seen or ignored by those on the frigate. In desperation the Spanish crew slipped the anchor cable, the vessel started to drift shorewards, and the pinnace turned its attention to another nearby frigate whose crew had fled to land. Polo's ship grounded, and its desperate occupants, including the traumatised Doña Juana, waded through chest-deep water to a small island.

Later the corsairs returned and plundered the deserted ship, hacked her rigging to pieces, smashed her boat and sailed off towards the mouth of the Chagre. They left aboard her a message in English: they were surprised, they said, that their flag of truce had been ignored; they wished no harm to anyone, and anyone who discussed things reasonably with them would be courteously treated; how much better it would have been to talk, and save the frigate, whose contents were not worth tuppence anyway. They were not afraid of 'those ships' (meaning Flores' galleons, whose topmasts were probably visible in the distance); 'with God's help it will cost them their lives before they defeat us'. It was signed, not with a name, but as from 'Englishmen who are well-disposed, if there is no reason to be otherwise; if there is cause, we will be devils rather than men'.[14] The original English letter has not survived, but even after the translation into and out of Spanish we can perceive the ironic humour, the smile cloaking the steel, which characterises so many of the later writings and speeches of Francis Drake.

If we accept that the attack on Polo's frigate was done by Drake and men from the *Swan*, perhaps with some French reinforcements, and if we believe Spanish depositions which say that the attack on Melo's ship was made by the same group who took Polo's frigate, then Drake's men were involved in the incursion of the two raiding vessels which ascended the Chagre with the aim of attacking Venta de Cruces. Probably the galliot referred to by García de Paz was French, and the shallop was the *Swan*'s pinnace.

Captain-General Flores was naturally faced with a flood of complaints from the local community. Here he was in Nombre de Dios, with two large men-of-war and a score of other vessels under his command, no doubt being handsomely wined and dined by officials, merchants, and anyone else who had an interest to pursue, while a few dozen ruffians in their puny vessels were free to commit looting, piracy and murder at will. He bestirred himself, rather slowly. Two weeks had gone by since the attack on Polo's frigate when Flores set out to keep the peace.[15]

A letter to Philip from the city of Panama summarises his achievement with a dry brevity:

> General Diego Flores de Valdés sailed in search of the corsairs with the *capitana*, the *almiranta*[16] and a caravel, well-supplied with artillery. It was expected that his going would have some effect. He found the corsairs. He reconnoitred them and returned without approaching them; he dared not risk his ships because the corsairs were hugging the shore.[17]

Flores' own report[18] makes it clear that his failure was due to the fact that the raiders were in oared vessels, which could escape simply by rowing into the shallows. He evidently made no contact with either the *Swan* or the *Espérance*, but he did recover three frigates which had been taken and abandoned, possibly including Polo's.

Flores revised his tactics. As he wrote his letter, dated 16 March 1571, he was preparing three frigates, equipped with oars and sails, 'craft from which they cannot protect themselves as they did from the galleons'. His plan was to escort fourteen or fifteen river barks, laden with clothing and at present cowering in Nombre de Dios, into the Chagre and then to pursue the raiders, whom he still thought at this point to be French. Before he finished his letter he received the news that an English ship with an oared pinnace was anchored off Cativa headland. The pinnace was the one which had attacked Polo's frigate,[19] and the ship, almost certainly, was the *Swan*. Flores would have been relieved to know that she was now his principal problem; the *Espérance*, either satisfied with her plunder or despairing of a successful assault on the Venta de Cruces now that Panama was alerted, had sailed away from Flores' show of strength and was heading north.[20]

After his own failure with the galleons, Flores entrusted the command of the second punitive force to his Admiral, Gerónimo de

Narváez. It was no more successful than the first, to the chagrin of the burghers of Nombre de Dios, who had financed it. This Spanish impotence raised Drake's audacity. His next attack is an early example of a mode of thought which underlay much of his later success and reputation: always consider the psychology of the enemy, and if everyone thinks something is out of the question, try it. The French had given up the idea of raiding the Venta de Cruces because they knew Panama had been forewarned; Panama knew that the French knew this, and was therefore complacent; Drake knew all this, and therefore raided the Venta de Cruces.

Here speculation ceases: the 1575 Spanish list of corsair raids says unequivocally that 'in the year of '71, the said *francisco drac* stole goods worth over 50,000 ducats from Lope Ruiz de Ceco and Baltasar Díaz'.[21] García de Paz also mentions the raid, and says that the goods (they were velvets and taffetas) had been unloaded and were sitting on the wharf. He mentions no casualties, whereas he gives a meticulous count of the dead and wounded in other incidents; the signs are that Drake met little resistance in an audacious and completely unexpected raid. The pinnace dropped down the river with her loot and waited for further plunder to arrive in passing craft. Three barks coming down empty were seized and sunk to prevent them taking the news to Nombre de Dios.

By early May the volume of Drake's booty was beginning to cause him problems. Gold and silver presented no difficulties to a raider, even in a small ship like the *Swan*; they could always be used as ballast. Another dozen barks were seized in the first week in May between Nombre de Dios and Porto Belo, though not necessarily all by Drake. The cargoes were bulky: clothing and merchandise worth around 150,000 pesos, plus a number of slaves, and two of the barks were kept by the raiders as transports.[22]

A few days later, in another, bloodier encounter off the Cativa headland, the *Swan*'s pinnace with twenty-three men aboard took a frigate coming from Cartagena. The owner, Salvatierra, was killed, other people were injured, and a friar was stripped and mocked by some energetic Lutherans. Parcels of royal despatches were ripped up and thrown into the sea, and the crew and passengers were put ashore on an uninhabited island. Later in life this sort of thing was not Drake's style; enemy casualties were few, he behaved with elaborate courtesy to prisoners, and he was not a man to strip friars naked. In 1571 he was young and fiery, and perhaps the savage example of the more experienced French influenced his actions. His outrage at the

Spanish treachery at San Juan de Ulúa, after all, was only three years old.

A day or two after this attack he had sailed west again past the impotent Flores, and between the Chagre and Porto Belo he found a group of eighteen small barks, of which he boarded and pillaged four. He took his pick of the cargoes, including some negroes, retained one of the barks, abandoned the other three at sea, and sailed back to Cativa. In addition to the *Swan* and her pinnace, he now had at least one, probably three, captured vessels laden with goods and slaves.

At this point, the evidence fails us. He returned to England in October 1571.[23] May to October is about three months longer than he needed to return to Plymouth directly. Perhaps he stayed on the Panama coast, picking up further plunder; perhaps he sailed his little fleet eastward to try to dispose of some of his plunder using Hawkins' methods. Taking slaves east across the Atlantic was taking coals to Newcastle; he needed a market which would take them off his hands, and his previous experience would suggest places such as Santa Marta and Río de la Hacha as possible unloading points, not only for the slaves but also for some of the clothing, linens and taffetas seized in and around the Chagre. He also probably spent some time seeking 'such intelligences as might further him'. Around the beginning of July he was exploring the Acla coast, east of Nombre de Dios, and between there and Tolu he found 'a fine, round Bay, of verie safe harbour for all winds, lying between two high points, not past halfe a cables length over at the mouth, but within eight or ten cables length everie way, having ten or twelve fadome water, more or lesse, fulle of good fish'.[24]

In this corsair's paradise Drake remained for some time, certainly long enough to establish himself ashore, clear paths through the lush forest, and hunt the game, which was so plentiful that he named the place Port Pheasant. His purpose was probably to careen and clean the *Swan*. The underwater hulls of wooden ships, especially in tropical waters, became covered with barnacles and weed, which could seriously impair sailing qualities. Careening involved laying the ship aground on some convenient shore, heeling her over sideways with large tackles attached to her mainmast, and scraping off the growth.

Later in July Drake may have ranged along the coast eastward. Towards the end of that month three vessels with English crews entered Borburata, which Drake knew from his experience with Hawkins, and tried unsuccessfully to trade. Also in July, an English ship with about fifty men aboard sailed into the harbour of Coro to take on water, but the landing was forestalled by the governor at the head of a force of Indians and Spaniards.[25] After the heady successes of the River Chagre and the coast of the isthmus, Drake may now have found the volume of his booty an embarrassment. Getting rid of the captured slaves, who were an extra drain on water and victuals, needed the skills of a Hawkins rather than a Drake still in his twenties.

However he disposed of his plunder, Drake must have been well pleased with his voyage. It was obviously a financial success; the policy of making advantageous but easily dissoluble alliances with the French had worked well; the Spanish defences had proved ineffective against the small and nimble oared vessels of the raiders, and Philip's empire had been penetrated to within a few miles of Panama and the ocean which lay beyond it. From his interrogation of prisoners Drake now knew about the situation with the *cimarrones*, and about the mule-trains which took the gold and silver from Panama to Nombre de Dios. The coast had been thoroughly reconnoitred, and an ideal base of operations found. As the *Swan* sailed home through the big seas of the autumn westerlies, Drake thought often of Port Pheasant. It was to play an important role in his next, more ambitious venture.

> And having ... gotten such certaine notice of the persons and places aimed at as he thought requisite, and there upon with good deliberation resolved on a third voyage, ... hee ... had such successe in his proceedings as now followes farther to be declared.[26]

V

THE WAY TO PURCHASE GOLD:
RAIDING THE MULE-TRAINS
1572–73

'And now let us see how a dwarf, standing on
the mount of God's providence, may prove an
overmatch for a giant.'

William Fuller, *The Holy State*, 1642

Sir Francis Drake Revived is an account written at Drake's instigation,
and checked by him, late in his life at a time when he was out of
favour with Elizabeth. His intention was to present it to the Queen.
It is almost entirely taken up with the story of his voyage to the Indies
in 1572–73, though its dedicatory epistle suggests that he had in mind
the compilation of a complete biography of his exploits. The voyage
is presented as the beginning of a campaign of personal retribution
against King Philip and his viceroy, Martín Enríquez:

> As there is a generall vengeance which secretly pursueth the doers of
> wrong and suffereth them not to prosper, albeit no man of purpose
> empeach them, so is there a particular indignation, engraffed in the
> bosome of all that are wronged, which ceaseth not seeking by all meanes
> possible to redresse or remedie the wrong received. Insomuch as those
> great and mightie men, in whom their prosperous estate hath bred such
> an over-weening of themselves that they doe not onely wrong their infer-
> iours but despise them being injured, seeme to take a verie unfit course
> for their own safetie, and farre unfitter for their rest.[1]

It is typical of Drake that he should fail to realise, even late in life,
that justifying his actions on the basis of personal outrage was hardly
likely to endear him to Elizabeth. Even in the years after the Armada,
it could only confirm her view of him as an erratic fighting-cock whose
private interests were always likely to disrupt his implementation of
royal policy.

Despite the successes of the previous voyage, Drake's standing and wealth in 1572 were not yet such as to furnish, or command support for, a large expedition. His backers were probably the Hawkins brothers; possibly also the Wynter family. Both had their fingers in many pies, and their financial contribution to Drake was limited. John Hawkins probably thought the voyage worth supporting as a small gamble with a slim possibility of very large profits to be gained by methods very different from his own, for Drake's intention was nothing less than a raid on Philip's treasure-stores in Nombre de Dios. To carry out this plan, conceived and developed during his two previous voyages, Drake had only two small ships, both from Plymouth: as well as the well-tried and kindly *Swan*, he had the *Pascha*, larger at 70 tons. A ship *Pasco* appears in lists of Hawkins' ships, and if this is the same vessel Drake already had experience of her, as she went on Lovell's voyage in 1566.[2] Drake called her the *Pascha*, so we will do the same. He captained her himself, with forty-seven men, and his brother John captained the *Swan*, with twenty-six.

They sailed on 24 May 1572, had an ideal passage with steady north-east winds, and sighted Guadeloupe on 28 June. After a three-day halt for rest and watering on the south coast of an island off Dominica, Drake set his course for the mainland. Five days later the mountains behind Santa Marta were sighted, but on this voyage Drake kept well off shore. There was to be no armed trading to send ripples of alarm ahead of him; he wanted to descend on Nombre de Dios like a hawk swooping on a sitting pigeon. Not until six days later, when he was off Port Pheasant, did he approach the coast.

When the ships had anchored off the mouth of the bay, Drake left his brother John in command and was taking a small boat party ashore to reconnoitre when they saw smoke rising from the woods. There was no reason to suspect the presence of Spaniards, whose nearest settlements were thought to be Tolu to the east and Nombre de Dios to the west, but Drake ordered a second boat to be manned, and they made their way ashore, armed with muskets.

When they landed they had difficulty in recognising the place, for all the clearings and paths cut the year before had been invaded by lush vegetation. There followed one of the almost novelesque incidents with which Drake's career, and the whole era, are studded: here on the fringe of the American wilderness, having crossed an ocean, they found a message addressed to him. Nailed to a great tree was a lead plate; it bore a warning from a Plymouth sea-captain:

Captaine Drake, if you fortune to come to this port, mak hast away, for the Spaniards which you had with you here the last yeere have bewrayed [betrayed] this place, and taken away all that you left here. I departed from hence, this present 7 of July, 1572.

Your verie loving friend,
JOHN GARRET[3]

Garret must have been guided to Port Pheasant by members of his crew who had been with Drake in the previous year. The smoke was from a fire lit in a great tree a few days earlier to draw Drake's attention. All this suggests that Drake's destination and his approximate time of arrival may have been known to some of the seafaring community of Plymouth, or that he had made some prior arrangement with Garret for a joint enterprise.

Although Garret has now sailed out of the story, the idea that there had been an arranged rendezvous is supported by the arrival only a day after Drake of another English ship, again guided by members of Drake's earlier crews. She was captained by James Rance, who had been with Drake and Hawkins on the unfortunate voyage, though as master of the *William and John* he had escaped the ordeal of San Juan de Ulúa. With him he brought two small prizes: a caravel which had been carrying despatches, and an oared shallop. Rance was admitted to the enterprise, 'upon conditions agreed on betweene them'.

When Rance arrived Drake was building a rough, five-sided fort out of timber with one side open to the sea and a fifty-foot wide clearing around it. The Portuguese master of the captured caravel later described a busy scene in his report: straw huts, three pinnaces on the stocks, carpenters, sailmakers and riggers working away.[4] The pinnaces were ready after a week, and on the morning of 20 July the little fleet set sail for Nombre de Dios. Two or three days later, at the Pinos Islands, they found two timber ships, and were told by the negro crewmen that the town was on the alert for attacks by the *cimarrones*, and that reinforcements of soldiers were expected from Panama. Drake put the negroes ashore on the mainland to join the cimarrons if they wished, confident that they were too far from Nombre de Dios to raise the alarm. Nevertheless, he was keen to press on, being 'loath to put the towne to too much charge (which hee knew they would willingly bestow) in providinge before hand for his entertainement'.[5]

The scope and audacity of Drake's plan almost beggar belief.

Leaving Rance in charge of the larger vessels in an anchorage which he called Port Plenty, he transferred seventy-three men, including twenty of Rance's, into the three pinnaces and the shallop. They had only twenty-four firearms and sixteen bows. The rest were mainly armed with pikes, and there were two drummers and two trumpeters. No ordnance; no reinforcements organised. With this tiny force Drake planned to surprise and storm an important colonial port with largely unknown defences, locate the gold and silver awaiting shipment to Spain, and make off with it. Nothing could better exemplify the change from the armed trading methods of Hawkins, with his polite applications for permits and testimonials, delicate allusions to his armed strength, gifts to venal officials and surreptitious sales. This was to be smash-and-grab, with all the risks that entails, against a town now permanently nervous, like all the coastal towns of the Caribbean mainland, of piratical visitations.

On 28 July 1572 the pinnaces reached the islands of the Mulatas. Drake landed his men, handed out weapons, did some drill and made a speech of exhortation in which he mentioned his personal campaign for redress and told them that Nombre de Dios lay unwalled and open to attack. By nightfall they were within two leagues of the point of Nombre de Dios bay. Drake's tactics reveal the extent of his reconnoitring in previous voyages: he kept the boats hard in to the shore to avoid being seen from the lookout house, and anchored until the night was dark. They then continued rowing along the shoreline until they were below the point of the harbour, with the high land above them, and waited for dawn. Drake had planned to attack between four and five in the morning. In the darkness, the silence and the waiting began to tell on the nerves of the men; there was whispered speculation about the strength of the town and the reinforcements coming from Panama. Drake put an end to this when the moon rose; he decided to attack at three o'clock.

The attack was almost foiled at the start when a Spanish ship, her sails still not furled after her arrival, saw the four suspicious pinnaces on the moonlit water. Her boat made for the town to raise the alarm. She must have had no ordnance aboard; a cannon-shot would have roused the town more effectively, and the boat was intercepted. A major justification for Drake's stress on secrecy and silence was found in the shape of a battery of six culverins and demi-culverins in the sandy bay where the pinnaces landed the men. The single gunner on watch fled to raise the alarm, and as Drake's men were dismounting the guns they heard tumult rising

47

in the town, with the church bells ringing the alarm and drums beating through the streets.

Drake left a dozen men to guard the pinnaces and set off to dismantle another battery of guns of which he had prior intelligence. This was on a hill on the east side of the town. It was found to be empty of guns, and the delay caused by this detour was crucial to the outcome of the raid. The town officers managed to rally and organise the townsmen so efficiently that the English thought they were faced with soldiers, whereas the Spanish sources make it clear that the opposition was mainly by armed civilians. The townsmen used the device of hanging strings with pieces of lighted match at intervals to give an impression of a line of waiting musketeers, a device probably invented to ward off attacks by the cimarrons.

With his main force, led by drums and trumpets, Drake marched up the main street. As they reached the market place they were met by a warm volley of shot from a group of thirty or forty defenders, and one of the trumpeters fell dead. Instead of retiring the English returned fire with muskets and arrows, and then charged with pike and sword. At the unexpected charge, coupled with the arrival on the Spanish flank of John Drake and John Oxenham with a smaller force which Drake had sent round by a side-street, the defenders broke and fled out of the town gate and onto the Panama road.

Drake gathered his men by the market cross, and sent a few to silence the alarm bell which was still pealing out from the church tower. The doors were locked, and Drake decided that there were more urgent tasks than breaking them down. He had taken a few prisoners, and told them to guide him to the governor's house and the treasure-store. His advance intelligence was that the *recuas* bringing the treasure from Panama were first unloaded in the courtyard of the governor's house; that the silver was stored in the same building, and the gold, pearls and jewels were taken to the royal treasure-house not far away.

At the governor's house the raiders found the great door of the courtyard open, and in the light shining from a lantern at the top of the stair they saw a saddled horse. They also saw, in a ground-floor room, a heap of silver. If we are to believe the description in the account approved later by Drake, it was 'a pile of barres ... of (as neere as we could guesse) seventie foot in length, of ten foot in breadth, and twelve foot in hight, piled up against the wall. Each barre was betweene thirty five and fortie pound in weight'.[6] Drake forbade his men to touch it, telling them that in the treasure-house, nearer to where they had landed, there was more gold and jewels than the pinnaces could carry away.

By this time the men left guarding the pinnaces were in a state of alarm. A negro from the town had braved musket-fire from the pinnaces and begged to be taken aboard. When he told them that there were a hundred and fifty soldiers in the town, and they saw groups of Spaniards moving about on the waterfront, they sent word to Drake that they were likely to be overwhelmed. Drake sent his brother John and Oxenham to stiffen them, and led the rest to the treasure-house. As they reached it a thunderstorm and an immense downpour of rain began. As they sheltered under a lean-to roof beside the building, with powder and bowstrings wet, the men began to lose heart. Mutterings about the threat from the town forces angered Drake; here he had brought them, he said, 'to the mouth of the treasure of the world'; if they missed their chance now they could blame nobody but themselves.

John Drake and Oxenham had now returned, and as the rain eased Drake stepped forward and told them and their men to break down the door. As he did so he staggered, fainted, and almost fell, and they saw his footprints in the sand darkened by blood pouring from a wound in his leg. He had received it during the skirmish in the square, and either was unaware of its gravity or had kept it a secret. The assault on the treasure-house was abandoned, by men who in some cases were glad to have a way out of these uncertain dangers, and in others saw their leader's life as more important than looting. They used Drake's scarf to put a tourniquet on his leg, and carried him back to the pinnaces. The day was barely breaking.

The raid had been a miserable failure. Only one man was lost, the trumpeter, but there were many wounded in addition to Drake. It is impossible to know how great a success it could have been. No doubt both the governor's house and the treasure-house could have been broken into if Drake's leadership had not been temporarily lost, but we do not know what quantity of bullion was inside them. Drake's intelligence in some ways was good; he did not find the guns on the hill where he was expecting them, but an emplacement had been prepared. Doubt has been cast, though, on the amount of bullion likely to be stored in Nombre de Dios at the time of the raid. The treasure fleet had sailed for Spain not long before, and it was unlikely that there would be any large accumulation of precious metals in the town until the next fleet was due in the following January. Obviously Drake must have had reason to believe the town was worth raiding, and he may well have found some silver, but it may be that the pile of bars gleaming in the light from the courtyard was somewhat inflated in *Sir Francis Drake Revived*, and the gravity of Drake's injury overstated, as a way of depicting the raid on Nombre de Dios as a heroic near-miss, rather than a misguided muddle based on poor information.[7]

Something was salvaged out of nothing: the ship which had tried to warn the town was taken as a prize before the pinnaces left the harbour. She was full of Canary wine. The shore battery, frantically remounted by the Spanish, fired a shot after her as Drake's men sailed her away, but to no avail. The raiders spent the next two days at the Bastimentos Islands, only a league from the town, resting, tasting the Canary wines, and restoring the wounded with the poultry and garden produce they found. The owner of the wine ship, Joan María, persuaded about seventy men to form a punitive force, but as they were embarking the man appointed to command them, Miguel Hurtado, was arrested to face a court case, and the pursuit was abandoned.

Instead, the governor sent an envoy under flag of truce to ask whether he was, indeed, dealing with the Captain Drake who had been harrying the coast in the last two years. He also wished to know if the English arrows had poisoned tips, and whether Drake needed any supplies. Drake, who could recognise a spying mission when he saw one, was now sufficiently himself to entertain the man cheerily and send him back with the reply that

> he wanted nothing but some of that speciall commodity which that countrey yeelded, to contente himselfe and his company. And therefore he advised the Governour to hold open his eyes, for before hee departed, if God lent him life and leave, hee meant to reape some of their Harvest, which they get out of the Earth, and send into Spaine to trouble all the Earth.

Despite these brave words, Drake decided to leave Nombre de Dios alone, and on the following morning he set off with two of the pinnaces to return to the ships anchored at Port Plenty. The other two pinnaces were sent, under the captaincy of John Drake and a seaman called Ellis Hixon, to explore the River Chagre. Diego, the negro taken aboard at Nombre de Dios, had offered to act as intermediary with the cimarrons, and John Drake's mission may have had more to do with establishing contact with them than with exploring the river, which Drake already knew from the previous year. When

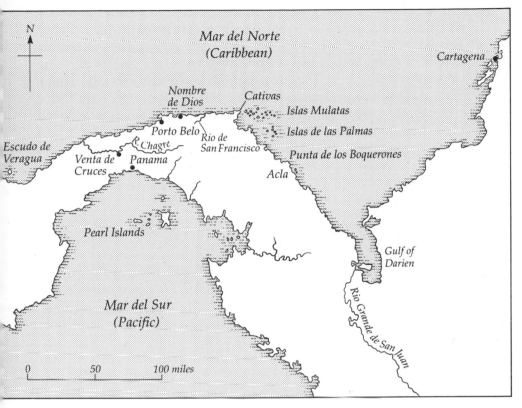

The Isthmus of Panama

the fleet reassembled around 7 August James Rance withdrew from the enterprise after a disagreement with Drake.

It was time to let the dust settle on the area around Nombre de Dios. Drake sailed east in light winds, and six days later his two ships and their pinnaces, now reduced to three, dropped anchor off Cartagena. They heard the booming of heavy guns coming from the port, and soon found out the reason. Drake led his pinnaces into the outer lagoon of the harbour, and found a frigate anchored. The crew had left one old man aboard and gone ashore to settle an argument about someone's mistress. The old man told Drake that shortly beforehand a Spanish pinnace had gone by towards the town under sail and oars, warning that French or English pirates were in the area. From the frigate's maintop the shipping in the inner harbour, warned by the gunfire, could be seen huddling in close under the castle batteries for protection.

Just beyond the next point of the harbour a big ship from Seville was lying, ready to sail for Santo Domingo on the following morning. The pinnaces rowed around to her and prepared to board, one at her starboard bow, one at her starboard quarter, and the third, with Drake, between them. The men had difficulty in climbing the high sides of the ship, and Drake, with his recent wound, must have found it harder than most, but the Spanish crew shortly fled below decks, and the pinnaces towed her away with her own anchor cables. It was a largely pointless incident, for there was little of value in the ship. Two smaller vessels captured on the following morning were equally unproductive, except inasmuch as the letters of advice which they carried revealed to Drake his own increasing notoriety, warning Cartagena that 'Captaine Drake had beene at Nombre de Dios, had taken it, and had it not beene that hee was hurt with some blessed shot, by all likelihood he had sackt it'.

It is an indication of the dominance and confidence of the English corsairs of the period that, having just raided the harbours of two major Spanish colonial ports, Drake should now release his captives, order his ships to the Islands of San Bernardo, only a few miles from Cartagena, and do some fishing. There followed an incident which reveals that Drake, bluff, outgoing and direct as he appeared, was also a man of extreme deviousness. It is surprising that he ever revealed the truth of the matter at all, and more so that the account in *Sir Francis Drake Revived*, read and approved by Drake, seems to show a good deal of pride in the episode.

From the start of the voyage Drake had been short of men to carry out his ambitious aims. Perhaps his plans had included Garret's crew, and their failed rendezvous had left him short. The lack had been temporarily supplied by Rance, but he had now left. Help from the cimarrons was in prospect, but it was not ashore but in the crewing of the pinnaces that Drake felt short of hands. The pinnaces were his main weapon in his present activities, and they needed full, strong crews to row the long distances involved. The small crews of the *Pascha* and the *Swan* made it out of the question to hold on to his Cartagena prizes, which he burned. To free more men for the pinnaces, he adopted a startlingly radical plan: the secret scuttling of the *Swan*.

The *Swan*'s carpenter, Thomas Moone, was Drake's only confidant in the business. Drake told him to go below in the middle of the second watch, bore three holes with a great auger just beside the keel, and put something over them to muffle the noise of the inrushing water. Moone's reactions were those of any good seaman with respect for a sound vessel: incredulity that Drake should destroy his own ship, relatively new as she was, after she had served him so well; fear that if Drake's brother and the rest of the crew caught him in the act they would kill him. Orders were orders; Moone did as he was bid, bored the holes, and spent the rest of the night in the lonely knowledge that the ship was sinking under him as his shipmates off watch slept.[8]

In the morning Drake, all innocence, climbed down from the *Pascha* into his pinnace to go fishing. He was rowed across to the *Swan* and called for his brother to go with him. John rose from his rest and told Drake he would follow shortly. As the pinnace crew bent their backs to row him away, Drake mentioned casually that the *Swan* seemed to be a little low in the water. John sent a man below to ask the steward to investigate, and when the steward jumped through a hatch into the bilges he found he was up to his waist, 'and shifting with more haste to come up againe as if the water had followed him, cryed out that the Ship was full of water'.

The hands rushed to the pumps. John Drake was rowed after his brother, told him the situation, and apologised for not joining in the fishing. He could not understand how there could be six feet of water in a ship which had had to be pumped only twice in the last six weeks. Drake proved himself a master dissembler, even offering himself and his crew to help with the pumping, but John said that his own crew could cope.

They went on coping through the morning; 'such was their love to the Barke ... that they ceased not, but to the utmost of their strength laboured all that they might till three of the afternoone'. They were barely keeping up with the leak; there was still four and a half feet of water in the bilges. Drake waited until their affection for the ship had been reduced by exhaustion, and proposed his plan to meet this emergency: he, by implication generously, would transfer to the pinnace until they could capture some suitable frigate; John Drake and the master of the *Swan* would take over the *Pascha*; the *Swan* would be stripped and burned to her waterline to keep her from Spanish hands. The weary men of the *Swan* agreed. 'Our Captaine had his desire, and men enough for his Pinnaces.'

On the following morning, 16 August 1572, Drake set a course for the Gulf of Darien and found a secluded anchorage where the *Pascha* might lie hidden while the pinnaces ranged about their business. He rested there a fortnight, partly to refurbish the ship and the pinnaces, partly to refresh the men. It was a pleasant interlude; an area ashore was cleared, huts were built under the guidance of Diego, the negro, who had become something of a favourite, and the smiths set up their forges. The men worked alternate days, and spent their free time practising their archery, hunting, or playing bowls and quoits.

Refreshed, Drake left his brother in the *Pascha* and took two pinnaces back down the coast for a probing foray up the Río Grande de San Juan. They rowed and hauled laboriously upriver, pestered by mosquitoes, and found by the waterside a group of warehouses guarded by a single Spaniard, who ran off. The buildings were full of dried bacon, biscuit, cheese and conserves. With the pinnaces filled with this windfall, and unharmed by a hail of arrows from a group of Indians who arrived from the town of Villa del Rey, the English moved downstream and returned to their anchorage. On the way they captured two small provision ships. Drake now had more victuals than he knew what to do with; like a squirrel preparing for winter, he built four storehouses, ten or twenty leagues apart, some on offshore islands, to serve unknown future needs.

His brother had given him good news. John, guided by Diego, had sailed the other pinnace along the coast and run into a group of cimarrons. He left two hostages and brought two of these potential allies with him, having arranged a meeting at a river he named, after his guide, the Diego. He had also found a safer anchorage near the river, between the coast and an island in the Mulatas group.

Drake set off with John and the cimarrons in the pinnaces for the arranged conference. His hope now was to forge an alliance with the cimarron leader to attack the *recuas* transporting the gold from Panama to Nombre de Dios. The proposal for an alliance was well received. The cimarrons had no great financial interest in the gold; their main interest lay in being tiresome to the Spanish. The gold they had already taken from the mule-trains had been thrown into rivers, otherwise Drake could have had it, but they explained to him that the water levels were too high to recover it in this, the rainy season of the year. Worse, the *recuas* carrying the treasure were suspended during this part of the year. This meant a delay of five months. Again Drake's earlier intelligence-gathering, excellent in coastal matters, had let him down in an aspect of operations ashore, this time an essential one.

By 19 September the *Pascha*, rather battered by a storm in Drake's absence, had been carefully piloted between the shoals to the new anchorage. Drake, obviously feeling that hard work was the best antidote to disappointment, set his men to building a fort on the nearby island, to be called Fort Diego. It was triangular, with walls thirteen feet high made of an earth bank and large tree-trunks brought from the mainland. Diego and the cimarrons quickly created two houses from palm-branches, and the *Pascha*'s cannon were brought ashore and installed on platforms made from the timbers of the captured vessels.

Drake himself spent most of October and November ranging to the east with Oxenham in two pinnaces, taking, searching and releasing small coastal craft and teasing the shore batteries of Cartagena and Santa Marta. Morale in the open pinnaces was lowered by cold and exposure, and when their supplies dwindled it was discovered that some of the caches of food had been found and rifled. By mid-November a sickness was affecting many men, and after a popular quartermaster, Charles Glub, had died Drake decided to go back to Fort Diego. The smaller pinnace, the *Minion*, was sent ahead to tell John Drake to make all ready for Drake's main preoccupation, the overland journey to attack the *recuas*. It was a long beat to windward, and it was not until 27 November 1572 that Drake reached the *Pascha* and received bad news.

John Drake and a young sailor called Richard Allen had died of wounds received in a hastily conceived and ill-equipped attack on a passing frigate. A few weeks later large numbers of the crew went down with a violent sickness, probably yellow fever. Among those who did not recover was Drake's other brother, Joseph. Drake held him in his arms as he died, and to clarify the cause of the disease he had his body opened up by the surgeon, 'who found his liver swolne, his heart as it were sodden, and his guts all faire'. The surgeon himself died four days after the post-mortem.

Drake's eyes ashore, the cimarrons, had remained in touch with the *Pascha* during his absence and since his return, and had been looking particularly for the arrival in Nombre de Dios of Philip's treasure fleet, which would indicate the imminent resumption of the mule-train movements. The fleet entered port on 5 January 1573, and Drake was informed soon afterwards. He confirmed the information by sending a pinnace, the *Lion*, to the outermost of the Cativas Islands, where she soon pounced on a frigate passing from Tolu to Nombre de Dios with produce for the fleet.

The cimarrons were indispensable to the success of Drake's overland excursion. Twenty-eight of his own men had now died, and he left a few with the trusted Ellis Hixon to look after the *Pascha* and guard his prisoners. This left Drake only eighteen Englishmen to accompany thirty cimarrons on the march towards Panama City. The relationship between the two groups, united in their hatred of the Spanish, appears to have been excellent. The cimarrons' main contribution was their knowledge of the country, but they also did more than their fair share in carrying provisions, supplemented these by their hunting skills, and at every night-stop quickly built half a dozen huts out of branches and palm leaves. Without them, Drake would have got nowhere. The march was very arduous, involving repeated climbs to cross wooded mountain ridges, and the fording of many rivers. They marched from sunrise to ten o'clock, and again from noon until four. Four cimarrons went ahead, breaking branches to show the way, and in the main column the English formed the middle section, with the rest of the cimarrons divided between the van and the rearguard.

One night was spent in a cimarron settlement, a substantial and orderly village of three streets, and a few days later there was an episode which has assumed some symbolic significance in Drakean legend. The cimarrons had promised Drake that they would show him a spot from which both the Atlantic and the Pacific were visible. Towards the end of the morning march on a fine, clear day Pedro, the cimarron leader, took him by the hand and led him to a tall tree in which steps had been cut and an observation platform built. The surrounding trees had been felled, and when Drake climbed up he did, indeed, see the Great South Sea as well as the Atlantic. He called the men up, and 'besought God of his goodnesse to give him leave and life to sayle once in an English Ship in that sea'. John Oxenham, sharing Drake's vision, 'protested that unlesse our Captaine did beate him from his company he would follow him by God's grace'. Both were to realise their ambition; indeed, Oxenham was there first, but God's grace was selective. Drake's venture into the Pacific was to lead to the glory of the circumnavigation, whereas Oxenham's incursion was to lead to his capture, torture and death at the hands of the Inquisition after some of the most outrageously anti-Catholic pillaging perpetrated by an Englishman.

As the column neared Panama, they emerged into grassland; for three days they could see the city intermittently through the hills, and eventually could make out the masts and spars of the ships riding at anchor. Only a few miles from the city Drake halted the march and hid his party in a wood, while a cimarron who had been a slave in Panama went ahead alone to find out the departure time of the *recuas*. They normally travelled by night over the first part of the journey, to

Venta de Chagre, to escape the heat of the day; in the later stages between there and Nombre de Dios they had the protection of the forest trees, and travelled by day.

The spy's news was good: the treasurer of Lima was on his way to Spain with his family, and would leave Panama that night with a *recua* of fourteen mules, of which eight would be carrying gold and jewels. Two other, larger *recuas* would follow, laden mainly with victuals. Drake ordered a rapid march to a point on the road two-thirds of the way to Venta de Chagre, and placed his men in ambush. The attack was minutely planned: the men wore their shirts outside their outer clothes so as to recognise one another in the night, and were split into two parties, positioned so that Drake's group could seize the heads of the foremost mules and the other group, under Oxenham and Pedro, the rearmost. So placed, they would not be shooting towards each other if shooting were necessary.

Crouched in the long grass about fifty yards from the road, the men waited in suspense for a long hour. Then, through the night air, they heard a distant ringing: the sound of the bells on the necks of the mules. They heard it first to the north, the direction of Venta de Chagre, and then, like an echo, from the direction of Panama.

Drake had given orders for anything passing towards Panama to be left unmolested; mules going in that direction were unlikely to be carrying anything resembling treasure. As the first train of mules came along everyone kept his head down except one man, Robert Pike, who had been at the brandy bottle. Forgetting Drake's orders, or perhaps confused about which way was north, he stood up and started forward to win the glory of seizing the first mule. A cimarron beside him dragged him down and lay on him, but too late: a horse-man riding with the *recua* saw the flash of the white shirt and spurred his horse into a gallop and on towards Panama. The *recua* coming in the opposite direction with the gold was only about a mile away. When the horseman came galloping through the dark and warned him of possible danger the treasurer ordered the mules to be led smartly off the road so that the other, larger *recuas* could pass by and on towards Drake.

When Drake's ambush was sprung, he quickly learned from the muleteers that his main prey was now lost, and on its way back to Panama. One man's drunken impetuosity had deprived the enterprise of gold worth 80,000 pesos.[9] In the bitter disappointment at having come so near to success, Drake consulted Pedro, and it was decided to head for Venta de Chagre and fight their way through it. Restoring themselves a little with supplies taken from the mule-packs, they set off along the narrow road through the woods, between walls of vegetation as dense as an English clipped hedge. Nearing the settlement, they ran into a group of well-armed travellers, including some Dominican friars and possibly a contingent of soldiers. When the Spaniards' challenge and demand for surrender drew a pistol-shot from Drake, they fired a ragged volley which wounded him and several others, one of whom later died.

As the hostile fire weakened, Drake ordered his men to fire in return with shot and arrow, and then to rush the enemy, but the Englishmen were overtaken by the cimarrons, dancing a kind of war-dance and yelling 'Yo pehó! Yo pehó!', which put the Spanish to flight. One of the friars and several others were killed. Drake spent about an hour and a half in Venta de Chagre, allowing some minor pillaging as a gesture to the cimarrons, but then pressed on as quickly as possible. Despite invitations from the cimarrons to rest in their villages he marched the men hard in the next few days, not stopping to relax until they reached a cimarron settlement a few miles from the anchored *Pascha*. From there Drake sent a cimarron to tell Hixon to pick them up in a pinnace. As a token to identify the man he sent a gold toothpick with 'By me Francis Drake' scratched on it, and the same afternoon the pinnace arrived.

The raid had taken a heavy toll of the men's condition and spirits. Their feet, particularly, were in such a sorry state from the rough terrain and stony rivers that the cimarrons made new shoes for them. A deeper pain, however, was the evaporation of their dreams of gold.

> Wee all seemed, to those who had lived at rest and plenty all this while, as men strangely changed ... in countenance and plight, and indeed our long fasting and sore travell might somewhat fore-pine and waste us, but the greefe we drew inwardly, for that we returned without that Gold and Treasure we hoped for, did no doubt shew her print and footsteps in our faces.[10]

A leader less charismatic than Drake might well have faced discontent and mutiny after this exhausting failure. His remedy, as usual, was more action, 'as knowing right well by continuall experience, that no sicknesse was more noysome to impeach any enterprise than delay and idlenesse'. First of all he made clear his intention to make another attack on the mule-trains when the dust had settled. He then invited ideas as to what to do in the meantime. There were three suggestions: seize a few food-ships and replenish provisions; look for ships bearing treasure; and (this from the cimarrons) raid the gold stores of the Veragua mines, to the west. Some of the cimarrons had worked in the mines and painted a tempting picture of 'a mightie Masse of Treasure ... in certaine great Chests of two foot deepe, three broad, and four long'. Their proposal was that they should guide Drake to the mines overland and come at the owner's house from the landward side for greater surprise. Drake was interested in the gold, but had had enough of forest and river for the present. He decided to split his forces to carry out the first two suggestions, though he did not dismiss the gold-mine from his mind.

Oxenham, in the pinnace *Bear*, was sent east to Tolu to look for provision ships to rifle, and Drake sailed west in the *Minion* to lurk in wait for ships bringing treasure from Veragua to the fleet in Nombre de Dios. He soon came across a frigate which provided some gold. Her pilot, one of the many Genoese serving in Spanish vessels in the Indies, offered to guide Drake by night into Veragua harbour, where a frigate laden down with gold was waiting to sail. After some hesitation Drake agreed, with his mind half on the treasure ship and half on the gold at the mine.

As they approached the harbour mouth they heard two shots, followed by two more in answer further into the bay. It was obvious that they had been seen, and with the wind now coming westerly Drake turned and returned to the *Pascha*. Oxenham had taken a fine new frigate, full of fat pigs, 200 hens and quantities of maize. Drake was so pleased with the prize that he put some guns into her and crewed her as a man-of-war. On Easter Sunday the men feasted on pork and chicken, and on the next day, 21 March 1573, he set off for the Cativas in his new frigate, accompanied by the *Bear*.

Two days later, about noon, they saw a sail to the west. As they approached her, she fired her lee-side guns in a friendly salute. She was a French privateer from Le Havre, captained by Guillaume Le Têtu;[11] he had been looking for Drake with a view to joining forces with him. Drake told him to follow, and when the ships came to anchor the Frenchman sent Drake a gift of a case of pistols and a scimitar said to have belonged to the king of France. Drake responded with the gift of a gold chain. At their first meeting Le Têtu gave Drake the news of the death of thousands of Huguenots in Paris in the massacre of St Bartholomew's Eve the previous summer. For one as fervent in his Protestantism as Drake, this hardening of the religious rift can only have worked to stiffen his hatred of papism.

Drake accepted Le Têtu as an ally, but with a certain edgy distrust.

The Frenchman had a larger vessel, with seventy men; the English were now reduced to thirty-one. Drake thought he needed more men for a second attack on the *recuas*. It is not clear why; the first attack had not failed for lack of men, and the cimarrons had been willing, undemanding and invaluable allies. He probably assumed that the Spanish, after their first scare, were now sending more soldiers with the *recuas*. Whatever his reasons, he accepted the Frenchman's help on the basis of equal participation and equal shares. Two cimarrons were brought aboard for the discussions, and after reprovisioning his own vessel and the French from one of his caches Drake set off in his new frigate and the *Bear* and *Minion* pinnaces (the *Lion* had been scuttled as surplus to requirements). The party consisted of twenty French, fifteen English and an unknown number of cimarrons. Leaving the frigate, with her deeper draft, at the Cabezas, Drake and Le Têtu landed at the mouth of the River Francisca,[12] not far from Nombre de Dios. The pinnaces were ordered to return to the frigate and to come back four days later. 'And thus, knowing that the cariages [i.e. the *recuas*] went now daily from Panama to Nombre de Dios, we proceeded in covert through the woods, towards the high way that leadeth betweene them.'

The ambush was to take place close to Nombre de Dios; so close, in fact, that when the party stopped to rest for the night a mile from the mule-train road they could hear the hammers of the shipwrights working in the harbour. In the morning, 1 April, they heard the mules approaching from Panama, and as the bells came closer the cimarrons danced in glee as they realised the size of the *recuas*. There were almost 200 mules in three trains, most animals carrying about 300 pounds of silver, some carrying gold.

The plan was the same as on the first raid, and this time there were no brandy-fuelled heroics to spoil it. The halters of the leading and hindmost mules were seized, and the ones in between obligingly stopped and lay down. The forty or fifty escorting soldiers put up a brief resistance during which a cimarron was killed and Le Têtu was wounded in the belly with small shot. After the guards had taken flight, some to raise the alarm in Nombre de Dios, the raiders unloaded the mules, buried about fifteen tons of silver and some gold in the gravel of the river and in holes made by land-crabs, and made off with what they could carry. Drake does not appear to have considered simply cutting the bells off some of the mules and leading them away with their loads.

When the routed soldiers reached Nombre de Dios the mayor,

Diego Calderón, ordered a drum to sound the alarm and set off with a band of about thirty men. They arrived about two hours after the start of the attack, followed the trail of the raiders into the forest and caught up with the stragglers, including the wounded Le Têtu and another Frenchman who had overburdened himself and fallen behind. Le Têtu, belying his surname, was promptly beheaded. The pursuit continued through the day, but was called off at dusk on a vile night of rain and storm. The captured Frenchman was persuaded to point out where the treasure had been buried, and was then executed. Le Têtu's head and that of the dead cimarron were exhibited in the market-place of Nombre de Dios.

The raiders marched on the next day through the sodden forest. The Spanish were confused about exactly where Drake had landed,[13] and a force of fifty men sent by Calderón to intercept him on his way back to the coast had a wasted journey. However, when Drake's party emerged from the woods near their landing-place and looked out to sea, they were dismayed to find, not their own boats, but a force of seven Spanish pinnaces searching the coast. Flores, the captain-general, had chosen them from amongst the fleet as soon as he heard of the raid, crewed them with ninety men with muskets and small ordnance, sent them to search the area of the River Francisca, and taken to his bed with tertian fever.

In Drake's party, spirits sank. Even when the Spanish pinnaces gave up the search in stormy conditions there was no sign of Drake's vessels. They were, in fact, struggling towards him under oars against the strong westerly wind. Into Drake's mind came the thought that their captured friends had been tortured into revealing the where-abouts of the ships, that these, with their depleted crews, had been seized by the Spanish, and that he and the raiding party were now shipless, helpless and at their enemies' mercy.

Drake's leadership never faltered. Many have said that he was lucky in his enterprises, which he was; luckier than Hawkins, far luckier than Oxenham or Le Têtu. But luck can be helped. If the pinnaces had been captured, perhaps the ships had not. The course of least peril was to make for the ships. To the twentieth-century landsman Drake's proposal of how to reach them looks like madness born of desperation. He simply refused to acknowledge that nothing could be done, and his solution was the natural one to a man more at home on water than on land, who had had the crafts of the sea in him from his boyhood: build a boat with whatever he could lay his hands on:

If the enemy have prevailed against our Pinnaces, which God forbid, yet they must have time to search them, time to examine the Mariners; time to execute their resolution after it is determined; before all these times be taken, we may get to our Ships if yee will, though not possibly by land, because of the Hills, Thickets and Rivers, yet by water. Let us therefore make a Raft with the trees that are heere in readiness as offring themselves, being brought downe by the River happily this last storm, and put our selves to Sea. I will be one. Who will be the other?

A man called John Smith stepped forward immediately; then two Frenchmen and some of the cimarrons. Tree-trunks were lashed together, a crude mast and rudder fitted, and a sail improvised from a biscuit sack. With a favourable wind, and under the blazing sun which had followed the storm, this piece of organised flotsam was pushed out, low in the water under the weight of its crew, and set off eastward. They sailed six hours under the unremitting sun, soaked to the armpits by every wave, and towards night they sighted two pinnaces, which altered course towards them. Their elation subsided when it became clear that they had not been seen, and they watched the pinnaces row in towards the coast ahead of them and vanish into a bay, obviously to spend the night. Drake's makeshift craft was manoeuvred to the shore, and leaping out he raced along the beach and around the point, followed by Smith and the Frenchmen, to be dragged on board the pinnaces by the crews, who thought the Spanish were after them.

Even now, sunburned, soaked and dishevelled, Drake could manage a joke. When he was asked how things had gone, he put on a miserable look and said 'Well ...'; and as their faces grew grave he smiled and pulled out a great quoit of gold from inside his doublet, 'thanking God that our voyage was made'. Aware of the danger to the men he had left, he ordered the tired crews to row on through the night. By dawn all the landing party and their plunder were aboard, and the pinnaces had set their sails and were running free to rejoin the frigate and thereafter the *Pascha* and Le Têtu's ship. The gold and silver were weighed and shared equally between the English and the French, and a fortnight later, having stripped the *Pascha*, Drake handed her over to his Spanish prisoners and set them free.

After one failure and one startling success against the *recuas*, most men would have sailed home satisfied. The French sailed away. Drake, amazingly, planned a third foray, partly to save Le Têtu, whose fly-blown head was by now decaying on its pole, but mainly to recover

*A typical sixteenth-century vessel, square-rigged on fore- and mainmasts
with a triangular lateen sail on the mizzenmast*

some of the buried treasure. He appointed John Oxenham and
Thomas Sherwell as leaders of a party of twenty-six, including sixteen
cimarrons. They were rowed ashore, probably at the same landing-
place as before, since they found waiting a desperate Frenchman who
had stayed behind to help Le Têtu. He told them that his Captain
was dead, and that all the treasure had been dug up, but Oxenham
pressed on. The Spanish had, indeed, dug up a large area near the
road, but the men managed to find thirteen bars of silver and a few
quoits of gold, and re-embarked three days later in good spirits.

Drake's final flourish showed the theatricality and devil which
might have got less lucky men into terminal trouble. The Spanish
fleet was now at anchor off Cartagena. Drake, with a fortune in gold

and silver below decks, had no need to go anywhere near them. Being Drake, young and elated, he sailed past in full view of the fleet, flying the flag of St George and with the ship decked out in pennants and streamers from the tip of her mainmast to the waterline.

Supplementing his supplies from a captured frigate carrying pigs, poultry, maize and honey, he spent a week at the Cabezas preparing for the homeward passage. The pinnaces were burned and their ironwork was given to the cimarrons. Pedro, the chief, and three of his lieutenants were invited to choose gifts, and while Drake was looking through his own chests to find some silks or linens for the cimarron women Pedro's eye fell on the scimitar given by Le Têtu. Not daring to ask for it directly, he asked one of Drake's men to broach the subject, offering to buy it for four quoits of gold. Drake was loath to lose the weapon, but he made the trade with a good grace, and put the gold into the common fund. He parted with the cimarrons on the warmest of terms, the first European who had used them without abusing them, in an alliance which left the Spanish incredulous and quaking in fear for the future of their Central American possessions if such associations developed further.

The voyage home was speedier than Drake could have hoped. Heavy rains in the Caribbean replenished his water-casks, making an expected call on the Florida coast unnecessary. Twenty-three days after passing the tip of Florida they sighted the Scillies, and on 9 August 1573 they sailed into Plymouth. It was a Sunday, and few people heard the preachers' sermons that morning, 'all hastning to see the evidence of Gods love and blessing towards our Gracious Queene and Countrey, by the fruite of our Captaines labour and successe'.

VI

To Anoy Hym by his Indyes
1573-77

> 'Of how great importance then ... is that
> Attempt which is by a British subject presently
> intended, ... who (God sparing life and health)
> hath secretly offered up to God and to his
> Naturall Soverayn and Country the employing
> of all his skill and talent, and the patient
> enduring of the great toyle of his body, to that
> place being the very ends of the world from us
> to be reckoned.'
>
> Doctor John Dee, *The Great Volume of Famous*
> *and Rich Discoveries*, 1577

Even though half had gone to the French, the proceeds of the raid on the mule-trains were about £20,000, a handsome return on such a modestly mounted voyage. The crews must have been well satisfied with their portion, but the share taken by Drake, as both commander and owner of one of the ships, was enough to set him up in life; barely in his thirties he was, in Camden's words, 'now growne abundantly rich'. From now on he was in a position to take his own decisions, make his own proposals, and live like a gentleman, no longer a dependant on Hawkins' support but a respected and envied figure in the mercantile community of Plymouth. He bought a house in the town, and more ships. As the years went by he acquired more properties, including mills. It would be interesting to know something of his wife Mary's feelings in this period, as she became used to fine clothes, rich linens, tapestries and tableware, and waited touchily for the pregnancy which never arrived. Drake's career of voyaging was temporarily dampened by a brief period when it looked as if there could be a reconciliation with Spain, and anything which appeared to threaten this was unlikely to gain favour with the Queen. Consequently we have few details about his activities in the four years after his return. He had a shipowning business to establish, and with his love of the sea and its craft it is unlikely that he did this from behind a desk.

His next documented involvement in furthering the national interest was in connection with the campaign in Ireland entrusted by the Queen to Walter Devereux, the Earl of Essex, who employed Drake's ships to ferry his troops and was impressed by his performance.[1] There is no evidence that Drake took part in any of the very bloody fighting. Two men involved in the campaign were to play a role in his future: John Norris, who directed the massacre of a force of Scots on Rathlin Island in July 1575, and Thomas Doughty, a literate and well-connected member of Essex's entourage.

This was a time when geographers and navigators were much occupied with schemes to enable England to catch up the ground lost to Spain and Portugal in the world's trading possibilities. The schemes put forward in the 1570s included the idea of looking for areas of the southern hemisphere not yet exploited by Spain, but it was principally the northern hemisphere which appeared to offer the possibility of finding an English route to the rich markets of the Far East without offending the Portuguese or, more particularly, the Spanish. As early as around 1530 a merchant called Robert Thorne, trading in Seville, had written to Henry VIII that 'there is one way to discover, which is unto the north, for out of Spaine they have discovered all the Indies and Seas Occidentall, and out of Portugal all the Indies and Seas Orientall'.[2]

The great geographer, mathematician and suspected necromancer John Dee supported the idea of a north-east passage to the Pacific around the north of Russia. Expeditions had probed in this direction since the early 1550s, and had led to trade links with Russia and the formation of the Muscovy Company in 1555. Stephen Borough's expedition of 1556-7 reached the Kara Sea; he was accompanied by his sixteen-year-old brother William, who was later to become Clerk of the Queen's Ships, Vice-Admiral to Drake, and his bitter enemy.

From the late 1560s some of the best-known figures of Elizabethan seafaring began to turn their attention to the other possibility, a north-west passage, which had been Thorne's idea forty years earlier; he thought there was a strait linking the Atlantic to the Pacific across the north of America. This passage came to be known as the Strait of Anian, and the idea of sailing through it to reach the Orient was developed by Humphrey Gilbert in a treatise written in 1566. This was printed in 1576[3] to publicise the voyage undertaken by Martin

Frobisher to look for the passage in the same year. The map accompanying the book shows the strait wide and welcoming in a latitude well below the Arctic Circle; it stretches west, from an archipelago which includes Canada and Labrador as islands, to join the Pacific at a point not far from Japan.

When Frobisher returned, a printed account claimed that he had found the eastern entrance to the strait, but this was in reality only a bay on the coast of Baffin Island.[4] Frobisher made another voyage and brought back 200 tons of what he thought was gold ore. The assayers found no gold in it, but a third voyage was organised, and after sailing into Hudson Strait but turning back to load more ore he returned to England and made no further attempts.

Despite these northern explorations, the southern latitudes continued to fascinate the English. Not only was it correctly thought that the extreme south of the American continent still had no firmly established Spanish presence; it was supposed that there were vast lands further south separated from South America by the Strait of Magellan. This unexploited Terra Australis is shown on maps as a great continent centred on the South Pole, and was thought to be a potential source of riches exceeding even Spain's possessions in the Indies. It was said to include some of the otherwise unidentified areas mentioned by Marco Polo.

In 1574 Elizabeth was tempted by a proposal from William Hawkins and Richard Grenville. They sought permission to look for lands 'southward beyond the equinoctiall' not yet in the possession of any Christian ruler. Whether they were aiming at Terra Australis or areas on the South American mainland was left, probably deliberately, ambiguous. In conversations with John Oxenham, however, Grenville said that his intention was to establish a settlement in the River Plate area, pass through the strait of Magellan and 'look for land to settle, or some islands, because England is full of people and short of land'. According to Oxenham the Queen gave Grenville a licence, and he bought two ships, negotiated for others, and tried repeatedly to persuade Oxenham to go with him. The Queen, fluctuating as she so often did between trenchant action and indecision, revoked the licence when she heard that there were Spanish settlements in Chile.[5]

Oxenham is also the source of a statement that Drake and he had often discussed just such a project, and that Drake had said that 'if the Queen would give him leave he would sail through the Strait of Magellan and set up a colony here [Oxenham was speaking in Lima] in some suitable area ... with the help of friends and relations he could bring two or three ships, and more when he had found a suitable place.'[6]

A companion of Oxenham, Thomas Gerard, said at the same time that Elizabeth was the only obstacle to such an enterprise: 'if the Queen dies many people will come through the Strait and settle; she is the one hindrance and England is full of people who wish to emigrate'. He had heard it said that if she were to die, Drake would come through the Strait. The same man said that the Queen had refused Grenville and Hawkins the licence after demanding a surety of £30,000 or £40,000 that they would not attack Philip's possessions, which they could not or would not pay.

All this suggests that Grenville and William Hawkins were interested mainly if not exclusively in the southern parts of South America, on both sides of the Strait, and that Drake knew all about the scheme and was not averse to the idea himself. To keep alive the idea of passing through the Strait to the Pacific, Grenville tried a different tack: he wrote to Burghley suggesting that it would be useful to look for the western end of the Strait of Anian by sailing up the Pacific, and he also painted an alluring picture of the commercial possibilities of crossing to China or of finding new southern islands rich in gold, rubies and pearls.[7]

The Grenville–Hawkins scheme must have been squashed by April 1576, for it was then that John Oxenham left English politicking behind and set off for the Isthmus of Panama. He went in company with an Irishman, John Butler, nicknamed Chalona by the Spanish. The voyage had no official backing, and involved only one small ship with two sectional pinnaces. A Spanish report says that they had with them two cimarrons carried off after the 1573 raid.

Oxenham's ship was one of many raiders in the Caribbean in 1576.[8] He left his ship hidden in an inlet west of Cartagena and ranged about in his pinnaces. He had no grand strategic ideas; he was simply interested in carrying on the business of pillage, at which he was very talented. Reports soon reached the *Audiencia* in Panama that he was working in concert with the cimarrons, and he spent the winter of 1576-7 in their settlement at Vallano. On the Pacific side of the isthmus he built a 45-foot pinnace, and in February he attacked the Pearl Islands off Panama, so beating Drake to the distinction of being the first Englishman to sail on the Great South Sea towards which they had gazed together in their previous expedition. He pillaged the islands, carried out some hearty acts of sacrilege, and after briefly contemplating a raid on the city of Panama seized a fortune in gold from a Guayaquil ship and headed back to Vallano. The Panama authorities acted swiftly, found some of his party unloading the pinnace, and subsequently captured Oxenham, Butler and most of the rest. They were sent to Lima and interrogated by the Inquisition, which extracted from them the information about the Grenville–Hawkins plan and Drake's interest in the Strait of Magellan.[9]

Meanwhile the proposal for Drake's own venture into the Pacific had taken shape. We do not know from whom the project originated; it probably came from Drake himself, after discussion with John Hawkins and the Wynter family. A memorandum by the Secretary of State, Francis Walsingham,[10] names the proposed investors in the venture as the Queen's favourite the Earl of Leicester, Walsingham himself, Christopher Hatton, who was Captain of the Queen's Bodyguard, William and George Wynter, John Hawkins and Drake. The Queen probably contributed; it was proposed that the royal ship *Swallow* should constitute her adventure, and as the ship was not used (perhaps because Elizabeth thought its use would make her involvement too obvious) her contribution was probably in money, like the rest.[11] Drake invested £1,000; Hawkins £500; the Wynters £1,250.

The project was wrapped in secrecy. What were its objectives? Walsingham's memorandum has been partly destroyed by fire; the surviving text, with the burned sections represented by dots, reads:

> ... the powlle ... the southe sea then ... far to the northwards as ... along the saied coast ... as of the other to fynde owt ... to have trafick for the vent ... of thies her Ma[jes]ties Realmes ... they are not under the obediens of ... prynces, so is ther great hoepe of ... spieces, drugs, cochynille, and ... speciall comodities, such as maye ... her highnes domynyons, and also ... shipping awoork greatly and ... gotten up as aforesaid into XXX de[grees] ... the southe sea, yf it shall be thowght ... by the fore named frances draek to ... far then he is to returne the same way whome words as he went owt, w[hi]ch viage by godes favor is to be performed in XIIth month, All thowghe he shuld spend V monthes in taryenge upon the coaste to get knowle[dge] of the prynces and cowmptres ther.

The plan seems to be very similar to Grenville's first idea: enter the Pacific, which in the existing state of knowledge could only be done by passing through the Strait of Magellan, turn north, and investigate the potential of the west coast of South America as far as latitude 30° south. The words 'as of the other' suggest that the east coast was also to be explored below the same latitude before passing the strait. Five months were to be spent exploring the coasts, and a year on the whole voyage. There is a show of legality in the reference to not upsetting 'the obediens of princes'.

These proposals are not coming from the Queen downwards, since the previous page records a request to Walsingham that she 'be made pryve to the trewth of the viage'. This implies that others are not to be made privy to it; indeed, they are to be misled about it: 'the coollor [i.e. colour] to be given owt for allixandria'. This ploy of maintaining that the voyage was bound for the eastern Mediterranean was continued successfully up to the time of departure to confuse Spanish intelligence.

The memorandum has the air of being the result of a conclave of the main promoters of the voyage to decide how best to present the idea to Elizabeth. Drake later gave a rather different picture of the planning of the project, at a time when he was keen to stress the Queen's involvement and his authority deriving from her. According to him the plan was conveyed to him by Walsingham and Elizabeth after he had been recommended as the right man for the job by the Earl of Essex. This is Drake's description of the conversations, as reported by John Cooke, who went on the voyage:

'... thus it was: my lorde of Essex wrote in my commendations unto secretorye Walsyngham more then I was worthy, but belyke I had deserved somewhat at his hands, and he thowght me in his letters to be a fite man to sarve agaynst the Spanyards,' ... where upon indede secretary Walsyngham dyd come to conferr with hym, and declared unto hym that for that her Maiestie had receyved dyvers iniuries of the Kynge of Spayne, for the whiche she desyred to have some revenge; 'and withal he shewed me a plott (quoth he) willinge me to set my hand, and to noate downe where I thowght he myght moaste be anoyed; but I tolde hym some parte of my mynde, but refused to set my hand to any thinge, affirminge that hir Maiestie was mortall, and yf it shuld please God to take hir Maiestie awaie, it myght be that some prince myght rayne that myght be in league with the Kynge of Spayne, and then wyll myne owne hand be a witness agaynst my selfe. Then was I very shortly aftar and in an eveninge sent for unto hir Maiestie by secretary Walsyngham, but cam not to hir Maiestie that nyght, for that it was late; but the next daye comynge to hir presens, thes or the lyke words she sayd: "Drake, So it is that I would gladly be revenged on the Kynge of Spayne, for dyvers iniuries that I have receyved,"' and sayd fardar that he was thonely man that myght do this exployte, and withal craved his advice therein. Who told hir Maiestie of the smale good that was to be done in Spayne, but thonly waye was to anoy hym by his Indyes.[12]

The Queen laid great stress on secrecy, swearing on her crown that if word of the plans reached Philip she would have the culprit's head. Great efforts were also made to keep the matter from Burghley, who could be expected to react strongly against it and to see the idea as a bomb hurled into a pond in which he was trying to keep ripples to a minimum. It would be surprising if Burghley, whose ear was very close to the ground, never heard a whisper of what was afoot, but Drake certainly thought he was unaware of the plans at the time of departure.

So Francis Drake, born on a Devon farm and raised on a Medway hulk, was now consulted on policy and tactics by his sovereign, and shared secrets with her which were kept from the highest in the land. Elizabeth's stress on secrecy, her words about being revenged on Philip (if we may believe Drake's report of them), and subsequent events indicate that their conversation went well beyond a confirmation of a permit to explore the uninhabited coast of Chile without treading on Philip's toes. In this interview or in later negotiations Drake's sphere of activity was almost certainly extended, perhaps under the influence of Grenville's second proposal for a search for the western end of the Strait of Anian. Two of the backers, Leicester and Walsingham, were also involved in Frobisher's venture which had reported finding the eastern end of the Strait. Everyone involved, the Queen included, probably expected Drake to make the voyage pay by acts of plunder not included in his formal instructions, but naturally this understanding could not be voiced publicly and Elizabeth would not dream of committing such an idea to writing in time of peace.

There is no indication that the real plan was to sail round the world, except that one person, John Wynter, acquired the idea now or later that the Molucca Islands in the south-west Pacific were part of the itinerary. As he was Drake's deputy on the voyage, his opinion is worth consideration. If the voyage were to include the Moluccas, then the known way to Europe from there was on westward, across the Indian Ocean to complete the circumnavigation. The adventurers' secrecy was well maintained, with the help of leaked misinformation: Philip's envoy in London, Antonio de Guaras, reported in September 1577 that Drake was assembling a fleet of little ships to raid Scotland.

VII

WHERE WYLL WAS LAW,
AND REASON PUT IN EXILE
1577–78

'... mischief, by Gods providence detected and
prevented in time, which else had extended
itselfe, not onely to the violent shedding of
innocent blood by murthering our generall, ...
but also to the final overthrow of the whole
action intended.'

Anon., *The World Encompassed*, 1628

Drake's little fleet set sail from Plymouth in the gathering dusk of the
evening of 15 November 1577. His flagship, the *Pelican*, was not
large, at 150 tons, but was his grandest command so far. She had
been built in Devon to his own order.[1] Her companions were more
on the scale which Drake had been used to on his earlier voyages:
the *Elizabeth*, 80 tons, was commanded by John Wynter; the bark
Marigold, 30 tons, by John Thomas; the fly-boat *Swan*, 50 tons, by
John Chester, and the pinnace *Christopher*, 15 tons, by Thomas
Moone, the co-operative carpenter now rewarded for his work with
the auger on the previous voyage.[2] Drake also took four partly built
pinnaces aboard the larger ships for assembly as necessary in the
calmer waters of the south. He had 164 men, some of them only
ship's boys.

The composition of the ships' companies was unusual for the times.
We are accustomed to the vision of the grizzled, hornpipe-dancing
seadog of Old England. Drake took with him many men in a less
romanticised version of this mould. He also took, however, a group
of blue-blooded young men, nine or ten on the *Pelican*. They were
described by a Spanish captive later as 'cadets of English noblemen'.[3]
These included two brothers, Thomas and John Doughty. Thomas,
who had been with Drake in Ireland, was regarded by at least one of
the gentlemen sailors, John Cooke, as a partner in the venture with

Drake and Wynter, 'eqwall companyons and frindly gentlemen.'[4]

The inclusion of these men was clearly a deliberate decision by Drake, and we shall hear something of his attitudes to them in a later chapter. He certainly came to regret the presence of some of them, and possibly all of them; the inclusion of an articulate group, without clearly defined duties, in the narrow confines of a crowded ship, their subordinate ranking vis-à-vis the officers less clearly delineated by social inferiority than that of the common seamen, was a doubtful idea from the first. Their inclusion by Drake has been seen as indicating vision, the conviction 'that the future greatness of his country was to be built up by the educated privateer or Gentleman Adventurer'.[5] Less charitably one might see it as a misguided insurance policy; we cannot be sure how long Drake expected to be away, but he knew it was to be a long and hazardous voyage. The fiction had been maintained that the voyage was to be a workaday one to Gibraltar and on to Alexandria, and the seamen had been recruited on this understanding. If they rose in revolt when they found themselves heading for Patagonia, a few smart upper-class fellows practised in sword-play might be invaluable allies to threatened and outnumbered officers.

Among the common seamen were several foreigners, including Great Nele, who was a Danish gunner, and at least two Dutchmen, Arthur (a trumpeter) and Little Nele. The Diego aboard, described as 'a black Moore', was probably the one who had become such a favourite after the raid on Nombre de Dios.[6] As the voyage progressed the crew was to be augmented by other foreigners with specialised navigational knowledge to suit Drake's immediate purposes: a Greek, another Dutchman, Spaniards and Portuguese, other negroes, even a South-American Indian.

One might have expected some pomp to accompany the departure of a fleet with such a grand design. Drake's concept of his own dignity was evidently growing with his reputation; he had gone to some lengths 'to make provision for ornament and delight': a group of musicians, lavish provision of table silver, and 'divers shewes of all sorts of curious workmanship whereby the civilitie and magnificence of his native country might ... be the more admired'.[7] As he sailed from Plymouth, however, his love of theatricality was restrained by the need for discretion about his destinations and purposes.

Any euphoria, public or otherwise, was soon quenched by the stern November realities of the Western Approaches. On the first morning, off the Lizard, the wind came SW, and the ships put into Falmouth. Late on the 17th a real storm blew up, continued through the night, and increased with such violence between five and ten o'clock on the following morning that the ships, even in the shelter of Falmouth, suffered serious damage. Both the *Pelican* and the *Marigold* had their mainmasts cut away to save them. It was decided to put back for repairs, but what with the prolonged storm and the time it took to clear the ships, it was not until 28 November that the fleet regained Plymouth, and it took another fortnight to fit and rig new mainmasts. Drake was in a bad mood; he had an angry argument with a steward, James Stydye, and dismissed him from the company.[8]

They sailed again on 13 December. Drake set the island of Mogador as a rendezvous in case of separation, but this time the fleet had favourable winds, and with no problems except the loss of a ship's boy off Portugal made a landfall at Cape Cantin on the African coast on Christmas morning. After sailing down the coast to Mogador and taking soundings, Drake brought his ships to anchor in the shelter of the island on 27 December.

The next few days were spent in putting together one of the pinnaces on the island, and in very edgy relations with the subjects of the Moorish King of Fez, some of whom came down to the shore shortly after Drake's arrival. A boat was sent to bring some of them aboard, leaving a seaman on shore as surety. Plied with food and the gift of clothes, shoes and a javelin, the two promised to return on the following morning with some of the produce of the country. They departed in goodwill and returned the hostage. The following day, as promised, about thirty camels arrived, and a boat was again sent ashore.

There followed another of the small dramas with which the actor involved must have thrilled his grandchildren and bored his neighbours. The boat's crew included John Fry, a seaman who had been to Africa on trading voyages, knew a few words of the language and was evidently keen to show them off. He jumped ashore, ran inland to greet the Moors, and was promptly seized and taken away at knife-point. The boat crew quickly re-embarked and rowed away. The whole affair had been a stratagem to gain information on the part of the King of Fez, who suspected that Drake's ships belonged to the King of Portugal, with whom his relations were poor. Drake huffed and puffed about recovering Fry and led a foray inland, where he found the Moors unwilling to accept the challenge. He did some sight-seeing in a ruined Portuguese fort, loaded some wood, and sailed away for Cape Blanco on New Year's Eve. (The abandoned Fry, proving that knowing a little of the language can get one out of trouble as well as into it, was allowed to sail home on an English merchantman not long afterwards.)

The New Year of 1578 began with foul weather and adverse winds. The first seaborne actions of the voyage occurred in the first half of January. In a series of easy pickings off the African coast Drake's new pinnace took three Spanish fishing-boats called *canters* on the 7th and a caravel on the 13th; the *Marigold* took another caravel on the 15th; and after rounding Cape Blanco late on 17 January the fleet found a Spanish ship riding quietly at anchor with only two men aboard.[9] All these prizes were taken into harbour, and Drake decided to rest for a few days to clean and revictual his ships.

He found the inhabitants desperate for water; they offered him a female slave with a baby at her breast ('in which sort of merchandise our generall would not deale', notwithstanding his West Indian activities with Hawkins). Drake gave them water for nothing, and even food, 'in eating whereof their manner was not onely uncivill and unsightly to us, but even inhumane and loathsome'.[10] During this stay, according to John Cooke, the men were trained 'in warlyke order', presumably ashore. Cooke's grammar is faulty, so that it is not clear whether the training was done by Drake, Thomas Doughty, or the whole group of gentleman sailors, but he does mention the special 'meanes and procurement' of Doughty, 'who was always carefull in that respecte and toke great paynes in that behalf'.[11]

Drake sailed again on 21 January. He left behind all the prizes except the best of the *canters*, the owner of which was recompensed with the gift of the little *Christopher*,[12] and one Portuguese caravel. His next call, mainly to refill his water-casks, was at Maio in the Cape Verdes, where he arrived on 28 January. He spent two days there, sending Doughty and Wynter with about seventy men to find water, and continued westward. South-west of Santiago he took a good prize: a richly laden Portuguese ship bound for Brazil.[13] The most important contribution she provided to Drake was her pilot, Nunho da Silva, the course of whose life was changed drastically and permanently.

Except for a couple of token cannon-shots 'in honour of our fleet and Generall' as the ships sailed by, the shore installations in the Cape Verdes kept their heads down and waited for Drake to go away, which he did on 2 February. He put the crew and passengers of the Portuguese prize into his new pinnace with some bread, fish and wine, and let them go. Having renamed the prize *Mary*, he put Thomas Doughty into her as captain, 'as his good and especiall friend',[14] and set his course 'to passe into the South Sea'. The River Plate was named as the next rendezvous. The chaplain of the fleet, Francis Fletcher, strikes a note of awe and portent in his journal:

> And so wee take our farwell from the antient knowne parts of the world ... to travill into the new discovered partes, ... by the Gracious Providence of God, the God of all the world, Who, hitherto, in His singular mercy and grace, has preserved us alive to see and behold more and more of his excellent workes.[15]

They crossed the equator on 17 February, and sighted the coast of Brazil on 5 April, after a generally straightforward crossing. Their worries about water, not properly dispelled in the Cape Verdes, faded when it rained every day from 10 to 27 February. The concern returned on 28 March, when the Portuguese prize went missing with the bulk of the water supplies, but she rejoined the rest on the following day. The crews' diet was enlivened with flying fish, dolphin, bonito and the numerous birds which settled on the ships and were easily clubbed or snared.

In respect of personal relationships, however, and the mental ease of the main participants, the Atlantic crossing brought a marked deterioration. An unbroken passage of sixty-three days provides ample time in which small wounds may fester, social resentments smoulder into flame, and professed friendship crumble under the pressures of doubt and eventual distrust.

Drake's relations with Thomas Doughty during and after the Atlantic passage have left an ill-defined stain on his reputation. Evidence for what happened between them is, in two senses, partial. Aspects of Drake's character emerge which make us glad that we were not his subordinates: ruthlessness in authority; a quick anger; an excess of family loyalty; perhaps even hypocrisy. Reading between the lines, one can perceive that his attitude to Doughty may have been affected by factors other than truly objective ones. There was the social difference between them. Drake was an entrepreneurial seaman on his way to becoming a gentleman; Doughty a gentleman temporarily at sea. Doughty clearly had a high opinion of his own role in setting up the voyage, and saw himself as having a say in the running of things, an opinion shared by John Cooke. We have seen Doughty taking on the traditional aristocrat's function of drilling the troops during the days in Africa, and entrusted, with Wynter, with the leadership of the foray in the Cape Verdes, perhaps emerging more and more as the leader of the military aspects of the enterprise, while

Drake remained the unquestioned master on the maritime side.

In view of the events which followed it, it is hard to be sure whether Drake's appointment of Doughty to the command of the Portuguese prize was an indication of ability recognised and rewarded, or Drake's way of distancing a man whose social airs and increasing self-importance were growing irksome in the small confines of the *Pelican*. There was certainly some kind of gunpowder in their relationship, and when the spark came to light it the explosion was savage and, for Doughty, ultimately fatal.

According to John Cooke's account, the spark was struck by Drake's brother Thomas, described by Cooke as 'not the wysest man in Christendom, ... and more gredy of praie than covetous of honestie or credite'.[16] Drake had transferred his brother to the Portuguese prize along with Doughty. He had also expressly forbidden the prize crew to tamper with the cargo, a prohibition which Thomas Drake ignored by breaking open a chest and rummaging in it. When Doughty took him to task he begged him not to report the matter, but Doughty did his duty and informed Drake next time he came aboard the prize. Perhaps he did so with some relish, for Drake took the reporting of his brother as a piece of malice against himself, swore great oaths and declared that he would not have it. Doughty was sent back to the *Pelican*. Thomas Drake not only escaped punishment, but was made captain of the prize in Doughty's stead.

Francis Fletcher's account[17] makes no mention of any contravention of orders by Thomas Drake, saying instead that shortly after Doughty was given the captaincy he was denounced to Drake on the *Pelican* by a group including John Brewer and Edward Bright for appropriating valuables from the Portuguese passengers. Drake went to the prize to investigate and found Doughty in possession of some Portuguese gloves, unidentified coins, and a ring, which he had been given in full view of everyone 'in hope of favour'. Drake, not in open anger at this point, but 'in discression', sent Doughty back to the *Pelican*, put Thomas Drake in his place, and remained in the prize for a while to oversee the departure of the Portuguese in the pinnace. When Drake returned to the flagship he was met by fresh accusations against Doughty by the crew, 'such as had him in dislike', for being too peremptory and authoritarian. Drake therefore 'remooved the said Doughty into the fly boat [i.e. the *Swan*] with utter disgrace'.

Fletcher's wording gives the impression that this dismissal happened almost immediately, while the fleet was still off the Cape Verdes. John Cooke, however, gives convincing evidence of a period of festering resentment and growing division of loyalties, some of the company, including Leonard Vicary, arguing Doughty's case with Drake, others sharing Drake's simmering distrust of him. Cooke, obviously no lover of Drake, says that 'he dayly sowght matar agaynste Mastar Dowghtye, sekynge at every mans hand what they could invey agaynst him', and hints that the incident which caused, or rather enabled him to dismiss Doughty to the *Swan* was deliberately contrived by Drake through the agency of John Brewer. Brewer, a trumpeter, who was in the Portuguese prize, 'chanced ... to goo aborde the Pelycane', where he was subjected to some horseplay in which Doughty laid his hand on Brewer's buttock. Brewer flew into a rage and, as he recounted to Cooke later, accused Doughty of treachery to Drake, who at this time was in the prize. When Brewer went back to the prize he spoke to Drake, who immediately sent a boat to bring Doughty. Before he could climb aboard Drake shouted to him, 'Staye there, Thomas Doughty, for I must send you to an other place', and ordered the sailors to row him to the *Swan*.

At the time of the landfall in Brazil, then, Drake was in the *Pelican*, Doughty in disgrace in the *Swan*, Thomas Drake captaining the Portuguese prize, now renamed *Mary*. The *Elizabeth* and *Marigold* were still in company, as was the captured Spanish *canter*, renamed *Christopher*. It was now that the Portuguese pilot, Nunho da Silva, began to earn his victuals. Looking for a sandy bay in which to careen the ships and rid them of the marine growth which was slowing them down after the passage through the tropics, Drake found himself shrouded in fog and surrounded by shoals, on which one of the ships grounded briefly. Only da Silva's knowledge of the coast brought them safely into open water. On 7 April a serious storm separated the *Christopher* from the rest; she rejoined a week and a half later at an anchorage which Drake named Cape Joy.[18]

The ships sailed coastwise down to the River Plate with no great incident except a small massacre of seals while the fleet was anchored from 16 to 20 April. They cruised in the estuary, took on water, and emerged into the South Atlantic on 27 April. That same night the *Swan*, with Doughty still aboard, disappeared in stormy weather which continued into May, causing Drake to decide that it would be sensible to reduce the size of his fleet. He spent the first week of the month looking for a harbour where he could conveniently reorganise, and was still looking on the eighth when the *Christopher* lost touch as well, only to turn up again on the 12th when Drake was investigating a possible anchorage. This was a trying time for Drake; throughout this foul weather, according to John Cooke, 'he wolde say that Thomas Dowghty was the occasyoner thereof, and ... that it came out of Tom Dowghty's capcase, and would avouch the same with greate oaths; which he at no time scanted [i.e. spared], they cost hym so lytle'.[19]

Had he not enjoyed the loyalty of brave men, 13 May could have been the end of Drake. He had gone to sound the bay in the *Elizabeth*'s boat, and was about ten miles away when a storm blew up with thick fog, blotting out the fleet, which was upwind of him. Captain Thomas riskily took the *Marigold* into the bay to save him and then anchored, but the rest of the ships, outside the shelter of the bay, were forced to weigh anchor and look for sea-room further off shore. On the morning of the 14th, in better weather, Drake, now reduced to a single ship, went ashore to make fires as a sign for reassembling. When the fleet came together again, it was without the *Mary*, so that Drake's anger against the still absent Doughty was now given a further spur by the apparent loss of his own brother Thomas.

He named the headland Cape of Good Hope. Parties went ashore to load water and wood, and had some contact with the local native population. The huge joints of ostrich meat being dried for winter were a cause of great amazement among the crews. The ships sailed again on 15 May and found a fair anchorage three days later in which Drake decided to reassemble the fleet. He sent Wynter off southward in the *Elizabeth* and went back to the north himself in the *Pelican* to look for the lost ships. He was quickly cheered by the sight of a sail. Unfortunately it was not the *Mary*, with his brother, but the *Swan*, with the hated Doughty. She was taken to the anchorage, unloaded, run ashore and burned to save her ironwork, to the entertainment of the local people. One of them was bold enough to snatch off Drake's cap as they danced around him, but Wynter joined in the dance with them and relations remained friendly. The *Elizabeth* had returned, reporting no sign of the *Mary*.

Doughty had evidently had a miserable time aboard the *Swan*, where Chester's authority as captain had been largely usurped by the master. On being confined in the *Swan* Doughty behaved with his usual haughtiness and indiscretion, arousing such hostility that the master, probably no gentleman in any case, began eating with the crew, and Doughty and Chester were given inferior rations. John Cooke quotes vivid reports of the ensuing argument: Doughty urged Chester to re-establish his control, went to the master and accused him of deliberately starving them. The master flew into a rage, and swore 'the suche rascales ... shud be glad to eate the tholes [i.e. the wooden pins in the gunwale of a boat] when he wold have it'. Doughty replied that his adventure [i.e. his financial investment in the voyage] entitled him to better usage. ' "Thow an adventure here?" quoth the mastar. "I will not give a poynt for the[e] nor thye adventure, and when thow comest home to injoye any aventure I will be hanged!" ' After more harsh words and a blow or two, the master went on, ' "Thow," quoth he, "wilt thow have victualles? Thow shalt be glad, yf we do not mete with the generall, the rathar to eate what falls from my tail on the anchor fluke ere thow gettest home agayn." ' (There were no lavatories in a sixteenth-century ship; the crew relieved themselves from the side of the forecastle, sometimes fouling the anchor which hung below.) All this in a tiny vessel separated from the rest of the fleet, with a South Atlantic winter coming on.

As soon as Doughty was back on the *Pelican*, the friction with Drake flared again. After 'some unkynd speches', including a sally by Doughty 'that the worst word that came out of [Drake's] mowthe was to be believed as [so]one as his othe', Drake struck him and had him bound to the mast. He was later ordered into the *Christopher*; he refused to go, saying that there were 'desperate and unhonest people', including the ex-master of the *Swan*, who wished him dead. Drake threatened to lift him out of the ship with a block and tackle, and in desperation Doughty and his brother John climbed out of the *Pelican* and were rowed to the *Christopher*.

As the now reduced fleet was on the point of weighing anchor, there came an incident so curious that John Cooke, despite his dislike of Drake, can scarcely have invented it. It gives weight to the idea that Drake was trying to accumulate all the evidence he could against Doughty. This time, he misjudged his man, Thomas Cuttle, who had previously been master of the *Pelican*. As the last of the shore party were embarking Drake had a conversation with him, evidently about Doughty. It enraged Cuttle, who was clearly a brave and principled man, though too impetuous for his own good. He waded into the shallow water in a tantrum, with his gun hanging from his shoulder, and shouted to everyone that he would not accuse Doughty falsely, that he knew of no treachery on his part, and would rather give himself to the cannibals than collude with Drake. The crews finished loading the victuals, climbed aboard, and began weighing anchor. If Cuttle had sympathisers, they kept their heads down. The lonely man of principle, no doubt feeling a little foolish by this time with the water lapping around his knees and his back to a continent of half-

England's maritime aspirations: Elizabeth directs her captains on the title page of Dr John Dee's *General and Rare Memorials*.

King Philip II of Spain.

Queen Elizabeth I.

The Eastern Atlantic islands on a sixteenth-century Portuguese chart. Two ships are shown in battle in the strategic waters off the Azores.

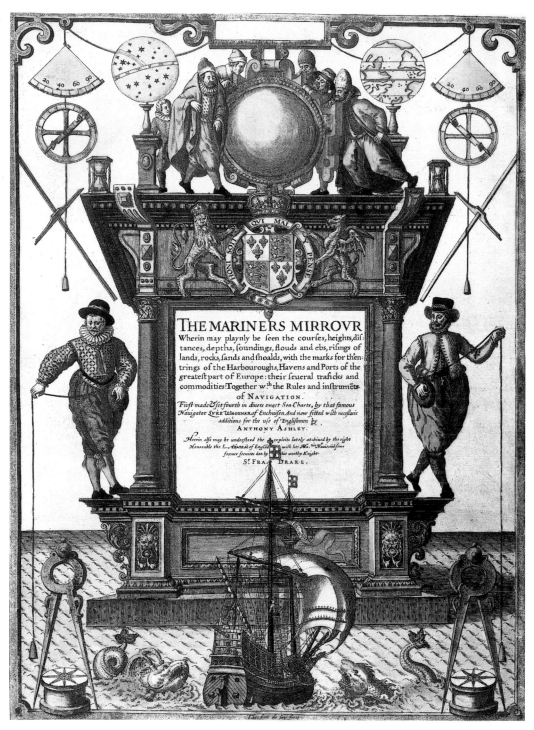

The title page of *The Mariner's Mirrour* (1586). The instruments in the upper corners are, from the top downwards, the quadrant, astrolabe, sand-glass and cross-staff. In the lower corners are compasses and navigator's dividers. The two seamen are taking depth soundings with the lead-line.

John Hawkin's ill-fated flagship, the *Jesus of Lübeck*.

(previous page) Spain's vulnerable empire: the south of the American continent on a Portuguese chart. Notice the unexplored west coast, and the supposed Antarctic continent extending south from the Strait of Magellan

naked savages, eventually fired his gun; whether in defiance, an appeal to like thinkers, or simple desperation we cannot tell. Drake had the decency to take this as a capitulation and sent a boat for him; Cuttle, still making a show of unwillingness, was persuaded 'by intreaty' to rejoin the *Pelican*.

The unhappy *Christopher* was again separated from the rest for three or four days, and when she rejoined Drake reorganised his crews and set her adrift. This involved another transfer of the Doughty brothers, this time to the *Elizabeth*. Cooke quotes a speech by Drake to the crew of the *Elizabeth* which shows how distrust and lack of sympathy had grown into naked enmity and accusation. He was about to send them 'a very bad cople of men, ... Thomas Dowghtie, whoe is ... a conjurer, a sedytyous fellow and a very badd and lewed fellow, ... and his brother, ... a wiche, a poysonar, and suche a one as the worlde cane judge of; I cane not tell from whence he came, but from the dyvell I thinke'. The brothers were not to be spoken to, and were not to be allowed to read or write. Drake went on to make ringing promises that even the ship's boys would be able to retire as rich men at the end of the voyage, returned to the flagship, and sent the Doughtys to the *Elizabeth*, where they were given the food and accommodation of common seamen. Doughty tried to bribe the bosun to give them a small and uncomfortable cabin with the promise of three pounds when they returned to England.

Drake's state of mind at this time must have been extremely strained. The repeated loss of contact with his ships; the disintegrating morale in the fleet; the suspicion of faction and fear of mutiny; the apparently growing polarisation between the gentlemen, with Doughty as their ill-used figurehead, and the true seamen; the continued absence and likely loss of his brother; even his private awareness of his own loss of restraint; all this, in deteriorating midwinter weather, with the unknown terrors of the Strait of Magellan ahead, did not assist clarity of judgement. No gold to cheer the crew; the easy victories of Africa and the Cape Verdes now far away. The only cheerful event at this time was the reappearance of the *Mary*, which he surely did not expect to see again on this voyage, on the evening of 19 June near the harbour of San Julián. Their latitude now was almost 50° south.

The voyage so far had achieved very little tangible or even symbolic success. If it was to continue, some decisive action was necessary to unite the company, be it in fear or in conviction. The events at San Julián are the most controversial of Drake's career, and were the subject of close scrutiny after his return home: he decided to try Doughty for plotting against him and the aims of the voyage.

On the last day of June Drake ordered all the crews ashore. He sat as judge, with John Thomas beside him with a bundle of papers, and had Doughty brought before them. The prisoner, asked by whom he wished to be tried for his seditious dealings, asked to be allowed to continue to England and be tried by law. In the ensuing exchanges Drake said that he would empanel a jury. Doughty demanded to see Drake's commission from the Queen, as proof that he had such authority. Whether Drake had such a commission, and whether he was confident that it empowered him to try Doughty, is not clear;[20] certainly this was not proved in the course of the trial, and in these early exchanges Drake appears to have been keen to change the subject and get on with things:

> 'I warrant you,' answered he, 'my comissyon is good enowghe.' 'I pray yow let us see it,' quoth [Doughty], 'it is necessarye that it shuld be here shewed.' 'Well,' quoth he, 'yow shall not se it; but well, my mastars, this fellowe is full of prating. Bynd me his armes, for I will be saffe of my lyffe; my mastars, yow that be my good friends, Thomas Hood, Gregory, yow there my mastars, bynd hym.'

Doughty's arms were bound behind him, and Drake berated him, accusing him of the poisoning of the Earl of Essex, and ranting about his claims to have introduced Drake to the Earl. A jury was set up under John Wynter, and John Thomas read the charges. Doughty listened to them without denial until the last, in which Edward Bright accused him of saying, in Drake's garden in Plymouth, 'that the qwenes majestie ... and counsell wolde be corrupted'; apparently a suggestion that Doughty could gain leadership of the expedition by bribery.[21]

In further argument Doughty mentioned that the Lord Treasurer had been given the plan of the voyage. ' "No, that hathe he not," quoth Mastar Drake. "How?" quoth Mastar Drake. "He had it from me," quoth Mastar Dowghty.' This statement was a great mistake on Doughty's part; the voyage was meant to be a secret from Lord Burghley, and Drake was evidently delighted by Doughty's slip: 'Lo, my mastars, ... what this fellowe hath done; ... his owne mowthe hathe betwrayed hym!'

Before the jury put their heads together one of them, Leonard Vicary, a Doughty supporter, was brave enough to question the legality of the proceedings, actually telling Drake, 'This is not lawe, nor agreable to justice'. According to Cooke's report, at least, Vicary extracted an undertaking from Drake not to execute Doughty: ' "I knowe not how we may answere his lyffe." "Well," quoth [Drake], "let me alone with that, yow are but to see whethar he be giltye ... or no." "Why very well," sayd Mastar Vicarye, "then there is, I trust, no matter of death." "No, no Mastar Vicarye," quoth he.'

The jury, after some discussion of the motives and honesty of Edward Bright, found the case proved. Drake stood up and walked down to the shoreline, taking with him everyone but the Doughtys and their guards, opened a bundle of documents, and explained their contents: letters between a Master Hankins and the Earl of Essex which disproved Doughty's claim to have introduced Drake to the Earl; letters of commendation from Essex to Walsingham; letters from Sir Christopher Hatton to Drake recommending John Thomas and John Brewer; the Queen's bill of adventure. Everyone must have been expecting him to clinch his self-justification by unfolding his commission, but ... ' "God's will! I have lefte in my cabyne that [which] I shuld especially have had" (as yf he had there forgotten his comyssyon)'.

Whether Drake had in fact, incredibly in the circumstances, left his commission in his cabin, or whether he thought that he was exceeding it, or whether he had none, as John Cooke insinuates, it made no difference. Doughty had already undermined his own chief defence by his speech to the crew of the *Mary* when he took the command:

> ... our said Generall ... hath sent me as his friend whom he trusteth to take charge in this place; ... As the General hath his authority from the Queen's Majesty and her Council, such as hath not been committed almost to any subject afore this time, to punish at his discretion with death or in other ways offenders, so he hath committed the same authority to me.[22]

Backed by the jury's verdict, Drake made a speech giving the crews a rather spurious choice: execute Doughty, proceed with the voyage, and become rich men and gentlemen, or give up the voyage, to the shame and impoverishment of themselves and their country. He carried them with him, some in greed, some in fear, some in honest conviction. By a show of hands, a theatrical irrelevance if the jury proceedings had any validity, Doughty's fate was sealed.[23]

Doughty was given two days to prepare himself and settle his affairs. He made a brave end. One account says that he was given a choice of his mode of execution, and that Drake offered to shoot him himself if he wished, so that he would die like a gentleman. Not surprisingly Doughty chose the block instead. After the two of them had taken communion and dined together, Doughty knelt down to pray for his Queen and the success of the voyage; asked for the forgiveness of the whole company, especially those who had incurred Drake's disapproval by supporting him; embraced Drake, calling him 'my good Captain', laid his head on the block, and was suddenly and brutally freed from all ambition and resentment by the descending axe. In case the trial process and the blood on the block had not made his message to the crews clear, Drake had the head held up before them and said, 'Lo, this is the end of traytors'.

Doughty's body was buried on an island in the bay, called by Drake the Island of True Justice.[24] Drake then made a speech threatening death to any man who committed so much as the eighth part of Doughty's offences. His behaviour in this period suggests that he had been faced with increasing evidence of antagonisms and resentment, and that Doughty's trial was organised, in part, *pour encourager les autres*. One such was probably John Cooke, whose support for Doughty is obvious: his description of Drake's behaviour includes such words as 'murder ... venome ... conceyved hatred ... moaste tyranicall blud spillyng ... tyranous and cruell tirant'. Cooke, because of events yet to be narrated, was writing in the supposition that Drake had perished; there is no evidence that he was anything like as forthright at the time, but clearly he was part of a group of Doughty sympathisers which included Vicary, Cuttle, Worrall, Hugh Smith and other 'gentlemen' voyagers. He complains of being kept ashore for a fortnight in only his doublet and hose, forbidden to fetch his cloak from the ship, through Drake's malice.

With the rigours of the passage into the Pacific awaiting him, Drake was determined to infuse a new spirit and community of purpose into the expedition. He ordered everyone to make his confession to the chaplain and to take communion on the following Sunday, and again threatened punishment for anyone reviving old resentments. On 11 August he commanded everyone ashore and conducted a ceremony of unification which combined threat, inspiration, patriotism and an appeal to greed; Drake at his most typical. His initial theme was the recent disunity, and here it emerges explicitly that the divisions as he saw them were principally between the gentlemen and the professional sailors:

Thus it is, my mastars, that we are very far from owr contry and frinds, we are compassed in on every syde with owr enemyes, wherefore we are not to make small reconynge of a man, for we can not have a man yf we would gyve for hym ten thousand pounds. Wherefore we muste have these mutines and discords that are growne amongest us redrest, for by the lyfe of God it dothe even take my wytes from me to thinke on it; here is suche controversye betwene the saylars and the gentlemen, and suche stomakynge betwene the gentlemen and saylars, that it dothe even make me madd to here it. But, my mastars, I must have it lefte, for I must have the gentleman to hayle and draw with the mariner, and the maryner with the gentleman. What, let us show owr selvs all to be of a company, and let us not gyve occasion to the enemye to rejoyce at owr decaye and ovarthrowe. I wold know hym that would refuse to set his hand to a roape, but I know there is not any suche heare; and as gentlemen are verye necesarye for governments sake in the voyadge, so have I shipt them for that, and to some farthar intent, and yet thowghe I knowe saylars to be the most envyous people of the worlde, and so unruly without gov-ernement, yet may not I be without them.[25]

None of this implies egalitarianism; Drake's words are largely metaphorical, an appeal to 'pull together'. Both categories are essen-tial, but their contributions are different, and must be loyally recog-nised as such. In one of his rhetorical flourishes Drake then offered anyone who wished to return home the use of the *Marigold*, but went on to qualify his generosity: 'let them take hede that they goo homeward, for yf I fynd them in my way I will surely sink them'. Nobody stepped forward; all agreed to sail on with him with a willing heart. Still not content, Drake made his power as leader crystal clear by discharging all the officers, including Wynter and Thomas, on whom no shadow of suspicion had fallen. He then reiterated Dough-ty's crimes and his own justifications and appealed to the crews' pride as Englishmen:

... yf this voyadge shulde not have good successe, we shuld not only be a skornynge or a reprochefull scoffinge stoke unto our enemyes, but also a greate blott to owr hole contry for evar, and what triumphe would it be to Spayne and Portyngale, and agayne the like would nevar be atempted.

The captains and officers were reappointed, and with a final promise of wealth Drake asked the men to work together in friendship in the difficult days to come and dismissed the gathering. The *Mary*, whose capture had lit the fuse which might have destroyed the voyage, was now leaking, and Drake decided to abandon her. On 17 August

1578 the reduced fleet of the *Pelican*, *Elizabeth* and *Marigold*, with a pinnace, sailed from San Julián and steered SW for the Strait of Magellan. There was illness among the crews in the increasing cold.

VIII

THE GREAT SOUTH SEA
1578–79

'The winds were such as if the bowels of the
earth had set all at libertie, or as if all the
clouds under heaven had beene called together
to lay their force upon that one place. The seas
... were rowled up from the depths, even from
the roots of the rockes, as if it had been a scroll
of parchment.'

Anon., *The World Encompassed*, 1628[1]

After running down the coast for three days Drake's ships found
contrary winds when they reached the mouth of the strait, and were
unable to enter it until the wind came east-north-east on 23 August
1578. Drake here ordered a little ceremony in which, as so often in
his career, it is difficult to sort out patriotism from pragmatism. He
ordered the fleet to strike topsails briefly as a salute to Elizabeth, 'to
shewe his dutifull obedience to her highnes, whom he acknowledged
to have full interest and right in that new discovery'. He also renamed
the *Pelican* the *Golden Hinde*, so linking her with the arms of Sir
Christopher Hatton, his friend at Court and a major investor in the
voyage. Both these aspects of the ceremony indirectly reinforced
points he had argued in Doughty's trial, as did the sermon on true
obedience which followed on the *Hinde*.[2]

Nunho da Silva's report of the passage through the strait has the
brisk nonchalance of the professional navigator: 'they passed along
without any let or hinderance either of wind or weather'.[3] On the 24th
they came to a triangle of three islands. Drake landed on the first, took
possession of it in the Queen's name, and called it Elizabeth Island.
This, too, may have been an indirect way of bolstering his claims to
hold the Queen's commission. The other two islands were named Bartholomew (it was St Bartholomew's Day) and St George; they were full
of penguins, whose habits and deportment caused great interest. Three
hundred were slaughtered and added to the food reserves.

In the western part of the strait Drake had trouble finding his passage, and at one point he ordered a boat out and went in it himself to find the way, but on 6 September the fleet emerged into the Great South Sea. Drake intended to take the whole company ashore for a service and to leave an engraving of the Queen which he had ready for the purpose. He was prevented by a change of wind to the north-west, the beginning of weeks of vicious weather and towering seas before which the ships were helpless and their crews incredulous.

The ships, driven southward as far as 57°, managed to stay in touch until the night of 30 September, when the little *Marigold* vanished, never to be seen again. The *Golden Hinde* and the *Elizabeth* turned back north-east on the following day and managed to regain the western cape of the Strait of Magellan on 7 October. The *Hinde* anchored briefly, but had her cable broken by the renewed violence of the winds, and on the morning of the 8th the *Elizabeth*, which had not anchored, was nowhere to be seen. She had re-entered the strait, where she rested until November, most of her men being 'very sicke with long watching, wet, cold, and evill diet'.[4] Shortly after this Wynter gave up the voyage and sailed for home.

Wynter's actions and thinking around this time are described contrastingly in different sources. Edward Cliffe, writing after Drake's triumphal return to England, blames Wynter for giving up, 'full sore against the mariners minds'. Wynter's own report paints a convincing picture different in several points from that of Drake's supporters. Firstly, he seems to have been at least as diligent in trying to rejoin Drake as Drake was to rejoin him. Secondly, he seems to have been clear in his mind that the expedition was going to the Moluccas (which it did), and that if he could not find Drake he had better make his way there. He sailed two days on an appropriate course for this after the weather lightened on 6 November. Thirdly, he gave up because of the crew's discontent, shortage of victuals, and the strenuous opposition of the master, William Markham, whose feelings about the voyage were probably general among the crews around this time:

> ... all was in vain, for the Master did utterly dislike of it, saying that he would fling himself overboard rather than consent to any such voyage to be steered, through which speeches and secret promises used by him, he caused a general dislike of the voyage. Sometimes he wished himself whipped at a cart's [tail] in Rochester. He said Mr Drake hired him for Alexandria, but if he had known that this had been the Alexandria, he

would have been hanged in England rather than have come in this voyage.[5]

Wynter sailed back through the strait for Brazil and England, eventually running into Ilfracombe on 2 July 1579. His account makes no mention of Drake having fixed a rendezvous in case of separation. This was Drake's normal practice, and other accounts say that he was expecting to rendezvous on the west coast of South America in 30° south. Despite Wynter's excuses, therefore, something of a cloud hangs over him, though he does mention that the winds made it impossible to head for Peru.

The *Hinde* had been battered southward again to 55° south. She anchored several times among the islands only to be forced repeatedly to face the fury of the sea. Eventually on 28 October, after fifty-two days of misery, the storm ceased. After a couple of days' rest among the islands Drake set his course north-west and then north, coastwise towards Peru. His company had been further reduced by the loss of eight men in a small pinnace. They were presumably about some exploratory duty when the weather separated them from the *Hinde*; they had no food, no compass and no chart. Somehow they made their way back through the strait and up the coast to the River Plate and Brazil. After terrible suffering one of them, Peter Carder of St Verian in Cornwall, survived to make his way back to England eight years later. Admiral Howard presented him to the Queen, who talked to him 'a longe houres space of my travailes and wonderfull escape and among other thinges of the manner of Master Dowties execution, and afterwards bestowed twenty-two angels* on me'.[6]

The island of Mocha lies off the coast of Chile. Drake anchored there on 25 November after three weeks without great incident. He went ashore and was kindly received by the Indian population, who gave him fruit and a couple of sheep (possibly llamas). He gave them some gifts, explained his needs, and went back to the *Hinde* with what he took to be an undertaking to allow him to fill his water-casks in the morning. When the watering party went ashore, led by Drake, they walked into an Indian ambush; two men who had gone on ahead were taken by the Indians, and the rest were received with a rain of arrows which wounded several men. Drake was hit by an arrow in his cheek; Nele, the Danish gunner, and Diego the negro later died of their wounds. The author of *The World Encompassed* explains the treachery as due to the mistaken idea of the Indians that their visitors

---

* The angel was a gold coin showing the Archangel Michael slaying the dragon.

were the hated Spaniards, an impression reinforced when one of the crew used the word *agua* to ask for water. Drake weighed anchor and continued north, looking for a haven in which he might await the *Elizabeth* and *Marigold*.

On 30 November the ship's boat was returning from an unsuccessful scouting expedition at Quintero when it came across a lone Indian fishing from a canoe. He was taken to the *Golden Hinde*, treated kindly, and set ashore by the ship's boat. In his gratitude he brought some of his fellow Indians, including their leader, with gifts of hens, eggs, and a fat pig. The leader offered to guide the *Hinde* to a place where there was a Spanish ship; this turned out to be Valparaiso, the port of Santiago de Chile, where the *Hinde*, after overshooting the port slightly, came to anchor at noon on 5 December.

The Valparaiso episode set the pattern for what was to come. The Spanish ship[7] was sparsely manned by eight Spaniards and three negroes. For them, in their colonial isolation, a ship sailing in to join them could only be Spanish, and an excuse for a party. They beat a drum in welcome and rolled out a butt of wine. When Drake's men swarmed aboard Thomas Moone thumped a Spaniard in the face, shouting 'Abassho pirra,[8] which is to say in English, Go downe dogg'. The Spaniards fled to the hold, except for one man who jumped from the stern and swam to the town, which Drake's men proceeded to rifle at their leisure over the next three days. They found ample supplies of Chilean wine, and took the plate and altar-cloth from the church. The Spanish ship contained further wine, but more interesting were the four boxes bound in iron and leather, full of gold from Valdivia. One of them was found concealed in a great chest of meal.[9] An official Spanish report values the gold at fourteen million pesos.[10] Another Spanish deposition also mentions a large emerald-studded crucifix among the spoils.[11] Drake sailed on the 8th, taking the captured ship with him. In one of his many inessential acts of decency he took his Indian pilot, Felipe, back home, and left him laden with gifts.

This call at Valparaiso was the start of a period of successful plundering on the west coast of South America which dumbfounded the colonial Spanish. It was not the first case of English marauding in the Pacific; John Oxenham's activities had already irritated Spain. Oxenham, however, had made a brief incursion into Pacific waters after crossing the Isthmus of Panama in what was essentially a Caribbean voyage of the kind the Spanish had come to expect. Spain's unpreparedness for hostilities such as those now begun by Drake is

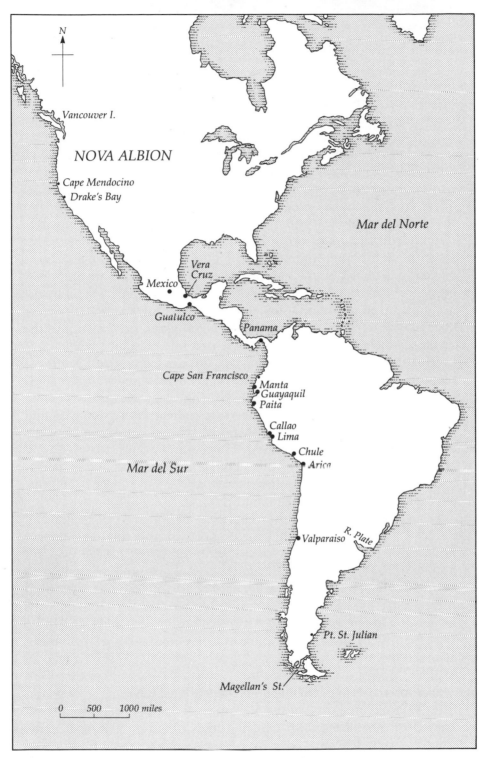

Drake on the West Coast of America

evident in the unprotected state of her harbours and ships, and in the casual confidence with which huge wealth in gold and silver was being transported by land and sea. For the authorities in Lima and Spain Drake's arrival out of the blue had an impact akin to that created in a modern emerging nation by the news that its unfriendly neighbour has just developed a ballistic missile.

The Spanish administration along the length of the west coast of South and Central America shook to its foundations. After an initial period of incredulous complacency at local level, virtual panic spread ahead of Drake as he proceeded north capturing ships at will, and the disquiet continued after his passing in the form of completely unfounded rumours of other English vessels in the South Sea. This stage of the circumnavigation is vividly documented by eye-witness accounts obtained by the authorities from Spanish sailors and passengers for inclusion in official reports. These are supplemented by the accounts given by John Drake and Nunho da Silva when they were examined in captivity later,[12] and by an *Anonymous Narrative* of the voyage, which can only have been written by a participant.[13]

Drake revelled in the activities of the next few weeks, and his tactical performance was generally masterful: he seized ships, retained them when he needed them, dispensed with them when they were no longer of use, employed a pinnace to excellent effect, took up and released local Indian and Spanish pilots for successive stages of the voyage, apparently killed nobody, lost only one or two men, and gradually filled the *Hinde* with a massive quantity of plunder. It was a time of euphoric success, self-congratulation, jokes at the Spaniards' expense, and affordable magnanimity.

From the crew of the ship captured in Valparaiso Drake had retained a pilot called Juan Griego (probably not his real, unpronounceable name; it simply means 'John the Greek').[14] He was still hoping to be rejoined by the *Elizabeth* and *Marigold*. Not wishing to hazard the *Hinde* by entering every harbour in the search, and worried that the small crew of the ship's boat might be seized by the Spaniards, he decided to put together another of his preformed pinnaces. On 19 December, with this aim, he entered a bay just north of 30° south, near the town of Coquimbo, and sent a boat with fourteen men to explore.

The Spaniards in the town had evidently been forewarned overland from Valparaiso; at two in the afternoon around a hundred of them arrived on horseback with two hundred Indians.[15] The boat crew, who had rounded up a couple of large pigs and some piglets, ran back to the boat and sheltered behind a rock, with the exception of Richard Minivy, who for some reason remained on the rock to outface the enemy. He fired his arquebus and drew his sword, but was killed. As the rest escaped in the boat Minivy's body was dragged ashore, his right hand cut off, his heart cut out, and his head severed and stuck on a spear. The Spanish made the Indians shoot the remaining carcass full of arrows. For the author of *The World Encompassed*, the example made of Minivy was merely what one could expect of Spaniards. The cutting out of hearts had been a feature of Europe's view of America since Bernal Díaz wrote down his account of Aztec practices in his history of Cortés's conquest of Mexico. The horrific details of Minivy's death, however, are not a piece of chauvinistic embroidery by the author of *The World Encompassed*; they are confirmed in the *Anonymous Narrative*. Nothing the crew saw of Latin-American society appears to have diminished their pre-conceived, Black Legend view of Spanish colonial behaviour, especially towards the Indians:

> Yea they suppose they show the wretches great favour, when they do not for their pleasures whip them with cords, and day by day drop their naked bodies with burning bacon, which is one of the least cruelties amongst many which they universally use against that nation and people.[16]

On 20 December[17] Drake reached a good anchorage in a bay called the Bahía Salada and set about building his pinnace ashore. The timbers were unloaded and the work went well. After a feast on New Year's Day the vessel was ready for caulking on 3 January,* and on the following day, a Sunday, Drake went ashore to see to the cutting of the topsails. She was launched on Friday, 9 January, and Drake set off to the south in her on the Saturday to look for his lost ships. It was a brief excursion; adverse winds forced him to return on the Monday.

In his absence the crew had begun moving ballast from the hold to get at some of the guns, in preparation for the livelier action expected further north. From 14 to 18 January the *Hinde* was careened, her bottom scraped, and her sides treated with grease, brimstone and tar. She almost capsized in the careening.[18] The gentlemen kept well out of these operations and spent their time fishing. On the 19th Drake set off, with his ship in good trim and with adequate supplies of

---

* Caulking involved sealing the seams between the ship's planks by driving tarry tow between them.

everything except fresh water, which continued to be a problem. In one of several contacts with the coastal Indians over the next few days false hopes were raised of finding the lost *Elizabeth* and *Marigold* when one of the crew misinterpreted an informant and reported him as saying that he had seen two other English ships pass by.[19]

Water continued to be short, but silver was easily come by: in one shore excursion at a place called Tarapaca a Spaniard was found lying asleep with thirteen bars of silver beside him. Something of Drake's own good humour and high spirits at this time shines through the account in *The World Encompassed*: '. . . we would not (could wee have chosen) have awaked him of his nappe; but seeing we, against our wills, did him that injury, we freed him of his charge, which otherwise perhaps would have kept him waking, and so left him to take out (if it pleased him) the other part of his sleepe in more security'. During another shore excursion a Spaniard and an Indian boy were found with eight 'Indish sheepe' (i.e. llamas), each laden with about a hundred pounds of silver.

> We could not indure to see a gentleman Spaniard turnd carrier so, and therefore without intreaty we offered our service and became drovers, onely his directions were not so perfect that we could keepe the way which hee intended; for almost as soone as hee was parted from us, we with our new kinde of carriges, were come unto our boates.

The llamas were taken on board and eaten. Drake had no trouble in replenishing food stores at this time; he bought fish from Indians who paddled out in canoes, and took more llamas from the timid Spanish authorities in a town called Mormorena. He was now in about 22° south, well to the north of the rendezvous point, and had given up the idea of finding his other ships. In Mormorena he also took aboard a Spanish pilot for the next stage of the voyage, and so arrived off the sleepy port of Arica, then a small place of about twenty houses, on 5 February.[20]

Lying in Arica harbour were two ships.[21] One, belonging to Jorge Díaz, had just arrived from Lima. In the other, Felipe Corzo's, was a Fleming called Nicolas Jorge. That evening he saw the sails of two ships against the western sky, and watched them come to anchor in the quiet harbour. Perhaps he noticed with some curiosity that one of them had cannon on deck. Curiosity was replaced by consternation when he saw the pinnace which accompanied the ships heading towards his own vessel, full of men and bristling with weapons. He and his shipmates made no resistance, and the *Golden Hinde* settled a little lower in the water under the weight of fifty-seven twenty-pound bars of silver which had been sitting, neatly piled, on top of Corzo's cargo. The ship from Lima was also seized; her cargo was transferred into Corzo's ship, and she was then burned.[22] Corzo's ship must have been the better one, and Drake presumably wished to retain different options for an uncertain future now that hope of being rejoined by the *Elizabeth* and the *Marigold* had faded. Nicolas Jorge was kept on the ship as a pilot with the prize crew.

Drake refrained from sacking the town, content to fire a few culverin-shots at it, but celebrated that night with trumpet fanfares and a musical entertainment aboard the *Golden Hinde*.[23] In the morning he seized three fishing boats and used one of them to send ashore three Spaniards whom he had taken prisoner. This was one occasion on which Drake's humanity (helped, perhaps, by his concern to conserve his water supplies) undermined his tactics. It would have been easy to slit the men's throats and throw them overboard. They are reported to have sailed ahead of Drake up the coast, warning of his approach and depriving him of some rich pickings.[24] In Chule, the port of Arequipa, Bernal Bueno's ship had loaded 500 bars of gold for Lima. The shipment was promptly unloaded and buried, so that when Drake's pinnace arrived it found an empty hold. He put a small crew in the ship to take her out of harbour, but realising now that speed was important he decided to slim down his fleet.

He transferred some casks of wine from the three prizes, hoisted their topsails and left them, crewless, to the wind. This may seem a profligate move, though his men would have been thinly spread between four ships and a pinnace. Even if some disaster were to overtake the *Golden Hinde*, he still had his pinnace and ship's boat; he had met very little resistance, though a greater wariness could now be expected from the Spanish. It probably seemed to Drake that he could increase the size of his fleet at will if need be, and that the important thing now was speed, which the broad-beamed cargo-carriers were hindering.

His target now was Callao, the port of Philip's great colonial capital of Lima, the City of the Kings. Apart from the potential for plunder, Drake was hoping to gain some bargaining power which might secure the release of John Oxenham and his companions, at present confined in the prison of the Inquisition in Lima. On his way he captured a small Callao-based trading ship, bound for Valles. Her captain, Gaspar Martín, was a fount of information about current shipping movements. His loyalty to his own welfare quickly overcame his loyalty to the Crown and his fellow captains, and Drake's eyes must have sparkled as he heard Martín's disclosures: Miguel Angel's ship was expected from Panama to load silver; so was Andrés Muriel's; San Juan de Antón's big ship, the *Nuestra Señora de la Concepción*, nicknamed the *Cacafuego*, had sailed only a few days earlier. She was bound for Panama, but was to make a few calls on the way, and she was heavily laden with silver.

Drake released Martín's ship, but retained some of the crew, including a Portuguese pilot.[25] He headed for Callao by the South Channel, piloted either by Juan Griego or the Portuguese. The *Hinde* struck a shoal briefly and Drake, suspecting treachery on the pilot's part, threatened to cut off his head, but the ship proceeded unharmed.

It is amazing that a man who had undergone the ordeal and humiliation suffered by Drake at San Juan de Ulúa, and was aware of the strong possibility that the authorities were expecting him, could contemplate sailing into the crowded harbour of Callao. Pedro de Sarmiento's account says that word had been sent from Chile but had not yet arrived, and blames the Peruvian authorities further south for not warning Callao.[26] Evidence given after the Callao raid, however, suggested that the warning from Chile had arrived. Drake's action was that of a man confident in his strength and riding a wave of success; nevertheless, he used a subterfuge.

He entered the apparently complacent harbour at the same time as a Spanish ship arriving from Panama, about three hours after nightfall. They anchored within hailing distance of each other. Drake made one of his Spanish prisoners shout across the water, asking where the other ship was from and saying that the *Golden Hinde* had come from Chile (which was no lie). The pinnace, with twenty or thirty men, and the *Hinde*'s boat, with six or seven led by Drake, then went quietly around another fourteen vessels, cutting their anchor cables. According to Drake's young cousin John's account this was done in the hope that the offshore wind would take the ships out of harbour so that Drake could seize them and use them as a bargaining tool to persuade the Spanish authorities to release Oxenham and his friends.[27] Guided, presumably, by their Spanish prisoners, the English located the ship of Miguel Angel which the communicative Gaspar Martín had told Drake was full of the king's silver, but they found that the treasure had never been loaded. It was still in the customs house, 200,000 pesos of it.[28]

The pinnace went alongside the ship from Panama to board her, but was fought off with the loss of a sailor called Thomas. The

Spanish crew thought better of it when Drake put a ball from a culverin through her; as they fled to the shore with the *Hinde*'s boat in pursuit a half-breed threw himself into the sea and was captured, and Drake then put a prize crew into the Spaniard. All this was in the middle of the night, which must have increased the confusion and panic in the Spanish ships and ashore, where the alarm had now been raised and bells began to ring. A customs house inspection vessel came out towards the *Hinde*, but soon departed when its crew realised the weight of her armament.

There was little wind, but with the help of the tide the *Hinde* and the Panama prize slowly emerged from harbour. It had been a stirring night, and was still bright in the mind of young John Drake years later, but effectively it had been a failure. Drake had taken from one ship a leather-bound chest, two feet long and ten inches wide, full of silver *reales*, and some silks and linens; a small reward for a raid of such audacity.[29] The one ship captured was hardly likely to be acceptable to the Spanish as an exchange for Oxenham. Indeed, the raid on Callao was counter-productive. Drake's progress up the coast of Chile and Peru, picking off a ship here and there, with an occasional foray ashore, had obviously been a matter of serious concern, but the raid on Callao was on a different level of impertinence altogether. Callao was the port of Lima, and Lima was the headquarters of the Spanish viceroy, governor and captain-general, Don Francisco de Toledo. The tweak administered to Philip's nose via that of his viceroy demanded action, and it was now that Don Francisco set in motion the first organised, if rather unenthusiastic, opposition to Drake's progress.

If the viceroy was cross about Drake's raid, the performance of his own subordinates in the next few weeks must have made him apoplectic. He had been roused from his bed at one in the morning with the news of the depredations in Callao harbour. He immediately issued a call to arms and sent a force of soldiers to the customs house to guard the treasure. From the chaos in the harbour two ships were somehow organised to pursue Drake, and the captured Dutchman, Nicolas Jorge, describes how the look-outs on the *Hinde* reported their sails emerging from the harbour while Drake was completing the plundering of the ship from Panama. At first, he says, Drake refused to believe that pursuit had been organised, but he abandoned the prize and made sail.

The pursuit was a fiasco. Jorge says that the two ships could have overtaken Drake, but other evidence suggests a dithering reluctance on the part of ill-prepared landsmen who had been shoved aboard in the chaos following the raid. The Spanish ships were short of provisions for a prolonged chase, and they soon gave up and returned to Callao to face the fury of the viceroy.

When he heard that the ships were back in harbour Don Francisco rode at once to Callao to forbid those aboard to land. The captains and soldiers were arrested and tried, and the chief officers received harsh punishments of exile or large fines. Five gentlemen who went ashore after the viceroy's prohibition were also tried; they pleaded that they were merely volunteers, had been badly seasick, and had gone ashore for a change of clothes. All of them were fined, and two were ordered to go on the next pursuit of Drake.[30] One feels that the viceroy was almost as cross with himself as with anyone else, for letting himself appear responsible for such a shambles. He now took his time, and did much better.

On the Monday after the raid Don Francisco presided over an extraordinary meeting of judges, justices of the peace, the attorney general and the provincial treasurer. He had no difficulty in securing authorisation to draw 1,200 *pesos* from the royal coffers as a fund to finance emergency measures. Drake, referred to in the report of the meeting as 'the tyrant' and 'the Lutheran corsair', was now acquiring bogeyman status akin to the vision of Bonaparte which pervaded the southern counties of England in the Napoleonic wars. The viceroy had received reports from released prisoners of his passage through the strait and depredations in Valparaiso. He told the meeting that Drake's other vessels were to rendezvous with him at Cape San Francisco in order to prey on the treasure ships on their passage from Peru to the isthmus, subsequently to return to England via China and 'the route of the Portuguese' (i.e. via the East Indies and the Cape of Good Hope). Drake was free with information like this in conversation with prisoners; sometimes he was boasting, sometimes deliberately leaking false or conflicting information to keep the enemy guessing. It is by no means certain that he had decided on his return course by this stage. Don Francisco also mentioned the threat to the vessels of Sebastián Pérez and San Juan de Antón which had recently sailed, the latter with 115,000 *pesos* of the king's silver and more belonging to private individuals.

The viceroy had already sent off warnings to other ports by the old Inca method of *chasques* or foot-messengers. He now proposed that a ship be sent the length of the coast to the north, to call at every port with orders for harbour watchmen to be organised. In Guayaquil His Majesty's war-galley was to be prepared. If the messenger-ship met any Spanish vessels, especially the two recently departed from Callao, it was to tell them to unload their silver in the nearest port. The viceroy also proposed measures of offence: two ships were to be prepared for war, with 200 fighting men aboard, to pursue Drake. Ultimately they were to be joined by the Guayaquil galley, whose role would be to probe the inlets and shallows.

By the time the two ships had been fitted out Drake had a fortnight's start. The command was given to Don Luis de Toledo. He managed to ship only 120 men instead of the intended 200. As Pedro de Sarmiento, one of the officers, reported later, everyone aboard 'left with a great desire to fight the enemy but with little hope of being able to overtake him'.[31] Of course they got nowhere near Drake; wherever they called – Santa, Trujillo, Paita – they arrived at least two weeks after him to find news of fresh predations. They were only four days into their pursuit when, far ahead and unknown to them, Drake was picking the fattest plum of his career: San Juan de Antón's ship, the *Cacafuego*.

When Drake abandoned the Panama ship off Callao he had left in her the Greek pilot, Juan Griego, and the half-breed he had captured later. His first aim now was to find pilots for the next stage of the voyage. Off Malabrigo he met a ship bound for Callao and seized a pilot called Domingo Martín, from whom he learned that the *Cacafuego* was not far ahead of him. He also put briefly into Paita and took a man called Custodio Rodríguez from his ship, along with sixty jars of wine. From Rodríguez he learned that the *Cacafuego* was now a bare two days ahead. Immediately after leaving Paita he took and released a ship from Panama, taking from her a negro who had been a cimarron, and shortly afterwards found a much more lucrative prize coming from Guayaquil with gold, rigging materials and provisions.[32] He also took from her 'a crucifixe of gold with goodly great Emerauds set in it'.[33]

The pilot of the Guayaquil ship, Benito Díaz Bravo, watched as Drake transferred artillery to the prize and tested her sailing qualities with a view to retaining her. While he had this in mind he put most of the occupants ashore, including a couple of friars. At ten o'clock on the following morning, however, he took the guns out of her again and handed her back to Díaz Bravo. Before he sailed away he had the ship's mainsail and topsail sent down, wrapped them around her anchor and threw them into the sea to prevent her from sailing to the nearest port to raise the alarm. Díaz Bravo later put the damage to the ship at around 4,000 *pesos* and valued the treasure at 18,000.[34]

Nevertheless, he was impressed by Drake's magnanimity. One of the *Golden Hinde*'s crew asked Díaz Bravo about the arms on the flag flying at the mainmast. When he replied that they were King Philip's the Englishman told him to strike them, but Drake, with a generosity born of euphoria, said 'Leave King Philip's arms where they are; he is the best king in the world'.

Díaz Bravo got off lightly in comparison with his ship's clerk, Francisco Jacome. This lad of twenty-one was transferred to the *Hinde* with four passengers and interrogated about the contents of the ship. Drake told them in full detail about his exploits so far, claiming that 'all the ships in the Pacific were in his power' and boasting that he would take the *Cacafuego*, pillage the coast of Nicaragua, and come again with a fleet of six or seven ships in two years' time. The prisoners were put back on their immobilised ship, but young Francisco had barely had time to sigh with relief when the boat returned for him. He was taken back to the *Hinde* and asked again about gold which he was thought to have concealed. When he told them nothing Drake ordered a rope to be put round his neck and tied to the yard-arm, and when he still refused he was dropped as if to hang him. The rope (presumably by design, given Drake's cheerful state of mind) was too long and the boy fell into the sea, to be retrieved and again restored to his own ship. Nunho da Silva's account says that the boy had taken two plates of gold, which were retrieved.[35]

If Drake had known how close he was to the *Cacafuego* he might not have wasted time on this little pantomime. The *Golden Hinde* steered away northward again in the forenoon, leaving Díaz Bravo to struggle into Manta for repairs. Drake offered a prize to the man who sighted the *Cacafuego* first, and this took young John Drake up into the maintop with his eyes peeled. It was only three in the afternoon when he sighted the quarry off Cape San Francisco. In his own account, given to the Spanish authorities when he was in prison, John describes how Drake towed cables astern to slow down the *Golden Hinde* so as not to alert the *Cacafuego* to her identity. Sailing after her at full speed would have given the game away, and a great reduction in sail to slow down would also have looked suspicious.[36]

Drake's pinnace was careful to stay out of sight on the off-side of the *Hinde*, and the *Cacafuego*, all unsuspecting, altered course slightly and bore towards the strange sail. The ensuing combat is richly documented by eye-witnesses on both sides.[37] At nine o'clock, with the dusk coming down, the *Hinde* was close enough to the Spanish ship to hail her. Drake used the same trick as in Callao, making one of his Spanish prisoners shout across to her, this time saying that the *Hinde* was Miguel Angel's ship. This alerted the Spanish captain, San Juan de Antón, who replied that he had left that ship empty in Callao. The *Hinde* closed in on the Spaniard's starboard side and someone, possibly Drake himself, shouted a garbled demand in Spanish for Antón to strike sail in the Queen's name, or be sunk. Antón's reply was on the lines of 'Come and do it yourselves, if you dare!'

By now the English were throwing grappling irons; a whistle blew, followed by a trumpet-call, and there was a volley of English small-arms fire followed by a rain of arrows, one of which wounded Antón. The *Hinde*'s gunner fired a culverin loaded with chain-shot which brought down the Spaniard's mizzenmast, and after another round and a further demand to strike sail Drake's pinnace came alongside on the port side of the *Cacafuego* and disgorged about forty archers who clambered up her sides. In this hopeless situation San Juan de Antón's bravado evaporated; he struck sail and surrendered.

Practical resistance to Drake was negligible. He must have expected more, if only from the ship's nickname, which suggests some previous feat of arms, though it is difficult to know against whom this could have been achieved (*Cacafuego* is usually translated as *Spitfire*, though it actually means *Shitfire*). The complacency of the Spanish in the Pacific before Drake's arrival is proved by San Juan de Antón's own statement that his ship, with her hugely valuable cargo, could not resist because she carried no cannon or even small arms.[18]

Antón was seized and taken on board the *Hinde*, where Drake was taking off his helmet and coat of mail. Drake embraced him cheerfully, told him to cheer up, for these things happen in war, and had him locked in the sterncastle under heavy guard. The other ten or eleven Spaniards on the ship were also transferred, five of them being sailors and the rest passengers (this presumably indicates that the *Cacafuego*'s crew was composed largely of negroes or, less probably, Indians). It was now night; the English sailors of the watch on deck looked across to the swaying lanterns of the *Cacafuego*, now occupied by thirty of their shipmates; John Drake put the gold chain which was his reward safely in his sea-chest; Francis Drake and the watch below exulted in an easy victory and went to sleep with visions of tomorrow's gold.

At nine in the morning Drake went across into the *Cacafuego*, leaving orders for Antón to be fed as an honoured guest at his own table. He stayed on the captured ship until midday to examine the

A fanciful depiction of the encounter between the Golden Hinde *and the* Cacafuego

cargo, and it was now that he realised that his voyage and his fortune were made. The registered silver and gold aboard was worth 362,000 *pesos*, of which 106,000 belonged to the Crown. There was another 40,000 in unregistered precious metals, and a quantity of jewels and precious stones.

Drake returned to the *Hinde* at three o'clock and with a fair wind set a course north-west for Central America. The ship was under foresails and mizzen only, probably to enable the *Cacafuego* to keep up, with her shattered mizzenmast. During the fair weather of the next three days the pinnace plied to and fro between the two ships transferring the treasure. Drake also took quantities of food, two casks of water, sails, canvas and rigging. It was a time of high good humour; he dined to the music of trumpets and viols. In his conversations with Antón he told him all about the voyage so far; teased him by alluding to the different options open to him for the homeward voyage; threatened to put him in irons and make him pilot him to Panama; complained about the treatment he had received from the Spanish in the Caribbean, and extracted information about where he might careen and clean the *Hinde*, now sorely in need of it. On a graver note, he more than once raised the question of the situation of Oxenham and his friends. Antón reassured him, saying that as the viceroy had not executed them yet he would hardly do so now; they would probably be drafted into the army and sent to Chile to fight the rebellious Indians. Drake gave him a message to pass on to the viceroy: if the English prisoners were killed he would take revenge on 2,000 Spaniards and throw their heads into Callao harbour.

As usual in his man-to-man dealings with other seafarers, Drake was generous in his triumph. Before he released the *Cacafuego* he gave many gifts to his prisoners: thirty or forty *pesos* in coin to each of them; tools; pieces of cloth from the Portuguese ship taken in the Cape Verdes; some weapons to a soldier called Victoria; a shield and a sword to the ship's clerk, Domingo de Lizarza, with a joke that now he could pretend to be a soldier; some fans with mirrors to a merchant called Cuevas to take to his lady. He was particularly generous to San Juan de Antón, giving him a German matchlock, a barrel of powder, two casks of tar, six hundredweight of German iron, and a silver-gilt bowl engraved with Drake's name in Latin: *Franciscus Draques*. He retained his good humour when he learned that Antón's pilot was hanging on to two fine gilt cups; Drake said to him, 'Señor Pilot, you have here two silver cups, but I must needes have one of them, which the Pilot because he could not otherwise chuse, yelded unto and gave the other to the Steward of our Generals ships'. The pilot's boy maintained the cheerful atmosphere with a joke of his own for Drake: 'Captaine, our ship shall bee called no more the *Cacafuego*, but the *Cacaplata* [= *Shitsilver*], and youre shippe shall bee called the *Cacafuego*; which pretie speach ... ministred matter of laughter to us, both then and long after'.[39]

On the day before he released Antón, Drake gave him a safe-conduct addressed to Wynter, telling him to treat the Spaniard well and, if it was necessary to take any of his cargo, to pay him double the value in goods.[40] Drake evidently still hoped that Wynter might be following in his wake. As Drake sailed away Antón kept him in sight until the *Golden Hinde*'s topsails vanished below the horizon, then set his own course for Panama and the unappealing prospect of official enquiries.

During the cheerful week in which the *Cacafuego*'s thirteen chests of silver *reales*, twenty-five tons of silver bars ('so mooch silver as did ballast the Goulden Hinde'), and eighty pounds' weight of gold had been stowed below, Drake began to feel that this voyage had achieved enough, and his mind turned increasingly to the passage home. Indeed, some of the gifts he made to his prisoners suggest that his generosity was aided by his need to prepare his heavily laden and increasingly cluttered ship for the long passage to come.

It is difficult to know how clear his plans were at this point. He showed Antón a large chart and told him that he had a choice of four routes by which to return to England: he could retrace his steps by the Strait of Magellan; he could cross the Pacific and go by the Indian Ocean and the Cape of Good Hope; he could go 'by Norway', which presumably meant an unlikely attempt to sail around the north of Russia; and he did not specify the fourth. Drake can hardly have been as completely undecided as this conversation suggested; he was trying to keep the Spaniards guessing. He also asked about possible careening sites on the Nicaraguan coast, to the north, and on the island of Lobos, south towards Lima; again, as Antón suspected, to confuse. When Antón reported to the authorities he was pretty sure, from other information he had gleaned, that Drake's immediate intention was to press on northwards up the coast of Central America.

IX

To the Northwarde of the Line
1579

'I am told that, with the aid of the captured
charts and the pilot of the China trade whom
they seized, they intend to go to China, raiding
the ports of Guatemala and New Spain on the
way. . . . This voyage will be their ruin.'

Diego García de Palacios, Judge of the Audiencia
of Guatemala, letter of 7 April 1579

There was a fever of speculation on the part of the Spanish colonial
authorities about Drake's probable route home. The viceroy in Lima
thought he would use 'the route of the Portuguese', westbound across
the Pacific.[1] One possibility not mentioned by Drake to Antón was
that he might go via the north coast of America and Newfoundland,
using the apocryphal Strait of Anian, called by the Spanish the Estre-
cho de los Bacalaos, after the Newfoundland cod fishery. Another,
which had the Spanish trembling, was that he might reverse Oxenham's procedure, cross the isthmus by land with the help of the
cimarrons, and seize a ship for a journey across the Atlantic.

The Spanish dilemma is clear from the tortuous logic of an influential lawyer called Valverde. Writing to Philip a little later from
Guatemala, he argued against the likelihood of a Pacific crossing: the
voyage was too long; Drake would run out of supplies; he would be
attacked by the Portuguese; he would face the perils of Islam; and,
clinchingly for Valverde's legal brain, 'as he has been proclaiming
that he intended to return by the route of China, we must believe the
contrary, for soldiers . . . are apt to proclaim what they do *not* intend
doing'. Drake's behaviour in the weeks which followed did little to
make things clearer for the Spanish. The fact that he continued north
did not rule out the possibility that he might go westward across the
Pacific; his best chance of fair winds for that crossing lay to the north,
in the area of the north-east trades.

The Spanish seaborne pursuit continued, haplessly and eventually acrimoniously. The rendezvous with the Guayaquil galley did not happen. In the middle of March 1579 the ships anchored in Manta beside Díaz Bravo's vessel and heard the news of Drake's pillaging and boasting, 'like a shameless robber who fears neither God nor man'. Two days later there was a heated debate about whether to pursue Drake coastwise or to cut across the Bay of Panama to the coast of Nicaragua. The latter idea, which might have enabled the pursuers to get ahead of Drake and surprise him by sailing south-east to meet him, was the one favoured by the true sailors in the party, notably Pedro de Sarmiento, who had a wealth of Pacific experience and had explored the Solomon Islands ten years earlier. The sailors lost the argument, and the ships stuck to the coast. When they reached Panama, short of food, they were able to hear the news of the loss of the *Cacafuego* from San Juan de Antón's own lips. Luis de Toledo had had enough of this wearisome command; he handed over to Diego de Frías, and amid renewed rumours of English vessels coming up from the south the ships, with another from Panama, set off to return to Lima. On the way they received the news that Drake had reached the island of Caño off the coast of Nicaragua.

He had anchored between the island and the mainland with the intention of careening the *Golden Hinde*, and took advantage of his time there to load water and supplement provisions by fishing. The *Golden Hinde* and the pinnace, lying about a mile off shore, were shaken by a substantial earthquake. The usefulness of the pinnace emerged again when Drake's lookouts on the island sighted a ship passing on her way to Panama. The pinnace, kept in readiness for just such an event, appeared from behind the island with two dozen well-armed men; it was about four o'clock, and the wind had fallen away, leaving the Spaniard an easy prey for the pinnace, which had the advantage of her oars. The captain, Rodrigo Tello, refused to strike sail at first, but after a trumpet blew in the pinnace and a volley rattled out from the arquebuses he surrendered. His ship was taken in to anchor beside the *Golden Hinde*, and a guard of Englishmen was left in her overnight.

Among six men transferred to the *Hinde* was a Flemish merchant, Cornelius Lambert, who later described the episode to the court of enquiry in Panama.[2] Like most of Drake's ex-prisoners examined by the authorities, he gave details of the English crew's numbers and skills, and Drake's impressive array of armaments: twelve large cast-iron guns; two of bronze weighing sixteen to twenty hundredweight; fireballs; chain-shot; arquebuses; bows and arrows, pikes, partisans, shields and coats of mail; details which must have made the population quake as the news spread and became embroidered. Lambert's account is supported by those of two other passengers: Giusepe de Parraces, who was wounded in the face and arm by balls from the arquebuses, and Diego de Mesa.[3]

On the morning after the capture Drake went across to inspect the Spanish ship, explored the shoreline in the *Golden Hinde*'s boat, and returned to organise a complicated unloading and transhipping of cargoes. He urgently needed to clean the hull of the *Hinde*, but had not found a suitable place to careen her. Careening involved putting a ship aground on a level bottom so that she was high and dry at low tide for scraping and any other remedial action. Drake now made use of the Spanish ship which had fallen into his hands, without any great treasure aboard, to achieve some of this aim without putting the *Hinde* ashore.

The Spaniard's cargo of sarsaparilla and timber was taken into her boat and Drake's pinnace, and probably dumped ashore. The remaining half-dozen Spanish crew and passengers were put in the pinnace, which was then moored astern of the *Hinde*, minus its oars, rudder and sails. Tello's ship was then brought alongside the *Hinde*, all Drake's guns and a large part of his cargo were transferred into the now empty ship, and the bullion was taken ashore. In the next five days the *Hinde*, now riding high in the water, was heeled over first to one side, then to the other, presumably by moving the remaining cargo and ballast, but possibly also with tackles mounted on the prize. All of her hull above the lowered waterline was cleaned and repaired.

Drake was still alert for possibilities of help with navigation. Two of the passengers on Tello's ship, Alonso Sánchez and Martín de Aguirre, were Pacific pilots, sailing to Panama on the orders of the viceroy of New Spain as prospective navigators to the Orient. They were carrying letters from the viceroy to the Spanish governor in the Philippines, two large navigator's maps of the Pacific, and a collection of charts. Drake had a little battle of wills with Sánchez, and used a mixture of bribery, cajoling and threat to try to make him agree to pilot the *Hinde* across the Pacific. Sánchez denied any familiarity with the route, saying that he was no more than a simple seaman who had visited a few places in the Far East (a claim refuted by other witnesses). Drake undertook to leave him at the first island they reached in the Philippines, and promised to give him a hundred *pesos* to send to his wife. The accounts of Sánchez's capitulation are interestingly varied.

According to his own version he agreed when he saw that he was to be taken by main force, willy-nilly, and only after making stern conditions of his own about being allowed to write letters of explanation to his wife and the viceroy. He makes no mention of the bribe, but Lambert (who says that Sánchez received a hundred *pesos*), Parraces (fifty *pesos*, with the promise of 1,000 ducats after the voyage) and Mesa (fifty *pesos*) seem pretty sure about it. He was allowed to write his letters under the supervision of Spanish-speaking members of Drake's crew.

Drake set sail again on 25 March, taking the Spanish prize with him, and accompanied by the pinnace, with her oars, sails and rudder restored. On the 27th he ordered his men out of the pinnace, put his prisoners into it, with the exception of Sánchez, gave them a keg and a half of water, and suggested they might make for the mainland. They had only about four miles to sail to Río de la Barranca, where they quickly reported Drake's latest outrage, forwarded Sánchez's letters, and caused another flurry of enquiry. In the fusty quarters of officialdom note was taken that Drake had retained a pilot with knowledge of the trans-Pacific trade; in Alonso Sánchez's house the windfall of Drake's bribe mitigated the absence of a husband and father who was absent most of the time in any case.

As he sailed on up the coast of Nicaragua Drake continued to put pressure on Sánchez. The pilot, who provides the only Spanish evidence for these days, may well have overstated things to the authorities in order to stress his loyalties after his earlier capitulation. His version was that he refused many offers of silver and gold made by Drake to persuade him to renounce Catholicism and go to England, and that Drake commented on his devotion to King Philip, saying that he must be a great captain. Sánchez also depicted himself as the saviour of the town of Realejo.

Here again we should beware of swallowing Sánchez's claims about his own sturdy heroism. They were made to the authorities in Realejo itself, and specifically to Judge Diego García de Palacios, whose life he obliquely claimed to have saved.[4] Obviously terrified of being suspected of collaborating with the Lutheran enemy, he told the judge a brave tale of his resistance: Drake demanded that he pilot him into Realejo harbour so that he could burn the town, seize the judge and hang him as a servant of King Philip; Sánchez denied all knowledge of the port. Drake offered bribes; Sánchez stood firm. Drake made threats; Sánchez was adamant. Drake ordered him to be hanged; Sánchez continued rock-like in his patriotism. They put a rope round his neck and hoisted him off his feet; no use. They did it again; he collapsed in exhaustion, the frustrated Drake gave up and sailed on to the north and Realejo was saved.

A final prize awaited Drake, and its capture was to be widely reported in Spanish circles in a way generally complimentary to him.[5] A Spanish trading vessel captained by Pedro Hernández had left Acapulco bound for Peru. Aboard her was a rich nobleman, a member of the Order of Santiago, Don Francisco de Zarate. This man's report to the viceroy of Drake's behaviour during the encounter which followed testifies to Drake's engaging generosity of spirit as convincingly as any eulogy by patriotic Englishmen.

Hernández's ship sailed placidly southward until Saturday, 4 April, when in the grey of the dawning the officer of the watch made out a ship astern and closing, and then a smaller vessel with her. As the *Golden Hinde* came within hailing distance his concern grew, and he shouted to her to keep off. There was no reply, so he hailed her again, asking what ship she was. A reply came back: she was Miguel Angel's ship. The Spanish was very good, for the respondent was, in fact, the demoralised Sánchez, another detail which he was careful to conceal in his own testimony. Drake swung across Hernández's wake, discharged seven or eight arquebuses, and ordered the ship to heave to. There was no resistance; all but half a dozen of the Spanish were asleep. The *Hinde*'s boat crew simply climbed aboard, seized the passengers' swords and keys and, rightly judging Zarate to be the most important man aboard, ordered him into the boat. Zarate thought his last hour had come, and commended his soul to God.

He was pleasantly surprised: Drake received him with courtesy and took him to his great cabin, where they had a long conversation extending through the day. Drake was disappointed with what he heard about the Spaniard's cargo, which included no treasure of any importance. He asked if Zarate knew the viceroy, the hated Martín Enríquez, and asked if any of Enríquez's relatives or friends were aboard. 'I would sooner find him than all the gold and silver of the Indies; I would soon show him how gentlemen keep their word'. At dinner Drake made Zarate sit beside him, gave him food from his own plate, and assured him that his life and property were in no danger. These courtesies were due partly to Drake's pressing need for information about where he could find water, but Zarate was of little help to him in this.

On the Sunday morning Drake was in high fettle. Dressing the *Golden Hinde* out with all her flags and banners, and wearing his own Sunday best, he went aboard the Spanish ship and helped himself to what he fancied. The cargo included silks, clothing and 'divers chests full of fine earthen disshes, very finely wrought, of fine white erth, brought by the Spanyards from the countrey of Chyna ... Of these dishes Drake took four chests full from them, also ... fine linen cloth and good store of taffata and other fine silks'.[6] Zarate, according to his own report, lost little, though he is said to have persuaded Drake not to take his rich clothing by giving him a golden falcon with an emerald set in the breast.[7] Drake apologised for taking what trifles he did, explaining that they were to be gifts for his wife, and gave Zarate a sword and a small silver brazier in exchange.

Zarate was hugely impressed by Drake: his silver and gilt tableware, perfumes and dainties; his popularity among his men; his maritime skills, assured authority and shipboard organisation. Zarate also commented to the viceroy, and expressed concern, about the careful paintings of the coast made by some members of the company (probably John Drake and Francis Fletcher). Zarate was on board the *Hinde* for over fifty hours. Drake talked to him at length about the voyage so far, and especially about the Doughty affair. He had no need to tell Zarate anything about it, but one gains the impression that he was still troubled in his mind over the execution of Doughty, and that he was glad to have the opportunity to unburden himself to someone outside the ship's company. He praised Doughty's character and went to some lengths to justify the trial on the grounds that the Queen's service required it; he even showed Zarate a document which he said was his commission from Elizabeth. Doughty's brother was still being regarded with distrust; Zarate reported that he was the only person not allowed to leave the ship during Zarate's time on board, and that a close eye was being kept on him.

By this time Drake had despaired of obtaining any serious help from Sánchez; perhaps he had concluded that the pilot's protestations about his ignorance of the trans-Pacific route were true. In his now habitual manner he retained a pilot from his latest prize; this time it was a 25-year-old Portuguese, Juan Pascual.[8] This man's testimony is of great interest; it was gathered by the Inquisition as part of the prosecution of his fellow-Portuguese, Nunho da Silva, for heresy, and consequently it has something to say about religious observance on the *Golden Hinde*. When Pascual first climbed aboard he found everyone at prayer, some kneeling, others seated. He was greeted warmly by Sánchez, who evidently saw him as his own salvation and immediately recommended him to Drake as a reliable pilot who could show him where to find water and fuel. In the ensuing days Pascual saw Drake conduct regular prayers before the midday and evening meals, kneeling on a cushion at a table, with the crew chanting the responses. The Spaniards aboard were allowed to withdraw into the bows, though da Silva, unfortunately for his future welfare, remained and took part, as did the negroes on board. Pascual also mentions that the crew heard sermons by another man, probably Fletcher, and that several of them, including da Silva, read religious books privately. Although it was Lent, Drake and everyone else ate meat, and the prisoners had to do the same or starve. Overt anti-Catholicism was rare; only the bosun, in Juan Pascual's recollection, went so far as to smash a small sacred image found in the booty.

Drake restored Zarate to his ship with some ceremony, returning the passengers' boxes and dispensing handfuls of *reales* to the Spanish sailors. His last words to Zarate were a request that he should convey his best wishes to 'certain Englishmen in Lima'. Zarate thought he was referring to a network of English spies, but Drake obviously meant Oxenham and his friends. Drake retained from Zarate's ship a good-looking black girl called María, 'which was afterward gotten with child between the captaine and his men pirats, and sett on a small iland to take her adventure'.[9]

Drake's business with the Spanish was now almost done. Although his intentions remained ambiguous, his course homeward, whether across the Pacific, up the uncharted and inhospitable coast of North America, or southward past the now alert and hostile ports of Peru and Chile, demanded that he provision his ships as fully as possible. He therefore 'thought it needfull that we should runne in with some place or other ... to see if happily wee could, by traffique, augment our provision of victuals and other necessaries'.[10] The unfortunate partner chosen for this 'traffique' was the little port of Guatulco, which Drake reached on 13 April 1579.

His entry into the harbour repeats a now familiar picture: a small outpost of empire, used to the presence of substantial wealth (it was an embarkation point for Peru and Honduras), complacent in its isolation and apparently oblivious to Drake's raids further south; a bold and unopposed arrival, followed by local panic and disorganisation; easy pickings. *The World Encompassed* describes the visit with its usual laconic humour, but the local Spaniards saw things very differently: as they made peaceful preparations for their greatest festival, Holy Week, their quiet lives suddenly exploded.

At eight in the morning the crew of a ship belonging to Juan de

Madrid, loading in the harbour, saw two sails off the coast and sent word to the mayor, Gaspar de Vargas. They thought the larger vessel might be a ship which was expected from Peru, and the smaller one a pearl-fishing boat. The ships neared the harbour entrance at about ten o'clock, and entered abreast. Someone commented on the size of the larger one, and it was noticed that she was rather low in the water. She lowered a boat, which approached the shore. Only when it was seen that the boat was bristling with arquebuses and bows did curiosity give way to alarm.[11]

The few Spaniards who could be mustered, together with a few Indians who were decorating the church for Holy Week, put up a brief resistance, but as soon as the small vessel fired her artillery most of them retreated into the woods overlooking the town and watched impotently as the English ransacked it. The enthusiastic Lutheranism of some members of the crew, led by the bosun, was given free rein: the church was pillaged, its plate, bell and vestments stolen, its altarpiece and crucifixes hacked to pieces, and the holy wafers scattered and trampled.[12]

The priest, Simón de Miranda, a relative of his, mayor of a neighbouring town, and the *encomendero* or Crown factor Francisco Gómez Rengifo were captured and taken aboard the *Golden Hinde*, as were three negroes found in the courthouse, accused of plotting to burn down the town. Rengifo's later deposition[13] describes the sacking of his home and the theft of 7,000 *pesos* in silver and gold. The bosun, sparsely bearded and pockmarked, seized a crucifix by the feet and smashed it against a table, saying that the Spanish were idolators and worshipped wood and stones. He kept up this performance when the prisoners were aboard the *Hinde*, wrenching a gold figure of the Virgin from a rosary worn by the priest, biting it and pretending to throw it overboard. A tall member of the crew was wearing one of the chasubles, and the church bell had been hung alongside the ship's pump.

The prisoners were put below deck, and Drake went ashore to oversee the plunder. On his return he ate a good meal with them: pork and chicken, with fish for the priest, after which there was an hour-long service of prayers and psalms, sometimes accompanied by four viols. Drake read a book described as containing 'many illuminated pictures of the Lutherans who had been burnt in Spain'. From Gómez Rengifo's description of specific illustrations, this was obviously Foxe's *Book of Martyrs*.[14] Drake said to him what he had said to others: he was acting in the Queen's name; his quarrel, and hers, where with King Philip and his viceroy; and he would not rest until he recovered the sum lost by Hawkins at San Juan de Ulúa.

Ashore, the mayor waited until the dust settled before descending from the wooded hills to assess the damage. That evening he sent off a letter to the viceroy[15] putting a brave light on his own part in the affair and suggesting the preparation of a punitive fleet at Acapulco, which he thought was Drake's next target. The problems of coping with Drake are illustrated by the fact that ten days passed before the letter reached Enríquez, and by the plaintive note of the viceroy's own letter to the king,[16] in which he says that although he is warning all the coastal settlements, 'they can do nothing more than take refuge in the woods ... There is no mode of defence ... In many places there are not more than four Spaniards, excepting in the port of Acapulco, and even there there are very few ... The ports are all without artillery'.

On the Tuesday afternoon, after replenishing his water-casks, Drake sent his three Spanish prisoners ashore. Two of the negroes took their chance to stay on board; the other was put ashore and vanished into the woods. Gómez Rengifo pleaded for some ship's biscuit and wine to save his family from starvation, and Drake sent him some oil, wine, flour and sugar. Wednesday and Thursday were spent in rifling the ship of Juan de Madrid, which was immobilised by cutting off her bowsprit and topmast. The *Golden Hinde* weighed anchor before dawn on Good Friday, 17 April.

Simón de Miranda, the priest, during his brief stay on board, noticed the apparent closeness of the relationship between Drake and Nunho da Silva. Drake spoke affably with the pilot, patting him and placing him next to himself at table, and da Silva took part in the prayers and psalm-singing. This makes all the more puzzling the fact that when Drake sailed from Guatulco he left da Silva behind on Juan de Madrid's ship. The version of da Silva's own account published by Hakluyt says twice that 'he let him goe',[17] but other sources suggest that the Portuguese was very unwilling 'to have bin lefft to ye Spaniard for a praye'.[18] Da Silva's log becomes fragmented in the week 6–13 April, and his final, brief entry is for the 13th, which may indicate that his mind was troubled by the awareness that he might be abandoned. Perhaps he lacked the knowledge of the East Indies trade which Drake thought he was going to need, and would only have been a drain on water and food supplies.

He was not thrown out in anger or haste, but if he had known for sure that he was going to be left he would hardly have participated so enthusiastically in Protestant worship in front of the local priest. He retained his possessions: sixteen shirts, several pairs of breeches, hats, etc.; an arquebus; lengths of damask; bedlinen; even oddments such as a pair of women's boots, a tin of saffron, a jar of oil, two pounds of soap and a length of hat-trimming. Gaspar de Vargas, the mayor, keen to restore his credentials after his puny defence of the town, seized da Silva and sent him to the viceroy, who passed him on to the Inquisition in Mexico City. Da Silva's depositions to the Inquisitors survive,[19] a helpful though not always consistent source for much of the voyage. He said that he was surprised to be left behind, that Drake had shown no intention of leaving him anywhere, and that he received no payment whatsoever.

A fellow-sufferer from the Guatulco raid tried to restore his own fortunes at poor da Silva's expense. When the mayor seized the pilot he placed his possessions in the care of the *encomendero*, Gómez Rengifo, who saw them as a gift of God. When the possessions were subsequently demanded by the Inquisition and sent by muleteer, they were found not to coincide with the inventory, and the *encomendero*, threatened with excommunication and a heavy fine, had to do some smart talking: some things, he said, he had never received; some he had seen da Silva sell to others; the missing Rouen lace was a gift from the pilot to Gómez Rengifo's wife; the hat-trimming had been given to Bernardino, a servant; and so on. A missing breviary had been left as a present for the priest, whom Gómez Rengifo had not seen since. The missing boots turned up on one of the *encomendero*'s maids. The soap had gone for good.

X

RETURNE AGAINE YE SONNES OF MEN
1579–80

'... the time of the yeare now drew on wherein
we must attempt ... the discovery of what
passage there was to be found about the
Northerne Parts of America ... through which
we might with joy returne to our longed
homes.'

Anon., *The World Encompassed*, 1628

The departure from Guatulco of the *Golden Hinde* and Tello's ship
began a new phase of the voyage. Drake may have considered undertaking the raid on Acapulco feared by the Spanish, but his thoughts
now were concentrated on his homeward course. His intentions at
this point remain ambiguous to this day. Two former possibilities
must by now have been abandoned: a return via the Strait of Magellan
would have been foolhardy,[1] and a crossing of the isthmus, given the
weight of treasure he now carried and the alarmed state of the
Spanish, unfeasible. He had provided himself with charts and information for the Pacific crossing to the Moluccas, but it is possible that
he still thought of the supposed Strait of Anian as providing a short
passage home. However, even if the strait proved to be there, it was
uncharted and possibly hazardous, and for a man with a fortune
under his deck the appeal of the known routes across the Pacific and
the Indian Ocean must have been great.

Drake sailed unmolested past California and onward a long way
north, but although contemporary accounts of this part of the voyage
are rather summary, he seems not to have put any great time or
serious effort into a search for the western mouth of a passage around
the north coast of America. The *Anonymous Narrative* says that he
sailed northwards

till he came to 48 degrees of the septentrionall latitude, still finding a very
lardge sea trending to the North, but being afraid to spend long time in

seeking for the straite, hee turned back againe ... untill he came to 44 degrees, and then hee found a harborow ... where he grounded his ship to trim her.[2]

The latitude of 48° north, confirmed by John Drake,[3] is almost that of the Juan de Fuca Strait. If Drake had gone even a few miles north of 48°, looking seriously for the western end of the North-West Passage, it seems unlikely that he would have missed the strait, or the chance to explore it, but it is not mentioned in any account. Other versions disagree with the latitudes given by the *Anonymous Narrative*, sometimes adding a good deal of creative detail. Hakluyt, who gives 43° north as the most northerly point (a little to the north of Cape Mendocino), says that Drake was forced to turn back by severe cold. He gives 38° north as the place where Drake careened his ship on 17 June 1579.[4] *The World Encompassed* agrees with the *Narrative* on 48° north and with Hakluyt on 38° north. It gives graphic details of the effects of the weather between 42° north and 48° north: numbing cold; iced-up rigging; meat freezing as soon as it left the fire; serious demoralisation among the crew, redeemed only by the cheerful example of the admiral.

The World Encompassed goes on at such length about the extremity of the cold and its possible causes that an uncharitable mind could interpret its account as an attempt to justify Drake's failure to pursue the search for the Strait of Anian seriously enough. It is patently untruthful, for example, in describing the coastal Indians as shivering in furs and crowding together for warmth (this was in California, in mid-June). Other accounts describe the Indians as naked, and *The World Encompassed* contradicts itself by saying that Drake gave them 'necessary things to cover their nakedness'. On the question of the strait, it concludes

> that either there is no passage at all through these Northerne coasts (which is most likely), or if there be, that yet it is unnavigable. Adde hereunto, that though we searched the coast diligently ... yet found we not the land to trend so much as one point in any place towards the East, but rather running on continually North-west, as if it went directly to meet with Asia; ... we had a smooth and calm sea, with ordinary flowing and reflowing, which could not have beene had there beene a frete; of which we rather infallibly concluded, than coniectured, that there was none.[5]

The identity of the bay where Drake stayed from 17 June to 23 July to put the *Golden Hinde* in a fit state for the homeward voyage has been the subject of much debate. He needed a bay secluded from the sea, in case the Spanish came looking for him; a suitable bottom on which to careen the *Hinde*; an anchorage at which his Spanish prize could lie, with some of the *Hinde*'s contents aboard her; and a site which could be defended against attack from the landward side. Within a few miles either side of 38° north are at least eight possible sites, some on the ocean coast, some in San Francisco Bay.[6] The likeliest appears to be Drake's Bay, which, though it has had this name only in modern times, sits exactly on the 38th parallel. A feature of it is its white cliffs, and Hakluyt makes a point of mentioning that one reason for Drake's naming the country Nova Albion was 'in respect of the white bankes and cliffes, which ly towardes the sea'.[7]

The crew pitched tents ashore and built a rough stone wall for defence, which proved unnecessary. The description of their contact with the Indians, the Coastal Miwok, is uncannily similar to Columbus's account of his reception in the Caribbean: a generous and tractable people, accepting the visitors as gods and taking a childish pleasure in simple artefacts; coming almost every day to offer gifts of feathers, skins, net bags, arrows; listening in wide-eyed joy to the crew's psalm-singing, and imitating their prayers. The Englishmen, just like Columbus, were quick to interpret formal speeches to Drake by the local chief as 'supplications, that hee would take the Province and kingdome into his hand, and become their king and patron'. *The World Encompassed* here reads like a translation of Columbus's *Journal* as Drake interprets the incomprehensible speeches of the Miwok as he will, incorporating their land into an embryonic English empire and into Christendom:

> ... they would resigne unto him their right and title in the whole land, and become his vassal in themselves and their posterities, ... because they were not onely visited of the gods (for so they still judged us to be), but the great and chiefe God was now become their God, their king and patron, ... wherefore, in the name and to the use of her most excellent maiesty, he tooke the scepter, crowne, and dignity of the sayd countrie into his hand; wishing ... especially that so tractable and loving a people as they shewed themselves to be, might have meanes to have manifested their most willing obedience the more unto her, and by her meanes, as a mother and nurse of the Church of Christ, might by the preaching of the Gospell, be brought to the right knowledge and obedience of the true and everliving God.[8]

Like Columbus, Drake left tangible evidence of his annexing of the country. He set up a strong post bearing a metal plate stating Elizabeth's sovereignty, with his own name, the date of his arrival and a specially cut hole revealing a silver sixpence with the Queen's head. Modern claims to have discovered the plate have been proved spurious by metallurgical investigation.[9] There have been attempts to make a case for Drake having established an embryo colony in the land he named Nova Albion. Some of these are based substantially on a supposed reduction in crew numbers before the Pacific crossing.[10] In view of the prominence given in different versions to the crowning of Drake by the Indians it would be odd if the establishment of a colony had gone unrecorded. If crew members did stay behind in California it is more likely that they did so as volunteers or deserters, wearied by the length of the voyage, unenthusiastic about crossing the Pacific, and possibly influenced by attachments to Indian women formed during their stay.

There is, however, intriguing evidence for the presence of a strain of European blood among Californian Indians not far from Drake's careenage. In the late nineteenth century a legend was recorded among the Indians of the Nicasio valley, about fifteen miles east of Drake's Bay, to the effect that some of the crew deserted and interbred with the Indians. When an expedition led by a Father Crespi explored the area in 1772, it found that the inhabitants included some who were fair in hair and complexion, and bearded (not a notable characteristic of the American Indian). Another priest, Father Francisco Palou, exploring Northern California two years later, met different groups of Indians who were tall, fair and bearded.[11] In the latter part of his time in California Drake, 'with his gentlemen and many of his company, made a journey up into the land, to see the manner of their dwelling, and to be better acquainted with the nature and commodities'. They found 'a goodly country, and fruitfull soyle, stored with many blessings fit for the use of man'.

The sustained presence of a group of Devonians fathering a sixteenth-century generation of the lucky inhabitants of this paradise must remain a pretty theory unless some more serious evidence turns up to support it, though it would be strange if at least a few blue-eyed, fair-haired babies were not causing gossip among the smiling and generous Miwok nine months after the *Golden Hinde*'s topsails sank below the horizon.

The ship was once again clean and trim when she set sail on 23 July 1579. Apart from an overnight call at a group of islands which Drake named the St James Islands, where he took on seal meat, her next landfall was on 30 September. Among some of the scattered islands of Micronesia she was repeatedly the target of outrigger canoes, each crewed by about fifteen men, who paddled out to trade coconuts, fish and fruit. They became so importunate and bold in laying their hands on whatever they fancied that Drake ordered a gun to be fired to scare them away,[12] and named the group the Islands of Thieves.[13] Continuing west on the same latitude the expedition sighted the Philippines on 16 October, and after watering in the Davao Gulf on Mindanao five days later Drake headed south towards the Moluccas.

Ever since Marco Polo's *Travels* opened the eyes and the imagination of Europe, the myriad islands of the South-West Pacific had loomed larger than their small land area could warrant in the thoughts of geographers, monarchs and entrepreneurs. The early exploration of the area had been carried out by the Portuguese; by discovering the Cape of Good Hope they had revealed a sea route to the Far East which, thanks to papal decree, had remained for a long time their monopoly. The living testimony of this today is the survival of the Portuguese language in the old colonies of Macao and Goa, but in the sixteenth century the Portuguese presence in the area was very alive, and extended into Micronesia.

Discoveries were still being made, and the Spanish had extended their exploration across the Pacific. By Pedro de Sarmiento's voyage to the Solomon Islands ten years before, and the established trade route between Central America and the Philippines, Spain, debarred from exploring eastward from Europe, had now extended her sphere of action far enough westward to check Portuguese expansion coming the other way around the world.

The appeal of trade with the islands off South-East Asia lay largely in their abundant spices. For a Europe which had not developed the crops and techniques necessary for overwintering cattle, spices were a scarce and expensive way of rendering salted meat palatable, and fresh meat interesting, for the tables of the well-to-do. For a shipowner the appeal of spices was obvious: their selling price relative to their weight and volume made them a hugely profitable cargo.

The various contemporary accounts of Drake's homeward journey give the impression that his course to and through the Melanesian islands, and the calls he made at them, were more or less fortuitous; to the ordinary crew members they probably appeared so. Once he had settled to return to England by a western route, however, which must inevitably take him within striking distance of the Moluccas, it would have been uncharacteristic of Drake not to investigate the chances of increasing the profits from the voyage by picking up some light and marketable spices. The fact that Wynter argued for proceeding to the Moluccas when he had lost contact with Drake suggests that a call there had been at least a strong possibility from the outset.

The Portuguese presence in the area affected Drake's activities, and worked to his advantage. He had a brief encounter with a trading vessel, probably Portuguese, from which he offered to buy provisions, a request refused on the grounds that the English were Lutherans. Drake chased the foreigner through the night, but gave up when she entered shallow water.[14] Once again he obtained local pilotage, in this case from two men found fishing, and around 4 November he sighted the Moluccas.

He steered initially for Tidore, guided now by a half-breed Portuguese, but off the coast of the neighbouring island of Ternate an embassy arrived in a canoe from the ruler of Ternate, the muslim Sultan Babullah, who currently 'held the Portingall as an enemy'. The Portuguese had killed his father, and he was preparing to expel them from their stronghold on Tidore. It is clear from his dealings with Drake that Babullah was exploring the possibilities of acquiring England as an ally and trading partner.

After an exchange of gifts the Sultan himself was rowed out in all his courtly pomp to receive Drake, and the *Hinde* was towed into harbour by three large canoes. Drums and gongs beat in welcome, songs filled the air, Drake's orchestra responded, and the *Hinde* fired off gun-salutes and volleys from arquebuses. It was Ramadan, but quantities of rice, sago, chickens, bananas and coconuts were sent out to the ship. However, Babullah's promise to go on board her himself on the following day was not kept. Instead his brother came and invited Drake ashore, offering to remain himself as a hostage, but Drake too was wary, and sent some of his gentlemen instead. They were entertained with impressive ceremony.

Drake bartered for several tons of cloves and ginger[15] before leaving on 9 November. Neither side had much confidence in the other, but Drake evidently thought that foundations had been laid for further negotiations which might give England a commercial toe-hold. (This belief was to lead to a follow-up voyage led by Edward Fenton in 1582, in which several of Drake's men took part.[16])

By now the *Golden Hinde* needed careening again, her water-casks needed repair, and the crew were 'sickly, weake and decayed'. After sailing five days west from Ternate Drake found a small, uninhabited, wooded island, where he anchored and prepared for a stay of several weeks. A stockade and tents were erected ashore, a forge was set up, and charcoal-burning was begun to provide fuel for it. The *Hinde* was careened and scraped clean; casks were repaired and refilled from a water supply on an adjacent island; the crew recovered in strength and spirit. They had time to observe the wildlife: swarms of fireflies; huge bats; crabs which astonished them by climbing trees. They called the place Crab Island.

When they sailed on 12 December they left behind the black woman María, now pregnant, and two negroes, 'to start a population'.[17] Drake had a bad time getting round the Celebes; after beating about in adverse winds among the tricky shoals, and eventually finding what seemed to be a clear passage west on 9 January, with a fine following wind, he was struck by a disaster which could have ended the voyage in oblivion:

> ... loe, on a sudden, when we least suspected, no shew or suspition of danger appearing to us, and we were now sailing onward with full sailes, in the beginning of the first watch of the said day at night, even in a moment, our ship was laid up fast upon a desperate shoale, with no other likelihood in appearance, but that wee with her must there presently perish; there being no probability how any thing could be saved, or any person scape alive.[18]

Their first resort was prayer. As this had no immediate result, and in order that 'we might not seeme to tempt God by leaving any second meanes unattempted which he afforded', Drake proceeded efficiently to practicalities, leading by example. The ship was pumped out and found to be sound, but remained fast. The next obvious step was to take out an anchor and try to kedge her off the reef; that is, to drop the anchor onto firm holding ground and winch in the cable in the hope the anchor would hold and the ship would move. Drake went in the boat and took soundings with a lead-line himself, but the reef was so steep-to that he could find no bottom, even a mere boat's length from the ship. Their hearts sinking, they considered the options: the boat would hold only about twenty, and the nearest known coast was twenty miles directly upwind. If they reached shore they would fall into the hands of infidels and probably be murdered. Staying on board the ship would mean drowning when she eventually opened up and sank.

They spent the night in further prayer. In the morning, after another failed attempt to find holding ground for an anchor, they listened to a sermon from Francis Fletcher, took Holy Communion and proceeded to the desperate measure of lightening ship by throwing overboard two of her guns and three tons of cloves. With this, and a change in the wind which had been pressing her against the reef, the *Hinde* was able to heel into deeper water.

> But when all was done, it was not any of our endevours, but Gods onely hand that wrought our deliverie; 'twas he alone that brought us even under the very stroke of death; 'twas he alone that said unto us, Returne againe ye sonnes of men; ... to his glorious name be the everlasting praise.[19]

The period of the crew's relief at their deliverance was enlivened by a curious piece of theatre. The words of Fletcher's sermon are unrecorded, but for some reason Drake decided to scare the man. An anonymous memorandum in the British Library[20] says that

> Drake excomunicated Fletcher shortly after that they were come of the rock in this manner, *viz*, hee caused him to bee made fast by one of the leggs with a ... staple knocked fast into the hatches in the forecastell of his ship. He called all the company together, and then put a ... lock about one of his legs, and Drake sytting cros legged on a chest, and a peire of pantoffles [i.e. slippers] in his hand, hee said, Francis Fletcher, I doo heere excomunicate the[e] out of the Church of God, and from all the benefites and graces therof, and I denounce the[e] to the divell and all his angells; and then he charged him uppon payne of death not once to come before the mast, for if hee did, he sware hee should be hanged; and Drake cawsed a posy [i.e. a poem] to be written and bound about Fletcher's arme, with chardge that if hee tooke it of hee should then be hanged. The poes[y] was, Frances fletcher, the falsest knave that liveth.

Despite the 'pantoffles', this was not just friendly horseplay. The same document contains a memo 'to enquire where Drake fell out with Fletcher, and how long hee wore his bracelett, ... where it was put on, and wher it was taken off again'. The reason must have been the content of Fletcher's sermon, which no doubt called on the company to repent of their sins, and perhaps recalled a specific one, the death of Doughty. Fletcher, on close scrutiny, emerges as something of a trimmer, himself not guiltless in Doughty's death, but perhaps his conscience and his duty as a priest overrode his self-interest in the crisis on the reef.[21]

The next two months were a time of slow progress westward,

calling at an occasional island for water, in winds initially adverse. Spirits were raised by two days (8–10 February 1580) at Barativa, whose inhabitants were 'cheerfully ready to relieve our wants with whatever their country could afford'. This may be a euphemism; it is followed by a description of the women of the island, naked above the waist. On Java, after changing his anchorage twice and exchanging gifts with the rajah, Drake led a party ashore on 13 March. The ship's musicians played and Drake drilled his pikemen before his host. This combination of musical entertainment with a show of strength was repeated when the rajah and his retinue visited the ship. In this friendly atmosphere Drake felt safe to careen the *Hinde* again, but here too European rivalries were present: John Drake mentions that there were Portuguese on the island, and that one was discovered on board the ship with some natives, planning treachery.[22]

When Drake sailed on 26 March the ship was clean, fresh and well victualled with an ox, hens, goats, coconuts, sugar-cane and bananas. From Java onwards, except for the usual concern about water, the voyage was without incident. They found their landfall on the African coast in 31°50 south, sailed coastwise past the Cape of Good Hope, and reached Sierra Leone on 22 July. They spent two days watering, enjoyed some oysters and lemons, and by 22 August were level with the Canaries. The final month, without sight of land or of another ship, must have seemed endless; it was not until 26 September 1580 that they reached home.

> We safely with joyfull minds and thankfull hearts to God, arrived at Plimoth, the place of our first setting forth, after we had spent 2 yeares 10 moneths and some few odde daies beside, in seeing the wonders of the Lord in the deep, in discovering so many admirable things, in going through with so many strange adventures, in escaping out of so many dangers, and overcomming so many difficulties in this our encompassing of this neather globe.[23]

XI

THAT GOLDEN KNIGHT OF OURS
1580–85

'The Queenes Majesty came aboorde his
weather beaten Barke; where beeing as highly
graced as his hearte coulde wish, with knightly
honour, . . . his name and fame became
admirable in all places.'

Edmond Howes, *The Annales, or Generall*
Chronicle of England, 1615

Drake's first act after reaching Plymouth was to send a messenger by
relayed horses to London to inform Elizabeth. She ordered him to
have the treasure brought ashore and put in a place of safety under
the supervision of Edmund Tremayne, and summoned him to Court.
He was probably not wholly confident of his reception or his future
at this point, after three years away during which he must often
have wondered whether the state of Anglo-Spanish relations and
Elizabeth's volatile mind would allow him to enjoy a welcome. He
knew he could expect hostility from Burghley. He took some of the
choicest pieces of plunder as gifts for the Queen, and emerged from
his interview with her in no doubt of her favourable attitude, but
aware too of the difficulties facing her. Bernardino de Mendoza,
the Spanish ambassador in London, reported to Philip that Drake
presented the Queen with a diary of the voyage and a large chart,
and that they talked for six hours.

News of Drake's successes against Spanish ships in the Pacific had
reached London long before, and so had Spain's protests and demands
for restitution. Elizabeth's advisers were divided on whether or not
to hold on to the treasure. Burghley, inclined as usual against entering
into open confrontation with Philip, and probably also in a long-
term huff about being kept in the dark before the expedition, argued
that the plunder should be stored in the Tower pending its restoration
to its owners. He had the support of some of his fellow members of
the Council, but not surprisingly Leicester, Walsingham and Hatton,

with the huge dividend on their own investment in mind, disagreed.[1]

Mendoza pressed Elizabeth for action against Drake, and was sent away with a flea in his ear.[2] Drake was sent back to Plymouth to oversee the registration of the treasure, an obvious necessity whatever its destiny, but was allowed *sub rosa* to extract £10,000 for himself. Some of the rest of the treasure, but far from all of it, was taken to the Tower of London. The country's foreign debt may have been a factor in the eventual decision to retain the treasure and distribute it among the investors, who received the stupendous return of forty-seven pounds for every pound adventured. The Queen's share was enough to pay off the debt and leave her £42,000 over to invest in the Levant Company. Drake, Hawkins and the Wynters became massively rich.

Elizabeth and her advisers were determined to keep the details of Drake's route after leaving Central America secret as long as possible. Mendoza probed for information wherever he could. One of his informants was Sir Christopher Hatton's trumpeter, who told him that Drake had returned by the Portuguese Indies, but Mendoza did not take this at face value, and reported to Philip that Drake had said the opposite and that the crew had been sworn to secrecy.[3] Walsingham responded to Mendoza's claims for restitution by asking Edmund Tremayne to question the crew of the *Golden Hinde* and to make sure that he got the right answers. Four of the company, Lawrence Eliot, Gregory Cary, John Chester and George Fortescue, testified that as far as they knew the amount of gold and silver taken had been small, and Drake had killed and tortured no-one. 'Only on[e] man I remember,' said Eliot, 'was hurt in the face, w[hi]ch o[u]r General caused to be sent for, and lodged him in his owne shipp, seet him at his own table and would not soffer him to depart before he was recovered.' The document bears the names of forty-five other crew members (some of them signed in the same hand).[4] The investigation ended in a whitewashing of Drake.

A similar official attitude of going through the motions was adopted towards John Doughty's attempt to have Drake brought to trial for his brother's murder. He took his case to the Earl Marshal's Court, the High Court of Chivalry and Honour. Drake delayed things by questioning the Court's competence in matters happening abroad, but the ruling went against him. The suit was never heard, because the Court's hearing of a case 'of things done out of this realm' needed the presence of both the Earl Marshal and the Chief Constable of England, and in 1581 the latter post had no incumbent. Elizabeth took advantage of this technicality to put a stop to the proceedings by refusing to appoint a Chief Constable when petitioned to do so by John Doughty.

The events which followed strongly suggest, though they do not prove, that Drake and powerful friends pursued young Doughty with any means possible. A Patrick Mason confessed under torture in May 1582 to being implicated with John Doughty and the Spanish agent Zubiaurre in a plot to murder or kidnap Drake. Zubiaurre, he claimed, had shown him letters from Philip promising 20,000 ducats as a reward, and had told him to procure the services of Doughty. In the light of Mason's confession, and of testimony from Drake concerning speeches made against him by Doughty at the time of the conferring of his knighthood, John Doughty was arrested and put into the Marshalsea. He had not been tried by 27 October 1583, when he petitioned to be tried or released, and what happened to him is not known.[5]

Philip's plots and claims in England were meeting with little success, but closer to home he had taken a major step by pressing and enforcing a justifiable claim to the throne of Portugal after the death of the childless King Henry the Cardinal in January 1580. This not only increased his territorial holdings, but also made Spain mistress of the Portuguese trade routes to Africa, the Far East and Brazil. More importantly in the eyes of Elizabeth and her seamen, it augmented Philip's fleet with that of Portugal and gave him an important Atlantic staging-post in the Azores. The Duke of Alba was entrusted with the military occupation of Portugal, and the troops in the Netherlands were now under the command of Philip's nephew, the Duke of Parma.

Close to England's other flank, Philip had been meddling in Ireland, landing troops on the south coast in support of the rebels. At one point Elizabeth began using the treasure in the Tower as a bargaining instrument, suggesting that if Philip left Ireland alone the bulk of his silver might be returned to him and the investors would be content with simply doubling their money, but fortunately for Drake and his fellow adventurers the Spanish troops were heavily defeated and the offer was dropped.

The Queen was in a mood for cocking snooks at Philip. On Court occasions she wore a new crown incorporating five huge emeralds brought back by Drake from the Pacific.[6] Even in the conferring of Drake's knighthood she did not summon the hero, but went to Deptford to be entertained by him on the weather-beaten *Golden*

Drake's circumnavigation, depicted in an emblem book. The Golden Hinde
*surmounts the globe, guided by a bridle steered by the hand of God. This motif
was used as the crest above Drake's coat of arms.*

Hinde. The ceremony was surrounded by feasting, banners and public
spectacle; a bridge collapsed under the weight of the spectators. Philip
could dismiss this sort of thing as merely an irritant, but he must
have looked more seriously on the news that she handed the sword
to a French courtier who accompanied her, a Monsieur de Marchaumont, and asked him to knight Drake. Marchaumont was in
England to pursue negotiations for a marriage between Elizabeth and
his master, the Duc d'Alençon, brother to the King of France, and
Philip could only construe the proposal for this loveless alliance as a
strategic move against him.

Drake gave Elizabeth magnificent presents to mark his knighthood,
including a 'very faire Baskett of silver to take up [i.e. clear] a Table,
graven with her Ma[jes]ties Armes, Rooses and Portcloses and divers
other workes', and a 'Sault of golde like a Globe', decorated with
green enamel to show the oceans.[7]

A title necessitated a coat of arms, and Drake's, as described in John Ferne's *Blason of Gentrie*, was suitably symbolic:

> This Knight for his speciall merit toward his Countrey, hath well deserved to beare in a field of the Cherubins, a fesse wavye ... His Fesse is watered in the semblance of the surging and unquiet waters of the Ocean, between two Starres, representing the extreames of that Axeltree whereupon Philosophy teaches the whole world to be turned about, ... under both of them hath this bearer compassed the globe and circumference of the Earth; ... His egregious, and prayseful Actes, not alone our present age doth well see, but also future posterities will lament their destinies, in that they lived not in his age. ... He was Knighted by our Soveraine, and I wish that everie Gentleman, to whom her Highnesse hath imparted that dignitie, had with as good a Desert, wonne his Knightly Spurres, as hath this bearer; oh then, how famous were England in the order of her Knighthood.[8]

Drake's incursion into areas of Spanish and Portuguese monopoly caused a ferment of ideas and projects for English voyages to the Southern Hemisphere. Even before the *Golden Hinde*'s return, young Richard Hakluyt's discussions with some of Wynter's crew had been the basis of a wild proposal to establish bases in São Vicente in southern Brazil and in the Strait of Magellan in order to dominate both coasts of South America.[9] Drake's successes, and especially the contact established with the Sultan of Ternate, underlay a visionary suggestion from Walsingham for a corporation to trade 'beyonde the Equynoctyall lyne': Drake, 'in consyderatyon of his great travayll and hazarde of his person in the seyd discoverye' was to be governor in perpetuity of the organisation and was to have a tenth part of all profits on goods brought into the realm from the new trade, and the Queen was to have a fifth of the proceeds of any gold and silver mines found. Both these proposals have Spanish models: Columbus was granted an eighth of the proceeds of any lands he discovered, and Philip took his fifth part of the precious metals from the American mines. Another idea taken from Spain was Walsingham's proposal for a 'howsse of contratays', based on the *Casa de contratación* in Seville.[10]

On a more immediate level, in December 1580 and January 1581 Mendoza was reporting to Philip a plan to send Drake around the Cape of Good Hope on a plundering and trading voyage to the Moluccas, where he was to be met by Henry Knollys, who was to go by the South Sea. Walsingham and Leicester were again involved, as were Hawkins, Martin Frobisher and John Wynter. This scheme was interrupted by Portuguese developments. Philip's principal rival in the argument over the throne of Portugal, Dom Antonio, had fled to France when Philip's invasion succeeded, but some of the Azores were loyal to him. The Moluccas scheme was therefore reshaped into a support project, designed largely to keep the strategically important Azores out of Philip's hands. Drake was to take eight ships, with smaller vessels and pinnaces, establish a base in Terceira, and range from it to attack Philip's returning treasure fleet. If he missed the fleet, he was to carry on to raid the West Indies.[11] In April Mendoza reported that 'it is decided that Drake himself shall not go, although, no doubt, he has arranged the matter through other hands in order that he may not be too conspicuous.'[12] There were repeated delays, and eventually in August the Queen blew cold on the idea, partly because of difficulties in obtaining French help towards the costs.

Interest in the Portuguese trading area continued. A plan to send ships to the Malabar Coast to trade for spices fell through. In September Mendoza reported that the Queen was planning a voyage of three ships under Frobisher; they were to leave at Christmas, test the East Indies for support for Antonio, and proceed to the Moluccas to trade. The Earl of Leicester was a major investor; so was Drake, who contributed his ship the *Francis*. There is, and was at the time, some ambiguity about the intended route. The instructions were that the expedition was not to use the Strait of Magellan 'except upon great occasion incident'. Whether this necessarily obliged it to go by the Cape of Good Hope is debatable; when concern was expressed during discussion among the planners that the Strait of Magellan would be too dangerous because Philip would have ships there waiting, Drake replied that this would be so much the better; the expedition could sail round the islands lying to the south of the strait, where he had established that there was open sea, in the knowledge that the Spanish were sitting, unknowing, in the strait. He also provided a chart showing the islands, and the Great Southern Ocean to the south of them.

This chart was taken on the expedition, which set off with four ships under Edward Fenton in May 1582. Young John Drake sailed as captain of the *Francis*. Frobisher had been discharged in February and accused of embezzling some of the funds. Not everyone who sailed with Fenton was impressed by Drake; Richard Madox, the chaplain, whose diary is an important source for the voyage,[13] refers to him sarcastically as 'that golden knight of ours'. He queries how Drake could have charted with such detail all the islands he found near the strait when he was there only seventeen days, eight of which were spent in rounding one cape. Madox was convinced that either Drake's chart had been stolen from the Spanish or Portuguese and its details passed off as his own discoveries, or he was 'a man who cast off all shame and dared boldly to determine things unknown and to present them to her majesty as explored and already claimed'.[14]

An interesting version of the Thomas Doughty affair emerges from a piece of gossip recorded by Madox. He was told by John Walker, the chaplain of another vessel, that he had learned from Henry Whitaker, the receiver for Plymouth, that Doughty had been cuckolding Drake with Mary, and had plotted against him on the circumnavigation to forestall his vengeance.[15]

The expedition was an ill-starred failure. There were allegations that Fenton had been bribed by the Spanish to frustrate it;[16] he turned back before reaching the strait to attempt a little plundering on the Brazilian coast. John Drake tried to go on alone in the *Francis*, but after running aground in the River Plate, he was captured by Indians, escaped into the hands of the Spanish and was taken to Lima, where he was interrogated about the circumnavigation. He was accepted into the Catholic Church as a penitent and never saw England again.

A more successful enterprise, in the capable hands of old William Hawkins, set off for the Cape Verdes, Africa and Brazil with encouragement from Dom Antonio. It ended up in the Caribbean and returned with a rich haul of treasure, hides and sugar. Drake had supplied two ships, one of them valued at £1,000, and his dividend must have been considerable.[17]

Fame, joined to money and aristocratic status, brought obligations; it laid one open to requests for patronage. Richard Hakluyt was quick to approach Drake after his knighthood with a suggestion that he should use some of his wealth to improve the standard of English navigation, which was acknowledged to be inferior, at least at the theoretical level and in respect of published manuals, to that of Spain and Portugal. Hakluyt proposed the establishment of a lectureship in navigation, 'a matter of great consequence and importance for the saving of many men's lives and goods, which nowe, through gross ignorance are dayly in great hazard, to the no smalle detriment of the whole realme'. Drake answered 'in most bountifull maner ... that he liked so well of the motion, that he would give twentie poundes by the yeere standing, and twentie poundes more before hand to a learned man, to furnish him with instruments and maps, that would take this thing upon him'.[18]

Unfortunately no suitable candidate could be found who would take the post for less than twice the proposed salary. Drake had not let his new-found wealth turn his head, however, and stuck to his offer, suggesting that another patron be sought to supplement it to the level demanded.

He was using much of his money to invest in buildings and land. Within two months of his return from the circumnavigation his agents, John Hele of Plymouth and Christopher Harris of Plymstock, were negotiating with Richard Grenville for the purchase of Buckland Abbey. The abbey was a mediaeval monastery church converted by Grenville to a solid, though rather inelegant and curious, house only in the 1570s. Grenville may have been short of money in an inflationary era, or he may simply have wished to live in the family house at Stowe.

The method of sale was rather unusual. The bargain struck with Grenville in 1580 was that Drake would lend him £3,400 against the right to inhabit Buckland, with its contents and 500 acres; if Drake wished to retain it in March 1584 it would become his without further payment; if not, he could return it and have his money back. So it was a peculiar mortgage-cum-leasing arrangement, with ultimate possession to be decided by Drake. In August 1581 he gave up the lease of a house in Plymouth, so this may be when he moved into Buckland, but in the following month he became mayor of Plymouth for a year, which would demand his frequent presence in the town. A more likely date is November 1582, when he took formal possession of the Abbey.[19]

Very quickly Drake became a major landlord in Plymouth, where in October 1582 he invested £1,500 in buying forty freehold properties, as well as some leaseholds. He also bought leasehold interests in the Plymouth Town Mills, and added country properties to his investments. One, the manor of Sherford, near Plympton, was a gift from the Queen in 1582; in the same year he bought the manor of Yarcombe in east Devon, and later that of Sampford Spiney, five miles from Buckland.[20]

His marriage came to an end in 1582 or 1583 when Mary died after thirteen childless years, many of them lonely. Drake was married again about two years later, this time to a well-born Somerset woman considerably younger than himself named Elizabeth Sydenham. A portrait of her painted in 1585 shows a confident, slim woman with a face and nose a little longer than might be thought ideal, redeemed by wide, bold brown eyes and a pretty mouth where a smile seems to be hovering. She is lavishly dressed and bejewelled, with an elaborate chain of gold filigree and precious stones around her waist, huge pearls at her ears, and richly worked ruby and emerald rings on both hands. Her head-dress and her full sleeves are dripping with pearls, and a four-stranded necklace of matched pearls reaches below her waist. If Drake needed any confirmation that he had left behind his humble origins, the portrait of this refined, elegant and confident woman, glittering with the spoils of the Pacific and the Caribbean, certainly furnished it.[21] Drake's own portrait was painted by the famous Court miniaturist Nicholas Hilliard. Sharp-eyed and short-bearded, with the points of his mustachios upturned, he looks the essence of the aggressive sailor grown rich.

His civic duties and private business involved him in frequent visits to Plymouth, sometimes on horseback, sometimes by river. While he was mayor what was referred to as 'the newe Compasse' was installed on the Hoe. A compass on a fixed spot is not much use, so it may have been a pelorus, a compass rose with a directional pointer for taking the bearings of ships in or off Plymouth harbour.[22] Another Drakean innovation was the wearing of scarlet gowns by the town council. As mayor he was also Captain of the Fort and St Nicholas Island, and his successor as mayor, Thomas Edmonds, evidently no warrior, petitioned the Crown to allow Drake to retain the captaincy. He was also chief magistrate, and received ten pounds for his expenses, of which he gave a pound to the town gaol.

In 1584 Drake was able to help Plymouth in a very material way in his capacity as Member of Parliament for Bossiney. The town needed a new water supply, and a scheme had been under intermittent discussion to bring water from Dartmoor by diverting the River Meavy into a leat, a stone-lined channel, and bringing it winding around the contours to discharge its surplus into Plymouth harbour. In this, as in his seaborne activities, it is difficult to know how far Drake was serving the public interest and how far his own. A Parliamentary committee, of which Drake was a member, looked at the bill and added to it the permission to use the flow to drive a series of mills. Drake was not finished with this matter, but national affairs shortly took his attention away from the diverting of watercourses and the grinding of corn.

The war which was not yet a war continued. Elizabeth was supporting the Dutch Protestants against Spain with money and men; Mendoza was expelled in January 1584 for plotting with Catholics against her life; Philip's concern about the growth in English sea-power and the overstretching of his own continued. English ship-owners, as usual, traded where they could. In 1585, as well as the carriage of men and supplies to the Dutch wars, there was plenty of work for them taking supplies of grain to Spain itself, where harvests had been poor. In May Philip saw a chance to make a political and economic point, and at the same time to strike at England's growing maritime strength: he ordered the seizure of a large number of English merchantmen lying in Spanish and Portuguese harbours.

The London shipowners, hitherto unsupportive of moves which might disrupt their profitable trade to Spain,[23] were thrown into an alliance of interest with the warmongers among Elizabeth's advisers, and even the more sober thinkers like Burghley agreed that, though it was not yet time to declare open war, Philip should be 'annoyed' sufficiently to deter him from any further acts of hostility, and particularly from launching an attack on England from the Low Countries.

Merchants who had suffered losses were granted letters of reprisal. These empowered them to seize Spanish vessels and goods in compensation of their own losses, in a legitimised campaign of armed privateering. Various other enterprises, encouraged but not run by the Crown, were concerted in the campaign to annoy Philip at sea. A special commission including Drake examined a proposal by Walter Raleigh to establish a colony in Virginia; permission was given, and seven ships commanded by Grenville left over a hundred men on Roanoke Island, which it was hoped to develop as a base for harassing Spanish shipping in the Caribbean. Drake's cousin Bernard, of the family of the Drakes of Ashe, swooped on the Spanish fishing fleet, disrupting the Newfoundland cod fishery, capturing 600 fishermen, and denying Spain a staple element in her subjects' diet. The most ambitious of the moves arising from Philip's increasingly threatening posture involved Francis Drake's return to the West Indies; this time not with one or two small ships and a few dozen like thinkers, but as the leader of a large fleet with a substantial army aboard.

This project, again, had its roots in a Southern Hemisphere scheme. A document dated November 1584[24] refers to the 'navy of the Moluccas', consisting of eleven ships, four barks and twenty pinnaces. Contributors to the costs of £40,000 included Drake, the Hawkins brothers, Leicester, Hatton and Raleigh, and the Queen was to pay half. A large body of soldiers was to be carried; this was evidently an invasion fleet rather than a company of trading ships. When Philip seized the English merchantmen in May 1585, the scheme for an attack on the Portuguese East Indies was given up, and the target became Spain's own ports in the Caribbean.

XII

THE GREAT WEST INDIES RAID
1585

Ye worthy wights that doo delighte
To heare of Novels straunge and rare,
What valors wonne by a famous knight
May please you marke I shall declare,
  Such rare exploytes performde and done
  As none the like hath ever wonne.

Thomas Greepe,
The True and Perfecte Newes, 1589

Compared with the little group of ships which had set out on the circumnavigation, those under Drake's command in Plymouth in September 1585 formed a substantial fleet, powerful in size, armament and crews. It was, in fact if not in law, a fleet organised for war, proceeding with a clear plan of campaign and logistically structured for a combination of land and seaborne combat. Spain's detention of the merchantmen, and the letters of marque issued as a result, provided an excuse for bothering Spanish shipping in Philip's home waters and for a possible (and massively disproportionate) plundering of his homeward-bound treasure fleets, but Drake had planned and roughly timetabled a further itinerary involving not only the devastation of specific cities in the Indies, but a project for establishing a land-based military presence there.

The campaign plan survives in a document written for an unknown party by an unknown hand.[1] The writer evidently had Drake's confidence. The estimates of spoils are interesting, and suggest that English espionage had been successful in probing the strength of Spanish defence installations. The transatlantic part of the plan is as follows:

28 NOVEMBER: arrive Dominica; take on water.

29 NOVEMBER: depart Dominica.

BY 2 DECEMBER: take capital of Margarita and another town on same island. Seize twenty pieces of brass ordnance.

THEN EITHER

BY 6 DECEMBER: sack Río de la Hacha; gather much spoil, including pearls.

OR

BY 18 DECEMBER: sack Santo Domingo on Hispaniola; spoil of 500,000 ducats (12 December); then sack Río de la Hacha.

[*Here the writer possibly conflated part of his text*][2]

30 DECEMBER: take Santa Marta (10,000 ducats).

BY 8 JANUARY: besiege and ransom Cartagena; probable capitulation after six days (a million ducats and twenty pieces of brass ordnance).

BETWEEN 8 JANUARY AND 25 FEBRUARY: proceed to Nombre de Dios; join forces with the cimarrons; sack and ransom the town. Drake to raid coast of Honduras with pinnaces, seizing some 200 small vessels, ransoming rich men (say, 100,000 ducats). A thousand men of the land forces to proceed up the Chagre with cimarrons and capture Panama (a million ducats). Possibly find time to raid the Island of Pearls.

AROUND 25 FEBRUARY: Reassemble at Nombre de Dios; sail for Cuba.

BY THE END OF MARCH: raze Havana; attack shipping; capture hides and sugar. 'If he finds the place tenable', leave a company of soldiers in Havana.

BY 10 JUNE, WITH GOD'S HELP: HOME.

For this ambitious enterprise Drake, as admiral and general, had at least thirty-three vessels when he left Plymouth. His flagship was the *Elizabeth Bonaventure*, 600 tons; his vice-admiral, Martin Frobisher, and rear-admiral, Francis Knollys, were in the *Primrose* and *Leicester* (sometimes called the *Lettice Leicester*) respectively, both of 400 tons; and Edward Wynter captained the 200-ton *Aid*. An important appointment was that of a lieutenant-general, Christopher Carleill, Drake's second-in-command in matters concerning the land forces, who sailed in the 150-ton *Tiger*. He was Walsingham's stepson, and had considerable experience on sea and land, notably in Ireland.

There were a further nine or ten ships of between 100 and 150 tons, and a flock of smaller vessels, including the little *Duck*, 20 tons, and at least eight pinnaces. Other pinnaces were taken in prefabricated form on the larger ships.[3] Two of the vessels, the *Elizabeth Bonaventure* and the *Aid*, were the Queen's; several were owned by John Hawkins, and at least three, probably more, by

Drake.[4] Thomas Drake had a command, the 100-ton *Thomas*, as did two members of the Hawkins family, William, the younger (the bark *Hawkins*), and Richard (the *Duck*). As well as Carleill, eleven captains were named specifically for land service. The ships' companies totalled 1,925 men. The initial victualling of such a fleet was a large enterprise in itself: 240 hogsheads of beef and pork; 60,000 salted cod; 600 hogsheads of pilchards; 140 tuns of wine; 600 tuns of beer; 300 hogsheads of peas; bacon, butter, cheese, oil, vinegar ... This was not an expedition; it was an invading fleet, in which the soldiers were to play the crucial role.

The voyage is well documented. The most complete account is the *Summarie and True Discourse of Sir Frances Drakes West Indian Voyage*, begun by Walter Bigges, one of Carleill's land captains, who died during the voyage. It was continued by a Lieutenant Croftes. There are also journals written by officers on three of the most important ships, the *Leicester*, *Primrose* and *Tiger*, this last being kept by Carleill until he handed the pen over to Edward Powell. These may be supplemented by other fragmentary accounts and letters, and by Spanish archival sources. The Caribbean exploits are also the best illustrated of any of Drake's engagements, thanks to the superb series of maps showing the geography of the towns attacked and the deployment of forces during the battles. These were drawn by Baptista Boazio, who was probably a member of the expedition in the entourage of Carleill.[5]

After sailing on the night of 14 September 1585 the fleet had a lively time on its way to Spain. Tacking against a contrary wind off Falmouth on the following night, the *Minion* and *Tiger* collided. The *Tiger*'s foresail was ripped to pieces, and there was a three-hour delay while she replaced it. On the 17th, with the weather now 'fayre and clere', Carleill and Frobisher dined with Drake on the flagship. Afterwards he took the two aside and told them that in any early emergency the fleet would put in at a French or Irish port, in order to give Elizabeth no opportunity for a change of mind about the voyage. He professed his great trust in the two men, as Carleill recorded in his journal,

> above all men elce, and with all requiringe in frindly sorte to be advartysed by us of any thinge which we coulde wyshe to have altered or amended; in so muche that for my owne parte I can not say that evar I had to deale with a man of greatar reson or more carefull circomspection.[6]

Drake was cementing the relationship of an exclusive triumvirate,

ꙮ The true and perfecte

Newes of the woorthy and valiaunt ex-
ployres, performed and dooue by that valiant Knight Syr
Frauncis Drake: Not onely at *Sauĉlo Domingo*, and *Carthagena*, but alſo nowe at *Cales*, and vppon
the Coaſt of *Spayne*.
1587.

ꙮ Printed at London by I. Charlewood,
for Thomas Hackett.

The title-page of Thomas Greepe's account of the Great West Indies Raid

the most notable exclusion being his rear-admiral, Francis Knollys. Knollys, the brother-in-law of the Earl of Leicester, had strong connections at Court. He certainly came to feel alienated from Drake, and the friction between them came to arouse memories of the Doughty affair. Drake and Carleill, in contrast, formed an excellent working combination, with reciprocal respect and complementary experience. There is no evidence of any differences of opinion between Drake and Frobisher on the voyage, but the vice-admiral had harsh things to say a few years later about Drake's self-interest, and may have found him irksome as a superior.

Drake briefly detained three French fishing vessels, homeward bound from Newfoundland. A mysterious encounter with a larger vessel, which hovered near the fleet for a day, led to the surmise that she was a French man-of-war, but she disappeared into the mists before her identity could be established. On 19 September the *Tiger* chased and seized a 150- or 200-ton vessel laden with a type of salted Newfoundland cod called Poor John. The master claimed she was French, from St Jean de Luz, but since all her voyages had been from Newfoundland to Pasajes, in the Spanish Basque country, and papal bulls in Spanish were found aboard, Drake concluded that she was Spanish enough to be taken as a prize, and later shared her cargo among the fleet.[7]

After the fleet had rounded Cape Finisterre on 24 September, Frobisher's pinnace seized seven small French grain ships, returning from Spain with salt. Drake incorporated one of them, *La Madelaine*, into his fleet, and renamed her with his own surname, with the intention of paying for her on his return, 'yf so it be adjudged'. According to Carleill, 'we ded this rather becawse we were informed by the other barques ... that she belonged to a very riche man that was a papiste and great enemye of those of the relygion'.[8]

After the shake-down stage of the voyage, Drake paused in the Ría de Vigo, in Galicia, to carry out minor reorganisation of crews and provisions. He could not resist making his presence felt. Anchoring at the islands off Bayona, he took 700 men towards the town in pinnaces in an aggressive manner, replying to the governor's messenger, an Englishman called Short or Sharpe, that 'we were men of warr and sought nothyng butt what we could winn by force'.[9] He showed his confidence by landing a force of men; a chapel was sacked and burned on one of the islands, and the governor tried to parley, disclaiming any influence in the question of the detained English merchantmen. From 27 to 29 September matters were suspended by a storm so great that the *Talbot*, *Hawkins* and *Speedwell* lost or dragged their anchors and had to put to sea; the *Speedwell* never rejoined, but limped back to England.

On the last day of the month the storm abated. William Hawkins reported to a conference of captains that he had seen three or four caravels sailing up the Ría to a point above Vigo. Drake sent Carleill in the *Tiger* with five smaller ships to investigate them. They were found to be carrying mundane cargoes, except that one was full of 'coapes and such other Church trashe' from Vigo cathedral. After Drake had moved more of the fleet up to Vigo there was a brief raiding foray inland, repulsed by a force of 200 Spanish. Four Englishmen were captured and decapitated.[10]

On 2 October, in the wretched weather which maintains the greenness of Galicia, a truce was agreed with the governor of Bayona, and with an exchange of hostages Drake was allowed to water his ships and bargain for supplies. Many Spaniards 'cam thicke abowte our shippes',[11] some being royally entertained by the general. The fleet stayed in the Ría de Vigo, pillaging a few small vessels, including a French ship with sugar and wine from the Azores, until the wind came more northerly on the morning of 11 October.[12]

Drake divided his ships into two roughly equal squadrons led by himself and Frobisher. The point of this may have been to range more widely in search of Philip's treasure fleet, but it is clear from the journals that the whole fleet stayed in company at least in the early part of the Atlantic stage and were together in the Caribbean.[13] There was more foul weather from the 12th onwards, and the *Primrose*, *Drake*, *Francis* and some of the pinnaces were separated from the rest on the 14th and 15th. The *Francis* rejoined after a few days, but was lost again on the 18th; the *Primrose* and *Drake* turned up on the 19th. The *Francis* was eventually found again towards the end of the month, off the Canaries.[14]

On 28 October Drake had bad news. He sent his pinnace to investigate a strange sail, which turned out to be a French man-of-war or armed merchantman, captained by a Monsieur Montaigne.[15] He told Drake that Philip's treasure fleet had passed by three weeks earlier. Even if he had not lingered in the Ría de Vigo, Drake would have missed his chance. Moreover, he received a hot reception from the island of Palma, whose shore batteries were well trained. After a ranging shot over the *Tiger* and *Elizabeth Bonaventure* the gunners put a cannonball through the flagship's gallery, where Drake was standing with Carleill and Frobisher (according to the *Leicester* journal it flew between Drake's legs), and another through the waist of the ship. Three other ships were hit, including Knollys' *Leicester*, but damage was slight. The fleet's withdrawal to sea is variously ascribed to the absence of an anchorage, the dangerous sea-surge, and the gale; not, of course, to the excellence of Spanish gunnery.

Drake had a brief look at the island of Gomera, but after consulting his captains decided instead to attack Ferro, where he landed with 600 or 700 men on 5 November. The islanders, helped by an English lad marooned there by French raiders who had attacked twice lately, convinced Drake that the place was too poor to warrant his attention, and he sailed for the Cape Verdes in the evening. While in the Canaries he had issued a set of orders governing discipline, especially in matters of pillage; unauthorised looting was to be punished by death.[16]

After a few days' productive fishing off the Barbary Coast, the fleet anchored on the east-north-east side of Santiago, in the Cape Verdes, on the afternoon of 17 November 1585. After some desultory fire from the shore batteries, Carleill landed with a force of close on 1,000 men, marched them through the night over difficult terrain to a point above the town of Santiago, and divided them into three companies. His efficiency was hardly necessary; a small advance party secured the town, all the inhabitants having fled to the hills. Carleill hoisted the great ensign with the cross of St George to inform Drake of the success, and the English settled in for twelve days of pillage and refreshment among 'gardens and orchards well replenished with divers sorts of fruicts, herbes and trees, as lymmons, orenges, sugar canes, cochars or cochos nuts, small and round onions, garlicke and some other things ...'.[17]

The plunder, however, was slight. The bells were taken from the church, and between fifty and sixty brass cannon were removed from the forts and shared around the fleet, but no real treasure was found. Nevertheless, the fleet's time on Santiago was not devoid of interest. Seven loaded caravels were captured; the village of Santo Domingo was burned; the steward of the bark *Talbot* was hanged for buggering two of the ship's boys; and there was a sudden surfacing of enmity between Drake and one of his senior officers.

It is clear from the *Leicester* journal that the anonymous but literate officer who wrote it cared little for Drake, and that some, at least, of the *Leicester*'s company distrusted the admiral and resented his favouring of Carleill and the *Tiger*. Jealousy is evident, for instance, in the diarist's comment on the distribution of the ordnance taken from Santiago

whereof Captain Carlell had a Culveringe of Brasse given him by the Generall, and Captain Powell [also of the *Tiger*] another whole Culveringe of Brasse for a memorial of the place. The rest were dystributed and put abourd divers of the shippes, the Lettice Lester reacevinge but 2 morter pieces which wold, as I thinke, not have ben receaved to any other shipp, being in respect of the rest of little worth.[18]

As we have seen, Captain Francis Knollys, despite his title of rear-admiral, appears to have been excluded from conferences to which Frobisher and Carleill were party, but there is no sign of overt hostility between him and Drake before the taking of Santiago. Indeed, he led a party from the *Leicester* as part of Carleill's force, for which he needed Drake's special permission as he was not a land officer. However, it appears that a brooding unhappiness was stirred into an outburst by Drake's decision to administer oaths of loyalty to his men.

Drake was not the greatest diplomatist. The time to impose such oaths is at the start of an enterprise, not two months later after several naval and military engagements. One can only conclude that he felt something in the wind, and that after the Doughty affair he wished to make his position cast-iron secure if action were necessary; but there was something in Drake's manner of doing things, his assertion of his own determination, which raised the hackles of men who were concerned for their own authority and dignity. This time the object of his distrust was Knollys, a courtier and sprig of the aristocracy. He and Drake were chalk and cheese.

Of the various journals, only the one produced on the *Leicester* goes into any detail about the affair. The *Tiger* account says nothing, though a newsletter written by someone on the vessel mentions the oaths,[19] and Carleill himself describes 'the setting downe some furthar direction to owr people, ... articles of ordar for their good behavioure both by sea and land'[20] as one of the matters on Drake's mind when they were at Vigo. The *Summarie* seems to approve of the oaths, as intended for the 'better government of the armie ... to acknowledge her Maiestie supreame governour, as also every man to do his utter-most endevour to advaunce the service of the action, and to yeeld due obedience unto the direction of the Generall and his officers'.[21]

The oaths were proposed on 20 November. On the previous day Carleill had allotted quarters in the town to the different companies. By those from the *Leicester* he was seen to have favoured the land officers and their men:

> The lifftenant generall ... plaied the harbinger himsealfe that day, but the distribution he made was so unequall as that sum had all, sum nothinge,

which was a discontentment to many, Captain Carlell himselfe and all the other Captains beinge placed in howses of greatest wealth.

Knollys and his company were kept on guard all day and all night on the western battery of the town. On the following morning, no doubt weary and irritable after a second night without sleep, and feeling that sentry duty was hardly a job for a rear-admiral, Knollys suffered the further irritation of having his company placed under the command of Captain Platt. This was not a reflection on Knollys; Frobisher and Wynter received the same treatment: their companies were now ashore, and were therefore put under the command of land officers. Later that day Drake convened his council of officers, and his chaplain, Philip Nicholls, showed them a draft of the oaths. The first was a general acknowledgement of the Queen's authority; the second was for Carleill alone, an assertion of loyalty and obedience to Drake; the fourth was for the rank-and-file. It was the third which caused the problem, though it reads innocuously enough:

> To all the Capteyns
> Furthermore thou shalte sweare that you will truly and dilligently to the uttermost of [thy] abylety during the whole tyme and course of this action to dyscharge the duty of Capten, as well in followinge obediently the articles and direction of the generall and his officers thereunto appoynted, as in doing right indifferently to every person under [thy] charge, so God help thee and by the Contents of the holy gospell.

Everyone agreed to sign except Knollys. He had no objection to the first oath; 'as for the rest he never sawe nor heard of before, therefore he requested further tyme to advise uppon them'. Drake agreed, with obvious irritation; Knollys made a copy of the document, and then had a heated argument with the chaplain about the point-lessness of the oaths. A Master Thorowgood and several gentlemen of Knollys' company joined in to support him, and the author of the *Leicester* journal was probably one of them; he wrote later that none of the oaths 'was necessary for us to be sworne unto'.[22] Possibly Knollys thought the content of the oaths axiomatic; possibly, because of the time chosen by Drake, applicable only to the land forces; possibly inapplicable to *Leicester* as a private vessel. More likely a simmering feeling of being excluded from Drake's confidence, a resentment of Carleill's power and the unfairness of the billeting, and anger at being relieved of his command of a company with which he had been on watch all night came together and produced a certain bloody-mindedness.

The following day was a Sunday. Nicholls, the chaplain, used his morning sermon for an overt attack on Knollys, saying that 'If there were any man so foolish or so proud or so fleshly harted as to refuse these oathes beforesaide, he thought him an Ill member in the action, and not worthy of the scocyety.' This did nothing to sweeten Knollys' attitude. After dinner, in front of Drake and all the captains, he asked Thorowgood to repeat the words exchanged with Nicholls on the previous day. At this point Drake lost control of his anger, and in the scene which followed his intemperate attacks on the men of the *Leicester* are so similar in wording to his criticisms of Doughty that captains such as Moone, Martin and Fortescue, who were with him on the circumnavigation, must have felt a strong sense of *déjà vu*. No paraphrase can improve on the drama conveyed by the *Leicester* journal:

Master Thorowgood . . . was cutt of by the generall being in his acustomed Furies, . . . saying that they did nothing but sowe sedition, and that by meanes of there factions he stood in feare of his lyffe, . . . to which speeches Master Thorowgood answered he was as true a subject to her Maiesty as any whatsoever, . . . and wolde to his power do her as good service as any man in this action. The generall tooke that to be spoken in comparison with him. Whereuppon he grewe in exceding furye, wishing that neyther my Captain nor any of them had entered into this action, to whom my Captain answered he sawe his choller so much to superbounde that he knew not what to saye, and as for the hard speeches he had gyven touching himsealfe and his gentlemen which were with him, he sawe no licklehood of remedy, especially where will stood for a lawe. Yea, saide the generall, *you are there defender and mayntayne them agaynste me*. My Captaine answered, he had reason to take there partes in any good and honest cause, in respect they lefte there Frendes and all that they had and betooke themselves to go with him in this unhappy voyage booth for them and him. . . . the generall answered him, they were a pack brought a pourpose, wishing he had never seene them, to whom my Captain answered, his meaning was to weary with discontentmentes, which he might easy do, for rather then he wolde continnewe such a hellish liff to consume him selfe with greefe in continuall dysgraces and to remaine still so offensive in his eyes without any thinge proved against him or his company, he desired his generall to have a ship or a barke for him and his company, and he wolde be suer to go farr yenought from troubling him any more this voyadge. He [i.e. Drake] tolde him presently before all the Captains that he shulde have [a ship] for him selfe and as many as wolde go with him, and rather then he shulde staye, he shulde have a shipp as good as the Ayde, for the which my Captain gave him great thankes and so departed.[23]

Drake pursued this matter over the ensuing days. On the 22nd he called all Knollys' company before the council of captains and demanded to know who wished to continue and who to return to England with Knollys. Forty or fifty of 'the properest men', despite unspecified inducements offered by Drake,[24] said they would go with Knollys wherever he went, and were immediately suspended by Drake. Drake went back on his intemperate offer of a ship as good as the *Aid*, and Knollys was given the *Francis*, of only 50 tons. He asked for the *White Lion*, which was refused, and could have had the *Bond* or the *Bonner*, both of 150 tons. He was confined meantime to the *Leicester*.

On the 23rd, obviously keen to do anything to prove his loyalty short of taking the oath, he sent his company to offer themselves to Drake for whatever service might be needed. They were kept waiting while the council of captains sent three questions to Knollys: was he content for his company to be at the General's disposal; was he resolved to depart from the enterprise; and if he did so, would he go directly to England. Knollys was still on his high horse. In his written reply (preserved in the *Leicester* journal), while protesting to have been and to remain 'as farr fourth as any others' in loyalty to Drake and the Queen, he declared that, having been accused of mutiny, he would rather be not only 'out of the socyety but under the waves as deep as there is any bottom'; he would return to England if properly victualled.

Drake was now definitely on the alert for mutiny. He summoned Knollys ashore to appear before the council, but as proceedings were about to begin there was a mistaken report of a fleet approaching, at which everyone was ordered back to his own ship. In spite of the bustle, Drake found time as the boats were departing to order Thorowgood, Chamberlayne and Willis, all Knollys' men, to be dispersed to other ships in the fleet. On the *Leicester* distrust of Drake had now extended to petty matters. The diarist writes of the captured caravels 'being emptyed by souch as the generall in his secresye had appoynted', and complains of the meagre share of the cargoes (three butts of wine and three dozen jars of oil) allotted to the *Leicester*.

XIII

A Newyeers Gifte: Santo Domingo, Cartagena and Florida 1585–86

When siedge is layd to towne or forte,
And then the same bee yeelded straight,
The valour's then of small report,
And the exploites of no great waight.
　　But where with force they bide the brunt,
　　Theyr conquestes are of great account.

Thomas Greepe,
The True and Perfecte Newes, 1589

On 29 November 1585, after making a bonfire of the small settlement of Porto Praia, Drake weighed anchor and set his course for the West Indies. The Knollys affair had not been settled to anyone's satisfaction, and the rear-admiral remained with the fleet. Drake must have been dissatisfied after the attack on the Cape Verdes. It had provided an easy but virtually profitless victory, and it had produced enmity between his officers and another display of rage from himself.

The call in the islands left a more serious legacy than ill-feeling. Between Plymouth and Santiago not a man had died, but after leaving the Cape Verdes

> we were not many dayes at sea, but there beganne amongst our people such mortalitie, as in a few daise there were dead above two or three hundred men; ... the sicknesse ... seazed our people with extreme hote burning and continuall ague ... In some that dyed were plainely shewed the small spottes which are found upon those that be infected with the plague.[1]

The fever remained with the fleet for weeks; most of those who recovered were left seriously weakened, and some were affected mentally. This was to have a very grave effect on the military and financial success of the voyage.

146

When he left the Cape Verdes Drake was several weeks behind his schedule, according to which he should by now have watered in Dominica. Fortunately the Atlantic crossing was speedy, and Dominica was reached on 18 December. After some cheerful barter with the islanders they proceeded to St Christopher, where a stay was made over Christmas to rest the crews and clean and air the ships. Drake had now abandoned the plan to attack Margarita, to the south, and headed instead for one of his main targets, Santo Domingo on Hispaniola.

Santo Domingo was a splendid place, reflecting the wealth and the free labour available to Spain's early colonial settlers. 'This Towne standeth verie pleasawntlie & is of a verie huge buildinge, All the walles of ther howses ar like the walles of our churches but higher, and such great Doores far greater then our churche Doores with such cost of Iron wourke that it is woonderfull.'[2]

The fleet was off Santa Cruz on 27 December, Puerto Rico a day later, and within striking distance of the target on New Year's Eve. The *Primrose* took two small cargo ships, from one of which Drake retained a pilot, a Greek, to help with the approach to Santo Domingo. That afternoon and evening were spent in transferring soldiers to the boats, pinnaces, and smaller ships, and at dawn on New Year's Day a landing was made at the mouth of the Hayna river, nine or ten miles west of the city. Drake had learned from the Greek pilot that Santo Domingo bristled with defences on the seaward side. Having supervised the landing from the *Francis* he returned to the fleet, leaving Carleill to conduct the land attack. The march began at about eight in the morning.

In essence the English tactics were similar to those used against Santiago, but this time there was some resistance. The Spaniards, having sunk two ships to block the harbour and moved a large galley so as to use its guns, were exchanging fire with Drake. They were taken aback when the word came of Carleill's approach overland, but even so eye-witnesses in the city thought the odds were against the English:

The eight hundred approached the city, marching leisurely to the sound of their fifes and drums, firing off their muskets and affecting in every way more security than they felt, in order to hasten the flight of our people ... The hurry and scurry of the disembarkation had kept the English from sleep; their muscles were stiffened with struggling through the sand on the road; the fearful heat when they reached the town at midday was consuming them; they felt the want of water – of which there is none to be had on those three leagues of march – more than at other times that of wine; they were in a foreign land, not knowing when their foes might be upon them. All those advantages favoured our people, who had, moreover, the sun at their backs, whilst its scorching rays struck full in the eyes of the advancing English.[3]

As Carleill approached the town between noon and one o'clock a ragged force of cavalry rode out to face him. They were soon dispersed by fire from the English arquebusiers. Carleill had divided his force into two, one to attack each gate of the town. Both gates were defended by ordnance, whose first rounds caused some casualties, but Carleill, seeing men falling to right and left of him, whipped his column into a pell-mell rush to prevent the guns from reloading. The gunners dropped their ramrods and ran back into the town through the gate with the English after them. Carleill led his men to the central square, where they were joined by Captain Powell with the party which had stormed the other gate.

The square was barricaded with material including effigies from the cathedral, and in the small hours the remnants of the Spanish garrison, who had taken refuge in the fort, abandoned it, some being taken prisoner and others skulking away into the countryside. A jewel of Spain's empire, confident in its impregnability against naval assault, had succumbed to a well-concerted but straightforward combined operation which demonstrated the ideal balance between sailor and soldier in Drake's force, the options given to him by the range of vessels at his disposal, and the inspirational leadership of Carleill. 'Thus,' the *Primrose* journal reported, 'the Spaniardes gave us the towne for a Newyeers gifte.'

The Spanish were left in a state of demoralised incredulity. Their despatches after the attack lack even the normal claims of heroic defence overcome by overwhelming odds.[4] Their well-fortified waterfront had been rendered pointless by Drake's simple stratagem of an assault by land, for which the raid on Santiago had been a useful rehearsal. The Spanish, as their letters make clear, had thought a land attack impossible:

> ... disaster has befallen us ... thirteen ships, apparently English, landed men at a place where no precautions had been taken, the Boca de Hayna. To the people here a landing there is more incredible than I can express.[5]

> ... the enemy had landed two thousand soldiers at the mouth of the

Hayna ... The city was entirely unprepared for this because the place is three leagues from the city, through thick, difficult jungle, with not a drop of water on the way.[6]

For the dean and chapter of the cathedral the calamity was a judgment on the city for the inhabitants' sins,[7] and later Fray Pedro Simón saw it as a punishment for the Spaniards' cruelty to the natives of the island, whose population of a million had been exterminated in a few decades.[8]

The better-off inhabitants of the city had fled to their country estates when Drake appeared. Negotiations for the ransom of the city were protracted, despite the pressure put on the residents by Drake's systematic burning of houses and pillaging of churches. The behaviour of the English in Santo Domingo did nothing to improve the Spanish view of them as anti-Catholic allies of the Devil:

> They began to carry out endless atrocities, especially in the churches and against the images. They smashed them to pieces, heaping shame and calumny on our faith, profaning everything ... they even opened the tombs of the dead and threw into them the offal and refuse of the cattle they slaughtered in the churches, which they turned into abattoirs. They used these edifices for even fouler purposes.[9]

The archbishop reported later that Drake defended some of the buildings he seized by putting crucifixes and holy images on the outside walls to deter the Spanish from shooting at them. Drake himself, however, impressed Philip's factor for Hispaniola, García Fernández de Torrequemada, as a man not wholly demonic when they were discussing the terms of ransom:

> Francis Drake knows no language but English and I talked with him through interpreters in Latin or French or Italian. [He was mistaken; Drake's knowledge of Spanish was adequate.] ... Drake is a man of medium height, fair, tending to stockiness; he is merry but careful. In command he is forceful, and is feared and obeyed by his men. He is firm in punishing. Alert, restless, well-spoken, ambitious, vainglorious, but generous and liberal; not a cruel man. These are the qualities I saw in him while we were negotiating.[10]

Some, though not all of this impression was supported by Drake's reaction to a gratuitous piece of cruelty by the Spaniards to one of his messengers, a negro boy who was sent with a flag of truce, only to be run through the body by an ex-officer of the captured galley.

The lad staggered back and died at Drake's feet. Drake ordered two Spanish friars to be marched to the site of the outrage and hanged, and sent a message that he would hang two prisoners every day until the murderer was punished. The captain of the galley brought the man in on the following day, 'but it was thought a more honourable revenge to make them there in our sight to performe the execution them selves, which was done accordingly'.[11]

Amid the plundering and euphoria the officers had to deal with a good deal of indiscipline among the rank-and-file; 'the Captens leading staves [i.e. officer's canes] did walke about the shulders of the poor souldeours and ... there were 30 or 40 committed to the Marshelsy [i.e. the prison cells, probably in the cathedral] for contempt and disobedyence'. An Irishman was hanged for killing his corporal. The captains' council had quarrels to settle at higher level too: Captain Powell and Captain Platt had come to blows; so had Captain Erisey and one of the ensigns; the master of the *Primrose* had a quarrel with Lieutenant Waterhouse, an officer of the vessel's contingent of soldiers.

The Knollys affair dragged on. By now both men were looking for an honourable way out of it, but Knollys had entrenched himself so deeply in his own pride that Drake could hardly give in to him without seriously undermining his own authority. On 6 January Knollys wrote a long letter to Drake, protesting his 'honest love and unfayned affeccon', mentioning his maritime experience, and complaining of the limbo in which he was now being kept,

> when accordinge to equitie and Justice I can nether be accused openly as an offender nether y[e]t excused accordynge to the innocencye of my accions, when I may nether remayne here in any estate or condicion in quyettness nor yet be sent home agayne as unworthye of this socyetie.

The letter, however, contains neither apology nor retraction:

> ... no course ... whatsoever shall make me playe the dysemblynge hipocrit nether carrye ii faces under one hoode; ... yf my self might have a good portion ... in doing somethinge agaynst my conscience, I protest I woulde not for all I can expresse, esteemynge yt vyle tromperye and trashe in respecte of the incomperable treasure of an unpoluted mynd.

He gives no indication whatsoever of a willingness to take the oaths, and goes on to press Drake for a final decision. Surprisingly, Drake let the matter splutter on indecisively. On 9 January Knollys attended the council under the charge of a marshal, and it was firmly decided that he and his supporters should sail for home on the bark *Hawkins* in three days' time. Emerging from the cathedral and finding Knollys and the others outside, Drake said, 'Gentlemen, ye maye take your pleasure where ye lest untill souch tyme as the bark *Hawkins* be ready, which shal be with all spede possible.'

On the following day he released Knollys from the custody of the marshal, and that night, after a dinner given by Captain Fenner, Captain Wynter tried to mediate. Drake, Knollys and Wynter withdrew into a separate room, and Drake almost pleaded with Knollys to take the oath, saying that he would be rear-admiral (presumably he had been demoted) and could have charge of his own company ashore if he wished. Knollys, calm and courteous, refused to budge, saying that as he had no land command his position should suffice. He did, however, say that he would not accept any land commission without taking the oath. They parted with an understanding that if he would take the oath he could have any office he chose, land or sea; if not, he would retain Drake's favour and his own reputation (at least, this is the interpretation placed on the discussion by the *Leicester* journal). Knollys was given a few days to come to a decision.

At dinner on the 14th Drake went so far as to drink Knollys' health before asking what he had decided. Knollys told him privately afterwards that his mind was unchanged on the matter of the oath. On the 26th, after a final meeting of the council to discuss the affair, Carleill emerged and told Knollys the verdict. He was to be aboard the *Hawkins* by the following night, taking Thorowgood, Chamberlayne and Willis with him. Drake had been driven into another brief rage by seeing Thorowgood, who he thought was eavesdropping, in the next room.

Knollys boarded the *Hawkins*, was given provisions, and ... remained with the fleet. Later in the voyage we find him, still named as rear-admiral, being given minor responsibilities, including a small command ashore.[12] So, after going to the brink, one of them conceded. Drake, after his initial outburst of rage, had already conceded a good deal, not least in the affability towards the stubborn Knollys which emerges even from the hostile entries in the *Leicester* journal. Either Knollys signed, or Drake reassessed his man, concluded that Knollys was more interested in his own dignity than in mutiny, and quietly let the matter drop. Reluctance to alienate the Earl of Leicester may have had something to do with his decision.

The half-million ducats expected from the Santo Domingo raid proved to be a huge overestimate. Drake's opening ransom demand was a million, to which the city responded with an offer of 10,000 or 12,000. Drake came down to 100,000, and the city offered just over 20,000. The dean of the cathedral reported Drake as saying that he would rather ransom the town for a lady's ring than accept this. When even the sight of the city being systematically destroyed produced an offer of only 25,000 ducats, Drake made the best of a bad job, salving his pride by a refusal to return a silk banner with a coat of arms which he had taken from the governor's house. The *Summarie* has some fun out of the deflation of the Spanish imperial pride embodied in the Latin motto on the escutcheon, *Non sufficit orbis* (The world is not large enough).

Santo Domingo, then, was a smashing military success, but the financial gains were very modest. Drake towed the great Spanish galley out to sea and burned her; set fire to at least twenty other vessels; confiscated over seventy cannon, mostly large pieces; and incorporated five Spanish vessels into his fleet. These included a ship of 200 tons, renamed the *Hope*, and one of 400, renamed the *New Yeeres Gifte*. He abandoned the *Benjamin*, the *Scout* and the old *Hope*. The freed galley slaves, Turks, Frenchmen and negroes, went with him, as did some slaves escaped from Spanish estates.

Drake was now over a month behind schedule, and the worrying losses by disease had continued. The fleet weighed anchor on the morning of 31 January 1586, 'beinge in number 24, smale and great', and set sail S by E for the Spanish Main. With stiff winds on the port beam they made good progress, though they were slowed down slightly by the Spanish prizes, which were inadequately ballasted. The intended raid on Río de la Hacha was abandoned; Drake's next target now was Cartagena, which he reached on 19 February, Ash Wednesday.

His task now was much more formidable than on his earlier visit when he had made an inconspicuous entry to snatch one ship. The city was protected against a major raid by natural geography and by fortification to such a degree that, in the words of the *Primrose* log, 'it was Impossible by mans reason for us to winne; ... In deede hyt was not likelie that anie man of us shulde escape'.[13] Access from the east by land was difficult because of swamps and creeks. Immediately west of the city extended a long peninsula which enclosed two lagoons, the nearer, the Caleta, almost completely landlocked, but linked to the further, outer lagoon by a channel called the Boquerón, overlooked by a fort. The outer lagoon was larger and linked by another, undefended channel with the sea. The only road access into the city crossed a bridge over a watercourse on the south side. In the inner lagoon lay two large, well-armed galleys, the *Capitana* and the *Ocasión*, and a big galleasse,* the *Napolitana*.[14]

The governor, Pedro Fernández de Busto, was forewarned of Drake's intentions, and had heard by despatch boat about the raid on Santo Domingo. Wild reports had arrived to the effect that the entire black population of Hispaniola had risen and joined the English, and all along the mainland coast frantic preparations were being made. The confusion was increased by reports of an Indian uprising in Santa Marta. In Cartagena Fernández de Busto had trenches dug and cannon mounted, and raised a defence force of about 450 men, plus 500 Indians. Don Pedro Vique, the commander of the galleys, wanted to engage Drake in the open sea, but the inhabitants complained that it was his duty to guard the city, and the galleys were stationed in the Caleta, which was closed with a chain on floats across the Boquerón. The Indians stuck hundreds of poisoned spikes upright in the sand between the city and the mouth of the outer lagoon. All the women except those needed to cook for the soldiers, and all the children and the infirm were sent out of the city with everything of value. Even the clergy, including the dean of the cathedral, were armed with rapiers and halberds.[15]

The governor's own report makes Drake's options clear. One possibility was a repeat of the pattern successful at Santiago and Santo Domingo, sending land forces to assault the main entrance to the town on the landward side. To forestall this the governor sent small units of troops to the anchorage beyond the fort and to the town bridge, and extra men to the fort itself. The second, unlikely, option was a landing and attack from the east, to forestall which more troops were disposed. The third, and in the governor's view the most likely, was an approach by landing men at Hicacos Point, where the outer lagoon joined the sea, and marching eastward along the shore.

None of these options looks inviting, but on the face of it, given that the town was forewarned, the first appears the least forbidding, and the third a tall order. Close to the town the peninsula was only about 150 yards wide, and at this point a stone-faced earthwork had been built, with a ditch, and cannon had been mounted. The two galleys were rowed close to this defence-work, and anchored so that their guns could sweep across the peninsula towards the sea. Anyone

---

* A galleasse was a kind of hybrid between a galley and a galleon, combining a large sail plan with a long row of oars on either side.

coming along the shore towards the city would have to face frontal fire from the ordnance behind the earthwork and crossing fire from the galleys on their right.

After a brief alarm caused by the sighting of a Spanish caravel at dawn, Drake's fleet was seen. At noon the ships were close to the coast, and a boat cruised along the shore to reconnoitre; Drake was probably in it. A couple of shots from the city's batteries missed him. The Spanish noticed that the ships were flying black pennants and streamers. This is not explained by the English sources; it may have been to do with Ash Wednesday, but perhaps the fleet was in mourning because of the continuing deaths from fever. Drake was fortunate to capture two black fishermen, who warned him of the poisoned spikes along the shore.

During the night word came to the city that Drake was landing men at Hicacos Point, and the governor sent about half his men to lie in ambush and attack the English column from the rear. Drake had, indeed, landed his force (about 1,000 men, according to Spanish sources) under Carleill, and they began their short march around midnight.

Frobisher had been sent to attack the Boquerón fort with pinnaces, possibly just as a diversionary move. He met a fierce reception: his own pinnace's rudder was shot away, 'and mens hattes from there headdes and the top of our meane maste beaten in peeces, and the oares stricken owte of our mens handes as they rowed and our Captaine like to have bin slaine'.[16]

On the peninsula Carleill's organisation, and success, were as usual. The first hazard the English met was the poisoned spikes. Few men were injured, and to avoid the spikes Carleill ordered the column to march below the tideline from then onwards. This was probably the cause of their success, because doing this not only protected them from the crossfire of the galleys on the right, but also brought them to the weakest part of the defence-work. This was not properly finished at the seaward end, where it consisted only of a line of wine-barrels filled with sand. Despite three volleys from the battery, spirited work by the English pikemen demoralised the defenders. Broken by the inspired leadership of Carleill, who leaped through a breach with a cry of 'God and St George!' and killed the enemy standard-bearer, the Spanish broke and ran towards the town. One Spanish report says that the retreat was caused only by trickery, when an Englishman shouted in good Spanish, 'Retire, gentlemen, for we are lost!'[17]

One Spaniard who emerges with some credit is the governor, Pedro

Fernández de Busto, not so much from his own report, which is modest, depressed, and free from heroics,[18] but from that of an anonymous writer who was in the thick of the defence at the Caleta. Fernández is described as a hero in defeat, organising briskly, beating his fleeing men back into battle with his sword, and remaining to face the enemy with the few he had left. This description of his competence, however, was very much a minority view, and he was severely criticised later for the disintegration of the defence.[19]

Once the battery at the Caleta had been stormed, the Spanish dissolved into chaos; in the half-light of dawn friend and foe were indistinguishable, and the English were soon in possession of the main square and, after some desultory skirmishing in which they suffered casualties from Indian arrows, the city. The fort held out against Frobisher all day, but was evacuated at nightfall. The galleys, trying to escape through the Boquerón, miscalculated the tide and ran aground. One was destroyed by an exploding powder keg, and Vique ordered the other to be burned. Vique was later prosecuted for fraud, and in his support he adduced his heroic role in the defence of Cartagena.[20]

The number of English dead reported in Spanish sources varies between 78 and 200, and they put their own dead as between seven and twelve.[21] The English numbered their own dead as under thirty.[22] They quickly entrenched themselves in the central area of the city, moved the fleet to a closer position in the outer lagoon, burned a few Spanish vessels, and sought what pillage they could. Drake was angered by the discovery of the royal despatches warning of his approach, in which he was referred to as a pirate. He then proceeded to open ransom negotiations, insisting that these be conducted directly with the governor and the bishop.

After the usual haggling and persuasive arson, Drake accepted 110,000 ducats as the city's best offer,[23] though he managed to augment this by another 1,000 for the return of the Franciscan priory, and a further 5,000, paid in jewels, gold and pearls, as the personal ransom of a prominent citizen, Alonso Bravo. Bravo's wife, having sent her jewels to Drake, died soon afterwards. Drake not only allowed her body to be brought to the priory for burial, but attended her funeral and marked it with muffled drums and cannon-fire. He obtained a further, unspecified amount as ransom for the estate of a Doña Luisa Alvarez.[24]

Spanish sources say that Drake was still speaking of raiding Nombre de Dios and Panama,[25] but there was now increasing pessimism, accentuated by the continuing deaths from fever, about proceeding to the isthmus. There had been little in the pillaging of Cartagena to cheer the men, the main spoils being sixty-two cannon,[26] and in a pointless little incident Captain Moone and Captain Varney had been killed by small-arms fire from the shore while seizing two insignificant vessels. Captain Fortescue, of the *Bonner*, died from a recurrence of fever, 'and was throwne over board without any other solemnety'.[27]

Drake consulted his captains about how to proceed, and the general weariness and flagging morale are apparent in a document setting out the feelings of Carleill and the land officers.[28] Dated 27 February, this states that they could hold the town, albeit with difficulty, having only 700 fit men, 'very many of the better mindes and men being either consumed by death, or weakened by sicknes and hurts', but they conclude that 'it is better to hold sure as we may the honour already gotten, and with the same to returne towards our gracious Soveraigne and Countrey'.

Here, too, Carleill and the land officers emerge with immense credit, offering 'to freely give and bestowe' their own share of the proceeds of the raid on Cartagena, for which they could justifiably claim the main credit, 'upon the poore men who had remayned with us in this Voyage, meaning as well the Sayler as the Souldier, wishing with all our hearts it were such ... as might seeme a sufficient rewarde for their painefull indevour'. One can see their awareness that the voyage, despite its victories, has been in some respects a failure, that 'the bountifull masse of treasure ... which was generally expected at our comming out forth of England' has eluded them.

The lack of enthusiasm for continuing to Nombre de Dios merely confirmed what Drake knew already. 'And thus,' says the *Summarie*, 'at Cartagena we toke our first resolution to returne homewards.' On Thursday, 31 March, having careened his ships and taken aboard some of the slaves who had escaped from the galleys and a few hundred runaway negroes and Indians, Drake sailed for Cuba. Thomas Greepe's ballad *The True and Perfecte Newes* depicts a triumphant departure with pealing trumpets, drum salutes, and cannon firing exultantly for a whole hour, but this has no support in eye-witness accounts. The departure was soon followed by bathos when the *New Yeeres Gifte*, which had caused problems ever since her capture in Santo Domingo and was now carrying many of the captured cannon to make up for her lack of ballast, sprang a leak in foul weather, and the fleet had to put back. This must have caused mutterings, for most of the captains had expressed misgivings about using her for this purpose before they left Cartagena.[29] There was consternation in the town when Drake reappeared, but he sent a messenger called Jonas, a Spanish-speaker, to reassure people. Over the next fortnight the *New Yeeres Gifte* was unloaded and finally set on fire. Drake commandeered all the bakers' ovens in the city to bake biscuit, and sailed again on 24 April 1586.

Havana was in a great state of fear. The English accounts say little about Drake's unproductive visit to Cuba, but Spanish reports of the defensive preparations make interesting reading. The Spanish demonisation of Drake is clear, for example, in a letter to the Crown from Alvar Suárez de Toledo.[30] Drake is referred to repeatedly not by his name but simply as *el corsario*, the pirate, and is said to have 'a familiar spirit with whom he talks'. Men were on watch all around the coast, and in Havana a force of 900 troops was drilled, trenches dug, forts erected, and cannon removed from ships and disposed ashore.

Drake arrived off Cape San Antonio, at the western end of Cuba, on 27 April, and three days later his pinnaces approached Havana and drew a few shots from the shore batteries, but no attempt was made on the city. Suárez's letter, obviously written in relief after Drake had sailed away, has the comical bombast of a Gilbert and Sullivan general: 'It was believed they would land, ... and certainly it was hoped that they would, for had they done so not a man would have returned aboard; they would have paid for what they have done, and for their evil, heretical lives!'

In the fleet, the fever had not abated; an escaped prisoner told Suárez that 'every day they were throwing corpses overboard'. Drake was having problems with contrary winds, and especially with short-age of water. He finally resorted to digging pits at Cape San Antonio to gather rainwater. After three frustrating weeks off northern Cuba the fleet made for Florida. The Spanish garrison of Santa Elena, though small, was a threat to the embryonic English settlement in Virginia, and was an obvious target for Drake. As he was looking for it on the Florida coast, helped by a Portuguese pilot, he came across a new Spanish fort near the town of San Agustín.

This time Drake went ashore himself with Carleill and the soldiers. Carleill himself put a cannon-shot right through the Spanish ensign, and that night led a small scouting-party across the river. After they returned, they were surprised to hear music approaching eerily across the water. Out of the darkness came a lone fifer, playing a well-known

Drake's fame abroad: a German engraving of 'Francis Drake, a noble Knight of England, aged 46'.

Protestant tune called 'The Prince of Orange'. He was a French prisoner, escaped from the fort, who revealed that the Spanish had now abandoned it. They had left behind their fourteen good brass cannon and a pay-chest of about 6,000 ducats.[31] Drake proceeded to demolish the town of San Agustín, burn the fort to the ground, and raze the trees and maize-fields around.[32] Captain Powell, who had done so well at Santo Domingo, was killed in the pursuit of the Spanish, and Lieutenant Waterhouse, of the *Primrose*, was killed by Indians.[33]

Although a call at the English settlement established by Raleigh at Roanoke, in Virginia, is not mentioned in any surviving plan of the voyage, it is likely that Drake and Raleigh had discussed the possibility, and Drake's actions in taking aboard escaped negroes and Indians from Santo Domingo and Cartagena suggest that they were intended to reinforce the little colony. Before leaving San Agustín Drake assembled his captains, and it was decided to attack Santa Elena and then go on to Roanoke. The Santa Elena raid was abandoned when soundings taken three leagues off shore found only four and a half fathoms. Lacking a pilot with local knowledge, Drake passed on up the coast, along which the smoke of many fires revealed the presence of Indians, some of whom had been posted as lookouts by the governor of San Agustín.

The fleet paused at Oristan to take on water and firewood and repair a mast,[34] and then on 9 June an exceptionally large fire caused Drake to send a boat ashore. It was met by a group of the Roanoke colonists, one of whom piloted the fleet to an unsatisfactory anchorage, the harbour at Roanoke being too shallow. When the leader of the colonists, Ralph Lane, came aboard on the following day, Drake offered either to take all the colonists back to England immediately, or to leave them the *Francis* and a pinnace with their crews, a few boats, and a month's supplies so that they could sail home later in the year.[35] Lane chose the second option, but he had barely put some of his men into the *Francis* when a serious storm blew up. It lasted three days and threatened to drive the whole fleet ashore. Many ships had their cables broken, and some, including the *Francis*, lost all their anchors, had to look for sea-room, and ended by sailing to England alone. After further consultation with his captains Drake renewed his offer to Lane, and this time the wearied colonists accepted the passage home. The fleet sailed on 18 June, was off the Scillies on 22 July, and anchored in Portsmouth on 27 or 28 July 1586.[36]

In material terms the voyage had failed. Santo Domingo and Cartagena had been partially destroyed and their garrisons stripped of ordnance, but cannon could be replaced and houses and churches rebuilt. The financial rewards were disappointing: the Queen and the other adventurers received fifteen shillings on the pound, and there were deeply resented delays in paying the soldiers and sailors. These were due partly to Drake's poor account-keeping after his financial clerk Cottell died on the voyage. Half the proceeds were in silver bars, plate or coin; other major items were gold, pearls, and brass ordnance.[37]

The human loss was frightful: 750 men dead, including some of Drake's best captains. Psychologically, however, the result was a stunning blow to Spanish pride, and an increased resolution on Philip's part to contain England before greater disasters followed. In England, the uninformed popular view was joyful and exultant.

XIV

CADIZ AND CAPE ST VINCENT
1586–87

> 'God mak us all thankffull agayne and agayne
> that we have althowgh it be letell mad[e] a
> begenyng upon the co[a]st of Spayne. Yf we
> can throwghly beleve that this which we doe
> is in the defenc[e] of our relygyon, and contrye,
> no doubt but our mercyfull god, for his christ,
> our savyours sake, is abell and will geve us
> victory.'
>
> Drake, after the raid on Cadiz, 1587

Philip's plans for the invasion of England had evolved through a succession of independent schemes, and had been interrupted and re-energised by some notable international events. The need ultimately to subdue England by force had been in the air for a quarter of a century, but despite the depredations of English privateers and Elizabeth's overt help of the Dutch in their struggle against Spanish rule, the king had held back from the decision throughout the 1570s and on into the 1580s. His efforts to pacify the Netherlands were a major drain on his resources of men and money. To put an invasion force on English soil and maintain it there afterwards implied a huge additional expense and, initially, a weakening of his forces in the Low Countries.

As early as the summer of 1583 the Marquis of Santa Cruz, Spain's most distinguished naval figure of the day, was drafting plans for a fleet to sail from Spain and land troops in the Thames estuary. London would be seized and held with the help of troops from the Duke of Parma's army in the Netherlands. Elizabeth would be dethroned; Mary Stuart would be crowned; the supply of English help to the Dutch rebels would be cut, and two bastions of heresy demolished by a single blow. Philip consulted Parma, but the project went no further until the early summer of 1585, when Pope Sixtus V, newly elected, began putting pressure on Philip to undertake some striking enterprise in support of the Church, and suggested that either taking Algiers from the infidel or invading England would be deemed a suitable project for papal support. The presence of the Pope's envoy in Spain coincided with the Roanoke project, the attack on the Newfoundland fishery, and Drake's destructive call in the Ría de Vigo which formed the overture to his great Caribbean raid. This succession of English outrages convinced Philip that the time had come.

Santa Cruz took out his 1583 plan, dusted it, and put large amounts of very expensive flesh on its bones. He proposed gathering a fleet of almost 80,000 tons to transport an invasion army of 55,000 men, with siege trains, pack animals and support services. The men would be landed by specially built assault craft, supported by galleys working close inshore to subdue the defences. The cost would be about four million ducats. It was to be essentially a naval operation departing from Spain. By April 1586 Santa Cruz was authorised to begin preparing a fleet, and the Duke of Medina Sidonia was raising troops and gathering support vessels in Andalusia.

The Duke of Parma had different ideas: he suggested shipping 30,000 troops in barges from Flanders for a surprise attack on the Kent coast and a march on London. Naval help from Spain would be useful to create a diversion, and to keep supply routes open afterwards, but this was a secondary consideration for the Duke, whose view was essentially that of the campaigning land-soldier planning for a wider river crossing than usual.

The upshot was that the two plans were amalgamated. The joint scheme was a massively impressive tapestry of action: Santa Cruz's huge fleet, swollen by the galleons of Portugal, large and well-armed merchant ships from the Mediterranean and Biscay, and galleys and galleasses for coastal use; Parma's efficiently martialled fighting men, hardened in the Dutch wars, waiting in readiness in their transports; a rendezvous of the two; a Channel crossing made safe by Santa Cruz's domination of the narrow seas; a landing on the Kent coast, and a march on London. At many levels there was meticulous attention to detail, not least in Santa Cruz's costings. Only in the seam between the scheme's two main portions was the tapestry flawed, and it was there that the stitching was to give way.

In view of the extent of the preparations necessary, it was decided to postpone the invasion until the autumn of 1587. If Philip's resolution had been in danger of fading, Drake's career of pillage through the Indies in early 1586 certainly stiffened it, and Elizabeth's execution of Mary Stuart in February 1587 was a burning of boats for both Spain and England.

Once committed, Elizabeth was bent on carrying the fight to the enemy. Her initial instructions to Drake for the 1587 raid against Spain must have delighted his heart: Philip's invasion preparations were to be disrupted by whatever actions Drake saw fit. He was to have a handy and powerful fleet made up of four large royal galleons, another owned by the Lord Admiral, whatever strongly armed London merchantmen he could organise, ships of his own, and sundry pinnaces and fly-boats.[1] His commission empowered him to commandeer any other English ships he might come across at sea and employ them as he saw fit. With his recent record of success in the Indies as evidence, Drake had managed to persuade the Queen to authorise raids on Spanish and Portuguese harbours and aggressive acts on land; his implacable hostility to Philip could now vent itself by repeating the crushing combined operations successes of Santo Domingo and Cartagena on Philip's home soil.

The commission is dated 15 March 1587, but Drake had begun recruiting men some time earlier, and only three days afterwards he had organised and signed agreements with London shipowners for the participation of seven large merchantmen. By the 25th the Queen's ships and four of the merchantmen had reached Plymouth, where four of Drake's own ships were waiting for them. The other London ships put into Dartmouth. Drake himself had joined the royal galleons as they passed Dover. A week later, after hurried victualling and preparation and the arrival in Plymouth of the ships from Dartmouth, Drake sailed.

His urgency to be away on 2 April stemmed partly from enthusiasm and partly from doubts about Elizabeth's resolution; another factor was the desertion of some of the crews. In a letter to Walsingham,[2] written from the *Elizabeth Bonaventure* when she was already under way, Drake attributed the loss of men to treacherous persuasion and rumour 'by some practys of some adversaryes of the actyon'. He had filled the spaces with more soldiers, and written to the local justices and the Lord Admiral demanding exemplary punishment for the absconders.

The letter to Walsingham reveals a vague expectation of hostility from certain unnamed parties, 'yll-affected, as there hath not wanted in other actyons, and it is lykely that this [action] will not go free'. However, Drake professes satisfaction with his ships' companies, including his vice-admiral, William Borough, and with the attitude of the merchantmen; '... there was never more likely in any fleete of a more loving agreement than we hope the one of the other. I thank God I finde no man but as all members of one body to stand for our gracious Queen and country against Antichrist and his members.'

His gracious Queen had, in fact, already relented somewhat against the Antichrist's Spanish ally; or, at least, she was by now organising a process of pretending that she had. On 9 April her Privy Council signed an order partially countermanding Drake's commission. Elizabeth must have been aware by that time that Drake had sailed, but the new order was sent by courier to Plymouth and a pinnace set off after him. The new order still encouraged Drake to 'doe your best indevour ... to gett into your possession, avoyding as myche as may lye in you the effusyon of Christian blood, such shipping of the said Kings or his subjectes as you shall finde at seas; ether going from thence to the East or West Indies or returning from the said Indyes into Spayn'. Elizabeth referred, however, to a perceived easing of Philip's hostile preparations and her own wish not to be seen war-mongering, and forbade Drake 'to enter forcibly into anie of the said King's portes or havens, or to offer violence to anie of his townes or shipping within harborough, or to doe any act of hostillity uppon the land'. In short, seize treasure ships by all means, but no repeat of Santo Domingo.

Did the Queen mean Drake to receive this order, or was this simply a continuation of her ambiguous policy of letting Drake have his head while covering herself against accusations of encouraging him? Certainly when Spain later complained about Drake's activities on this voyage the countermanding order and the sending of the pinnace were used by Burghley as evidence of the Queen's good faith. By human design or by the will of God, the pinnace never caught up with Drake; with nine days' start to make up, this is not surprising. Her captain, on his return, pleaded stress of weather, and his crew supported him on oath. He had, however, found sufficient fair weather to capture a prize laden with sugar and Brazil wood worth £5,000, which went into the pot for the final share-out.

Drake had augmented his fleet on his first day out after pursuing a couple of strange sails. They turned out to be from Lyme; Robert Leng, who sailed on the voyage and wrote an account of it,[3] describes them as men-of-war, so they were probably privateers. They agreed willingly to Drake's 'courteous comaundement' to join the fleet; a chance to share in the ultimate spoils of a major voyage with Drake would be a great attraction to such West Country entrepreneurs.

Having sighted the coast of France on 5 April, and sailing towards Cape Finisterre, the fleet was dispersed by five days of violent weather, and the *Dreadnought* suffered a serious leak. On 16 April they reassembled off the Tagus, all except a little pinnace, which was lost. The *Golden Lion*, in which William Borough was sailing, captured an enemy fly-boat that day, and with it the information that Cadiz harbour was full of shipping. As soon as Borough passed this on to Drake the decision was made to seize this chance, and only three days later the fleet was approaching Cadiz Bay.

The harbour at Cadiz was formed by a long peninsula, with the town at its tip, and was divided into the upper and lower bays by a point at El Puntal, half-way along the peninsula. Facing El Puntal across the channel was the fort of Matagorda. Drake's fleet arrived in the bay completely unheralded. An account by Agustín de Horozco, a customs officer in the town,[4] gives a picture of a port even less alert to danger than the distant cities of the Indies had been ten years earlier. The harbour was full, the wharves were bustling with their normal business, and the streets were lively with seafarers of different races and tongues: Spanish, Portuguese, Italians, Flemings, Frenchmen and negroes.

Drake's ships were rather strung out as he approached the bay in the late afternoon, and Borough, middle-aged and cautious, suggested a conference of captains to discuss the best approach; the delay would be slight, and they could still enter the outer bay by eight o'clock with everyone knowing what they were about. Drake would have none of it; he saw his target, was confident of surprise, and had the right wind. He took the *Elizabeth* straight on into the outer bay, with Borough's *Golden Lion* and the rest following behind as best they could.

They found the harbour teeming with ships: about sixty were riding at anchor in the roadstead, and many smaller vessels lay close in to the town's fortifications or in the River San Pedro, which flowed into the harbour. The larger ships included a great Genoese argosy, a huge carrack belonging to the Marqués de Santa Cruz, a score of confiscated Dutch vessels, and five great Biscayans, one loaded for the Indies and the rest with provisions for Philip's fleet in Lisbon. Drake came among them like a hawk among dozing chickens.

The town's defence fluctuated between spirited shows of defiance and what may kindly be called discretion. The Spaniards' main floating resource was a squadron of nine galleys and an eighteen-bench galliot under Pedro de Acuña.[5] They had put into Cadiz while

165

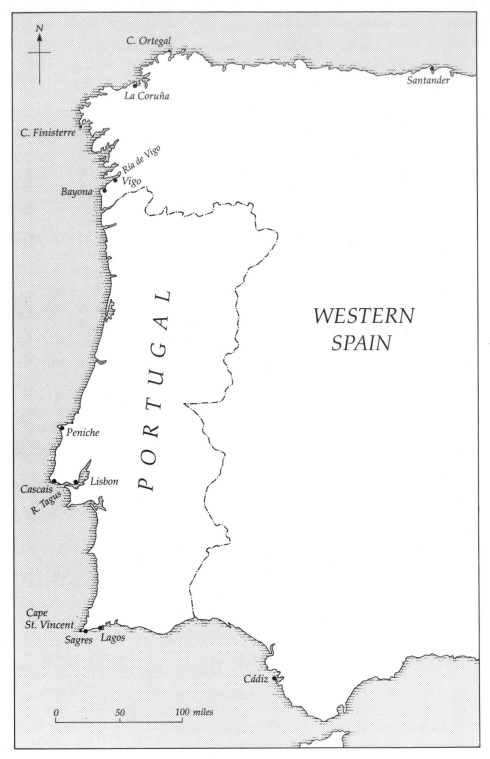

N

C. Ortegal

Santander

La Coruña

C. Finisterre

Ría de Vigo

Vigo

Bayona

WESTERN
SPAIN

P O R T U G A L

Peniche

Cascais

Lisbon

R. Tagus

Cape
St. Vincent

Sagres   Lagos

Cádiz

0   50   100 miles

Portugal and Western Spain

on their way towards Cape St Vincent, and had been kept there by unfavourable winds. Two of them (crucially, as things turned out) were in the San Pedro river; the rest were lying close to the castle.

Acuña sent the galliot and one of the galleys out to reconnoitre. When they were within musket-shot of the *Elizabeth* Drake hoisted his ensigns and his gunners opened fire. Acuña's vessels quickly turned tail and scuttled back to safety, the rhythm of the oarsmen in the galliot being disrupted by a cannonball which shattered part of her walkway and killed four or five of them. Drake met more serious resistance from an unexpected quarter. The big Genoese ship, fully laden and crewed, had been waiting to sail with her cargo of cochineal and sugar. She carried thirty or forty guns, but one might have expected her captain to do his best to appear conspicuous only in his neutrality. Inexplicably, she laid into Drake's ships with a will, refusing to surrender, and was sunk with all guns blazing, 'sore against all our wills', according to Robert Leng. This was not compassion; he was thinking of the loss of the valuable ordnance.

The harbour was now open to Drake's pleasure; he came in, in Horozco's words, 'with more speed and arrogance than any pirate has ever shown'. Acuña sent some of the galleys against him,[6] but they were hopelessly outranged by Drake's guns, and their only success was the recapture, with five men of its prize crew, of a small caravel seized by Drake the day before (even Horozco calls it a mere *navichuelo*, a little wee boat). Before nightfall Drake's whole fleet was comfortably anchored in the channel leading into the inner bay. Some of the smaller shipping in the harbour had taken refuge in the San Pedro river; other craft had made for the uncertain protection of the returned galleys.

The town was initially leaderless and panic-stricken. Twenty-two women and children were crushed to death in a stampede to take refuge in the castle, whose main doors had been closed against Drake's expected assault. The night was cold and very dark, and the presence of many different nationalities gave rise to fears of internal betrayal. Somehow a scratch force of men was assembled in the square, and companies were sent to the battery of San Felipe and to the bridge over the river which was the only access to the town for reinforcements coming from the landward side. Fifes and drums were organised as alarm procedures, barrels of pitch provided a smoky and flickering illumination, and watchmen were posted along the shore and in the countryside.

Drake, by now, 'havinge, by Godes good favor and sufference, good opportunitye to ponishe the enemye of Godes true Gospell and our dayly adversarye',[7] was hard at work in fire and pillage in the harbour, seizing stores of biscuit and provision and putting the unwanted vessels to the torch in an unprecedented storm of destruction. Later estimates of the quantity of shipping destroyed varied from 7,000 to 10,000 tons. He made no serious attempt to molest the town, though Horozco mentions that two boats were sent to capture the bridge, and were repulsed (and the city thereby saved) by the two galleys which were lying in the river.

In the town there were repeated alarms; soon after midnight the drums beat and news spread that Drake had landed near the San Felipe battery, but it was only a galley which had run aground. As the night went on reinforcements began to arrive, with impressive speed: two small ships brought soldiers from Puerto de Santa María across the bay; a troop of fifteen horsemen came from Chiclana, with more horse and foot behind them, who strengthened the bridge defences; more turned up from Jerez and Medina Sidonia around sunrise, and around midday the Duke of Medina Sidonia arrived in person to take control of things.

From early morning the town batteries began firing, but Drake was out of range. Two demi-culverins were dragged to a point overlooking the inner part of the bay, closer to the anchored fleet, and began firing, concentrating on the nearest ship, Borough's *Golden Lion*. When the firing started Borough was not aboard; he had gone in search of Drake to find out what was going on. He had a tiresome search, going first to the *Elizabeth*, where he was told that Drake was in the inner bay with the *Merchant Royal* and the pinnaces. By the time Borough reached the *Merchant Royal* Drake was on his way back to the flagship, where the vice-admiral eventually caught up with him. After a brief conversation about the redistribution of supplies Borough returned to his own ship to find that she was under fire from the improvised shore battery, and that a ball had removed one of the legs from his master gunner. The master was taking steps to warp the ship out of range and down towards Puerto de Santa María, and Borough told him to carry on.*

Acuña, seeing the *Golden Lion* separating herself from the main fleet, singled her out for an attack from the galleys, and Drake, tetchily no doubt, had to detach the *Rainbow*, some of the merchantmen and

---

* Warping involves taking an anchor out in a boat, dropping it at some distance from the ship, and moving the ship towards it by turning the capstan to wind in the cable.

his own pinnace to help her. Reinforced, and with a helpful wind to fill his sails, Borough chased the galleys off and anchored with his little flotilla in a new position in the outer bay, well away from hostilities.

Drake decided to take advantage of the same wind to get the rest of his ships out into the bay, and with salvos of cannon, hoisting of banners and a great noise of trumpets he weighed anchor. He made little progress seawards before the wind dropped completely, and re-anchored, to the dismay of the townspeople, who spent a second evening and night on the alert. They turned some of their remaining vessels into fireships and towed them out with the galleys, but to such small effect that Drake was able to joke that the Spanish were doing his work for him.

Early on Friday morning the breeze gave him his chance, and he sailed. His way was lit up by the burning ships, according to Horozco. The customs man grudgingly admired the seamanship which enabled Drake to get the whole fleet away without one of them grounding in the shoals, but marvelled too at his luck in having a fair wind to take him into harbour and an even fairer one to take him out again. Borough, too, probably pondered with mixed feelings on the lucky wind which made his own earlier, and very proper, reservations seem so stuffy and misplaced.

The galleys followed the fleet out to sea, snapping at their heels and doing no damage whatsoever. After three or four leagues Drake anchored off the Caleta de San Sebastián and sent a boat to Acuña under flag of truce to suggest an exchange of prisoners. Acuña replied with a gift of sweetmeats and a promise to convey the message to Medina Sidonia, but Drake soon decided that the Spanish were wasting time, 'for to accomplyshe some other ... devellish practyse'; he took advantage of the east wind and sailed away.

Calm was coming back to Cadiz; women went back to their houses, messengers were sent to halt the relief columns coming from Seville and elsewhere, and the Duke, confident that in the now strong easterly wind Drake would not return, went home. There was speculation about an alliance between England, the King of Fez, and the Turks, which some saw as the only explanation of Drake's boldness. Backslapping and self-congratulation replaced terror, and a euphoric procession was organised from the cathedral to the monastery of San Francisco to thank God, 'whose strong arm helped this weak and unprotected city and humbled the pride of the enemy'.[8]

*

This image of the Cadiz incident as a victory for Spain took root and was soon being embroidered. Even Fray Pedro Simón, who admired Drake and saw him as the punitive instrument of God, succumbed to jingoism:

> So valiant was the resistance made by Don Pedro de Acuña that not only did the heretic fail to take Cadiz, but he lost many of his ships and a large number of Englishmen were killed. Thus were the thresholds of the gate of Spain watered with the blood of those wolves, in order that the scent might keep their fellows away from our doors; for it is said of that animal that on smelling the blood shed by one of his own race he will go no further but will retreat. So also is it done with crows, where there is a plague of them, for if one be hanged to a post all the others will take flight.[9]

Within a score of years, an established myth of a Spanish victory; a national and ideological inspiration; a Dunkirk. After trauma comes selectivity, followed closely by legend.

The English had a different perspective on God's role in the raid. An anonymous participant, possibly Captain Fenner, wrote in the days following:

> [We] came out againe ... without the loss of any one man at the action, or any hurte but only the master gunner of the *Golden Lyon*, whose legge was broken with a great peece from the towne, but the man like to doe well, God be thancked. ... It may seem strange or rather miraculous that so great an exploict shold be performed with so small losse; the place to endomadge us beyng so convenient, and their force so great, ... but in this as in all our actions hearetofore, though dangerously attempted yet happily performed, our good God hath and dayly doth make his infinite power manifest to all papistes apparantly, and his name be by us his servants continewally honored.[10]

Drake's own despatches, imbued with the same religiosity and satisfaction, are none the less tinged with foreboding induced by his new awareness of the massive Spanish war preparations. In a letter to Walsingham on 27 April he told him that 'the like preparation was never heard of nor known', and he repeats the warning in a postscript: 'I dare not a'most write unto your honour of the great forces we hear the King of Spain hath out in the Straits. Prepare in England strongly, and most by sea. Stop him now, and stop him ever. Look well to the coast of Sussex.'[11]

Drake's aim, now, was 'to intercept their meetings by all possible means'. In Cadiz he had learned that a squadron under Juan Martínez de Recalde was cruising off Cape St Vincent, but by the time he arrived in the area Martínez de Recalde, warned by Philip, had taken refuge in the Tagus. Drake therefore decided to patrol the waters off the Cape and the Algarve coast to intercept passing shipping, particularly vessels on their way from the Mediterranean to join or provision Philip's war fleet in Lisbon. This was probably integral to his plans from the start.

He now had a further, more serious, disagreement with his vice-admiral. Drake decided on a land operation. He had, after all, a large force of soldiers and land officers who had not yet set foot on shore. On or before 29 April he told his officers on the *Elizabeth* of his intention to land and attack the castle of Sagres, near Cape St Vincent. We do not know if he had consulted any of his captains; he certainly did not consult William Borough, who came aboard the *Elizabeth* on the 29th to find the plan being discussed openly on deck. After Drake had told him of his scheme in what must have been a strained meeting, Borough returned to the *Golden Lion*, brooded on the matter overnight, and then composed a long letter to Drake brimming with accumulated resentment.[12]

He complained that since leaving England none of Drake's council meetings had included any serious debate, that Drake had simply imposed his own intentions, or had invoked support previously negotiated with his favourites; that any longer meetings had been simply blandishing displays of hospitality at the end of which the captains had 'departed as wise as we came'; and that Drake had not given instructions to the fleet as he should (here Borough was probably alluding to the entry into Cadiz harbour).

The letter went on to accuse Drake of arrogance and stubbornness, and of playing fast and loose with the expedition's orders. It also complained huffily of Drake's inexplicable favouring of captains of less experience over one who had been Admiral of Her Majesty's fleets. The letter argued a conservative but reasonable case against a shore expedition: no evidence of a good watering-place; a possible change of wind which might force the anchored supporting ships out to sea; the lurking presence of Acuña's galleys, now reinforced from Gibraltar; and doubts among the land officers about the vulnerability of the proposed target. And what was to be gained? 'Noe matter of substaunce, neither shall any man be bettered by itt, but a satisfyinge of your minde that you may saie, Thus I have donne uppon the Kinge of Spaines land.'

This last, perceptive accusation, from a man whom he had come increasingly to despise, was too near the bone for Drake. On 2 May he called Borough to the flagship and in the presence of his chaplain and Captain Fenner accused him of insubordination, had him arrested, and sent him back to the *Golden Lion* in the charge of Captain Marchant of the land forces, who was to take command of the ship.

The land operation went ahead. To the men who had sacked Santo Domingo and Cartagena it must have looked like a picnic, but events were to show that Borough's fuddy-duddy reservations had contained a good deal of sense. Drake's initial target was Lagos, about twenty miles east of Cape St Vincent. He used the pattern of the West Indian successes, landing 1,000 men five miles along the coast to march towards the town through cornfields and vineyards while he and the fleet hovered off the harbour. The Spanish land forces were obviously in a state of alert after Cadiz; the column was shadowed by groups of horsemen, who stayed out of shot but had increased to about 400 by the time Lagos was reached. The town gave Drake's land captains an unpleasant surprise: the landward side had been made impregnable with newly built walls well furnished with ordnance, and judging by the number of ensigns flying on the ramparts there appeared to be at least 3,000 defenders, though in reality there were far fewer.

The column marched around the walls, and then marched back again, suffering casualties from cannonballs and small-arms fire. It was decided that an attempt on the walls would be profitless. Gunfire from Drake's ships killed a Spanish horse and injured a few men, and the English column retired. On their way back they had to form squares several times to meet an expected attack from the cavalry, but there was no serious clash of arms. In the afternoon they re-embarked, and on the following morning a relieved and self-satisfied garrison watched the English fleet sail away towards Cape St Vincent. So far Borough, now in confined quarters on the *Golden Lion*, had been proved right.

Drake now returned to his earlier plan to attack Sagres, which was dominated by a castle in a strong defensive position, supported by several minor fortifications. On 5 May he took 800 men ashore himself near a small fort at Aveleira, whose garrison fled to the castle, leaving their brass ordnance behind them. He also sent some ships to burn the boats and houses of a fishing village to the east.

Sagres Castle was a daunting prospect. It sat on a headland, with high cliffs on three sides, and the approach on the landward side was barred by a wall forty feet high and ten feet thick, with a single gate. Drake despatched thirty arquebusiers to rattle the defences for a while, but after the captain of the garrison refused to surrender he decided to burn down the gate. This was a perilous task, for the layout of the fortifications enabled the defenders to defend the gate with crossfire. As the arquebuses kept up a rapid fire on the loopholes and ramparts, Drake himself led men to pile faggots against the gate, and after the captain of the garrison had been wounded the castle surrendered.

Drake spared the defenders and their families. On the following day the monastery on Cape St Vincent and a fort adjacent to it were captured without difficulty, the buildings fired, and the guns seized. The English reports mention no anti-Catholic dimension in the attack on the monastery, but according to Horozco 'they performed with all their usual drunken feasting and devilish atrocities; they stole whatever they fancied, and did not set fire to the place until they had committed innumerable acts of wickedness against the images of the saints, like the perverted heretics they are'.[13]

In the next three or four days, from his base in Sagres harbour, Drake turned his attention to the local shipping. In the ten miles of coast eastward from Cape St Vincent he destroyed forty-seven small cargo vessels and fifty or sixty fishing boats. Many of the cargo ships were carrying material for Philip's fleet in Lisbon, and Drake mentions particularly, in a letter to Walsingham, that he had burned large amounts of timber and galley oars, and enough barrel staves to have contained 25,000 or 30,000 tons of water or wine for the Spanish galleons.

Sagres was a stirring success, with few casualties, but the gains ashore were not large. Buildings had been burned, but the main fortress remained, easily restorable. These land installations, in any case, could have done little to hinder Drake's pillaging and burning of shipping, any more than had those at Cadiz. One of Drake's motives, perceived and criticised by Borough, was evident too to a man more in sympathy with it, Robert Leng: the raid was made 'to satisfye [Drake's] valyant mynde in doeing some worthye exploytes upon our enimyes lande'.[14] The strategic point, however, was to secure an anchorage and a harbour base for cleaning his ships, refreshing his men, and above all hindering the passage of supplies from Andalusia to Lisbon and thereby the preparations of Philip's fleet.

By 10 May 1587 Drake was riding at anchor off Cascais, at the mouth of the Tagus. A group of seven or eight galleys and some desultory fire from the shore batteries were treated with the same disdain as those at Cadiz. Drake used a small captured caravel to send a message to the Marquis of Santa Cruz in Lisbon, offering to exchange prisoners for any Englishmen in the galleys, and asking cheekily if it was Philip's plan to attack England that year. The Marquis, smarting from the destruction of his own large ship at Cadiz, had been making frantic preparations against a similar attack on Lisbon, and not surprisingly gave Drake a dusty answer. The Spanish, as Drake must have hoped, were unable to fathom his next move; they foresaw a repeat of the great West Indies raid, and Medina Sidonia wrote to the governors of the main West Indian towns alerting them.[15]

After Drake had sailed south again to Sagres, an escaped negro eluded the horsemen pursuing him and was brought aboard the *Elizabeth*. He told Drake that ten galleys had arrived in Lagos. According to Horozco[16] these were commanded by Martín de Padilla, Admiral of the King's Galleys, and kept an eye on Drake all the time he remained on the Algarve coast, exchanging fire with him. This is not the picture given by English sources; Leng says that Drake went immediately to Lagos and the galleys, unable to match the English broadsides, took refuge inshore.

It is not clear why Drake abandoned his effective blockade off Cape St Vincent and set off for the Azores on 22 May. On only the previous day he had sent three fly-boats and the captured French ship back to England with sick and injured men, writing to Walsingham that one of the fly-boats should be sent back to join him, which suggests that he planned to remain at the Cape.[17] The only ready explanation is that he had received intelligence from some captured vessel of an approaching target which must have aroused memories of the *Cacafuego*: a huge Portuguese carrack, the *São Phelipe*, homeward bound with her hold packed with the exotic riches of the Far East: pepper, cinnamon, cloves, mace, silks, calico, ebony, indigo, silver and jewels.

For four days after setting off for the Azores Drake's progress was delayed by violent storms which scattered his ships. All the London merchantmen disappeared. This can hardly have been coincidence. Perhaps they thought that they had done enough at Cadiz, without chasing off into the Atlantic. They may have been less convinced than Drake about the potential of the *São Phelipe*, if indeed Drake had told them about her. They all got home, and eventually shared in the profits.

A more serious cause of anger for Drake was the disappearance of the *Golden Lion* and the hated Borough. Many of the *Lion*'s crew were Borough's own men, and had been angered by his detention. Now weary and on short rations, they mutinied against Captain Marchant. There was no violence; one of the quartermasters handed over a written complaint stating that forty-six men were sick and provisions low, and demanding that Marchant take the fair wind which was now blowing and turn for England. After some not very spirited dissuasion by himself and the master, Marchant asked to be put aboard the pinnace *Spy*, and by common consent Borough took over command and set a course for England.

The extent of Borough's involvement in the mutiny is unknown, though his resuming of command, as he was certainly aware, was mutiny in itself. This seemed preferable to him to awaiting Drake's uncertain pleasure, as he testified later:

> I stood ever in doubt of my life, and did expect daily when the Admiral would have executed on me his bloodthirsty desire as he did upon Doughty. Now seeing it was so, and that by the providence of God this mean was wrought to save me, ... what reason had I to strive against them for coming away? If the ship had stayed by the Admiral I had assuredly been put to death.[18]

When Drake heard from Marchant he set up a court martial and did, indeed, sentence Borough to death. The only evidence was that of Marchant and the master of the *Lion*, so either the trial was a startling breach of justice, or these two had something convincing to offer about Borough's complicity in the matter. On Borough's later evidence, when Marchant and the master were being put in the long-boat he was continuing their efforts to dissuade the crew from mutiny. Either Marchant had something different to tell the court, or Drake's passion made any evidence pointless.

Reduced now to nine vessels, Drake reached the island of São Miguel on 8 June, and sighted a sail on the same evening. Thinking it could be a man-of-war, the ships lay in stays (that is to say, they backed some of their yards as a way of remaining more or less stationary) to let the pinnaces rejoin them in the night. At daybreak they were astonished by the immense size of the foreigner. She was flying the red cross of Portugal, which she lowered and raised several times to show her identity, possibly in the belief that Drake's ships were Spanish. 'But we,' wrote Robert Leng, knoweinge what she was, wolde put out noe flag untyll we were within shott of her, when we hanged out flages, streamers, and pendentes, that she might be out of dout; ... we hayled her with cannon shott, and havinge shott her thorowe dyvers tymes, she shott att us, sometymes att one, sometymes att an other. Then we began to applye her hotelye, our flyebote and one of our pynnisses lyinge thwarte her hawsse, att whom she shott, and threw fyer workes, but did them noe hurte; for that her ordenaunce lay soe hye over them ... s[i]x of her men beinge slayne, and dyvers sore hurte, they yelded unto us; whome when we boorded, we founde to be ... the greatest shipp in all Portugall, rychly loden, to our happye joy and great gladnes.[19]

This massive prize brought out the genial side of Drake; he freed the negro slaves loaded by the *São Phelipe* in Africa, gave them presents and put them and the Portuguese crew into one of the fly-boats to go where they chose.[20] He now abandoned thoughts of returning to continue his coastal blockade, sailed for home, and was back in Plymouth on 26 June 1587.

On every count the voyage had been a success. Spain complained, of course; Burghley's emollient responses survive, filled with prot-estations of the Queen's efforts to forbid Drake's assaults on harbours and assurances of her displeasure.[21] The threat of an invasion by Philip's armada had been distanced, not only by Drake's depredations off the Algarve coast, but also because Santa Cruz, worried for the safety of the Indies treasure fleet, had wasted three months by taking his galleons out of Lisbon to pursue Drake when he went off to the Azores.

Drake's opportunism, reinforced by his luck, had now confirmed the belief in Spain that he had powers of wizardry, and worked with the aid of a familiar spirit.[22] The *São Phelipe*'s cargo, unloaded at Saltash, proved hugely valuable; the initial estimate of £97,610 was later increased to £108,000. The pepper alone was worth £40,000. Drake took into his own care a chest full of gold cutlery, rings, girdles, bracelets, ear-rings, pomanders and precious stones as a placatory gift to Elizabeth.[23] The merchants, despite their ships' desertion, received their share of the profits, and were bold enough to insist on a little extra to take account of the provisions seized at Cadiz, which had been used to victual only the Queen's ships, and of the prize taken by the returning pinnace. The crews were happy; as well as their due wages the Queen gave them an extra two months' pay as a bonus, and Drake himself gave an extra six months' pay to every

Insula Elizabetha

Terra
Gene   *australis*
cognita

Cape fortunate

port St Julian

The Bay of Birds
Cscaled

our first aquaintance
of Giants

from the Riuer of Plate to the
supposed streight of Magilanus
doth the Land of Giants reach
that is from 36 degrees to
52 beyond the Equinoctiall

Cape Joy

Terra Demonum
pars Brasiliæ

Elizabeth Island, with the open Antarctic Ocean now revealed, drawn by Drake's chaplain on the circumnavigation, Francis Fletcher. (The south is to the top of the drawing.) Also marked are Port St Julian, where Doughty was killed, the River Plate, and 'our first acquaintance of Giants'.

The port of Guatulco on the west coast of central America, which Drake reached in April 1579. Part of an English sailor's atlas, based on one captured from the Spanish.

Drake, aged 43, with the symbols of his circumnavigation and knighthood.

Buckland Abbey, bought by Drake with the proceeds of the circumnavigation.

Drake's portrait painted in 1581 by the famous miniaturist Nicholas Hilliard.

Elizabeth Sydenham, Drake's second wife, painted in 1585 at about the time of her marriage to Drake.

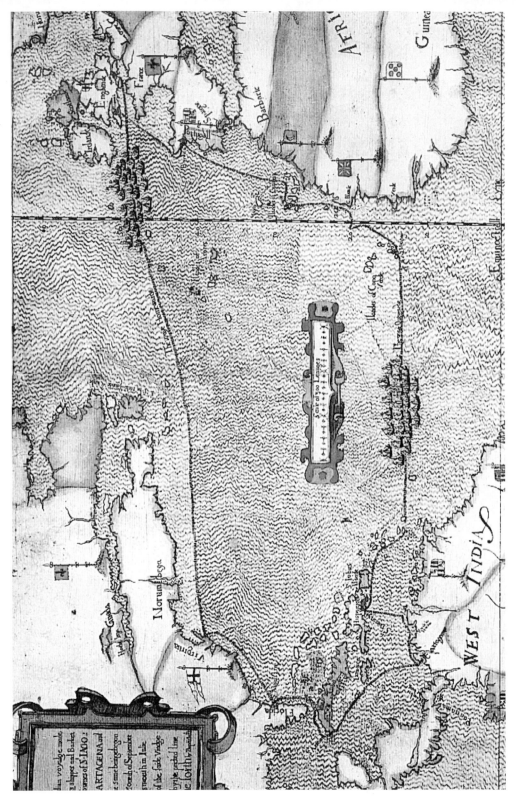

The route of the Great West Indies Raid, 1585–86.

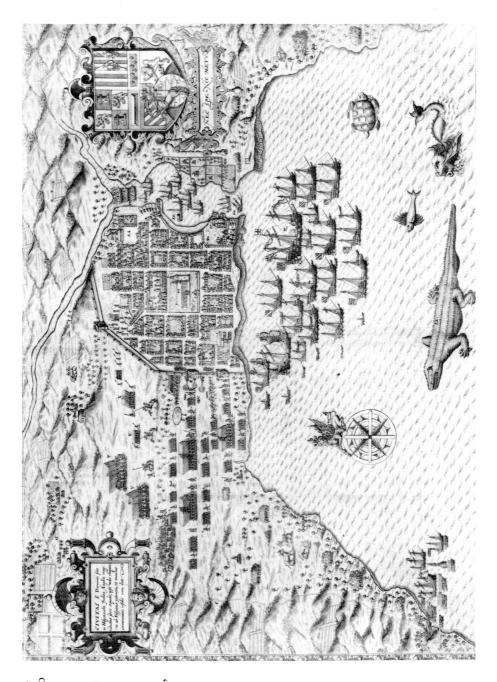

The Boazio map of the
raid on Santo Domingo
in January 1586. The
landing at the Boca
de Hayna is shown at
bottom left, and to the
left of the town wall
Carleill's two columns
are approaching the
gates. Drake, in the
Elizabeth Bonaventure,
is anchored off the
town with the main
fleet.

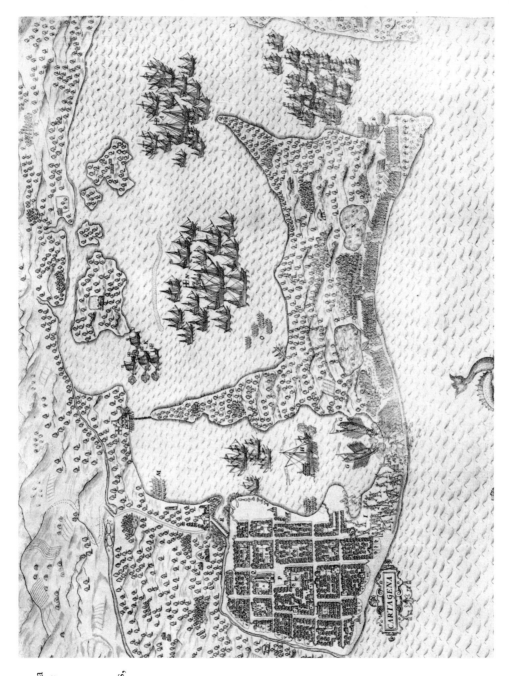

Boazio's depiction of the attack on Cartagena in February 1586. The English force, having landed at Hicacos Point, marches along the shore, braves the cross-fire of the galleys, and storms the Caleta battery. Meanwhile Frobisher's pinnaces attack the Boquerón fort (top centre).

man who had been at the taking of the carrack. He petitioned to have this expense (over £6,500) refunded by the Crown. Even some of the *Golden Lion*'s crew were paid their due wages.

This left the matter of Borough and the mutineers. Drake's joyful reception did not dispel his anger at the conduct of his vice-admiral; he had, remember, condemned Borough to death in his own area of jurisdiction, the high seas. He now succeeded in having him tried for mutiny. The surviving evidence from the trial shows that Drake had cooled down over the letter of reproach which had prompted him to arrest Borough. He could now allege the more tangible crime of mutiny and desertion, and he decided to reinforce this by presenting Borough's action in warping the *Golden Lion* out of danger at Cadiz as cowardice in the face of the enemy.

Only six years earlier, Borough had put his great admiration for Drake on public record. In his *Discours of the Variation of the Cumpas*, which aimed to introduce into English navigational practice some of the achievements of the Spanish and Portuguese, he had rejoiced that 'our Countrieman Sir Francis Drake for valorous attempt, prudent proceeding, and fortunate performing his voiage aboute the worlde, is not onely become equall to any of them, but in fame farre surmounteth them all'.[24]

Borough survived the trial unscathed. He defended himself fluently and convincingly, accused Marchant of craven weakness in the face of mutiny, and appealed to his judges' awareness of two skeletons which continued to rattle in Drake's cupboard: he justified his staying with the *Lion* after the mutiny by his dread of suffering Drake's summary justice, like Thomas Doughty; and he stressed Drake's failure to understand the moves of a fellow-combatant under fire at Cadiz by reviving an older memory:

> Sir Francis Drake, in urging this matter so vehemently against me, ... doth altogether forget how he demeaned himself towards his Master and Admiral, Mr John Hawkyns, at the port of San Juan de Ulua, ... when contrary to his said Admiral's command he came away and left his said Master in great extremity; ... which matter if it had been so followed against him (for that he could no ways excuse it) might justly have procured that to himself which now most unjustly, bloodily and maliciously by all devices whatsoever he hath sought and still seeketh against me.[25]

One can almost smell the rancour in the room as the two men faced each other. Drake inspired admiration, sometimes reluctant;

patriotism and love. He left no man indifferent, and he aroused in some an irritation which could easily be turned into a black and seething hatred. Most were discreet enough to cloak it; Borough, a mature and forthright man who had the loyalty of his crew and who emerges from these events as no coward, confronted Drake and survived. There were powerful men in the land who did not share the feverish popular admiration of Drake. Omnipotent at sea, his will was still trammelled by legality and distrust when ashore.

XV

Esta Felicisima Armada
1587–88

'I put my hope in God that He will favour this
service. . . . May His hand guide you and keep
you. Have a mind to your own health, which
you are to devote to such a holy enterprise.'

Philip II to the Duke of Medina Sidonia,
July 1588

'There was never any force so stronge as there
is now redye or makyng readye against your
Majesty and trewe relygyon, but that the Lord
of all strengthes is stronger, and will defend
the trewth of his word.'

Drake to Elizabeth, April 1588

The Marquis of Santa Cruz brought his weary fleet into Lisbon on
29 September 1587, having shepherded the treasure ships safely
past Cape St Vincent. Between then and the end of January he was
bombarded by letters from Philip demanding that he restore his ships
to fighting condition and sail for Flanders. It was a time of desperate
pressure for both men, and both, to some extent, crumbled. The
ships suffered fresh damage in a serious storm in November; the
organisation in the fleet, the shipping of ordnance and the distribution
of provisions were beset by problems. Santa Cruz's mental and physical strength gave way under pressure and he took to his bed. Philip,
too, exhausted by his long hours of self-imposed work at despatches
and reports and driven by an obsession with an enterprise which now
engulfed him, suffered a nervous collapse around Christmas and was
confined to his bed for four weeks.

When the king emerged he sent the Count of Fuentes to Lisbon to
light a firework under Santa Cruz, with the power to dismiss him if
necessary, but the old warrior, the architect of the Armada, was only

179

a few days from death. Fuentes found a demoralised fleet, with provisions rotting and men dying from typhus. On 20 January 1588 there were 12,600 troops attached to the fleet. By 13 February it could scarcely muster 10,000. Santa Cruz died on 7 February.[1]

Fuentes' reports to Philip made it clear that the fleet needed a shake-up by a man with a clear brain and a grasp of organisational detail. A mere efficient bureaucrat would not do; Santa Cruz's successor would not simply have to make sure the biscuit supplies were adequate, but would also have to lead the Armada into action. Philip's senior naval men, such as Juan Martínez de Recalde and Diego Flores, were disappointed; the King chose the Duke of Medina Sidonia. The Duke's organisational abilities had been proved over the years in his administration of the Andalusian end of the transatlantic convoys, and he had shown decisive military leadership in reacting to Drake's raid on Cadiz. He was, however, no sailor, and he was appalled by the letter of appointment.

In mid-February he wrote a reply pleading to be excused; he had, he said, no relevant experience, and indeed on the few occasions on which he had been afloat he had been seriously seasick. There was more to it than this: not only was the Duke aware of the chaotic situation in the fleet, but he had deep misgivings about the whole enterprise. Two days later he wrote a second letter arguing a comprehensive case against the project. Philip read the first letter, and dismissed modesty and *mal de mer* as inadequate reasons for declining such a noble role in Spain's destiny. He never saw the second letter; it was suppressed by his secretaries, who took it upon themselves to write to Medina Sidonia in terms of polite but steely blackmail. The Duke succumbed, partly to pressure and partly to his own dutiful conscience, and by the end of February was bending his mind to matters of naval detail in Lisbon, where his energies soon galvanised the project.

Meanwhile, in the Netherlands, an additional 15,500 Spanish and Italian troops had been assembled to form the Duke of Parma's invasion force. A fleet of 170 barges and boats, with over forty larger vessels, had been gathered in Antwerp, Dunkirk and the coastal havens of Flanders. Parma, nevertheless, was by no means confident, and he had written several times to point out to Philip that his transports were small and unsuitable for a Channel crossing except in fair weather. They had little defensive armament, and would be vulnerable immediately on leaving harbour to an attack by a lurking squadron of the Dutch. Parma's main cause for concern was the lack of any detailed plan for linking up with the fleet from Spain. This crucial aspect of the Armada enterprise was never seriously addressed, and it was to be a major reason for the Spanish failure.

Any pretence of secrecy about Spain's intentions had long since vanished. There was a vigorous school of thought in England that the best mode of defence against the Armada was to strike the first blow. Drake, of course, was one of its main proponents. On 30 March 1588, as Medina Sidonia's preparations were nearing completion, Drake wrote to the Privy Council from Plymouth. He had been sent there by Lord Admiral Howard to command a large proportion of the available ships, including the royal galleons. Howard and Lord Henry Seymour had remained in the eastern Channel with ships furnished mainly by London and the coastal towns. Drake, fully aware of the two aspects of Philip's plan, was emphatically in favour of carrying the fight to Spain:

> If ... the K[ing] of Spaigne meane any invasyon in Englande, then doubtlesse, his force is, and wil be greate in Spaigne, and thereon he will make his groundworke, or foundation; ... but if there maye be suche a staye or stoppe made, by any meanes, of this fleete in Spaigne, that they maye not come throughe the seas as conquerors, ... then shall the prince of Parma have suche a checke therebye, as were meett. The advantaige and gaine of tyme and place, wil be the onlie and cheife meane for our goode, wherein I most humblie beseech yor good L[ordship]s to pe[r]sever, as you have begun, for that with feiftie saile of shippinge, we shall doe more good uppon their owne Coaste, than a greate manye more will doe here at home, and the sooner we are gone, the better we shall be able to ympeache them.[2]

Howard was of the same mind. By early June he had joined Drake in Plymouth, where their joint force amounted to sixty fighting ships. Howard was in the *Ark Royal*, Drake in the *Revenge*. Seymour's squadron remained off the Downs.

Howard was delighted with his own flagship. The *Ark Royal*, newly built in 1587, would have seemed revolutionary to a sailor of fifty years earlier. Henry VIII's naval vessels were intended mainly to transport large bodies of land forces to foreign shores. Ship-to-ship encounters, if they occurred, were expected to involve a rapid closing with the enemy, as archers fired a rain of arrows, and a bloody assault by boarding parties armed with pikes. The idea of bombardment with cannon was secondary. The balance shifted towards naval gunnery in mid-century, while William Wynter was Surveyor of the Navy, but it was the appointment of John Hawkins as Treasurer in 1578 which transformed both tactics and ship design.

In the ten years preceding the Armada action, new royal warships were what was termed 'race-built'; they had a greater proportion of length to beam, and much less pronounced fore- and sterncastles, which improved their sailing performance. They also carried a greater number of heavy guns. The fleet was geared essentially, not to transporting armies overseas, but to the defence of England. In Philip's big galleons, full of men and supplies, the weight of ordnance was only three or four per cent of their total tonnage. In contrast the 250-ton *Aid* carried 27 tons of ordnance, nearly eleven per cent of her tonnage; Drake's *Revenge* could mount 70 tons of guns, fourteen per cent of her tonnage.[3]

It was not only the weight of guns, but their efficiency, that mattered. The Spanish had been slow to develop a gun mounting specifically for naval use. Spain's naval gun-carriages were no different, in essence, from those of her land forces: they had the same two large wheels and long trail which took up a lot of deck room and made them slow to manoeuvre. England had adopted the more compact and efficient naval gun carriage, with four small wheels, which enabled rapid reloading and the use of repeated broadsides, for which the new, sprightlier ships were well suited.

A few days before Howard joined Drake in Plymouth Medina Sidonia, stoically quelling his awareness of the test he was about to impose on his stomach, had led his revivified fleet out of the Tagus and turned north for the English Channel. Morale was again high in his 130 ships, and the troop numbers had risen from the 10,000 of February to almost 19,000. It had been impressed on everyone that this great enterprise enjoyed the favour of God, in whose service it had been conceived. The duke's achievement had been magnificent; he could have sailed a fortnight earlier but for north-westerly winds which kept him in the Tagus.

Once at sea, he was faced with new problems. The fleet, limited to the speed of its slowest vessels, struggled for a fortnight to reach Cape Finisterre, and rations were cut to slow the rapid drain on victuals caused by the increased numbers of men. Three dozen of the abler ships sailed into La Coruña to replenish supplies, but the rest remained off shore overnight to enter on the following morning and were scattered by a violent storm.

Medina Sidonia reacted by pleading with Philip to call off the project, going so far as to suggest that perhaps God had indicated that he did not favour it after all. Philip, of course, had no such doubts, and his reply, stiffened by the irrefutable illogicality of a divinely appointed monarch, told the Duke to reassemble and repair the ships and get on with things; if their cause had been unjust, then this storm might indeed have been an indication of God's displeasure, but since they were fighting a righteous war, this could not be the case.

The storm had pushed the duke's ships far to the north, and some were sighted off the Scillies. With a change of wind they returned unmolested to La Coruña, but Howard and Drake were now aware that the Armada had been at least partially dispersed.[4] They were desperate to seize an advantage in Philip's home waters, and cursed the southerly winds which kept them in Plymouth. In Elizabeth's fleet, as in Philip's, victualling was causing concern because of the delays to the Armada's progress, and Howard had to appeal to the Council for £5,000 or £6,000 to pay for extra stores after Drake and Hawkins had laid out some of their own money.[5]

The arrival of extra provisions coincided with a change of wind, and on 4 July the fleet set sail. This time the weather was on Medina Sidonia's side. It took Howard and Drake a fortnight to make their way through storms and calms to a point about sixty miles from the Spanish coast, where the wind came south and they turned for home. The same wind which forced them back to the Channel brought the Armada out of La Coruña, and the weather continued to favour the Spanish until 29 July, when Howard and Drake received the news that the enemy had been sighted off the Lizard: '120 saile, whereof there are 4 g[alleasses] and many ships of greate burthen'.[6] Medina Sidonia had lost his galleys, which had been unable to cope with the heavy seas in the Bay of Biscay and had turned east to take refuge in French ports.

As the Spanish came along the Cornish coast they could see the English alarm spreading ahead of them in the smoke of the coastal beacons.[7] The English fleet was lying in Plymouth, to where it had returned a week before, short of victuals. Overnight the ships were warped out of harbour, and at about three in the afternoon of 30 July they had their first sight of the enemy sailing easily towards them before the south-west wind. The Armada was a daunting sight, sweeping up towards Plymouth in a great crescent with trailing horns; a sight unparalleled in the experience even of Drake, Frobisher and Hawkins, let alone of the younger captains and seamen; an arc of great ships, between two and three miles wide.

The events of the night of 30 July were crucial. In seaborne warfare the ship with the weather gauge, that is to say the one further upwind than its opponent, has all the advantage of manoeuvrability and initiative. With the wind in the south-west, the Armada had the weather gauge of the English. If Howard and Drake had lingered in Plymouth until the Spanish had passed on eastward, the English could then have emerged and been upwind of the Spanish, but of course Medina Sidonia would have allowed no such thing; he could have left a substantial flotilla of his major vessels off Plymouth to bombard an English fleet lying helpless while the rest of the Armada sailed on to rendezvous with Parma. Having warped out of harbour as soon as the tide permitted, the English aimed to get upwind of their opponents as soon as possible.

They did this neatly and comprehensively. Under cover of darkness the main body of the English fleet sailed on a long reach just west of south, directly across the face of the oncoming Armada and then around its southern tip. Another group, possibly the last ships to leave harbour, proceeded by a riskier course to gain a similar position behind the Armada's northernmost ships. This involved a high order of seamanship, probably with lanterns extinguished so as not to alert the enemy: a series of six tacks in a width of sea limited by the coast to starboard and the Spanish to port. Some historians have assumed that this group of ships was commanded by Drake.[8] The manoeuvre bears his stamp, but there is no firm evidence of this.

At daybreak on 31 July, then, Medina Sidonia was nonplussed to find the English in full strength upwind of him to the west. He could do nothing except maintain his formation and await the attack, which began at nine o'clock in the morning.[9] After one of Howard's smaller ships, the *Disdain*, had sailed forward and fired a formal shot of challenge, the English were able to use the wind to sail in line astern across the trailing horns of the Spanish crescent, discharging broadsides as they went, and then to turn and sail back on the reverse tack firing their guns on the other side. The Spanish could not respond with the same weight of gunnery except by breaking formation, which was the last thing Medina Sidonia wanted. The advantage of the crescent formation was that ships attacking it from the rear could only concentrate on the outermost vessels; if they tried to get at the ships in the centre they risked being, as it were, embayed in the arc of the crescent, where they would be vulnerable to attack by the ships in the horns.

The battle continued until one o'clock with a succession of passes and broadsides from the English. Howard was conducting the assault at long range; both sides knew that if the two fleets closed and boarding parties came into play the advantage would lie with the larger ships and crews of the Spanish. The Lord Admiral's report[10] claimed no great damage to the enemy, and Drake, too, made little of this opening action: 'We had them in chase, and so cominge upp unto them, there hath passed some cannon shotte betweene some of our fleete and some of them, and as farre as we perceive they are determined to sell their lives with blowes.'[11] The main targets were two ships of Juan Martínez de Recalde's squadron, the flagship *San Juan* and the *Gran Grin*. Drake, Hawkins and Frobisher were all involved in the attack on the *San Juan*.

The two Spanish disasters of the day were self-inflicted. The big *San Salvador* was disabled, and a large proportion of her crew killed or dreadfully injured, when some of her powder-barrels exploded, probably through a carelessly dropped match or fuse. She was carrying a large amount of the fleet's money. With her sterncastle blown apart and her steering shattered, there was no alternative but to abandon her on the following day after her pay-chests had been removed. Another of the more powerful ships, the *Nuestra Señora del Rosario*, leader of the Andalusian squadron, broke her bowsprit when she collided with the *Santa Catalina* during a manoeuvre to support Recalde. In the rising sea her foremast, its stays slackened by the damage to the bowsprit, broke off at deck level and fell against the mainmast, leaving her completely out of control. She was commanded by Don Pedro de Valdés, whose cousin, Diego Flores, was with Medina Sidonia to supply the sea-going experience which the Duke lacked. Diego Flores had been with the treasure fleet in Nombre de Dios in the 1570s, when Drake's pinnaces had made him and his galleons look foolish.

The crippled *Rosario* was briefly assisted by vessels detached from the fleet, but on the advice of Diego Flores, who saw the likelihood of a disintegration of the battle formation, Medina Sidonia recalled them and sailed on, leaving Valdés to fend for himself. Shortly afterwards the 200-ton *Margaret and John* sailed up to the wallowing *Rosario* and fired a defiant volley of muskets into her before rejoining the English fleet.

When darkness came down on the night of 31 July, it was the understanding of at least some of the English captains that Drake, in the *Revenge*, had been ordered by Howard to light a large lantern at his stern, take up position at the head of the fleet, and serve as a guiding light by which the other ships might keep their stations. Martin Frobisher, as we shall see, was emphatically of this opinion. Drake, however, did no such thing. Frobisher and the rest looked in vain for the light, and by the morning of 1 August they had become so dispersed that much of the day passed before they had properly regathered.

This incident is perhaps the most striking case of the factor we have seen many times before in England's hostilities with Spain: the uneasy balance between the national and the private interest. In this momentous situation, with his fortune made long ago, and with the Armada proceeding largely undamaged on its mission to seize England, depose his Queen and eradicate his religion, Drake's piratical instincts again proved irresistible. At dawn on 1 August, far from leading the fleet, the *Revenge* was far astern of it, within two or three cables' length of the disabled *Rosario*. Valdés responded to Drake's surrender demand with the initial show of defiance befitting a Spanish aristocrat, but he was not a death-or-glory man. Peeved at being abandoned by the fleet, he soon changed his tune, as he reported to Philip from captivity later:

> Uppon assurance of good usage, I went aborde him, uppon his worde, to treate of the conditions of our yelding, wherein the best conclusion that could be taken was the safetye of our lyves and curteous entertaynement; for performance whereof he gave us his hand and word of a gentleman, and promised he would use us better than any others that were to come to his hands, and would be a meane that the Queene should also do the lyke, whereupon, fyndyng that this was our last and best remedye, I thought good to accept of his offer.[12]

The *Rosario* was stripped of her pay-chests and plate. Some of the large quantity of ducats aboard her[13] disappeared mysteriously; it has been suggested that only about half of it reached Elizabeth's treasury.[14] Even the amount aboard is disputed; Valdés said that there were 20,000 ducats, but Vicente Alvarez, the captain, said that there were 52,000, plus large amounts of the officers' personal funds, plate and precious stones.[15] How much of it passed into Drake's permanent keeping nobody knows, but heavy suspicion fell on him over the whole episode of the *Rosario*. It is remarkable that, of the two Spanish ships disabled in the first day's engagement, one should have been seized by Drake and the other by his kinsman and early mentor, John Hawkins, who went aboard the *San Salvador* to take possession of her. She was taken to Weymouth on the following day. Drake left the

300-ton *Roebuck* to take the *Rosario* into Torbay, where they arrived on 5 August.[16] The treasure remained on the *Revenge* as she rejoined the fleet.

On Tuesday, 2 August, after a night of calm, the overall situation was changed by the weather: a north-east wind blew up which gave a temporary advantage to the Spanish. In a confused and indeterminate action off Portland the fleets exchanged fire from 5 o'clock in the morning until late evening, using huge amounts of powder and shot. Frobisher's *Triumph* and five other ships suffered a prolonged assault from the galleasses. Only when the wind veered to the south-south-west did Medina Sidonia break off the engagement and continue eastwards after a sharp attack from a group of the royal galleons and some of the merchant ships.

So far Medina Sidonia had done nothing wrong. The Armada had maintained its cohesion and was on course; the English had merely nibbled at its strength. It was now, however, that the deficiency in the grand design which was to nullify the duke's energy and meticulous organisation became all-important: the sketchiness of the planning for the link-up with the Duke of Parma. Medina Sidonia had already despatched pinnaces to warn Parma of his approach and to ask for details of his preparations and plans, to no avail. If there had been some sweeping English success in the Netherlands; if Seymour's ships in the narrow seas had linked up with the Dutch and landed men to destroy Parma's transports; if Parma's regiments were not yet assembled in the right places, it would be folly for the Armada to go any further east in the Channel. Much better to anchor in the Solent, wait for information from Parma, and leave options open. Medina Sidonia had stated this intention, and his reasoning, in a despatch to Philip when he was still off the Lizard.[17] On 2 August he was still in the dark about Parma's state of readiness.

On the following day Howard was content to shadow the Spanish. He reorganised his fleet into four squadrons commanded by Drake, Hawkins, Frobisher and himself. The Armada, too, had changed its formation, and was now bunched in a roundel. On the morning of 4 August Hawkins and Howard began trying to pick off further stragglers. The *Santa Ana* came under heavy attack from close quarters, and was rescued by the galleasses. As the action continued Frobisher led his squadron east of the Isle of Wight and into the mouth of the seaway, where he was soon threatened by some of the larger Spanish galleons. There was little wind, and Frobisher had lowered boats to tow him away from the threat when the wind freshened from the south-west, giving the advantage to the English and causing Medina Sidonia to break off the action again and continue eastward. That evening he sent another despatch to Parma, warning him of his imminent arrival and telling him to sail to meet him as soon as possible.[18]

Exactly what Drake was doing between 2 and 5 August remains unclear. He had rejoined the fleet promptly after taking the *Rosario*,[19] but none of the descriptions of the events of 4 August mentions him or the *Revenge*. It has been suggested that he anticipated the afternoon's change of wind, worked his squadron seaward, and led it on an attack from the south-west which caused Medina Sidonia to turn away eastward.[20]

In the heated actions of 2 and 4 August both fleets had expended much of their powder and shot, though the English were receiving some new supplies from ashore. On the morning of 5 August an increasingly worried Medina Sidonia sent another despatch to Parma asking not only for information but also for shot in various sizes.[21] This Spanish shortage of shot was far from uniform; marine archaeologists have revealed that some of the vessels later wrecked had their shot-lockers pretty full.

Howard now contented himself with keeping the Spanish in sight. On 6 August the Armada anchored off Calais, and at eight o'clock that night Medina Sidonia watched the English fleet anchoring upwind of him, increased now by the arrival of Lord Henry Seymour's ships. At seven on the following morning, at long last, he heard from Parma, and his heart sank; the force from Flanders would not be ready to embark for days to come. He knew now that, without some positive intervention from God, whose approval he had doubted from the first, he had lost the great game.

The English had followed him up the Channel like sheepdogs snapping at the heels of a flock, and now they had him penned; upwind lay the whole strength of Howard's united squadrons; downwind lay the treacherous banks and shoals of the Flanders coast. On the evening of 7 August his lookouts reported that two dozen of the smaller English vessels were coming closer, and he sent word round the fleet to lower boats with grapnels, for the English, as he well knew, were in a perfect situation to use fireships.

Nobody in the English fleet had anything like as much experience as Drake at destroying enemy ships in a restricted compass, and he would certainly be prominent in the organisation of the attack. Shortly before midnight the Spanish saw seven or eight pinpoints of flame in the darkness, and watched them grow and come nearer.[22] Despite the efforts of the Spanish boat crews to tow them away, the combination of wind and tide brought them inexorably towards the Armada. Many of the duke's ships simply cut or slipped their cables and stood off downwind. Collisions in the darkness disabled at least one large vessel, the flagship of the galleasses, which ran aground. Medina Sidonia himself re-anchored, and had established a controlled formation with some of his abler ships at dawn on 8 August, soon after which Drake led most of the English fleet into a close-quarter attack. Howard's attention was occupied for two hours by an attempt to seize the grounded galleasse. Drake's attack developed into a bitter ship-to-ship engagement, much of it within musket-shot.

The Spanish defence was heroic, and on it depended the duke's chance of reassembling the units of his fleet which had run from the fireships and downwind towards the Flanders coast. The flagship *San Martín*, the *San Marcos*, the *San Juan*, the *San Mateo*, the *San Felipe*, the *San Juan de Sicilia*; all were battered from the morning until three in the afternoon, by which time they had suffered serious damage alow and aloft; several were holed below the waterline, and most of their shot had gone. William Wynter's report gives some idea of the intensity of the action:

> Great was the spoile and harm that was done unto them; ... out of my ship there was shotte 500 shotte of demi cannon, culveryn and demi culveryn, and when I was furthest off in dischardgeing any of the peces I was not out of the shotte of their harquebus, and moste tymes within speeche one of another. And surely every manne did well, and ... the slaughter and hurte they received was great, as tyme will discover it, and when every man was wery with labour, and our cartridges spent, and munitions wasted, I thinke in some altogether, we ceased and followed the enemy.[23]

The English ships were damaged, but not to the same extent, and none was incapacitated. Drake's *Revenge* was struck many times, and the dockyard survey which followed the Armada victory reported her as needing a new mainmast, 'beyng decayed and peryshed with shotte'.[24] It is clear, however, that some of the Spanish ships had fired few shots in the action. This has been attributed to archaic gunnery techniques in Philip's navy, and particularly to the failure to use the tactic of repeated broadsides. The English crews were well drilled in this; it expended large quantities of shot, but the physical and demoralising effects of broadsides at close quarters were probably a significant factor in the English victory.

With the wind as it was, the Armada's only course was to make its way into the North Sea, where Howard, with his shot-lockers empty, 'set on a brag countenance and gave them chase, as though we had wanted nothing, until we had cleared our owne coaste and some parte of Scotland of them'.[25] Drake wrote exultantly to Walsingham on the evening of the Calais action, though at this point nobody believed that the fighting was over, and new supplies of powder, shot and provisions were of vital concern:

> God hath geven us so good a day in forecynge the enemy so far to Leeward, as I hope in God the prince of parma and the duke of Medonya shall not shake hands this ffewe dayes, and when so ever they shall meet, I beleve nether of them will greatly rejoice of this dayes Servis. ... Ther must be great care taken to send us monytyon and vittuall whether so ever the enemy goeth.[26]

Two days later he was still expecting a renewal of the fighting, but was in his chirpiest mood, with a victor's wind in his sails, his handwriting at its very worst, and a joke on his lips:

> We have the armye [i.e. the Armada] of Spayne before us and mynd, with the grace of God, to wressell a poull with him. There was never anything pleased me better than the seeing the enemy flying with a sotherly wynd to the northwarde. God grant you have a good eye to the Duke of Parma, for with the grace of God, yf we live, I doubt it not but ere it be long so to handell the matter with the Duke of Sidonya as he shall wysh hymself at St Mary Port [i.e. Puerto de Santa Maria, near Cadiz] among his orange trees.[27]

By the time Drake wrote again to Walsingham on 18 August the Armada had been beset by storms in the North Sea, had vanished northward, and was on its way to the celebrated shipwrecks on the west coasts of Scotland and Ireland. The letter combines Drake's usual religious triumphalism with an unusual, frank weariness produced by two weeks of battle and vigilance:

> ... To conclude, lett us all with one accord [praise] God, ... who of his only [will] hath sent this proud enemye of his truth where he hath tasted of his power.
> Aboard her Majesty's shipp the Revenge, ...
> Your Honour's most redy to be commanded, and yet now half sleeping,
> Fra. Drake.[28]

In the aftermath, Drake's disappearance on the night of 31 July brought no official censure, and Howard's reports of the incident are untinged by criticism. The Lord Admiral had behaved rather similarly himself in withholding the *Ark Royal* from the main engagement off Calais to try to seize the stranded galleasse. Martin Frobisher, however, was deeply suspicious of Drake's motives and outspokenly critical of him. Frobisher had been in the thick of things in the actions off Portland and the Isle of Wight, and he and Hawkins had been knighted by Howard between the Solent and Calais.

On 21 August one of the *Revenge*'s crew, Matthew Starke, arrived in Harwich with a message from Howard for Lord Sheffield, who had commanded the *White Bear*. He found him in bed at the house of a Mr King. Later he was recalled to the house, where Hawkins, Frobisher and others asked him about the condition of the fleet, and whether the ships were all at Margate. In the course of the conversation Frobisher began slandering the absent Drake, accusing him first of lack of commitment in the opening action:

Sir Fra[ncis]Drake reporteth that no man hath done anye good service but he, but he shall well understand that others hath done as good service as he, and better too. He came braginge up at the first, indede, and gave them hys prowe and hys broade syde, and then kept his lowfe [i.e. steered clear] and was gladde that he was gone agayn, lyke a cowardlye knave or traytor – I rest doubtfull, but the one I will sweare.

The last sentence is not clear, but Frobisher probably meant that Drake might or might not be a coward or a traitor, but was certainly a knave. He went on sarcastically:

He hathe don good service indede, for he tooke don Pedro, for after he had seen her [i.e. the *Rosario*] in the evening, that she had spent her masts, then, lyke a cowarde, he kept by her all nyght, because he wold have the spoyle. He thinketh to cossen us of our shares of XV thousande duckatts, but we will have our shares, or I will make hym spend the best blood in hys belly, for he hath had enowgh of those cossenyng cheats allready. He hath ... used certayne speeches of me, which I will make hym eate againe, or I wyll make hym spende the best blood in hys bellye ... he reporteth that no man hath done so good service as he, but he lyeth in his teeth.

Frobisher then interrogated Starke about the events of the night of 31 July, as Starke later reported:

Then he demanded of me yf we did not see Don Pedro overnyght or no.

Unto the which I answered No. Then he told me that I lyed, for she was seen to all the fleet. Unto the which I answered, I would laye my heade that not anye one man in the ship did see her untyll it was mornynge, that we were within two or three cables length of her. Whereunto he answered, I marye [i.e. Ay, marry!], sayth he, you were within 2 or 3 cables length, for you were no further off all nyght, but laye a-hull by her. Whereunto I answered No, for we beare a good sayle all nyght, off and on.

Then he asked me to what ende we stood off from the fleet all nyght, whome I answered that we had scryed 3 or 4 howlks [i.e. hulks], and to that ende we wrought so, not knowinge what they weare. Then saide he, Sir Francis was apointed to beare a lyght all that nyght, which lyght we looked for, but there was no lyght to be seen, and in the mornyng when we should have dealt with them, there was not above fyve or syx next unto the Admyrall, by reasone we sawe not hys lyght.[29]

All this was reported by Starke when he returned to the fleet, and set down in writing, probably at Drake's insistence. Starke's signature is witnessed by three captains and by the masters of both the *Revenge* and the *Ark Royal*, which probably means that Drake had brought the matter to Howard's notice, and was taking very seriously accusations made in the presence of Hawkins, other senior officers, and a common seaman.

Nothing except Starke's replies to Frobisher survives as evidence in Drake's defence in the matter of the stern lantern, but at least some of his fellow officers saw his action in seizing the *Rosario* as simply what any man of sense might have done in the circumstances. On the other hand, there were a dozen Queen's ships with the capacity to subdue the *Rosario*, including Frobisher's 1,100-ton *Triumph*, but none of them except the *Revenge* broke station. The captain and officers of the *Margaret and John*, which had merely peppered the *Rosario*'s towering sides with musket-shot before sailing away to rejoin Howard, petitioned for a share of the spoils on the grounds that their approach had frightened off the ships which Medina Sidonia had briefly detached to help Valdés. Had it not been for them, they claimed, all the treasure and the men would have been taken off by the Spanish.[30]

The men, officers, and especially Pedro de Valdés were a significant part of the spoil because of their potential for ransom. Valdés and the officers were sent ashore by Drake on 10 August, on the express orders of the Queen.[31] Drake's reply to the order gave a strong hint that he thought Valdés should be his to ransom:

Don Pedro is a man of greatest estimatyon with the King of Spayne, and thought next in his army to the Duke of Sidonya. Yf they should be given from me unto any other, it would be a gref to my friends. Yf her Majesty will have them, God defend but I should think it happye.[32]

Frobisher's feelings over the *Rosario* affair evidently carried little weight with the Queen, who fell in with Drake's wishes. After being interrogated on 14 August Valdés, with two other officers, was sent to the house of Drake's cousin Richard in Esher.[33] Aware that his own detention might be protracted, he took thought for his ordinary seamen and soldiers, whose ransom and repatriation he was negotiating with Walsingham in September.[34] Valdés himself was not ransomed until 1593, much later than some of the other noble prisoners. Drake made his enforced stay as pleasant as possible; another prisoner reported in 1592 that 'Francis Drake, to whom always he hath recourse, hath arranged everything, so as he goeth a-hunting and to other pleasure parties'.[35] The same letter says that Drake was extremely unpopular in England, disliked by the aristocracy as a parvenu and by the rest of society as the cause of the wars.

XVI

THE PORTUGAL PROJECT
1588–89

'We were requested not long ago (ye worthy
warriors of the Lord) ... to show our minds
particularly concerning ... whether we thought
a professor of the true Reformed Religion may
without offence to God aid a Popish king to
recover his kingdom. ... We were glad to hear
that so great commanders in our Prince's affairs
were so divinely minded.'

A group of London ministers to Drake and
Sir John Norris, February 1589

Having survived the Armada by a succession of favourable incidents
in which seamanship and gunnery were acknowledged to have been
helped by winds and storms directed by the hand of a Protestant
Deity, England proceeded by mismanagement to lose the opportunity
granted her to reduce Philip's naval strength to insignificance.
So much depended on that strength: Spain's seaborne support for
her presence in the Low Countries; her supplies of shipbuilding
timber, pitch and cordage from German and Scandinavian ports;
and most importantly, the transatlantic convoys which brought the
gold and silver which underpinned her military effort and her
trade.

Despite the celebrated shipwrecks on the rocks and beaches of
Scotland and Ireland, many of the Armada ships returned to Spain,
battered but basically sound and repairable. Given England's very
slight losses, there was general agreement in the weeks after the
Armada action that it would be a good idea somehow to harry the
Spanish in their home ports. As early as 9 August 1588 Burghley was
writing to Walsingham:

I wish if [the Spanish] pass about Ireland, that 4 good shipps, well manned
and conducted, might follow them to ther ports, wher they might distress

a great numbre of them, being wether beaten, and wher the numbres of the gallants will not contynew on shippboard.[1]

It was thought that most of the surviving ships would reassemble at Lisbon. However, with Philip's ability to defend the seas around the Azores so seriously reduced, it soon occurred to Elizabeth to try to improve the Crown's precarious financial position by seizing his treasure ships as they came from the Indies.[2] Walsingham approached Howard with the suggestion, and found him not unenthusiastic about the idea, but pessimistic about its immediate feasibility.[3] The Lord Admiral's first move was to consult Drake, and on considering the condition of the fleet they quickly concluded that the state of the ships, which all needed careening and cleaning, made the project impossible in the short term. Drake himself took Howard's written reply to Walsingham, and added his own forceful views man to man, on 27 August. John Hawkins too, a week later, was writing to Burghley:

> It is not fit for me to persuade in so great a cause, but I see no reason to doubt the spanyshe fleet; and our shippes utterly unfyttyd and unmeete to follow any enterpryse from hence without a thorowgh new trymmynge, refreshynge, and new fornyshynge with provysions, growndynge, and freshe men.[4]

The plan to attack the treasure fleet was not abandoned; it was subsumed as a third element in an ambitious project involving the destruction of the remnants of the Armada, as suggested by Burghley, and the elevation to the throne of Portugal of the Pretender, Dom Antonio. The success of this plan depended on four things: the assembling of a formidable naval and military invasion force; the presence in the Tagus of the Armada ships; a popular uprising in favour of Dom Antonio in support of a rapid seizure of Lisbon; and swiftness of execution to leave enough time to waylay the Indies fleet in the Azores. The first of these was achieved, very impressively; none of the others materialised. The financial foundations of the project were messy: the Queen could not provide all the money; those she appointed to carry out her aims had a financial interest themselves; and the result was a conflict between royal and private priorities, a situation in which some of the aims of the voyage could only be pursued to the detriment of others.

We do not know who originated this composite plan. There are hints, but only hints, of English support for Dom Antonio in letters from Walsingham to Henry Roberts and from the Queen to Mulay Ahmed of Morocco early in August 1588.[5] Burghley was floating his idea of attacking the Spanish ships in harbour around the same time, and before 27 August Walsingham had sounded out Howard about the Azores excursion. In late August or early September the idea of combining the three plans was discussed and hardened into a project, and a proposal for its financing and execution was invited from Francis Drake and a veteran soldier of the campaigns in the Low Countries, Sir John Norris.

Their scheme, slightly modified after discussion,[6] committed the Queen to contributing six ships 'of the second sort' with guns and three months' victuals, two pinnaces, and the captured *Nuestra Señora del Rosario* and *San Salvador*. She was also to extract from London shipowners, 'by authority or contract', twenty further ships of 150 tons or over, furnish guns and victuals for them, and provide substantial numbers of small arms and £20,000 in cash. The rest of the finance, £43,000, was to come from private adventurers: £20,000 from Norris, his relatives and friends; £10,000 from the City of London; £2,000 from Drake; £6,000 from Drake's friends; and £5,000 from the Leadenhall Company, the group dealing with the profits from the *São Phelipe*. The crews of the Queen's ships were to be paid by the private investors. Twelve thousand men were to be raised: a third from the Queen's Dutch allies; a third English volunteers; and a third pressed men.

Only the elation of recent victory and the vision of forcing Philip to peace by finally smashing his navy, crippling his immediate economy, and possibly prising Portugal from his clutches could have induced Elizabeth to enter into this bargain. Her commitment was, in fact, open-ended, since in the event of the fleet's departure being delayed by more than ten days she was to pay for the extra victualling costs, and if she cancelled the scheme she was to indemnify the adventurers. Financial gain was not the Queen's highest priority, whereas the friends of Drake and Norris, and the London shipowners, some of whom were no doubt coerced into participating, would look to have a decent reward, and had much more interest in the treasure fleet than in burning Philip's navy or in Dom Antonio's future, though the Pretender promised considerable trading concessions in the event of success.[7]

Even Norris and more especially the fanatically Protestant Drake, eager to deal any blow against Philip, must have wondered about the confusion of purposes. Destroy the remnants of Philip's navy, yes;

seize his treasure, certainly; even assault one of his major cities with land forces; all this was familiar work. But to risk their own lives and those of thousands of their Protestant countrymen, not to mention their personal fortunes, to replace one Catholic monarch with another was an odd business.

This last question was the subject of some moral debate. The misgivings of Drake and Norris were such that in November a Mr Nicholas, described as 'preacher of God His Word to that most Christianlike army which Her Majesty sendeth forth against the enemies of Christ', approached the ministers of several London churches individually to ask their views. This may have been Phillip Nicholls, Drake's chaplain on the 1585–86 voyage. The ministers met, discussed the question at length, and reported in February 1589 in a document addressed expressly to Drake and Norris.[8] Not surprisingly, the divines were cautious about crossing Elizabeth. They expressed no enthusiasm for Dom Antonio, but saw the furthering of his claims justified as a way of weakening the greater Papist enemy. This may or may not have been the response Drake and Norris were hoping for, but at least it kept their consciences clear.

Another fly had flown into the ointment of the three-fold plan in September, when Walsingham received a letter from a spy in St Jean de Luz informing him that, far from being gathered in Lisbon, the remains of the Armada were lying in Spanish ports on the Bay of Biscay, 'crying out on Sir Francis Drake, saying that he is a devil and no man'. They had mostly taken refuge in Santander, but seven were as far east as Pasajes, near San Sebastián.[9]

This complication in the profitless aspect of the voyage was to exacerbate the differences between the Queen and the other participants in the enterprise. A diversion to Santander, let alone further east, needed a favourable wind, and a good wind for getting there was a bad wind for getting out again; the fleet could find itself pinned in the Bay for weeks by the same westerlies which would blow Philip's treasure ships past the Azores and to safety. Drake did not refuse to attempt Santander; he did not, as far as we know, argue against it; but at some stage he decided that if there was any defensible way of avoiding the diversion he would leave Santander out of the itinerary.

Drake, now in his late forties, was having health problems at this period. Howard's letter to Walsingham of 12 August 1588 describes him as 'not very well', though he was evidently getting about.[10] He had suffered some spinal or muscular injury; Drake himself, writing to Sir Julius Caesar to excuse himself for not attending the Admiralty Court in January 1589, said that he was

> touched with some grief before my coming out of London, with a strain I took in quenching the fire ... and notwithstanding I have and do use all possible good means by physic following the advice of Doctor Fraunch, I do yet find little ease, for that my pain, not tarrying in one place, is fallen now into my legs and maketh me very unable to stand without much grief.[11]

Norris, however, was all energy, notably in the Low Countries, to where he was despatched in October to negotiate the provision of the Dutch auxiliary forces.[12] Elizabeth's instructions to the two leaders, as drafted by Burghley in late February,[13] set out two clear priorities in the opening paragraph:

> Forasmuch as the chief and principall end of the setting forth of our armie under your charge tendith chiefly to two purposes, the one to distresse the King of Spaines shyppes, the other to gett the possession of some of the Islands of Azores thereby to intercept the convoyes of treasure, ... we would have you directe the whole course of your proceeding in such sort as may best serve to accomplyshe and performe the said two ends and purposes.

They were to seek out Philip's ships in any of the ports of Guipuzcoa, Biscay or Galicia, and were also to attack any vessels found in Lisbon. The addition of Galicia to the range of possibilities suggests that further intelligence had been received, but Elizabeth may have come to regret the inclusion, since it gave Drake a loophole to choose Galicia and ignore the Bay of Biscay ports further east. The scheme to take Lisbon and install Dom Antonio as king is included in the instructions, but is wrapped in ifs and buts:

> And in case upon inquirie you shall find that neyther the love borne unto him is so great as he pretendeth and that the forces of the King of Spaine are such as nothing can be attempted without verie great hazard, our pleasure is that you shall then forbeare to attempt aniething towards Lishburn ... other than the destroying of the shippes there. But in case you shall find upon good ground that the partie that Don Anthonio hath there is great, ... as also that the King of Spaine hath not drawne downe into that realm anie such great forces, ... then wee think it a thing most honorable to be performed.

If Portugal could be induced to rise in support of Dom Antonio, the Azores project could be made much easier, since his authority as king would extend to the islands and he would be likely to authorise full use of harbour and watering facilities because of his gratitude. After long and detailed instructions about relations with Dom Antonio, hedged about with reservations, Burghley reiterated the Queen's main desire: the destruction of Philip's naval ships, to ensure the success of the voyage's other aspects and to protect against a repetition of the Armada:

> to the end that, ... the said shippes remayning entyer and undistressed, they may not, seeing such a number of shippes and mariners employed under you out of the realm upon that coast, take encouragement in the time of your absence to attempt somewhat against this our realm or our realm of Ireland.

By mid-March most of the expeditionary force had been gathered at Dover. The contributions of the Dutch had been slow in arriving. Expenses exceeded the initial estimates, and there were problems in finding enough troopships. This last difficulty was removed by a windfall when Drake was sailing for Plymouth on 16 March: around sixty Dutch fly-boats of 100 or 200 tons, on their way to France to load salt, were seized and incorporated into the fleet.[14] They were sorely needed, because Drake and Norris had enthusiastically raised considerably more men than had been at first envisaged; the number was probably nearer to 17,000 than 12,000. This increase, together with a further delay of a month due to unfavourable winds, caused serious victualling and financial problems; Drake and Norris had spent all the money in their hands, and had to dip into their sea-stores to feed their ever-increasing force. They had to appeal to Elizabeth for more money, and by invoking the clause in their pro-posal under which she was to pay for extra victualling caused by adverse winds, and coupling it with an allusion to the likelihood of widespread rioting by hungry and unpaid crews if the expedition had to be cancelled, they persuaded an increasingly irritated Queen to part with more money.

Elizabeth's temper was tested further by the development of a bizarre subplot. On 3 April her wayward favourite, the young Earl of Essex, left London on horseback without her permission and galloped to Plymouth to join the expedition. Elizabeth sent his uncle, Sir Francis Knollys, in pursuit, but by the time Knollys reached Plymouth the Earl had put to sea on the Queen's own ship, the *Swiftsure*, accompanied by a number of his friends, including Sir

Roger Williams, the Colonel-General of the Infantry, and a group of his own men.

Essex was deep in debt, and must have counted on a dazzling success in Portugal and the Azores to restore his fortunes and cajole the Queen into forgiving him. Drake and Norris almost certainly knew something of his intentions, but played the innocents. When Knollys arrived they sent him off in a pinnace after Essex and wrote to the Privy Council that the *Swiftsure* had vanished and they 'had entered into some mistrust and suspicion of the Earl's departure to sea', and were using all possible means to procure his return. Knollys' pinnace returned in unfavourable weather, and the *Swiftsure* was forced into Falmouth, but there is no evidence that Drake and Norris contacted Essex overland during the next ten days while the wind kept the ships in harbour, though Drake did claim to be seeking him by land and sea and to be expecting daily to hear from him.[15] The tone of Elizabeth's later correspondence barely stops short of accusing Drake and Norris of complicity in the affair; in the draft of a letter of 4 May some of the phrasing included and then scored out is very revealing of her rage at being crossed and her suspicion of treachery.[16]

Drake and Norris had hoped to sail early in February 1589. Every day's delay was another day's grace for the shipwrights, riggers and sailmakers working on the rehabilitation of Philip's navy; another day lost from the demanding Santander–Lisbon–Azores itinerary. Drake and Norris began preparing the ground for missing out Santander. On 6 April they wrote to the Privy Council:

> We have of late receaved verie credible advertisement that there are arrived to the number of *200 saile of shippes* of divers nations at *the Groyne* [i.e. La Coruña] *and other* portes of *Galizia* and Portugal, with stoare of munition, mastes, cables, and other provisions for the enemye. And therefore we resolve with all the speed we maie, if the wind will not suffer us to beare *with Biscay* and those partes, to attempt the destroying of the shipping in the foresaid coasts of Galizia and Portugal.[17]

The letter goes on to ask for extra provisions to be sent after them, either to Cape Finisterre or the Bayona islands. Their thinking is transparent. They had decided to avoid going to Santander and Pasajes if there was the least excuse for going straight to Galicia. Lisbon, with its promise of spoil, was their main target, followed by the chance of intercepting the treasure ships off the Azores; going to Santander, or worse, Pasajes, would risk becoming embayed for weeks, which would jeopardise the prospects of gain, or even breaking even, for their friends the investors. La Coruña was a compromise which would enable them to claim that they had done their best to carry out the Queen's orders before proceeding to Lisbon.

Essex, who must have had some discussion with Drake about the plans for Lisbon before he vanished in the *Swiftsure*, certainly did not head for Santander. Nor did anyone else when the fleet, at long last, set sail from Plymouth on Friday, 18 April 1589.

XVII

AN HUMOUR OF VAINGLORY:
LA CORUÑA
1589

'By reason of our army staying in Galicia ...
before we arrived at Lisbon, they had twenty
days' respite to arm and put themselves in order.
But had our army not touched at the Groyne
and sailed straight to Lisbon as the Earl of
Essex did, neither soldier nor captain can deny
but the town had been ours.'

Sir Roger Williams, *A Brief Discourse of War*,
1590

Numerically, the fleet was large; easily the biggest ever commanded by Drake. The additional Dutch transports had increased the total number to about 180. They were divided into five squadrons, each led by one of the Queen's ships.[1] Drake led the first squadron in the 500-ton *Revenge*, with his brother Thomas as captain; the second squadron was led by Captain Sackville in the 500-ton *Nonpareil*; Thomas Fenner, the vice-admiral, was in the 400-ton *Dreadnought* at the head of the third; and the fifth was led by William Wynter in the 300-ton *Foresight*. The fourth squadron was to have been led by the *Swiftsure*, Captain Goring, but she had gone with Essex. Possibly the only other large royal ship, the *Aid*, originally named as a liaison vessel, took over the leadership of the *Swiftsure*'s squadron under William Fenner. Drake was later criticised for completely ignoring the division into squadrons in his conduct of the expedition,[2] but as there was no real naval action to test the organisation of the fleet in this respect the criticism may be unfounded. There were about 23,000 men aboard, of whom only some 4,000 were mariners.

Despite these impressive statistics, it was not a perfectly equipped force with which to invade a foreign country and usurp its monarchy, especially since its logistical support was so vaguely organised, and its intentions so distractingly focused. Two of Elizabeth's aims, destroying Philip's ships and seizing his treasure, were jobs for mariners; 19,000 of the men aboard were dead wood except for the execution of the third aim, putting Dom Antonio on the throne. Feeding and watering such a large body of men was a serious concern to Drake and Norris; there was a shortage of ordnance suitable for storming Lisbon; and a large proportion of the army were inexperienced and pressed men. Even the size of the fleet is misleading; only four of the Queen's ships (excluding *Swiftsure*) were of 300 tons or greater, and most of the private vessels were under 200 tons.

After a couple of days of west-south-west winds in which the ships became scattered, Drake lay off Ushant to let them regather, and found that about twenty of them, mostly Dutch transports, were missing. On Monday 21 April the wind came round to the north-east,[3] which would have been welcome enough to a shipmaster with instructions to go to Santander, or even to Pasajes. Drake claimed later that the wind was too easterly to set a course for Santander, but this does not hold water: some of the separated ships, no doubt glad enough to have given Drake the slip, sailed to La Rochelle, so Drake could certainly have held a course for Santander at least. The wind was even fairer, however, for Galicia; after a brisk passage which must have raised spirits after all the delays, the fleet sighted Cape Ortegal on Wednesday, 23 April 1589, and at four o'clock on the following afternoon they were anchoring in La Coruña roads.

Drake's interest in La Coruña was no surprise to Philip. Whether he had been warned by the report of a spy, or whether he had come to know his enemy well enough to foresee his thinking, the arrival of the fleet was expected. In a despatch as early as the end of October the king had underlined a warning to be alert for possible attacks on ships in Spanish ports, 'especially La Coruña, for they are determined to send and burn them'.[4] In March, again, on receipt of intelligence about English preparations, he had written a marginal memo 'to give notice of this to La Coruña and Santander'.[5]

Drake found the port almost empty. If the '200 sail of divers nations' existed anywhere outside the persuasive imagination of Drake and Norris and their letter to the Privy Council, they were anchored somewhere other than La Coruña. The only vessels of any note in the harbour were one large Armada galleon, the *San Juan*; a 1,000-ton Biscayan ship; and two other large cargo vessels, one of which was being careened. There was a smaller ship with a cargo of pikes and muskets, a few minor craft, and two galleys.

The bay or harbour of La Coruña is large and pincer-shaped. The point of the peninsula which forms the western side of the bay was occupied by the high town, strongly fortified and half-surrounded by the sea. Immediately to the south of this fortress area, and encircling it from the bay to the sea, was an area called the base town. A hostile vessel entering the bay had to contend not only with the batteries of the high town, but also with those of an island fort, San Antonio, in the mouth of the harbour. Drake was also faced with the two galleys, which emerged into the roadstead as he was anchoring.

Battering the ramparts of the high town with gunfire from the sea would have been a long and unfruitful business. Norris had an army of men, at least some of whom were thirsty for action, and many of whom were thirsty for women and drink. Everyone was hungry for spoils. The two leaders decided on a plan similar in some respects to the one which had succeeded at Cartagena. The base town was defended against attack on the landward side by a wall and a dry ditch; the waterfront of the base town, in contrast to the high town, was unfortified.

Drake and Norris wasted no time. Soon after the fleet arrived the pinnaces and boats began landing men about a mile from the town. The intention was to take the base town that night. In about three hours there were 7,000 men ashore, but as the night turned to storm and rain the attack was postponed, and the men took whatever shelter they could in the hamlets, mills and stables outside the town. During the night and on into the morning the men ashore were under fire from the Spanish ships and the galleys, but when two demi-culverins had been landed and returned the fire, the galleys made off towards El Ferrol, across the bay. The English gunners worked to such effect against the other ships that by evening, in John Evesham's words, 'we might stand upon the land and see through the ships as through glass windows, we did so tear them with our pieces'.[6]

Norris reconnoitred the base town defences that morning and decided on a three-pronged attack. The unfortified waterfront was to be assaulted by Vice-Admiral Fenner and Colonel Huntly with 1,200 men in long-boats and pinnaces, with small cannon aboard to soften up the defenders as they approached the shore. Five hundred men under Captains Wingfield and Sampson were to enter around the seaward end of the wall if possible (rather as Carleill's men had done at Cartagena), or otherwise to storm it with scaling ladders. The eastern, or harbour end of the wall was to be stormed by Colonel Umpton and Colonel Brett with 300 men. Two shots from the demi-culverins were to be fired into the town to co-ordinate the assault. Things went well, though not perfectly. Between midnight and two o'clock the long-boats and pinnaces were filled with soldiers. The signal was fired a little in advance of low tide; too soon for Wingfield and Sampson, who found too great a depth of water preventing them from simply entering around the end of the wall, and had to use scaling ladders against strong resistance.

Fortunately the boat landings from the harbour were largely unopposed, and a Captain Hendar's company not only cleared the wall of defenders at the harbour end, enabling Umpton and Brett to enter easily, but continued round the wall and took the defenders at the other end in the rear after Wingfield and Sampson's men had been beaten back twice. All the defenders who could took refuge within the ramparts of the high town, and the English soldiers and their Dutch allies ran unchecked through the base town, committing murder and pillage fuelled by Spanish wine.

On the galleon *San Juan*, already severely damaged by Norris's demi-culverins, the crew had watched the invaders pour ashore into the base town. With no hope of saving their ship, they loaded most of her guns with a double charge of powder, set fire to her, and escaped as best they could. She burned for two days, with sporadic explosions; when the English were finally able to board her they found only sixteen of her fifty guns whole, the rest having been shattered by their double charge or melted by the heat.[7] Even the fragments were taken to be melted down and recast in England. The other ships were easily seized, and their guns removed.

There was no spoil of West Indian dimensions in the base town, which consisted largely of fishermen's cottages and warehouses, but there were plenty of provisions to gladden the heart of commanders of a large army: 2,000 pipes of wine, 1,000 jars of oil, large amounts of preserved beef, salt fish, beans, peas, wheat and biscuit. Unfortunately the distribution of this windfall among the fleet was ill-organised; some ships received nothing and suffered great hardship later. Much of these provisions, and the stores of cordage, small arms, etc., were said by a captured victualling commissioner called Juan de Vera to be the basis of supply stocks for a new Armada to invade England. Drake's and Norris's report[8] naturally made much of this aspect of things to justify their attack on La Coruña; of their earlier justification, the phantom 200 sail of ships, nothing more was said.

In the taking of the base town 500 Spaniards were killed, many of them innocent townspeople cowering in cellars. A day later a raggle-taggle force of about 2,000 Spaniards, mustered from the surrounding countryside, marched to relieve the town, but after losing about eighteen men in a short exchange of fire with the men guarding the gate they took to their heels and were chased a couple of miles through the fields, where more of them were killed. The English then seem to have wandered at will seven or eight miles inland, burning, ravaging and seizing cattle and sheep.

If Drake had been in sole command, the attack on La Coruña might very well have ended at that point. As on earlier occasions, he had successfully raided a harbour and destroyed its shipping, reducing defending galleys to impotence; he had landed a military force which had stormed the town's defences and seized or destroyed large amounts of enemy war materials and provisions. Everything pertinent to the stated aims of the expedition had been achieved, to the limited extent to which it could be achieved in this port. The sailors, however, were greatly outnumbered by the soldiers, not only at rank-and-file level, but also among the officers, and the force ashore was under the direction not of Drake, but of Norris. To such a seasoned and enthusiastic player in the great game of war, his spirits raised by an easy victory, the ramparts of an enemy town presented a challenge beside which reasoned long-term objectives might fade temporarily into abeyance. Norris decided to take the upper town by direct assault on the walls.

His attempt was twofold. An attack from the sea being out of the question, he installed two demi-cannons and two culverins in a cloister in the lower town, with his brother Sir Edward, Master of the Ordnance, in charge. The intention was to batter a breach in the walls of the upper town on the south side. Further round the wall the pioneers began digging a mine under one of the towers. Drake, meanwhile, was busy with his pinnaces attacking the island fort. He was criticised later for not keeping a better eye on the two galleys, which brought reinforcements and supplies to the town from the seaward side.[9]

After setting up his battery Norris tried to negotiate. In an episode which smacks of the Middle Ages, he sent a lone drummer to the walls to summon the defenders to a parley. The drummer was promptly shot. The outrage at this indecency was felt as keenly inside the walls as out; the culprit was thrown from the wall with a rope round his neck and protestations from the defenders of fair play in the future. A brief parley about prisoners and surrender came to nothing; this was hardly surprising in view of the drunken slaughter in the base town.

Both Norris's assault schemes stuttered and eventually failed. The first couple of rounds from his cannon broke one of the gun carriages and shook down the wall of the cloister, leaving his gunners open to fire from the ramparts which killed several men, including Mr Spencer, Edward Norris's lieutenant. Norris ceased fire overnight, reorganised his position, and resumed firing in the morning. After three days of digging the mine was thought adequate, and by then the cannon had opened a small breach in the upper half of the wall. The assaults at the two points were co-ordinated; the men made ready, and the train of powder was lit. Most of the explosion blew outwards, the mine having been made too high, and the tower still stood. Two more days' digging took the mine well into the foundations, and this time half the tower fell down, leaving a large breach and a pile of rock and rubble.

The leading troops of the assault parties, the 'forlorn hopes' as they were called, with ensigns waving and pikemen to the fore, rushed to clamber up the two breaches. As they reached the top of the confused pile of masonry the men attacking over the mine heard a rumbling roar, and turned to see the rest of the tower collapsing over their fellows lower down. Twenty or thirty were crushed; Captain Sydenham was pinned down by a mass of masonry on his legs, and the assault dissolved in panic.

The men at the other breach fared little better. Having clambered up to the gap in the top of the wall and begun thrusting at the defenders with their pikes, the forlorn hope felt their footholds moving as the pile of rubble gave way beneath them. They slid and tumbled over one another and retired in confusion through a narrow lane where they suffered casualties from the musketeers on the ramparts. At one of the breeches the heroic behaviour of a woman, María Pita, who continued fighting and exhorting the defenders even after seeing her husband killed, is said by local legend to have been a major factor in repelling the attack.[10]

The following day, after ten or twelve men had been lost in brave but fruitless attempts to extract Sydenham, news reached Norris of a threat from a Spanish force of 8,000 or 10,000 men preparing to relieve the siege, and presently encamped at Puente de Burgo, five or six miles away. He set off with nine regiments, leaving Drake with five to maintain the presence in the base town. Norris's vanguard, under his brother Edward, came on a small force of the enemy, and after an initial charge beat them back from rock to rock and wall to wall towards the bridge at Puente de Burgo.

The Spanish retired over the bridge, which was long and only wide enough for three men to walk abreast, and rejoined their main force encamped on the other side. The English, unprotected against intense Spanish musketry, lost about 150 men in two fruitless assaults on the bridge before it was finally carried; the defence dissolved, to be followed by riot and slaughter. 'How many two thousand men ... might kill in pursuit of foure sundry parties, so many you may imagine fell before us that day', wrote Captain Anthony Wingfield.[11] Drake and Norris reported to the Privy Council that over 1,000 of the enemy had been killed, and regretted not having been able to increase the number: 'Had we had some companies of Irish kernes to have pursued them, there had none of them escaped'.[12] Norris sent companies this way and that to burn and spoil, and the sky that night was lit up by 'the countrey more than three miles compasse on fire'. With some captured munitions and food, and some fancy clothing and plate abandoned by the Spanish officers, a satisfied Norris marched his men back to La Coruña.

The attempt on the high town was now given up (largely, it was later claimed, because Drake and Norris had not been provided with the heavy ordnance they had requested for such purposes). After an abortive attempt to set fire to some houses on the top of the wall on the waterfront, and when the entire lower town had been put to the torch, the army re-embarked on 8 May.

The fleet weighed anchor on the following morning, with the wind in the south-west,[13] an ideal quartering wind for Santander. Drake and Norris must have known that the repairs to Philip's ships in Santander were well advanced, since it was common knowledge in La Coruña that the whole fleet was to rendezvous in the Galician port at the end of May. Norris went aboard the *Revenge*, where Drake and he consulted with Thomas Drake, Sackville of the *Nonpareil*, and their masters, Thomas West and Robert Wignal. Later Drake and Norris laid much of the responsibility for the decision now taken not to go to Santander on the shoulders of these senior mariners,

the masters withal, and especially Weste and Wignall, refusing utterly to undertake the conduction of the navy thither. Whereunto the Generals were the more easily induced to condescend, remembringe a former advice given by Sir John Hawkins declaring how perilous it would be for such a navy to enter into that Bay out of the which the same would hardly have bene broughte agayne untill time and victuall had bene so farre spent as that thereby the enterprise would have bene utterly overthrowne.[14]

Drake's old vice-admiral, William Borough, who complained so bitterly of lack of consultation during the Cadiz raid, must have shaken his head sardonically when he heard about this piece of supportive committee work.

Drake and Norris, rather surprisingly for 'two so overweening spirits',[15] appear to have got on very well during the Galician operation. There was certainly a reciprocal respect between them, and their combined actions had gone smoothly. There is a hint in a letter from Thomas Fenner to Burghley that the easiness of their relationship was perhaps a surprise; he begs 'that my gracyous Mystress herebie maie have knowledge of the greate love and concord betwene our generalls, nothinge dowtinge the contynuaunce of the same'.[16]

The two brothers-in-arms sent Sir William Knollys off to England with a letter to the Privy Council saying that they were taking the first fair wind for Portugal, understanding the bulk of Philip's navy to be in Lisbon. They proposed to return to Santander later if possible, though their lack of heavy ordnance would make an attack on Santander a doubtful proposition.[17] In the absence of a fair wind for Portugal, they battled their way close-hauled through a foul one for days trying to round Cape Finisterre. Men had begun to fall sick; a few more of the Dutch transports seized their chance and ran for La Rochelle. In Santander and Pasajes the shipwrights and riggers carried on unmolested, restoring Philip's ships to fighting condition. Edmund Palmer wrote a month later:

> If Sir Francis had gone to Santander as he went to the Groyne, he had done such service as never subject had done, For with twelve sail of his ships he might have destroyed all the forces which the Spaniards had there, which was the whole strength of the country by sea. There they did ride all unrigged and their ordnance on shore and some 20 men in a ship only to keep them. It was far overseen that he had not gone thither first.[18]

XVIII

Viva Dom Antonio!: Events at the Tagus

1589

'When we arrived, had our navy entered, we
would have entered the town, or the world
should have witnessed so many Englishmen had
been buried in that place. . . . Notwithstanding,
we gave them the law 30 days in their
countries.'

Sir Roger Williams, *A Brief Discourse of War*,
1590

When Elizabeth read Drake's and Norris's account of the events at
La Coruña and their departure for Lisbon, her blood turned to vitriol.
First the excessive costs; then the departure of Essex, still unaccounted
for; now a total neglect by her commanders of her most pressing
instruction and a demand for more soldiers, guns and supplies. The
draft of her reply of 20 May, full of angry rephrasings and scorings-
out, reminds them that

> your first and principall action should be to take and distresse the King
> of Spains Navye and shippes in porte where they laye, which yf ye did not
> ye affirmed that ye were content to be reputed as traytors . . . We find that
> contrary thereunto ye have left two of the chiefest places where the said
> Kings shippes laye and passed to the Groyne, being a place of least hurt
> to be done to the enemy.[1]

The letter blames the shortage of provision and powder on Drake
and Norris, points out that the favourable wind which brought Sir
William Knollys so quickly to England would have taken them to
Santander, and repeats her demand that their main target should be
Philip's navy. By now she was even less keen on any long embroilment
with Portugal:

Ye may proceede by such means as most convenyently ye may to the restoring of Don Antonyo without making these your proceedings to be any quarrell and without any long abode in Portugall otherwise than to sette him there, but to direct your course to the Islands of Azores according to your instructions. ... we must putt you in mynde that you suffer not yourselves transported with an humour of vainglory which will offuscate the eyes of your judgement.

A few days earlier she had said to Thomas Windebank, a Clerk of the Signet, that 'they went to places more for proffitt than for serviss'.[2]

By the time the Queen was putting her emphatic signature on this letter, things had happened off the coast of Galicia which would have made her even angrier. On 13 May a large ship of war appeared: the long-lost *Swiftsure*, with Essex and Sir Roger Williams. Essex had been ranging down the coast of Portugal, and almost to Cadiz, waiting for Drake and the opportunity to distinguish (and enrich) himself in a dashing action against Lisbon. He had captured a few grain ships off Cape St Vincent, and led a small foray ashore near Vigo on his way north again. The inhabitants of Vigo must have come to feel that plundering their region was an obligatory preparatory overture for English expeditions rounding Cape Finisterre at this period; the broad, safe anchorage in the *Ría* made the area a natural target.

Drake and Norris probably groaned inwardly at the sight of the *Swiftsure*. In Plymouth they had fudged the issue of their complicity, but must have known that the Queen suspected them. At the time of Essex's reappearance they had almost certainly not yet received the letter drafted by Elizabeth on 4 May in which her distrust sizzles out of every sentence.[3] Much of her earlier rage against her favourite had by now shifted towards Roger Williams; she thunders against his treachery, demands his demotion and arrest, and hints that it would be within the authority of Drake and Norris to try him and execute him. Essex was to be sent home immediately. The Queen's phrasing would make strong men tremble:

... you will answere for the contrary at your perille. For as we have authoritie to rule, so we looke to be obeyed and to have obedience directly and surely contynued unto us, ... otherwise we will think you unworthy of the authoritie ye have and that ye knowe not how to use it, ... which if you do not, you shall looke to answere for the same to your smart, for these be weighty actions, nor matters wherein ye are to deale by cunning of devices to seek evasions as the custom of lawyers is; neither will [we] be so satisfied at your hands. Therefore consider well of your doings herein.

It is possible that this letter was never sent. If a good north-east wind had brought it to Drake and Norris before the *Swiftsure* hove into view, they would, surely, have taken some measures against Essex, or at the very least against Williams. Not only was the Earl accepted into the expedition, however; he was granted his demand that he should lead the vanguard of the land forces against Lisbon. In his insufferable way he had already created his own little army command on the *Swiftsure*, like a child playing with toy soldiers. Blind to his own naivety and self-importance, he explained later that

> I could take noe second place, having att the same tyme and in the same Armye place above the Generall. But thoughe I had no chardge, yet I made my brother Generall of the Horse [the whole expedition had only forty-four horses], my faithful friend Sir Roger Williams Colonell General of the Infanterie, seven or eight of my fast friends Colonells, and 20 at the least of my domesticks Captains, soe as I might have authority and party enough when I would.[4]

When the army landed at Peniche in Portugal on 16 May it was, indeed, led ashore by the Earl, his brother, and Williams. It is not clear whether the landing was mismanaged or the place ill-chosen; Wingfield's account says that the boats and pinnaces were in gunshot range from the castle, and that men waded ashore up to their armpits in water. One boat capsized in heavy seas and twenty-five men were drowned. Peniche is about fifty miles north of Lisbon, so that any element of surprise remaining after La Coruña was surrendered. Peniche had, in fact, been selected as the landing-place well before the departure from England, and Philip had been informed of the fact by a traitor in Antonio's household, Manuel de Andrada.[5] The thinking may have been that the march from Peniche to Lisbon would give time for Antonio's support in Portugal to rally to him and to organise the surrender of Lisbon from within. Drake afterwards, and possibly in advance, thought the choice of Peniche was a bad one.[6]

Initially, however, despite the awkward landing, things went well; Dom Antonio must have been encouraged by the events of the first twenty-four hours. As soon as Essex had enough men ashore he divided them into two troops. Leaving one to keep the landing-place he led the other across the sandhills to engage a force of defenders. After some close-quarter work with the pikes in which a Captain

Pugh was killed and a few rank-and-file injured, the enemy broke and withdrew inland, leaving the town completely unprotected. The Portuguese commander of the castle garrison, called on by Norris to surrender, opened the gates on the mere assurance that Antonio had landed. On the following day, while the army's small force of cavalry was being brought ashore, a group of friars came to assure the Pretender that within two days his supporters would have rallied to him in strength.

So far, so good; but the army had been increasingly weakened by sickness, desertions and casualties; it had very few cavalry and no heavy ordnance. It was also fifty miles from its objective, with no way of transporting munitions except on the backs of the soldiers, though this was soon remedied by the seizure of carts. The plan was for Norris, with the bulk of the army, to march overland to Lisbon, and for Drake to take the fleet into the Tagus to rejoin and support him. One company of foot was left in the castle at Peniche, and six more in the ships. The two commanders parted and Norris led his men away southward, set on their way by a cordial Drake, who,

> although hee were to passe by Sea, yet to make knowen the honourable desire he had of taking equall part of all fortunes with us, stood upon the ascent of a hill by the which our battalions must of necessity march, and with a pleasing kindnesse tooke his leave severally of the Commanders of every regiment, wishing us all most happy success in our journey over the land, with a constant promise that he would, if the injury of the weather did not hinder him, meet us in the river of Lisbon with our fleet.[7]

The events of the next few days were to strain this cordial relationship, and Drake's decisions were to cast a shadow on him over and above the doubts raised by earlier actions for which responsibility was shared with Norris.

After five days' march Norris was three miles from Lisbon. There had been one or two brief skirmishes with hovering enemy cavalry and foot, and false alarms of impending encounters with entrenched forces, but the invaders had marched virtually unchecked. The army was carrying few supplies of its own, but pillaging the countryside had been banned as a gesture towards Antonio, and victualling began to give concern from the second day onwards. The situation was eased after Sir Roger Williams approached Antonio for help, or at least permission, to obtain supplies from the villages. Fourteen men of Drake's own regiment were killed by an enemy force which was accepted into their camp professing support for Antonio, and many men sickened and died after drinking contaminated water. Others, weakened by hunger, fainted in the heat, and 'divers were saved by ... the Earl of Essex, who commanded all his stuff to be cast out of his carriages and to be laden with sick men and gentlemen that fainted'.[8]

Despite the many cries of 'Viva Dom Antonio!' along the road, tangible signs of a popular uprising were slow in appearing. A group of barefooted peasants arrived, as did some more friars and a few gentlemen on horseback, and a lady gave the Pretender a bowl of plums and cherries, but the rest of the population were biding their time.

Drake, meanwhile, had left a ship and two fly-boats at Peniche to serve the garrison, and was taking the rest of the fleet south. He anchored off Cascais, in the approach to the Tagus estuary, on 20 May, unworried by some tentative fire from the small battery in the castle. The next day he landed with about 1,500 men, and was met by a few Portuguese sympathetic to Antonio who guided him through the town. Apart from a couple of ineffective shots from the castle, the town was occupied without resistance, and people came out to give bread and wine to the soldiers. One of the minor horrors of war emerges from John Evesham's account: 'This town was, at our first coming to it, a most sweet town and cleanly kept; but when our soldiers had kept it one week, it was a place most loathsome.'[9]

A fleet lying at Cascais could play no part in an attack on Lisbon other than by re-embarking the army afterwards. Norris needed Drake at Lisbon, and that was where Philip's warships were lying. Drake's arrival in Lisbon roads should have coincided with Norris's attack on the city itself. On the estuary, between Drake and the city, were some formidable obstacles: the fort of São Julião, with its sixty cannon and a strong garrison of horse and foot; and a force of twelve galleys lying under the protection of the castle batteries and waiting for Drake to make a move. Sir William Monson, writing a few decades later, described São Julião as 'one of the most impregnable forts to seaward in Europe'.[10]

On the morning of 25 May came the news that Norris was on the outskirts of Lisbon. This was Drake's cue to sail. Instead of doing so, he called a council of captains and masters.[11] Their opinion, 'for sundry good reasons', was that it would be highly dangerous to pass up the estuary to Lisbon. Why it should be more dangerous now than when the original plan of the voyage had been made, or when they had waved Norris on his way a few days before, nobody has explained. It is interesting that at two key points in the voyage, after La Coruña and now, the masters should have been included in the discussions. They were mariners, not tactical decision-makers; their function was to sail their ships to comply with the requirements of Drake and his council of captains. The reason why a mariner would be reluctant to sail into the Tagus was the same as the one which had made the masters unwilling to sail east into the Bay of Biscay to Santander: the fear of not getting out again. If the wind were to fail, or turn to a strong westerly, the ships could be pinned in the Tagus at the mercy of the galleys and whatever ordnance the Spanish chose to bring against them. When Columbus took refuge in the Tagus in the battered *Niña* in 1493 he found that the westerlies had kept ships waiting to sail for weeks, and in 1588 the Armada was pinned in the Tagus for a fortnight, consuming provisions, until the north-west wind changed. None of this, however, alters the fact that this aspect of the situation had been known by Drake from the outset.

Another of the 'sundry good reasons' may have been the sickness and weakness of the crews, many of whom were incapable of hauling on a rope. Nevertheless, Drake, by his own account, decided to ignore the views of his masters and captains, and prepared to move up to Lisbon if he could. The possibility of being trapped by a change of wind had not deterred him at Cadiz, nor at Cartagena, and it did not deter him now. Nor did the strength of the fort; Drake probably shared Monson's view that 'the passing in by it was not the greatest danger, for with a reasonable gale of wind any fort is to be passed with small adventure'.[12] He ordered two-thirds of his strongest and best-manned ships to move to the south side of the estuary, away from the guns of the fort, ready to take the first good wind for Lisbon.

The good wind came on the 27th, too late. On the previous night Norris's men marched into Cascais, having abandoned the attempt on Lisbon. In the absence of evidence of any serious internal support for Antonio, it had never looked like succeeding. The army had run short of provisions, powder and shot. In sporadic street-fighting in the outskirts Norris lost several officers and men, and without heavy artillery he stood little chance of taking the inner town unless there were some revolt within the walls.

There were attempts inside Lisbon to muster support for Antonio, but they were easily and savagely suppressed.[13] Two monks who plotted with one of the Pretender's retinue to admit the invaders through the garden of the Trinidade monastery were betrayed by their prior and had their heads chopped off and put on public display.

Men of any position who were suspected of favouring Antonio were arrested. After a couple of days Norris debated with his senior officers on whether to continue the siege and send to Cascais for artillery. Some supported the idea; others, with no faith in Antonio's promise of the imminent arrival of 3,000 Portuguese reinforcements, argued for giving up.

Norris, warned of the approach of a Spanish relief force under the Duke of Braganza and Don Francisco de Toledo, decided to hold on for one more night; if the Portuguese reinforcements came, he would send for artillery and continue the siege; if not, he would march away. On the following morning, when 'all [Dom Antonio's] horse could not make a cornet of forty nor his foot furnish two ensigns, though they carried three or four colours', Norris retired to Cascais.

On 1 June word came that a large enemy force was marching towards São Julião. Norris and Essex were delighted at the thought of action after so much frustration, and again the mediaeval roots of Tudor warfare resurfaced: Norris sent a trumpeter to challenge the Spanish to a pitched battle near Cascais, and Essex indulged his own Arthurian fantasies by sending an individual challenge to Lieutenant-General Count Pedro de Fuentes; he would, he said, be waiting at the head of the vanguard 'with ... a red scarf upon his left arm and on his casque a great plume of feathers of sundry colours, where he meant to stand so close to him that would give a like signant of himself as his rapier should be long enough to encounter with the longest pike that should be used against him'.[14] Both challenges were ignored.

Cascais castle had by now surrendered feebly, but although there was some talk of a renewed attempt on Lisbon[15] morale had sunk very low, and assessments of the state of the army were appalling. John Evesham later wrote that nearly 2,000 soldiers had died between the landing at Peniche and the arrival of the land forces in Cascais, very few of them because of enemy action,[16] and on 2 June Drake and Norris reported in a letter to the Privy Council that the army had only 5,735 fit men and 2,791 sick.

The day after writing that letter, weary of Portugal and the empty promises of the Pretender, they decided to sail to the Azores to carry out the third, and potentially the most remunerative, aim of the expedition. On the 6th they received the Queen's energetic letter of 20 May, which was cool on the subject of Portugal and distinctly warm on the subject of disobedience, and this can only have confirmed their resolve to salvage something profitable and impressive from the voyage by waylaying the Indies fleet.

Drake weighed anchor on 8 June. By dawn on the following day the sails were drooping in a dead calm. This was an ideal situation for the Spanish galleys, whose flotilla had been increased to twenty-one by the arrival of nine more from Andalusia, and they seized their opportunity. They were wary of taking on Drake's larger ships and concentrated on some of the smaller stragglers, some of which were short of powder and shot. The *William*, owned by John Hawkins, came under heavy attack and was abandoned by her master and crew after they had tried to set fire to her. Drake's galleons were doing all they could to make progress to help the stragglers, with upper sails set to catch the lightest offering of a breeze and the boats towing them by the bows, and the *Revenge* managed to put a shot close enough to the galleys to make them abandon the *William*. They turned their attention to her boats, one of which was swamped with the loss of all its occupants, including Captain Calverley of the land forces.

Another small vessel, under Captain Minshaw, fought hard and long, but was finally seen to be on fire and was lost. John Evesham and his shipmates on the *Gregory*, becalmed and alone well to the leeward of the fleet, saw three galleys rowing towards them. A shot was fired to attract the attention of the larger ships, and the crew prepared to sell their lives dearly. They were saved by the *Dreadnought*, which struggled towards the *Gregory*, towed by her three boats and helped by a providential breath of wind catching her sails. The *William* was reboarded by the English, but with her crew mostly drowned men could not be spared to bring her away, and she was stripped and burned.

The galleys' achievements, in conditions favouring them, had again been rather meagre, but the manning situation in the fleet had by now grown really serious. Not only had there been large losses through sickness; during the stay at Cascais Drake had captured about sixty French and Dutch cargo vessels heading into the Tagus with wheat and provisions, and his decision to bring these away with him had further depleted the crews of his own ships. John Evesham reckoned that when Drake left the Tagus he had 230 ships, including the prizes and several victualling ships arrived from England. To hold them together, undercrewed and full of sickness as they were, proved impossible.

Drake's sailing instructions for the fleet were intended to enable

A Catalan depiction of a square-rigged ship attacked by oared galleys

them to rendezvous in the event of separation, but had the opposite effect. The captains were told that 'if the wind were Northerly we should plie for the Azores, but if Southerly for the Iles of Bayon'.[17] This gave great scope for subjective interpretation, of which some were glad to take advantage. The wind blew southerly and strong, and the cohesion of the fleet disintegrated. Many of the ships stayed with Drake, but most, through stress of weather or by desire, separated. Norris, in the *Aid*, with two dozen others, lost Drake and reached the Bayona islands first. Men were dying all the time. Drake found a wind briefly offering for the Azores as he neared the Ría de Vigo, and altered course southward again, but 'remembering how unprovided he was for that journey, and seeing that he had lost company of his great ships', he changed his mind and sailed into the Ría, where he found Norris waiting. Only fifty-three of the fleet reached Vigo.

Some of the smaller ships, separated from the larger groups in ones and twos, were now in a desperate state of weakness and hunger, and took advantage of the strong southerly winds to make the best of their way to England. Others, more conscientious, lingered further south. Young William Fenner's ship, 'being separated from all company, wandered as a lost sheep in search of the Generals, and chased day by day by the galleys, often being almost taken, was delivered when past hope of long life'. With her hungry and thirsty crew she struggled towards Porto Santo near Madeira, where the men were refreshed for a few days after taking a pinnace laden with plums and apricots, and then found another lonely wanderer under Captain Cross. They anchored together off Porto Santo, and were joined by seven others on the following morning. They landed, took over the island, rested for a couple of days, and having ransomed the town for a generous supply of cattle, fruit, wine and water, set sail for England.[18]

Drake and Norris anchored above Vigo on 19 June. On the following day they ordered ashore the 2,000 or so fit men remaining in the fleet and marched in a pincer movement on the town. As Vice-Admiral Fenner bombarded it from the roadstead Drake led troops from one side, and Captain Anthony Wingfield from the other. They found the place strongly barricaded, but almost completely deserted. After laying waste the surrounding countryside and setting fire to the town they re-embarked on 21 June, discarding the idea of attacking the fort at Bayona for the familiar reason of lack of heavy artillery.

Drake and Norris now decided on a final attempt to sail to the Azores. The original plan, to take over some of the islands with the help of the kingly authority of Dom Antonio and to use them as a base from which to ambush the treasure fleet, had probably been abandoned, and it was decided to send some of the ships home, to join the many which had already gone on their own initiative. The plan was that Drake would take twenty of the best ships, as well-manned and victualled as possible, to look for the treasure ships, and Norris was to take the remaining thirty-three to England. First the whole fleet was to move down to the lower estuary to reorganise provisioning.

Again they lost contact; Drake, possibly seizing a brief chance of a fair wind, continued on past Bayona and out into the open sea. Norris, perplexed, tried to follow him, but was forced back into the estuary by the tide and a change of wind. On the following day a north-north-east gale let Norris out, but forced him southward for two days before fair weather and a south-west wind allowed him to change course for England. When he sailed into Plymouth on 2 July he found Drake and the Queen's ships waiting for him. After two days of favourable winds, Drake had given up the Azores venture when the wind changed, and sailed the tired remnants of his fleet home.

Some of the smaller vessels were almost ghost ships in the final weeks of the voyage. The *Gregory*, straggling as ever, had stayed on loyally off Bayona, looking for Drake after the cargo ships with which she was in company had sailed away for the Channel. She had eight sound men left to haul her yards round as she beat to and fro. She was joined by another straggler, the *Bonner* of Plymouth, and they decided to stay in company and make for England. John Evesham, the master gunner, wrote a weary, bitter end to a sad story:

> So the 18 day in the morning we set sail, having sometimes fair wind, sometimes contrary, and daily our men fell down sick, and I myself upon the 23 day at night fell sick, at which time we had no more sound men but the 2, and 2 yonkers. So the *Bark Bonner* being in our company, our captain and master made their case known to them, who very friendly did lend us 2 sailors and 2 soldiers and promised not to leave our company till God sent us into England, which promise they performed. So, by the help of God, having fair weather, upon the first day of July we came into Plymouth, where we found Sir Francis Drake with divers others of the fleet, and daily came in more and more of them. Where we continued without pay or anything else.[19]

On almost every count the voyage had been a failure. On the financial level, it was a disaster; the investors, not least the Queen, lost heavily. Thomas Fenner complained to Walsingham that the voyage had cost him £1,000, almost half his fortune.[20] Some of the private shipowners may have done reasonably well, if they were sharp. It proved very difficult to gather final accounts for the proceeds because many ships took advantage of the fragmented state of the fleet to avoid Plymouth and make for other ports with whatever captured material they had aboard, such as the wheat captured off the Tagus. Unlike Portuguese coins or Spanish cannon, a pile of wheat unloaded quickly into a granary is very difficult to tell from a pile of wheat carted from English farms.

Efforts to trace vanished material were continuing a year later: the *Greyhound* of Aldeburgh yielded up three brass guns; Sir Edward Norris had to hand over a quantity of linen; £7,000 in gold coin, landed in Plymouth and then reloaded into the *Unity* of London and hidden in her powder store, was seized when she reached the Thames. Concealed with the money was 'a certain waistcoat of a carnation colour, curiously embroidered with gold', perhaps stripped from the corpse of a Spanish officer after the slaughter at Puente de Burgo, or left in his tent as he fled.[21]

The expedition's most remarkable loss was in human life. Elizabeth's instructions to Drake and Norris had mentioned the many loyal subjects under their charge, and had required them to 'have a

speciall care for their preservation, down to the meanest person ...
both for their lives and for their health and every ways for their well
doing'. Different participants' estimates of the losses vary, but all are
startlingly high. Most of the deaths were from the unspecified sickness
which was blamed initially on the La Coruña wine, though it was
clearly some infectious disease; it continued to attack new victims
right to the end of the voyage. Of Thomas Fenner's 300 men on the
Dreadnought all but three were affected by it, and over a hundred
died.[22] Of the fifty soldiers aboard the *Griffin* of Lübeck, thirty-three
died and were thrown overboard on the voyage home between Bayona
and Sandwich, and two more died as soon as she anchored.[23]

There were originally 107 English officers of captain's rank or
higher; thirty-two of them died, a few in action, but mostly from
sickness. The Spanish estimate of total English losses, 18,000, is
certainly very exaggerated, but all the English reports which give
figures show that more than half the rank-and-file soldiers and
common seamen died. Some of the survivors were more fortunate in
their captains than others: Thomas Fenner, despite his large personal
losses, sold a hundred pounds' worth of silver plate to buy food and
medicine for the remnants of his crew, only eighteen of whom were fit
to work when the ship reached Plymouth. There was great resentment
among the surviving soldiers and sailors when it proved impossible
to pay them. Some formed riotous mobs in London, and others took
to highway robbery. Some had still had no pay in June 1590.

It would have been easier for Elizabeth, the nation, and no doubt
Drake and Norris themselves, to accept all this if the financial and
human losses had been sustained in achieving something, but none
of the aims of the voyage had materialised. The damage to Philip's
navy, in the context of the huge outlay on the voyage, had been
derisory; the Azores venture had got nowhere, and the treasure from
the Indies reached Spain unmolested; the Portuguese excursion had
fizzled and died.

Norris and Drake were expecting the Queen's anger, and Norris
wrote to Walsingham on 4 July, 'afraid that Her Majesty will mislike
of the event of our journey', and asking for support.[24] Drake,
especially, was open to criticism on several counts. In winds which
had enabled other ships to sail to La Rochelle before and after the La
Coruña episode, he had deliberately not gone to Santander; at a time
when William Fenner's ship and eight others had managed to reach
Porto Santo, he had failed to get anywhere near the Azores; and when
Norris and Essex were besieging Lisbon and awaiting his appearance

off the city, he had lingered at Cascais. For this last failure, according to William Monson, Drake 'was much blamed by the common consent of all men, the overthrow of the action being imputed to him'.[25] The Queen's instructions had, after all, been that the shipping at Lisbon was to be attacked even if the land assault on the city failed.

The two leaders were called to appear before a Privy Council inquiry late in October 1589.[26] The inquiry said nothing about the abandoning of the Azores venture. Drake and Norris were charged with failing to go to Santander before and after the siege of La Coruña, and of landing in Portugal 'contrary to theire instructions, not standinge assured of any suffyciente party to back theire enterprise'. Drake was further accused of not taking the fleet to Lisbon, 'the wynde servinge well for that purpose at his firste arrivall in Cascais, as is testified by sundry of the masters'.

Their defence to the first charge was based largely on the consequences of a surprising degree of disorganisation in the fleet when it set sail. They said that they had not imparted their destination to the captains before leaving Plymouth, and by the time the unwieldy fleet had dispersed and [mostly] come together again for orders the wind had changed and was unfavourable for Santander. We have already seen their unconvincing reason for not taking the wind for Santander on leaving La Coruña: the masters' unwillingness. To the accusation of having landed in Portugal without having tested the political winds ashore, they replied, plausibly enough, that they could not destroy the ships in Lisbon without having forces ashore as well as afloat; 'neyther was there any means to try what party Don Antonio had, but onely by landinge their forces'.

To the individual charge, Drake claimed to have been willing and eager to join Norris on 26 May, awaiting only the return of a favourable wind. His reply to the inquiry fudges the issue of what he was doing, and why, and exactly when, between 20 May, when he reached Cascais, and 26 May; in particular, it says nothing about when the favourable wind turned against him. Whether the inquiry probed any further into this crucial aspect is not known.

Drake and Norris invoked the support of Anthony Ashley, Elizabeth's observer on the voyage, who had apparently reported favourably on their efforts, if not on their achievements.[27] Neither of them was punished. They were lucky, and knew it. By the late summer Philip's ships in Pasajes had been repaired and re-rigged, and sixty had sailed for La Coruña and Lisbon.[28] By October the hulls of six new galleons of between 700 and 1,000 tons were complete and caulked on the stocks in Santander; six more of the same in Bilbao; four more in Pasajes; all to be fitted and rigged by the following Easter for summer duty.[29] Philip's navy was restored, and growing.

Drake and Norris may have escaped punishment, but they did not escape a fall from favour. Norris had to wait a year and a half for another command. Drake's professional exile was longer. Allowing the Queen even the suspicion that her wishes had been deliberately flouted by one who had sailed so close to the wind in the past was bound to have consequences.

It may be, however, that Drake's long period ashore following the Portugal voyage was in some degree self-imposed. There is no evidence that the Queen's displeasure took any practical form; perhaps Drake, older now and in poorer health, was sickened by the loss of so many men in an enterprise for whose lack of success he was widely blamed, though it had offered few opportunities for purely naval engagements, and the real failures had been those of the land forces.

XIX

DRAKE ASHORE
1589–95

> 'I shall be sailing from this island tomorrow for
> Santa Marta. I do so at considerable risk, for
> it is understood that the course is blockaded by
> corsairs, which the pilot tells me is the normal
> state of affairs. God will arrange the outcome
> as may best suit his service. In that of Your
> Majesty one must accept such things, and much
> more besides.'
>
> Governor Manso de Contreras
to Philip, June 1592

After the grand strategic design of 1589 had failed so comprehensively, England's attempts to weaken and deter Philip were
carried on by more individual methods for several years. The early
1590s were the heyday of the privateer. It was a mode of war which
suited the shipowners, their crews and the Queen. The owners, denied
their trade to Spain and Portugal, equipped their large merchantmen
and small barks as efficient vessels of war to pursue on an individual
basis the attacks on Spanish shipping which some had learned to
perform as part of Drake's fleets in the 1580s, but at which others
were already past masters. Individuals and syndicates in London; the
City itself; gentlemen and aristocrats like Sir George Carey, the Earl
of Hereford, Sir Walter Raleigh, the Hawkins family, and most
notably the Earl of Cumberland put their money into privateering.
Even Lord Admiral Charles Howard's ships contributed to the stream
of captured goods flowing into the country. The main organising
centres were London, Southampton, Chichester, Bristol and Plymouth.

The booty was not usually bullion; the vision of intercepting and
seizing Philip's American gold and silver on its way past the Azores
never faded completely, but nor did it materialise. Philip had adopted
a fresh system for bringing home his treasure, using a new class of

strong, fast frigates which sailed alone and were even harder to waylay than the convoys had been. The privateers' prize cargoes were more workaday, but by their sheer quantity were a serious weakening of Spain's economy: wines, hides, sugar, oil, silks and linens, brazil-wood and sarsaparilla. The values were usually respectable rather than vast, hundreds of pounds rather than thousands; some voyages lost money, but there was always the hope of a bonanza such as the £25,000 in silver, gold, jewels and exotic produce brought home by the *Julian* in 1589, or the £16,000 in gold, pepper and ivory seized by the *Prudence* of Barnstaple in 1590.

Ships which had been part of Drake's fleets at Cadiz or La Coruña now ranged as lone predators or in small groups: the *Merchant Royal, Edward Bonaventure, Moonlight, Tiger, White Lion*. Thomas Fenner, who had sold his silver to help his starving crew after the Portugal débâcle, began restoring his fortunes in privateering ventures with other members of his family. John Watts of London, who had contributed ships to the Cadiz and Portugal ventures, continued activities in which he and his captains were already well versed. In the years 1589–91 at least 236 English ships, mostly of between 100 and 150 tons, were operating as privateers. Sometimes two groups formed brief alliances and achieved a major success, most notably in the capture of the great Portuguese carrack the *Madre de Dios* in the Azores in 1592. The Earl of Cumberland's five ships, totalling 1,100 tons and led by the 500-ton *Red Dragon*, which was as powerfully armed as a Queen's ship of the same size, teamed up with a fleet sent out by a syndicate including the Queen, Raleigh, John Hawkins and the City of London and subdued the carrack after a long struggle. Her cargo, probably worth close on a million pounds, was pillaged by the sailors, and much of it disappeared surreptitiously in various ports, but even so there was £140,000 left for the adventurers to squabble over.[1]

The West Indies, too, were plagued by privateers. In 1595 the treasurer of Santo Domingo reported that

> the corsairs have been as numerous and as determined over the last four years as if these were their own home ports. They lie in wait on all the sailing routes, ... especially those coming to this city. ... Not a ship approaching or leaving this port can escape them. If this goes on this island will be depopulated or we will be forced to trade with them instead of with Spain.[2]

Privateering was a trade for young men or hungry men, and Drake was neither. Secure in his fortune, despite the temporary coolness with the Queen, he devoted his attention to the more placid environment of Buckland and Plymouth for a year or two. The matter of the town water supply was taken up again. Having served on one parliamentary committee which approved the bill, Drake had later chaired another committee which rejected a petition against it by local millers, who saw it as a threat to their business. Plymouth now entrusted Drake with the construction of the leat. Some of the cost of digging (£200) and compensating the landowners (£100) was borne initially by Drake, and other wealthy men including Richard Hawkins paid for the piping of the water within the town. This was not pure charity on Drake's part; his rent on mills and land was reduced by the town for some time afterwards as a method of reimbursing him.[3] Digging began in December 1590 and was finished in the following April.

Drake's whole role in the matter has come under scrutiny. As the future lessee of the six corn mills driven by the leat, he obviously stood to benefit from its construction. Moreover, whereas the original plan had been that the leat should discharge into Sutton Harbour and scour it, it was routed to discharge into Mill Bay, where it powered an old tidal mill of which Drake had recently taken over the lease from the Hawkins family.[4] Once again public service and private interest are hard to separate.

The leat was a great success, and provided Plymouth with water for three centuries. The council's annual survey of the leat was marked by the Fyshinge Feaste, at which Drake's memory was toasted first in water from the head-weir, then in wine, with the words 'May the descendants of him who brought us Water never want Wine'. This was followed by a meal of trout from the Meavy. There was a nineteenth-century controversy as to whether the toast should be 'who *gave* us water'; it was claimed that this was the older form, that Drake had *given* the water, and that the council's water charges were unjustified.[5] The leat's builders did their work well: when it was repaired early in the 1939-45 war as an emergency water source, the cost was only £200.

The failed attempt on the impregnable high town of La Coruña, contrasting with the ease with which Drake had entered badly defended and complacent ports in the Indies, made him realise the vulnerability of Plymouth, poorly fortified and likely to be an early target of any renewed attempt on England by Philip. In the winter of 1589-90, with news of Spain's increasing naval preparations, fears of invasion caused trepidation in the town:

The Harborowe lyinge without anie defence to make longe resistance, the towne uppon this late reporte was strucken with such feare, that some of them had convaied their goods out of the towne, and others no doubt would have followed, if they had not ben stopped by the cominge of Sir Fr[ancis] Drake, who the more to assure them brought his wife, and familie thither.[6]

Petitioning Elizabeth to contribute to the building of a fort on the Hoe and supplying it and the St Nicholas Island with ordnance, Drake and the council pointed out that

the said towne lyeth open to the enemy, not defended by anie forte or rampier, but that he maie by the landinge of a small force in the night, become master of their Ordinaunce, and so possesse him selfe of the towne.

These are the thoughts of a man who had done exactly that at Nombre de Dios twenty years earlier. The ordnance defending the port was mostly borrowed, and the Queen was asked to supply eight or ten cannon. Drake himself was to contribute money, and he had already taken steps and led by example in the establishment of a watch-keeping rota:

hereafter Sir Fr[ancis] Drake hath taken order that there shall be watch and warde every night kept in the towne no lesse than if it were a towne of garrison. Of which watch every Master in his torne as Capten is to have the charge, and to watch with them him selfe untill midnight, and then to be releeved by his deputie, who shall likewise be a man of good substance and truste. This watch did Sir Fr[ancis] himselfe beginne on friday laste.

The Queen gave permission, but her finance came grudgingly: all the pilchards landed in Devon and Cornwall were taxed, and £100 per year was given from the proceeds towards the fort. The building was begun, but the pilchard men were predictably slow and argumentative with their taxes, and progress was slow.[7] Drake never saw the fort completed; from 1592 onwards his thoughts were returning to wider horizons.

The sight of the city of Panama, spread out before him with the great ocean which was its *raison d'être* stretching southward beyond it, had not faded from Drake's mind since the hours of suspense when his cimarron ally was reconnoitring the departure plans of the muletrains twenty years earlier. By the early winter of 1592 he was involved again in the most ambitious plan so far conceived to attack the city. It is likely that Drake himself was the main instigator. Earlier in the year he had probably presented Elizabeth with a copy of his account of the 1572 voyage, and evidently her resentment over the Portuguese fiasco was now abating. Drake must have been helped in his persuasion of the queen by having the sober John Hawkins as coproponent of the plan, and by January 1593 they had impressed her to the extent of being authorised to use three royal ships and twenty private vessels.[8]

By the spring, however, the venture was 'waxinge colde' in comparison with Richard Hawkins' scheme for a South Sea voyage.[9] It was under discussion again in June 1594, with the active interest of the Earl of Essex, who may have been thinking of taking part himself.[10] In December the Queen provided Drake and Hawkins with exchequer funds for 'a speciall service to be by them done on the sea'.

They were not slow in dipping into them; by the beginning of March 1595 they had spent £22,000, and were talking of their first estimates as too low. Items in the accounts of the venture range from £2 for bowstrings to over £4,600 for grain and peas, and include £3,000 for beer and £942 for wines (a third of them Spanish). Over £150 was spent on flags and streamers, and £14/11/- on 'sundry instruments of music for 8 musicians and 9 trumpeters'. These last items were destined to be greatly underused in the kind of pomp and euphoric hospitality with which Drake had entertained his officers and prisoners in previous voyages. In contrast, the £246 spent on items for 'physic and chirurgery' was to prove sadly inadequate.[11]

Spanish spies were confused about the destination of the fleet during the preparations in the spring of 1595. Was it the Indies? Santo Domingo and Panama were alerted. Was it Lisbon? Eight or nine thousand people left the city in panic in March and April. Was it the treasure fleet? If Drake and Hawkins had managed to sail by 1 May, as intended, Spanish doubts would have continued and the voyage might have fared better, but by the late spring Philip had enough information from a range of sources to be sure that the target area was the West Indies.[12] By midsummer he knew still more. The Spanish had seized Blavet, on the coast of Brittany, and galleys operating from there were able to monitor English preparations by capturing West Country fishermen in the Channel. Philip's admiral in Brittany, Don Diego Brochero, was able to send him detailed intelligence about the fleet, the number and size of ships, weight of armament, etc. in the early summer.[13]

Judging by the names of individual ships reported to Philip, however, the fishermen did a fair job of misleading Brochero, or said anything they thought might save their skins; they were right about the *Hope* (reported to Philip as the *Hop*); they were wrong about the *Ark Royal* (*Arca Real*), *Golden Lion* (*León Dorado*) and *Dreadnought* (*Dretroch*), none of which was in the fleet; and the *Quiteve* and *Demodernare* are unidentifiable. The tonnage of the ships was much overestimated: the *Hope* was said to be 800 tons instead of her true 600, and the tonnage given for these six vessels totalled 4,700, whereas the six largest vessels in the fleet totalled just over 3,000.

In Trinidad the garrulous Sir Walter Raleigh had captured a Spanish explorer, Antonio de Berrío, to whom he had described Drake's and Hawkins' plan. Raleigh later released Berrío in exchange for some of his own men, and the Spaniard wrote to Philip in July:

> ... they have twenty large royal galleons and another forty smaller ships, not counting numerous other adventurers who have joined them. On the ships they have a great number of flat-bottomed boats ... Their orders are to go directly to the mouth of the River Chagre, without calling at any populated part of the Indies, and put two thousand men into these boats to proceed secretly to Panama. The ships will go to Nombre de Dios, with the intention that word will be sent of their presence and troops will be despatched there, and the river will be left unprotected. Their aim is to take Panama, fortify it and make themselves masters of the South Sea. They then intend to take and destroy Cartagena and winter in the Indies, destroying all the coastal towns they can.[14]

Ambushing mule-trains was one thing; seizing Panama was an altogether more ambitious project, and establishing a fortified base in the city and in Nombre de Dios for controlling the South Sea and sacking the ports of the Caribbean represented a new dimension in English official aspirations. Raleigh was not the only contemporary who saw a prolonged occupation of Panama as part of the scheme; Sir William Monson also saw this as Drake's and Hawkins' intention, and so did Thomas Maynarde, who went with them.[15]

Preparations for the voyage dragged on into the summer of 1595, and its desirability began to be questioned in the light of evidence of fresh Spanish naval preparations. By the time the fleet was ready at the end of July reports had been received that Philip was preparing to invade Ireland that very summer, and England in 1596. In July Captain Carlos de Amezola led four of Brochero's galleys out of Blavet and attacked some Huguenot villages on the Normandy coast.

This probing force then landed a raiding party of 400 men at Mouse-hole in Cornwall on 25 July. Penzance, Newlyn and several nearby villages were burned. Philip was reported to be assembling three large fleets in Cadiz, Lisbon and the ports of Galicia and Biscay.

In this situation the clarity of the project disclosed by Raleigh to Berrío began to be muddied, and was never afterwards as clear-cut. A suggestion from the Queen that the fleet should linger off the Irish coast to block Philip's invasion was met with a refusal, though Drake, Hawkins and Sir Thomas Baskerville, the leader of the land forces, did promise to tackle any Spanish fleet they might meet on their originally planned course. By 14 August the Queen was confusing matters even more by asking Drake and Hawkins to spend time reconnoitring Philip's preparations on the Iberian coast, and by suggesting that they should spend up to a month waiting to intercept the treasure fleet expected at the Azores in September. At the same time she demanded that the total length of the voyage be limited to six months to ensure their return in time to help defend England against the invasion believed to be planned by the Spanish for the summer of 1596.[16] The same letter blames Drake and Hawkins for the delay in sailing.

Their huffy reply points out that their fleet, with dismantled pinnaces and hundreds of soldiers cluttering the decks, is completely unfitted to linger a month in the Atlantic to seize the treasure ships. If that is the Queen's real desire, the ships should be re-equipped and crewed on a different basis, and the Queen would have to bear the cost; otherwise they should be left to get on with the original and still the main aim of the voyage. They do not quite say 'Make up your mind, woman', but this is clearly their feeling, and the letter borders on insolence: '. . . we are lothe to be tedyous, knowinge your heighnes dothe myslyke yt, and therfore do referre the consyderacion of this weightye matter to your pryncely Judgment.'[17]

In their agitation Drake, Hawkins and Baskerville spent much of 13 August composing letters. In one, to Burghley, they restated their frustration and the effect of the Queen's indecision on the finances of the voyage. They also wrote to the Earl of Essex in similar terms, threatening 'the lyke dyscontentment or worse than that of the portyngall viage'.[18] In a much longer letter to Essex with the same date, Baskerville pleaded with him to dissuade the Queen from her insistence on a time limit of six months. Once more we see the conflict of interests involved in the financing of Elizabethan naval projects. Baskerville's concern is for his own investment in the voyage:

I Am alredy halfe ruinid, and shal be wholy If the Jorney goe nott forward
acording to the first platte, which I fear is or wil be wholy alterid ...
I beseech your Lordship therfor ... thatt Itt will pleas you now to
second the Jorney In such sorte thatt we maye goe forward in our first
Course withoutt Lymyting us so strycke a tyme, wherby we may nott
only undo our selfes in our purcis butt also In our reputacions, for
who is so unadvised that will undertake to perform such a vyag in six
months.[19]

Essex's interest in the project was considerable, and left its mark
on the list of officers. Baskerville had been induced to take part by
the Earl, as had his second-in-command Sir Nicholas Clifford, and
several of the land captains had previously served in actions with
Essex.

On 16 August Burghley drafted a stiff letter from the Queen,
refusing to allow the voyage to proceed without a clear undertaking
from Drake and Hawkins to return by the middle of May 1596.[20]
Otherwise they were to begin selling off provisions with as little loss
as possible and accept the blame for the abandoning of the project.
The stiffness of the letter was probably increased by Elizabeth's
awareness that she had moved from her original position. The
despatch of this ultimatum was forestalled by an excited letter from
Drake and Hawkins which finally won the Queen's approval for the
voyage.

They had received news that a Bristol bark had come home after
capturing a Spanish frigate in which were several passengers. They
had formerly been in a large treasure ship which had taken refuge in
Puerto Rico after being dismasted in a storm and losing touch with
the homecoming fleet. According to a Portuguese who was the main
informant, she carried a treasure worth two and a half million
ducats.[21]

After all the peevish arguments, organisational minutiae and royal
changes of mind, this news rekindled enthusiasm for the voyage in
everyone. To Drake it must have seemed, literally, a godsend which
would meet a major demand of the Queen's without completely
undermining the Panama plan. We see through the letter a brisk,
rejuvenated Drake, the smash-and-grab raider of Cartagena and
Nombre de Dios, weary of administration and fired by memories of
the actions in Caribbean harbours of which he had been deprived for
ten years. No tiresome beating to and fro in the Atlantic for a month
waiting for the treasure fleet, with the crews quarrelsome and sick in

stinking ships; instead, a sitting target; a purse of gold lying by the wayside; a *Cacafuego* or *São Phelipe* immobilised:

> She lyethe ther unrygged and her ordenance put a shore. Yt ys abowt two monthes past that the maryners that dothe dyscover this came from thence and left ther ship in that port; which cannot come from thence without order from the kynge. We have sent to Brystow for the masters mate of the shipe, and a portyngall that hathe dyscoveryd this matter, and do mynd with gods favour to take that place with all spede, yt lyethe in our way and wyll no way impeache us.

Elizabeth agreed, and a few days later the news was out.[22] The original plan, as divulged to the Spanish by Raleigh, was admittedly over-ambitious, and flawed in its apparent neglect of the later logistical support which its success would have entailed, but it had at least a clear strategic aim and a logical sequence: take Panama with the help of whatever surprise was left; consolidate it as at least a temporary base; and lay about other targets in the Caribbean and the South Sea with Panama and Nombre de Dios as centres of operations. The surprise element had been reduced, and the planned attack on Puerto Rico now risked losing it altogether. The time available for the Panama operation had been whittled away, and only the most dashingly successful operation at Puerto Rico could avoid its further reduction. The logic of the original sequence of operations had now been reversed, and the old vision of plunder and personal interest had usurped broader naval strategy.

Wishful thinking, too, clouded judgement. Despite the alluring picture they drew for the Queen, Drake and Hawkins could hardly have entertained the idea that the Spanish galleon would be sitting there with her crew and cannon ashore and the treasure left on board, but they certainly underestimated Philip's wish to keep his gold and the steps taken in Spain and Puerto Rico to ensure that he retained it. They perhaps underestimated, too, the effect on Spanish colonial defences of thirty years of intensive privateering and Drake's 1585–6 raid. The days when one could land in a lonely cove in South America and find a man asleep with a mule laden with gold bars dozing beside him were past. In 1572–3 the cimarrons had been crucial to Drake's success, and again in 1585–6 they had been important to his plans, but they had now been bloodily reduced by Spanish campaigns to wipe out the threat of a long-term alliance between them and the English.

Even on the level of small practicalities, hard facts were neglected.

The overland march to Panama in 1573 had been handicapped by a lack of strong footwear; the men had arrived back at the coast lame and with their shoes in tatters. For the 1595 voyage over 2,000 pairs of shoes were bought, but again they were inadequate and were to disintegrate as soon as land campaigning began.

In its long-delayed departure, confusion of aims, and conflict between the interests of strategy and plunder; even in the insertion of a new and potentially time-consuming target which might undermine the main venture, the 1595 voyage showed that the lessons of the Portugal excursion had not been learned. Another similarity was the division of command. This time, however, the division was more misconceived; another departure from clarity. In the great 1585 raid Carleill had been in charge of the land forces, but the overall command had been Drake's. In the Portugal voyage, Drake and Norris had been joint leaders, but there was a clear division of responsibility between Norris as general ashore and Drake as admiral at sea. In 1595 Carleill's role was to be played by Baskerville, sub-ordinate not to one overall leader, but two: Drake and Hawkins. This joint appointment was not only to strain relations between two very different personalities and cause divisions and loss of morale in the fleet; in certain instances it was to affect tactics and hinder success.

In at least one participant's view the juxtaposition of Drake and Hawkins was a deliberate ploy by the Queen to restrain Drake. Thomas Maynarde, a relative of Drake's by marriage who accompanied him and attended council meetings on the voyage, wrote a perceptive narrative of events. Maynarde was very much a Drake man; he saw Drake's faults clearly enough, but loved him in spite of them. Drake had needed the sober-sided Hawkins in his persuasion of Elizabeth, but their incompatibility as joint commanders was evident to Maynarde, who described Drake as

A man of greate spirit and fitt to undertake matters, In my poore oppinion better able to conduct forces and discreetly to governe in conductinge them to places where service was to be done, th[a]n to comande in the execution therof. But assuredly his very name was a great terror to the enemie in all those partes havinge hearetofore done many thinges in those countries to his honourable fame and profitt. But entringe into them as the childe of fortune it maye be his selfewilled and peremptorie command was doubted. And that caused her majestie (as should seeme) to joyne Sir John Hawkins in equall commission. A man oulde and warie entringe into matters with so laden a foote, that others meate woulde be eaten before his spit could come to the fire. Men of so different natures that what one desireth the other would commonly oppose against. And though theyr warie cariages sequestred it from meaner wittes yet it was apparently seene to better judgments before our goenge from Plymouth, that whom the one loved the other smaly esteemed.

XX

Defeat in the Canaries

1595

'We were of one mind: we would fight the
enemy on the beach, and we would fight him
to the death.'

Próspero Casola to Philip, October 1595

The fleet which was to seize control of the Isthmus of Panama
consisted of six large royal galleons and twenty-one private vessels.
They ranged in size from the 660-ton *Garland* to two little Ramsgate
ketches, the *Nannycocke* and the *Blessing*. Several of the private
vessels were seasoned privateers, four of them belonging to the
well-known London entrepreneur John Watts. Drake's flagship,
the *Defiance*, 550 tons, was a relatively young ship, lately re-
launched after major repairs. Of the other royal ships the *Adventure*,
captained by Thomas Drake, was almost brand-new, and the
Garland, Hawkins' flagship, was about five years old, but the
Foresight, again captained by William Wynter, the *Hope* and
the *Elizabeth Bonaventure* had all seen more than twenty years'
service.

At least fourteen pinnaces, possibly over twenty, were taken in
parts. There is no firm evidence to support Raleigh's statement to
Berrío that some of these were specially designed flat-bottomed craft
for approaching Panama by river, though it is clear from the accounts
that nine were bought complete, at £40 apiece, and the others specially
built.[1] The accounts do mention two 'flat boats', but these were
specifically for carrying timber and cost only £2 each. There may
have been some misunderstanding between Raleigh and Berrío about
the special shallow-draught boats; it was impossible to travel all the
way to Panama by the Chagre, the upper course of which turns away
from the city after Venta de Cruces, which could be reached by
normal pinnaces.

The concept of the joint command, already weakened by the defensible placing of Drake and Hawkins in different ships, was further

diluted by their own decision to split the fleet into two squadrons. This may have been an early decision, welcome to both men; Maynarde wrote that Drake and Hawkins each victualled his own squadron, neither adequately:

> Agreeinge best . . . in givinge out a glorious title to theyr intended jorneye, and in not so well victualinge the navie as (I deeme) was her majesties pleasure it shoulde be, both of them served them to goode purpose, for from this havinge the distributinge of so great sommes theyr miserable providinge for us would free them from incurringe any greate losse, whatsoever befell of the jorney.

The friction between the two soon produced its first wisp of flame. The fleet sailed on 28 August 1595, and on 2 September, after making only 200 miles, Hawkins ran up a flag on the *Garland* to call a council of captains, important masters and gentlemen. This may have been prearranged to finalise practicalities which would have wasted more time if discussed in Plymouth and could have given Elizabeth another chance to change her mind. The meeting was acrimonious; Drake complained that his squadron was carrying 200 more men than Hawkins' and that the *Defiance*, in particular, was overcrowded. Hawkins blamed Drake for recruiting more men than they had agreed, 'and this drewe them to some cholericke speeches'. With both men on their high horse and incapable of climbing off it the matter was not resolved, and the meeting passed on to questions of sailing orders, rendezvous points and victualling allowances. Hawkins 'revealed the places whether wee were bound, in hearinge of the basest mariner', wrote Maynarde critically.

A week later Drake called the council to the *Defiance* and proposed a call in the Canaries, for watering and plunder. He was supported by Baskerville, who as we have seen was 'halfe ruinid' by the preparations for the voyage and was consequently keen to augment the venture's profits. Hawkins utterly refused to consider it, on three grounds: there could be no need to rewater so soon (unless, he said sarcastically, it was necessary because of Drake's overmanning); an attack would put the whole enterprise at risk; and the main purpose of the voyage would be delayed. 'Now the fyer which laye hid in theyr stommackes began to breake forth, and had not the coronell pacified them it would have growen farther.'

Calming down, at least outwardly, they agreed to discuss it further at dinner on the *Garland* next day. Baskerville was sure he could take

Las Palmas in four hours and persuade the inhabitants, by some selective arson, to ransom it within four days. John Troughton, captain of the *Elizabeth Bonaventure*, reported in his journal that there was talk of Hawkins' pressing on to Puerto Rico and leaving Drake and Baskerville to do whatever they chose,[2] but the old man eventually succumbed to persuasion with an ill grace, and the fleet remained together for a practically unplanned assault on Gran Canaria. Hawkins is not mentioned in any of the reports as taking an active part in what followed; it was, in his view, 'labore lost, with much hazard of all'.[3]

At the north-east corner of Gran Canaria is a mountainous peninsula called Las Isletas, probably because to approaching ships its several peaks appear over the horizon like a group of little islands. It is joined to the main island by a thin neck of land, to the east of which is a round bay, and at the southern end of which lies Las Palmas. In the sixteenth century there was a lookout position, the Atalaya, on the southernmost summit of Las Isletas, and on the southern shore of the promontory a fort overlooked the bay. The most vulnerable place for a landing was the Caleta de Santa Catalina, a smaller, sandy bay to the south of the main bay, and separated from it by a point. The Caleta was defended by earthworks, and the town itself was walled. Slightly further south was another fort called Santa Ana.[4]

Shortly after daybreak on 26 September the agricultural workers emerging from their houses in the town looked at the sky, as usual, wondering if the thin mist and light drizzle were going to clear. Rising from the Atalaya they saw a column of smoke. A warning fire was lit whenever more than five sails at a time were sighted. Shortly afterwards the sound of a cannon-shot rolled across the bay from the fort on Las Isletas, passing on a message from the lookouts. Antonio Lorenzo, captain of one of the town's companies of troops, saw the smoke from the cannon and went to the house of the governor, Alonso de Alvarado, whom he found about to mount his horse. They were joined immediately by other officers, and having given orders for drums to beat through the town and the troops to be gathered in the square, Alvarado galloped off towards Las Isletas to see for himself.

As he rode he saw the first of the English ships appearing round the easternmost point of the promontory, El Golfete. He was met by a messenger from the fort with the news that seventeen or eighteen ships had been sighted. He ordered the man to ride on, warn the town, have the bells rung, and tell the officers to take the half-dozen artillery pieces outside the walls and down to the shore. Shortly after Alvarado had reached the fort and received its commander's assurances of competence but also a request for more powder, two more messengers arrived from the Atalaya with the news that the enemy had twenty-eight ships and as many smaller vessels.

It was now about seven o'clock. In the next hour or so Drake (Hawkins was probably keeping out of all decisions) anchored his fleet in a line north–south from El Golfete, and the townspeople saw the threat which faced them. Drake took his time, uncharacteristically. It may be that he took extra precautions because of the rift with Hawkins and the fear of an aftermath of I-told-you-so. Between ten and eleven o'clock he sent one of the smaller ships forward to reconnoitre along the shore, past the Caleta de Santa Catalina and down to the fort of Santa Ana. He went himself in one of the *Defiance*'s boats to take soundings off the Caleta and to lay buoys to guide the landing, after which he returned to the fleet. In Las Palmas the lieutenant-governor, Antonio Pamochamoso, watched him go and then ordered a boat out to remove the buoys, but by the time it was ready the English had weighed anchor and the assault was beginning.

Drake had put 500 or 600 men from the larger ships into twenty-seven boats, with instructions that after landing the boats were to return to the galleons to land as many again. The boats were in line abreast, and were preceded by three ships. There was a ship at each end of the line of boats, and another ten in a triangle behind them. The orderly formation approached the Caleta with banners and ensigns flying; in the middle of the line, in a twelve-oared boat with a red banner, Baskerville waited to lead the men ashore. Drums rattled; trumpets pealed; and around noon the leading ships began firing at the shore defences. It was a brave sight, and an impressive display of seamanship. Unfortunately it did not work.

Spanish accounts are agreed that it would probably have worked if Drake had been quicker. Ashore there had been a certain amount of dithering, with conflicting views about how to confront him. Avarado had given orders to man the earthworks at the Caleta and prevent Drake from landing, but at one point, perhaps awed by the size and organisation of the landing force, he had shown signs of giving in to the view of some of his captains and withdrawing within the town walls. He was rallied by the energy of his deputy, Pamo-chamoso, who made a stirring speech, and the earlier plan was resumed. Two of the town cannon were hauled down to the Caleta, arriving when Drake's nearest ships were within musket-shot. After a further delay four more arrived, hauled by oxen which, goaded by sword-points into an uncontrolled gallop, ended up fortuitously at exactly the right place.

Companies of arquebusiers who had been withdrawing towards the town were turned and ordered back down to the shore pell-mell, and the defence began in earnest. Some Spanish accounts give a stirring, and almost convincing, picture of Alvarado galloping up and down the beach with drawn sword, animating his men and waving the enemy on to their deaths. The English gunners had little effect, whereas the Spanish guns, having done little damage to Drake's ships with cannonballs, changed to firing bags of musket balls at the boats nearing the beach, with withering results. Spanish accounts put the English dead in this phase at between 200 and 400 (though English prisoners later told the Spanish that only about forty had died).

The three ships in advance of the boats went so close to the shore that one of them grounded briefly, but not one of the boats managed to land any men. The action moved southward along the shoreline, with three unsuccessful landing attempts, until the previously enthusiastic Baskerville retreated. A ship was holed below the waterline and had to be towed away as her crew manned the pumps and tried to stop the leak. Other ships continued south to exchange fire with the fort of Santa Ana before breaking off and rejoining the main fleet at about two o'clock in the afternoon. The fort at Las Isletas took little part in the action, and the commander was criticised for firing so few shots when the English were in range. His excuse was that he was short of powder and was reserving it for future eventualities. One shot from the fort smashed the binnacle on an English ship and killed five seamen.

The boats took the demoralised men back to their ships, and the raid was abandoned. The English had been humiliated, with nothing whatsoever to show for it. Drake must have had difficulty in facing Hawkins. Baskerville revised his estimate of the time necessary to take the town to four days, but Drake decided to cut his losses and that night the fleet moved down the coast to tend the wounded, take on water, and no doubt to apportion blame.

Spanish celebrations in the town were unrestrained, and in the days to come, in an eruption of poetic elation, odes and ballads were composed in praise of the heroic defenders. Some more thoughtful heads, however, knew how lucky the town had been; one anonymous pen commented sardonically that this so-called victory of ours was won principally by the grace of God. Drake was blind; if he had sent in his launches and ships half an hour sooner he would not have found a single man on the beach ... and he could have landed his men and seized the island. He lay at anchor for three hours, giving our people time to rally from the countryside, and then he thought all our men were in the earthworks, when we had only a hundred and fifty there. It really is a joke to think how the island escaped![5]

Not only the Spanish thought Drake was too slow in attacking. Thomas Maynarde, too, in the secrecy of his own journal, was critical:

... undoubtedly had we lanced under the forte at our first cominge to anchor we had put fayre to bee possessors of the towne, for the delayes gave the enimie great stomackes and daunted our owne, and it being the first service our new men were brought into it was to be doubted they would prove the worse the whole jorney folowinge.[6]

One English account[7] mentions heavy, breaking seas as the reason for the failed landing attempt, but neither Maynarde nor John Troughton says anything of the kind. Eight years earlier Drake had sailed jauntily into Cadiz bay, leaving the rest of his fleet to follow him as best they could; now, with the caution of middle age and the fear of proving Hawkins right, he had spent so much time in reconnoitring an uncomplicated target, laying buoys which made his intentions unmistakeable, that a small force of defenders, whose determination made up for confused leadership and shortage of ordnance, had beaten off his meticulously organised landing force. As Maynarde says, it was a poor augury for the rest of the voyage.

The state of the sea may have been against Drake, but if that was so it was a mistake to launch the attack. Baskerville's capacity to inspire must be called into question; perhaps Christopher Carleill would have done better. Maynarde, who usually speaks his mind, says nothing in criticism of Baskerville, but Troughton shares the anonymous Spaniard's view that his withdrawal showed undue caution:

To this place ... did the Spaniardes drawe 2 or 3 very small peces of ordynaunce, with which, and with som companyes of soldiers, made some show of resistance, whereuppon notwithstandinge most of our smaller shippinge, who accompaned our bottes with their Artillery, Sir Thomas made his retreat without puttinge foot aland.[8]

It would be interesting to read Baskerville's own version (his account of the voyage survives only in draft form, and does not describe the Canaries action), and perhaps even more interesting to read the one sent by Hawkins to his wife, which probably distanced him from the opprobrium of failure and asked her to let Burghley and the Lord Admiral know the facts. The letter is lost; Lady Hawkins wrote to Sir Robert Cecil that Sir John had 'thought it not amiss to set down himself what befell ... lest it should be misreported.'[9]

As the fleet sailed down the coast on the Friday night, its lanterns were watched by peasants who reported to Alvarado on the following day that it seemed to be heading for the bay of Gando. Four companies of foot and a troop of sixteen cavalry were sent in pursuit in case of another landing attempt, and four scouts were ordered ahead urgently to keep an eye on the ships. On Sunday the fleet anchored off Arguineguín in a sparsely populated and undefended area about forty-five miles from Las Palmas and landed around 500 men. The purpose was twofold: to take on water and to restore morale. Drake had a large tent erected ashore, and there was musical entertainment.

Relaxation was short-lived. One of the land officers, Captain Grimston, went ashore with eight or nine men to see Hawkins, and landed some distance from the main company. The Spanish scouts, with help from a band of peasants, fell on them, killed Grimston and some others, and took two prisoners, a Frenchman called Bluq and an English barber-surgeon, Daniel Equisman. A Polish sailor called Gasparian, captured earlier by some English ship and pressed into the fleet, escaped from one of the water-parties and handed himself over to the Spanish. The three were interrogated,[10] as a result of which advice vessels were despatched from the Canaries to warn the ports of the Indies. To judge by their testimonies, both Bluq and Equisman were either ignorant of the fleet's exact targets in the Indies, or cagey about disclosing them. Bluq regarded Drake (*Francisco Draque el viejo*, 'old Drake') as being in overall command.

The advice vessels sent from the Canaries were to play no great part in matters, for Philip had already acted on his intelligence reports to protect Puerto Rico and save his silver. A squadron of five large frigates left Sanlúcar on 15 September and arrived in the Canaries on the 28th, the very day on which Drake and Hawkins left Arguineguín. They were commanded by Don Pedro Tello in the *Texeda*, and carried 250 soldiers and 300 seamen and gunners. News of the Canaries raid, and of Drake's intentions, reached Spain late in October. A week later a decision was taken to send a fleet after Drake to the Caribbean, but it did not sail until almost two months later.

XXI

Gold may be Bought too Dear: Puerto Rico

1595

> 'Great was the difference betwixt the Indian
> cities now from what they were when Drake
> first haunted these coasts; ... Whilest the King
> of Spain guarded the head and heart of his
> dominions in Europe, he left his long legs in
> America open to blows; till finding them to
> smart, being beaten black and blew by the
> English, he learned to arm them at last,
> fortifying the most important of them to make
> them impregnable.'
>
> William Fuller, *The Holy State*, 1642

Drake and Hawkins had an uneventful passage across the Atlantic until the night of 26 October, when the ships were scattered by a storm. This would not worry the two leaders unduly, as the fleet had been told to rendezvous at Guadeloupe. Drake was sufficiently unconcerned to alter course and call at the island of Marigalante, where he was rowed ashore and was given fruit by a group of Indians from Dominica. He gave them a yellow flannel waistcoat and handkerchief. He remained at anchor overnight, and on the morning of 29 October reached the south coast of Guadeloupe, where he was rejoined by Hawkins.

Four days later, they received disturbing news from Josias Cape, of the *Delight*. This 50-ton vessel had been blown to leeward of the fleet in company with the 35-ton *Francis*, whose rudder was damaged, and the smaller ship had fallen into Spanish hands. The luck, or divine providence, which had saved Gran Canaria had continued to smile on the Spanish, and Drake's three-day delay in the Canaries had proved crucial. Philip's five frigates had, all unwitting, shadowed the English across the Atlantic. Tello's landfall in the Indies was

242

tentative and confused; his pilots mistook Deseada and Antigua for Martinique and Dominica, and on that basis he decided to make for Guadeloupe for water. He then changed his mind, and his course, but shortly found himself, after all, off Guadeloupe, where he sighted two sails which proved to be the *Delight* and the struggling *Francis*. Tello's vice-admiral, Gonzalo Méndez Canzo, soon subdued the *Francis*, two of whose crew were killed and the rest taken prisoner. Tello gave up the attempt to catch the *Delight* when he saw the topmasts of nine of Drake's ships nearer the island.

He sank the *Francis* and proceeded to interrogate her crew, who were not long in confirming that Drake and Hawkins were heading for Puerto Rico, and that they had enough supplies for further activities in the Indies. Tello must have exulted in his luck. On being told that the English were likely to sail from Guadeloupe within a day, he gave orders for all his frigates to get under way, extinguish all lights, and make for Puerto Rico as quickly as possible. They arrived on 3 November, sent a boat ahead of them to make sure that Drake and Hawkins had not beaten them to it, and sailed into harbour.

Drake, in fact, had not yet moved from Guadeloupe. In his dismay at the loss of the *Francis*, and his awareness that her crew was unlikely to hold out against Spanish persuasion, he had immediately proposed that all or part of the fleet should chase the frigates to prevent them warning Puerto Rico. Most of the captains supported him, but Hawkins would have none of it, and 'Sir John prevayled for that hee was sickly, Sir Francis beinge loth to breed his further disquiet'.[1]

This was a mistake worse than the raid on the Canaries. In the Atlantic crossing Tello, presumably under a press of sail, had gained no ground on the English, who were restricted to the speed of their slowest ships. If Drake and Hawkins had sailed promptly from Guadeloupe, with the faster ships making all possible sail, they should have either caught or outspeeded Tello, and also arrived at Puerto Rico before the advice ship from the Canaries, which reached San Juan on 5 November.

Instead the English lingered on at Guadeloupe, trimming the ships, watering, mounting cannon and setting up some pinnaces, until 4 November, by which time San Juan was busily preparing its defences. Still there were delays: the fleet anchored off one of the Virgin Islands on 8 November to divide the soldiers into companies and parade the colours. Hawkins was now seriously ill with a sickness which, according to one account 'began upon newes of the taking of the

Francis'.[2] Only on 11 November was the fleet considered ready to sail for the attack on Puerto Rico.

In the town of San Juan preparations had been energetic. There was discussion as to whether it would be worth loading the silver onto the frigates and despatching them; if the authorities had known how long Drake was going to take to arrive, this would probably have been the best idea, though Tello was not happy about the condition of his frigates. It was decided to leave the silver in the fort, and to be ready to throw it into the sea as a last resort. The frigates were moored in line abreast across the entrance channel of the harbour, and two large ships were sunk ahead of them. One of these was the *Begoña*, which had brought the silver and been the cause of all these endeavours. An invader trying to enter the harbour was therefore limited to a narrow channel between the nearest frigate and El Morro, a formidable tiered defence-work on the western point of San Juan Island. The channel at the other end of the island was not navigable. The only land access from the mainland was by a causeway at the south-east corner of the island.[3]

The governor mustered a force of over 10,000, mostly civilians, but including 700 soldiers and 50 cavalry, as well as the men from the frigates. Four hundred and fifty of the soldiers were distributed to possible landing places, and the rest to El Morro and the parade-ground. As well as the guns on the frigates, many of which could not be trained because of their line-abreast formation, another seventy were spread around the island, twenty-seven of the best being mounted in El Morro, another five below it, and four more in the fort of Santa Elena, 500 yards into the harbour. The narrow channel, therefore, was very well protected from three different angles. To make up for a lack of small weaponry the frigates were supplied with quantities of stones.[4]

Drake's fleet was sighted at dawn on 12 November, sailing in close order. As it neared San Juan one of the smaller ships and several boats went ahead taking soundings, and in the early afternoon the whole fleet dropped anchor off the eastern end of the island, where the Spanish were not aware of an anchorage. As the anchor cables ran out, so did John Hawkins' life. He had known he was going; sixty-three was then a fair age at which to die. His affairs were in order, but he had modified his will in the last few days to leave £2,000 to Elizabeth. He was given a sailor's funeral, with no great pomp and circumstance. Other matters were pressing.

Maynarde, like others no doubt, was expecting an immediate

attempt on the island, but he was disappointed by a delay similar to that in the Canaries:

> I made my men ready presently to have lanced, knowinge that our sodaine resolution would greatly have da[u]nted the enimie and have held our [men] in opinion of assured victory, but I was countermanded by authoritie and duringe the time of our deliberation the enimie labored by all meanes to cause us to disanker, so workinge that within an hower hee had planted 3 or 4 peeces of artillery upon the shore next to us, and playenge upon the *Defiance* knowing her to bee the admirall whilest our generalls sate at souper with Sir Nicholas Clifford and diverse other, a shotte came amongst them wherwith Sir Nicholas Brute Browne, Captain Stafford ... and some standers by wer hurt ... Sir Nicholas died that night ... my brother Browne lived 5 or 6 days after and died.

Some accounts say that this shot struck Drake's stool from under him.[5] The Spanish guns had been ineffective at the start, but the gun which hit the *Defiance* was a demi-culverin brought to the battery late in the day, and it had a good man training it. It fired only five shots: the first cleared the fleet, but the next three all struck capital ships, which were preparing to weigh anchor when the last shot went through Drake's great cabin. Drake sent his scouting vessels past the town westward to take fresh soundings off the island of Las Cabras, across the harbour entrance from El Morro, where he anchored at eight o'clock next morning. After reconnoitring the approaches to the harbour entrance Drake called a council of captains, and it was decided to raid the harbour that night to burn the frigates. Maynarde and a Captain Poore were chosen to lead the attack.

At ten o'clock twenty-five or thirty fully manned boats and pinnaces (led as far as the harbour mouth by Drake, according to Spanish sources) were rowed in the darkness under the guns of El Morro and towards the frigates. They carried fireballs and other incendiary material. Unsurprisingly, in the nervous state of the town, they were seen and came under heavy fire from the frigates and from El Morro and Santa Elena. The boats clustered round the frigates and hurled fireballs into four of them, including the *Texeda*. Fires started in all four, but were put out as the frantic crews fended off the boats and threw down stones to smash holes in them. In the *Magdalena* fires were twice put out, but at the third attempt the blaze took hold at the stern and grew out of control. Her captain and crew jumped overboard and tried to swim between the milling boats to the other frigates. The captain reached the *Santa Isabel*, but the bosun and four of the crew were captured.

The fighting continued bitterly for another hour, in a harbour now lit by the great flames from the burning frigate, and the English grew demoralised and confused. In Maynarde's words,

> The burnte shippe gave a great light, the enimie therby playenge upon us with thyr ordinance and smale shotte as if it had been fayre daye, and sinkinge some of our boates; a man could hardly comande his mariners to rowe, they foolishly thinkinge every place more dangerous than where they were, when indeede none was sure.[6]

The English accounts do not number the losses, but they were evidently very high. Maynarde is again critical of Drake's tactics. His own view was that 'it had binne an easier matter to bringe [the frigates] out of the harborowe than fire them as wee did, for our men aboard the shippes numbred 160 peeces of artyllerie that played on us duringe this service ... but great comanders many tymes fayle in theyr judgment'. His ebullience fades as he lists his own friends who were killed in the action; 'I had cause of more greife than the Indies could yeilde mee of joye'. Spanish sources say that eight or ten boats and pinnaces were sunk, and between 200 and 400 Englishmen lost; the beaches were strewn with corpses on the following day.[7]

Expecting a repeat of the night attack, the Spanish spent Friday 14 November moving and refining their defences and constructing earthworks. Drake took the land breeze at about eight o'clock in the morning, stood out to sea, and worked his way eastward. Tello watched him from the *Texeda* and concluded that his plan was to turn with the change of wind and run directly into the harbour under sail, between El Morro and the frigates. At four in the afternoon the fleet had, indeed, turned and was running directly towards the harbour mouth. Tello hurriedly sank two laden cargo ships and the *Texeda* to block the entrance, and Drake re-anchored near the Isla de Cabras. At nightfall Tello withdrew his three remaining frigates into the harbour to save them from further attack.

In the council on the *Defiance* on the Saturday there were open differences of opinion. Most of the captains thought that going on with the attack would risk the whole voyage, but a Captain Rush said privately to Maynarde that so far they had barely looked at the defences, let alone tested them. Maynarde voiced his opinion to the council that if they were resolute they would take the place, and 'no towne in the Indies could yeilde ... more honnor or profitte'. Drake replied, 'I will bringe thee to 20 places farre more wealthye and easier to bee gotten', and seemed to have determined to give up. Baskerville, who still had not put a warlike foot on shore during the voyage, was also anxious to be away. On Hawkins' death he had moved from the *Hope* to the *Garland*. On the 15th, demoralised and with many wounded, the fleet weighed anchor and sailed away from San Juan. 'Heere I left all hope of good successe,' wrote Maynarde.

Drake, too, was depressed. He pulled his beard in vexation when he learned form the captured bosun and sailors of the *Magdalena* how few men had been in the frigates, and blamed Hawkins' caution at Guadeloupe which he thought had robbed him of Puerto Rico. The wind fell away to a calm, and the ships' sails hung idly for two days while Drake brooded in his cabin. Philip's silver, thirty-five tons of it according to the prisoners, was still in the fort, and three of Tello's frigates had survived to take it to Spain.

On the 19th the fleet anchored in the Bay of San Germán, at the western end of Puerto Rico. The ships took on water, oranges and bananas, and four days were spent putting together pinnaces to replace those lost at San Juan. With all hope of taking the island now abandoned, Drake gave the bosun and seamen of the *Magdalena* clothes, and set them ashore with a letter for the governor. Only Spanish versions survive; the gist was:

> I know Your Lordship to be a noble gentleman and a soldier. I write to let you know that whenever I have had dealings with one of your nation I have treated them honourably and mercifully, and I have set many of them free. When our men burned the frigates, certain Spaniards escaped the flames. After their capture they were treated honourably, as is the custom of war. From them I have learned that Don Pedro Tello's flagship seized a small vessel of ours with twenty-five or more men. If they are treated well and fairly, I shall be my usual self; if not, I shall be forced to be otherwise. I am sure that your city contains soldiers and gentlemen, and that our men will be treated well and given their freedom according to the rules of war ... I remain your servant in everything except the matter which lies between us.[8]

This letter became quite celebrated in the Indies, and versions of it are included in several reports.[9] It had some effect; John Austyn, one of the crew of the *Francis*, reported later that 'the Englyshe men receaved some favour, both in their imprisonmentes and their dyett'. They were taken to Spain with the treasure, and Austyn managed to escape and find a passage home in an Irish ship. He was back in

Plymouth by March 1596, before the fleet returned.[10]

The lessons of the Canaries and San Juan had not been learned. If Drake had arrived unexpected at San Juan his landing would have been largely unopposed and the town, without Tello's frigates and the ships sunk in the harbour mouth, might well have succumbed to the fleet's superior fire power. The possibility of surprising his principal targets, Nombre de Dios and Panama, was evaporating daily, but he seems to have been in no hurry to press on towards what had been the central aim of the voyage from the outset.

Perhaps he assumed by now that the rest of the Indies had been forewarned and that haste would make no difference; perhaps his prisoners had told him about the despatch boat sent by the governor to Santo Domingo as soon as the news of Drake's approach arrived with Tello. The warning flew ahead of him, relayed from Santo Domingo; on 25 November, the same day that he finally left Puerto Rico, it reached Cartagena; a day later, Río de la Hacha; a week after that, Panama.

XXII

AND LAST RETREAT DOTH CALL: PANAMA
1595–96

'There are three sundry places where this citie
may without difficulty be taken and spoyled
by the Pirates. The first is on the North seas in
a certaine place ... called Acle; ... the other
place is Nombre de Dios, although this is a bad
place, and naughtie wayes, and full of waters
and a very dirtie way, ... and another very
badde way, which is the going up of the
mountaines of Capira, which are of height three
quarters of a league. ... The other entrance is
up the river of Chagre.'

Bautista Antoneli's report to Philip on
Panama's defensibility, 1587

As if he were seeking to rediscover the days when he had first sailed
these waters as Hawkins' protégé, Drake crossed to the mainland far
to the east of the isthmus. After skirting Curaçao, which he thought
at first was Aruba, he sailed west along the coast and doubled the
Cabo de la Vela. He now spent three weeks in actions reminiscent of
his early voyages, revisiting some of the settlements where he had
come first in Hawkins' slave ships. No pretence of trade now, though;
no suborning of poorly salaried officials; but thoroughgoing sack,
looting, kidnapping and ransom, in an attempt to restore the voyage's
balance-sheet.

From the Cabo de la Vela he sent Baskerville with all the land
companies in pinnaces and boats to raid Río de la Hacha. They found
the town lightly defended and almost empty of people and goods.
With five days' warning the inhabitants had carried everything of
value into the woods and buried it, and many of the soldiers had fled
after them. The fleet arrived shortly after the pinnaces, and Drake

began a systematic combing of the area twelve miles around the town. With the help of some negro slaves and captured soldiers the English found large amounts of jewels, silver, pearls and silks, and took numerous prisoners. Drake also took 150 men east to La Ranchería and came back with a small haul of pearls from the fishery there.

Despite these successes, he was deceived into spending longer in Río de la Hacha than his gains justified. After over a week negotiations began for the ransom of the town and prisoners. A figure of 24,000 pesos was agreed, to be paid in pearls, but when the ransom arrived four days later Drake decided it was worth only half the agreed sum and rejected it. After a further delay of three days the governor, Manso de Contreras, came to see Drake. Despite offers and threats Contreras refused to ransom the town, and told Drake frankly that the negotiations had been simply a delaying tactic to gain information on the English strength and time to warn Cartagena, which he had now done overland and by sea.

With Drake in the mood he was in, Contreras may have been lucky to escape with his head; no hostage or security had been given for the governor's presence, merely Drake's word. He kept his word, gave Contreras two hours to get away, and put the whole of Río de la Hacha and La Ranchería to the torch, 'the churches and a Ladies house onely excepted, which by her letters written to the General was preserved'.[1] Baskerville, meanwhile, had sailed west with three ships and four or five pinnaces to burn the village of Tapia and some nearby settlements.

On 19 December the fleet weighed anchor and sailed along to join Baskerville. Drake took with him a hundred negroes, mostly from the pearl fishery, for a purpose which at this point was not clear. The small gains at Río de la Hacha were more than outweighed by the delay in Drake's progress towards Nombre de Dios. Panama had had another nineteen days to organise its resistance, and in the fleet, ominously, men had begun to die of fever. Captain Gilbert York of the *Hope*, elevated to Vice-Admiral after Hawkins' death, lived only as far as Río de la Hacha to enjoy his promotion. Thomas Drake was made captain of the *Hope* in his stead.

Santa Marta, which the fleet reached on 20 December, was even less productive than Río de la Hacha. Its inhabitants, long fore-warned, had removed everything of value, including the gold stores of the nearby mine, and after taking the lieutenant-governor and a few others prisoner Drake set fire to the town and departed. More men were dying from fever, including Captain Worrell, the trenchmaster.

In the heady years of the 1570s Drake's next target would normally have been Cartagena. Realising the extent to which the whole of the Main was aware of his approach, however, and perhaps influenced by the disturbing rate of sickness in the fleet, he decided to leave Cartagena alone and carry on, at last, to Nombre de Dios. The 80-ton *Phoenix* and the pinnace of the *Garland* lost contact in a storm, and the pinnace, with nine men, was captured by two galleys from Cartagena. Piers Lemon, who captained the pinnace, escaped after being taken to Spain and made his way back to England.[2]

The laments and protests about the defenceless state of the ports of the Indies which had been reaching Spain from colonial authorities for a quarter of a century had caused remarkably little change by the start of the 1590s. Constant awareness of the threat from privateers had brought about improvements in local organisation and reaction, but little in the way of fortification and military investment. Lately, however, an Italian engineer named Bautista Antoneli had been sent to report on and redesign the defences of the main cities.

With the protection of Panama in mind, coupled with his awareness of Drake's successes in the seventies and his recent preparations, Antoneli recommended that Porto Belo be fortified, and defence-works installed on the River Chagre and at the Capirilla pass, on the road from Nombre de Dios to Panama. The Panama authorities did little about it, beyond writing to the viceroy in Lima for help and stationing a few dozen soldiers in Nombre de Dios and at the mouth of the Chagre. Towards the end of November it was assumed that the threat from Drake would not materialise, and these guards were withdrawn. Early in December the warning from Admiral Tello arrived, followed soon afterwards by news from Cartagena of Drake's arrival at Río de la Hacha.

By now Lima had responded by sending a frigate to Panama with reinforcements under a capable commander, Alonso de Sotomayor. The Panama authorities delayed things further by arguing about the terms of his commission, and it was 21 December before Sotomayor met Antoneli and orders were given at last for an organised defence against a now pressing threat. Even then action was slow. If Drake had left Las Palmas alone; if he had accepted the ransom at Río de la Hacha when it was first brought; if he had sailed on past Santa Marta. ... Any one of these would have brought him to Nombre de Dios in time to attack Panama via the Chagre, or overland, or both, when neither route was seriously defended. Hawkins' reservations were to be vindicated, by the narrowest of margins.

Nombre de Dios put up a brief resistance from the fort which Drake had found undefended in 1572, but the small garrison force soon retreated into the woods. A small amount of booty was found: twenty bars of silver and one of gold, 'and this was all the place yealdid, ... for their treasur with other goodes they had sent long befor into the southe sea'.[3] The following day was spent in resting and preparing for a march to Panama along the mule-train route.

Sotomayor had by now done some purposeful reconnoitring and organising. He was quite resigned to the loss of Nombre de Dios. He saw more prospect of defending Porto Belo, but there too he had given orders for a delaying action and a tactical withdrawal if necessary. The Chagre had been closed by a boom of logs about fifteen miles from the mouth, and a defence force of fifty men left there in improvised forts. Sotomayor had also inspected possible defence positions on the mule-train route, but there were still no defences on the road on 29 December, when news reached him that Drake had anchored at Nombre de Dios. By that time Baskerville, with 600 or 700 men, was already on his way up the road towards Panama.

The English rank-and-file were probably in good heart when they left Nombre de Dios. The failures at Las Palmas and San Juan had not been of their making; they had not set foot ashore there. They had just had three and a half weeks of cheerful pillaging and burning at Río de la Hacha and Santa Marta, and had now taken Nombre de Dios as easily as picking an apple. It was raining, and each man was laden with his musket, forty bullets, his bandoliers of powder and another pound and a half of powder in his pockets, and a supply of biscuit which was supposed to be eked out for nine days. But Panama lay now just a long march away; for this they had been recruited; this had been their talk in the idle hours in the trade winds, when even the sailors had little to do except reminisce, speculate, and repeat the tall tales of gold and the old exploits of Drake.

They soon became aware of the realities facing them. Drake had chosen the wrong season. The first few miles made this clear; the clay of the track had been so softened by the continual rain and churned by the hooves of the mules that the men sank to their knees in it. They were under intermittent sniping fire from the Nombre de Dios garrison which was retreating ahead of them, and at several points they found the track flooded by rivers so that they had to wade thigh- and even waist-deep for long distances, or clamber over slippery rock, past swirling pools where 'he that missid foting was drownid without remedy'. Their shoes began to disintegrate, their biscuit was ruined, and much of their match and powder was soaked by the unremitting rain. They spent a miserable night huddled together at an inn, the Venta de la Quebrada, which the Spanish had partially burned. Baskerville wrote later that 'hear we fownd our selfes in greatt misseris ... yett the hopes of thatt rich place mad[e] us to think of no extremyty, and therfor as son as the day aperid we put forward'.

It was now 30 December, and ahead of them the road had at last been blocked, by a Spanish force greatly inferior in numbers, but in a position which it was determined, and well able, to hold. At a point called La Capirilla, not far from the Venta, the track, barely a yard wide, passed along the side of a gorge, with a steep drop on the right and a densely wooded hillside rising on the left. Sotomayor had sent Captain Juan Enríquez Conabut to this point with forty men only the day before, and they had now been joined by another forty or fifty of those retreating from Nombre de Dios. They had created makeshift defences by cutting down trees which fell across the track. At eight o'clock in the morning the English vanguard appeared.

Their attack was brave (even the Spanish accounts say so) but doomed. For three hours they battled to break through the fallen trees, sometimes managing even to seize the barrels of the Spanish muskets, but on such a narrow front they could make no headway. Some, notably Maynarde, with Captains Poore and Bartlett, tried to work a way round the barrier by climbing the hillside to the left, but the thick cover was difficult and was made worse by more felled trees. With many men dead and wounded, Baskerville consulted his captains. Powder was almost gone; the Spaniards could be heard felling more trees to block the track for some distance ahead, and the supply position was bad. Even the normally belligerent Maynarde agreed that to go on would be folly. Baskerville gave orders for the dead to be thrown out of sight, and the army withdrew to the Venta de la Quebrada carrying its wounded. There the injured who could ride were put on horses; they included Baskerville's brother Nicholas. The rest were left in the Venta in company with a few enemy prisoners, and a note asking for decent treatment for them.

The assault force was totally exhausted and demoralised on its return to Nombre de Dios on 2 January 1596. 'This Jorney brake wholy thoss tropes I caryed with me,' wrote Baskerville. Maynarde felt the same: 'Yt would have bin a poore dayes service that we should have done upon an ennimie had they been there to resist us ... This marche hath made many swere that hee will never venture to buy goulde at such a price againe.' Poor footwear had played a part; so had inadequate food supplies ('In this March a paire of shoos was sold for thirty shillings, and a Bisket Cake for ten shillings.'[4] With Antoneli's advice, Sotomayor knew what he was doing, and did it with brisk efficiency once he had overcome bureaucratic hurdles. But the real victors were the terrain and the weather of Panama.

While Baskerville had been in the interior, Drake had been burning Nombre de Dios and the few small vessels left in the harbour. On 4 January, dismayed by Baskerville's defeat, he called a council. From Maynarde's account emerges a picture of a shrunken man; a Drake so wearied by fruitless effort that he seemed unwilling to take on himself the burden of decision or persuasion. The atmosphere of general disillusion, tending to bitterness, emerges from Maynarde's words:

> Like as upon the cominge of the sun, dewes and mistes begin to vanish, so our blinded eyes began now to open, and wee founde that the glorious speeches of an 100 places that [Drake and Hawkins] knew in the Indies to make us rich was but a baite to drawe her majestie to give them honorable imployments and us to adventure our lives for theyr glory, for now cards and mappes must be our cheefest directors, he beinge in these parts at the furthest limit of his knowledge.

Drake's proposals were tentative, with no basis of experience, and Baskerville's reply was terse and almost insubordinate:

> There [i.e. on the chart] hee founde out a place called Laguna de Nichoragua, upon which standeth certaine townes, as Granada, León and others; also the bay of [Honduras][5], a place known to be of smale wealth ... He demanded which of those we would attempt; our Coronell saide both one after another, and all to[o] little to content us if wee tooke them.[6]

On 5 January the fleet sailed west for Nicaragua. Five days later it anchored off the island of Escudo, where a small Spanish frigate was taken. It had been sent along the coast from Nombre de Dios to warn other settlements, and the crew told Drake that none of the places along that coast was worth raiding. He stayed here twelve days, cleaning and watering his ships and putting together more pinnaces, which suggests that he may still have had in mind the possibility of ascending the Chagre. However, a Spanish report,[7] quoting information received from English prisoners captured later, says that Drake's plan was 'to go from there [i.e. Escudo] to a river in a bay thirty or forty leagues away, from where they thought there was a channel to the South Sea'. Unless this is based on a misinterpretation by the seaman of Drake's plan to ascend the Chagre, it suggests that he was aware of the geography of the Lake of Nicaragua and the rivers San Juan del Norte and San Juan del Sur.

The sickness which had affected the fleet since it reached the mainland was now taking a greater toll, accelerated by the weakened state of the men who had been on the march, and by shortage of provisions.[8] During the stay at Escudo Captains Platt and Egerton and 'divers others' died, and by now the total original complement had been reduced by a fifth.[9] Maynarde describes Drake as still sunk in depression, with an occasional desperate attempt at cheerfulness:

> I demanded of him why hee so often conjured mee beinge in England to staye with him in these partes as longe as himselfe, and where the place was. Hee answered mee with greife, protestinge that hee was as ignorant of the Indies as my sealfe and that hee never thought any place could bee so changed, as it were from a delitious and pleasant arbour, into a waste and desarte wildernesse, besides the variablenes of the winde and weather, so stormie and blusterous as hee never saw it before, but hee most wondred that since his cominge out of England hee never sawe sayle worthye the givinge chace unto. Yet in the greatnes of his minde hee would in the end conclude with these wordes: It matters not man, for God hath many thinges in store for us, and I knowe many meanes to doe her majestie goode service and to make us ritch, for wee must have gould before we see Englande.

In these sad final weeks of his last voyage, Drake's thoughts turned back to the simpler days before grand schemes for the restoration of monarchies and the seizure of territories filled his life, and he remembered the things he enjoyed most: the sight of a foreign sail; the mariner's trickery; the pursuit and plunder; the cheerful entertainment of his prisoners. Maynarde, young, reckless and critical, softened as he saw the old man's sadness:

> ... goode gentleman, (in my conceite) it fared with him as with som careles livinge man who prodigally consumes his time, fondly perswadinge himsealfe that the nurse that fedde him in his childhood will likewise nourishe him in his ould age, and findinge the dugge dried and withered, enforced then to behould his folly, tormented in minde, dieth with a starved bodie. Hee had beside his own adventure gaged his owne reputation greatly in promisinge her majestie to do her honorable service and

to return her a very profitable adventure ... And since our returne from Panama he never caried mirth nor joy in his face, yet no man hee loved must conjecture that hee tooke thought thereof. But heere hee began to grow sickly.

The sickness grew on him quickly, and towards the end of the stay at Escudo he took to his cabin with dysentery. The fleet sailed on 23 January for Porto Belo, and by the night of the 27th Drake was close to death, and knew it. Like Hawkins at Puerto Rico, he had time to set his affairs in order, as far as that was possible given the doubtful outcome of the venture. His will had been drawn up at the start of the voyage, with the acknowledgment that 'all men are borne to die, that the time of our departure of thys mortall life is most uncertaine ... as also for that I ... am now called to action by Her Majestie, wherein I am to hazard my life'. He had bequeathed properties in Plymouth and the contents of Buckland to his wife, given forty pounds to the poor of Plymouth, and entailed his estates on Thomas Drake. So Thomas, having inherited a feather bed and a Bible by being his father's youngest and favourite son, now acquired a fair portion of the wealth of the Indies simply by outliving his brothers.

In Drake's last hours, a codicil was added to the will, leaving an estate to Jonas Bodenham, his first wife's nephew, and another to Francis Drake of Esher, the son of his cousin Richard. Bodenham and Thomas Drake were to fall out and come to litigation over the terms of the will. Drake also gave farewell gifts to some of his officers and to young William Whitelocke, who had been with him on the Portugal voyage and was now serving him in the *Defiance*.

In the small hours he rose and asked Whitelocke to help him put on some of his armour, 'that he might dy like a soldiour',[10] but he was soon brought to his bed again, and died an hour later. Depression probably reduced his resistance to the disease; Baskerville wrote that he died 'as I thinke throughe greffe'.[11]

Baskerville took over command of the voyage. One of his first tasks was to oversee Drake's funeral. Like most wills, Drake's had been drawn up by a landsman, used to standard formulas: 'I bequeath my soule to Almightie God, my onelie maker and redeemer, and my bodie to the earth to be buried and entombed'. God may have received his soul, though some of his contemporaries, not all of them Spanish, would have argued otherwise; the earth was cheated. With the fleet at anchor off Porto Belo, only a few miles from the scenes of some of his most startling exploits, he was laid in a lead coffin and lowered into the sea, 'the Trumpets in dolefull manner echoing our ... lamentation for so great a losse, and all the Cannons in the Fleet were discharged according to the custome of all sea Funerall obsequies'.[12]

For many in the fleet Drake's death marked the complete ending of hope, and their hearts turned to England. Baskerville called a council on the *Defiance*, showed his commission, and was accepted as General, but he did not command the loyalty of all the sea-going captains. His plan, incredibly, was to return to Santa Marta, or if the winds were contrary, to head for Jamaica, but in mid-February, with deaths multiplying and rations now reduced to a miserable level, William Wynter in the *Foresight* allegedly took advantage of poor weather to leave the fleet, and several other vessels disappeared at the same time.[13]

The Spanish fleet sent to pursue Drake had left Spain just before Christmas, commanded by Don Bernardino de Avellaneda. He had eight large galleons and about a dozen other ships. Drake may have been warned of this by pinnaces sent for the purpose on 20 December. Avellaneda reached Cartagena on 17 February, sailed on the 21st, and ran into Baskerville and his remaining fourteen ships at the Isla de Pinos, off Cuba, on 1 March. After an intense but indecisive encounter, in which Baskerville's naval organisation seems to have been capable, the English continued their course homeward. In the passage to England the remaining unity of the fleet disintegrated: the *Elizabeth Bonaventure*, the *Little John*, the *Hope*, the *Jewel*, became separated one after another. Eventually Baskerville was left with only the *Garland*, *Defiance*, *Adventure* and *Phoenix*.

In the spring of the year the ships came singly and in little groups into the harbours of the West Country, with the news of the deaths of Drake and Hawkins, and of many another Devon man. Some participants salvaged what they could from the wreck of their hopes by embezzling bullion, pearls and munitions. Baskerville was accused of fraud, and charged Wynter with desertion; pay was long withheld from officers and men alike; penniless sailors starved. Royal expenses were saved by charging men for their clothes and for the shoes which had fallen apart on the march to Panama. The worst indifference to the crews' hardship was shown by Hawkins' widow and Thomas Drake, who refused to pay their share of the wages bill.[14] Baskerville and his wife began working out how to live on only fifty pounds a year.[15]

XXIII

HE WHO ALIVE TO THEM A DRAGON WAS

'There are people who will say that this whole
account is a lie, but a thing isn't necessarily a
lie even if it didn't necessarily happen.'

John Steinbeck, *Sweet Thursday*

If Drake had lived two hundred years earlier, and the pattern of his
life had been the same, his place in literature and legend would have
been among those crestfallen representatives of prosperity gained
and lost with whose fate mediaeval people consoled themselves (or
frightened others who were doing well). The Goddess Fortune turned
her wheel and brought him low; grim Death levelled him with the
common seaman. The solemn men of the Middle Ages would have
found him a perfect example.

In his own, more cheerful times, and later, he plays a brighter role.
On the Spanish side, certainly, the scale of Drake's achievements is
essential in enhancing Spain's role in combatting and finally defeating
him, but no-one uses him as a basis for moralising generalisations. A
proud nation needs decent opponents to nourish its legends; without
Bonaparte, Nelson's farewell to Hardy would have been a more
private and mundane affair, and Wellington boots would have had a
different name. Like Bonaparte in British eyes, Drake was both hated
and admired by the Spanish.

In the 1560s he had no separate identity in their vision of English
maritime villainy. Their early accounts of the action at San Juan de
Ulúa make no mention of him, though later the Spanish were made
well aware of his involvement there by released prisoners' reports of
his complaints about Martín Enríquez's treachery.[1] During his first
two voyages in the 1570s, too, he was simply one among many
indistinguishable foreign corsairs. It was the 1572–3 voyage, with the
startling attacks on Nombre de Dios and the mule-trains, and ensuing
intelligence reports from England, which brought his name to Spanish
notice.

He did not become instantly familiar to Spaniards. Pedro de Zub-iaurre, the Spanish agent pursuing Panamanian compensation claims in England, did not mention Drake's name when he wrote to Philip about his progress in September 1573, but self-importantly implied that he knew the name of 'this corsair'.[2] Even though Drake is not named, we can see in Zubiaurre's excited scrawl the seeds of Spanish mythification of their great enemy: 'He is one of the most skilled mariners in England; ... no-one else in England would dare to do likewise'. By this time, however, Philip's secretaries could put a name to Drake, though a wrong one. The king's letter to his ambassador in London following the Nombre de Dios raid in 1573 calls him *frances diaz*, which must be a scribal corruption of either *draq* or *drac*.[3] The name soon became all too familiar to the Spanish; as *draque*, *francisco draque* or *el draque* Drake began to appear with frequency in Spanish documents of 1574–6, and as time went on he was sometimes referred to familiarly as *el capitán francisco*.

It was the reports of the circumnavigation which filled out Drake's image in the eyes of the Spanish. The amazing navigational feats involved, the alarming raids on ship and shore, and his self-pro-claimed and often reported campaign of personal vengeance against Enríquez began to give him a mythical dimension. The idea that his successes were helped by supernatural powers began to circulate, but those who admired him most were those who came into closest contact with him physically and professionally. The soldiers and sailors against whom he fought; the masters, pilots and passengers whom he captured and released, found him a generous opponent, and hard to dislike. It is, of course, easy to be in a good humour with people from whom one has just taken a fortune in bullion. These people's testimonies reveal a rather swaggering, boastful man, but for a sixteenth-century Spaniard pride was no bad thing; it was often the thing a proper man relinquished last. He treated most of them well, frightened a few to speed his immediate purposes, indulged in no serious torture by contemporary Spanish standards, and released them unharmed and sometimes with gifts.

At the same time as his celebrity as an individual was increasing in Spain and the Indies, Drake was coming to be looked on as an archetype of various concepts. In the 1580s he is sometimes referred to simply as *el corsario*, as if he were now the only corsair in existence, and when the war had become open and official he was an embodiment of Englishness for both sides.

He was also strongly identified in Spanish eyes, as in his own, with anti-Catholicism. His crews are commonly referred to not as *los ingleses*, but as *los luteranos*, the Lutherans. One Spanish account[4] describes his successes as 'extremely serious, not so much for the sheer quantity of plunder as for the use to which the treasure is put in our Kingdom for the fostering of the Catholic Church, ... and lamentable because of the iniquitous abuses which it will go to support in the schismatic countries'. Drake's reputation in this respect may have been increased by outrages committed by others, particularly Oxenham and Butler in 1576. Their enthusiastic smashing of crucifixes, defiling of altars and insulting of priests probably went beyond what Drake would have thought necessary, although the bosun of the *Golden Hinde* seems to have done his best in this respect. Drake's religious services on board and his infliction of Protestant martyrology on his prisoners were fully reported to the authorities, and the concern he expressed for Oxenham and his men when they were in the hands of the Inquisition in Lima tarred him with the same brush.

The circumnavigation occurred in an era when Spain's imperial achievements had made grandiose epic poetry fashionable. Some of the poetry is generous in its recognition of Drake's greatness. The circumnavigation figures largely in *La Argentina* by Martín del Barco Centenera,[5] who is fulsome in his praise, and sees Drake's only flaw, his heresy, as a misfortune rather than a crime:

> This noble English gentleman
> Was skilled in navigation.
> To seaman's skills, and pilot's craft,
> He added martial prowess.
> Shrewd and astute ...
> [then another ten complimentary adjectives]
>
> But since the one, essential thing,
> The love of Christ, was lost to Drake,
> He turned his mind to piracy,
> Where no-one ever equalled him.

There follows a full description of Drake's exploits on the west coast of South America, and we finally see him rounding the cape of Good Hope into the Atlantic, blithe, unscathed and cheerful, with his ship ballasted with gold from the *Cacafuego*.

In another Latin-American epic written about a dozen years after Drake's death, Juan de Miramontes' *Armas antárcticas*,[6] there is similar praise, and the ideological content is greater. England is perfidious as well as heretical, but Drake is nevertheless a figure to be admired:

> This realm inconstant, changeable in faith,
> A captain raised whose glittering memory
> Will last undimmed through future centuries,
> Admired and eulogised eternally...

The question of England's heretical posture and its embodiment in Drake is treated ambiguously. The poet's admiration for Drake does not make any easier his task of justifying the success of such an enemy of the True Faith, and any Spaniard trying to do so was treading on dangerous ground. The theme of insincere conversion, a preoccupation of the Inquisition, emerges during the stormy passage through the Strait of Magellan, in which the seamen in one of Drake's ships vow to become Catholics if they survive the storm:

> This one says humbly, 'I do vow to Christ
> That if He saves me from these storm-tossed seas
> All my poor clothing I will sacrifice
> Upon the altars of the Church of Rome.'
> 'I vow,' another said, 'that what is left
> Of my poor life I will devote to prayer
> In pious and religious monasteries,
> In lowly service and humility,'

Drake's bravery and seamanship bring him through the storm, and in the incident of the *Cacafuego* the poet goes so far as to portray him as the agent of God, whose success, despite his heresy, is divinely arranged as a way of humbling an overproud Spain.

The taking of the *Cacafuego* and Drake's other prizes became common knowledge in Spain and Spanish America, and passed into history and literature. The eye-witness accounts by his released prisoners provided particularly lively material, much of it very creditable to Drake. In his biography of Alonso de Sotomayor,[7] whose energies foiled the attempt on Panama, Francisco Caro de Torres wrote generously of Drake's life and death:

> He decided, with great courage, to make the attempt. He was overtaken by a fever which killed him, just as the fleet was reaching the mouth of the Chagre.
>
> This river, therefore, is famous for having been the scene of the death

of so great a sailor. ... With all this fame and fortune he remained courteous, decent and hospitable to his prisoners, as we know from Captain Ojeda. Don Francisco de Zarate, whom he encountered in the Pacific, ... was generously entertained; they discussed important matters, and Drake gave him back all his property – silver, servants, a female slave and his ship – with great humanity and courtesy. This is a virtue which cannot be overpraised, even in one's enemy.

Similar praise of Drake's humane behaviour is found in the account of his victories in the Pacific in *Armas antárcticas*. Here the stress is on his concern for women and the Spanish sailors:

> With smiling face and words of comfort,
> Noble in gesture and courtly in manner,
> He dispelled their pallor and fear.
> ... he allowed no-one to touch
> The clothes, the jewels or the boxes
> Of any lady; instead he gave them gifts.
> Generously he gave the wages for the voyage
> To all the Spanish seamen, boys and pilot.

There is some evidence that Drake figured in the *romances de ciegos*, the popular, ephemeral ballads which were a news-bearing medium in the sixteenth century. They were delivered orally or sold as single sheets in the streets. That Drake had become synonymous with English piracy is evident from a ballad by Góngora, which alludes to him incidentally in a passage criticising vagabonds:

> What care you that Drake
> Our nation's ships distrains?
> What care you, though he take
> The treasures that are Spain's?[8]

In an anonymous ballad, it is the heretical aspect which is stressed:

> My brother Bartolo   is sailing for England,
> To kill El Draque   and capture the Queen,
> And the Lutheran lords   of her royal table.
> And after the war   he will bring me a present:
> A Lutheran boy   with a chain round his neck;
> And a Lutheran girl   to be Grandmother's maid.[9]

Most Spanish literature on Drake, however, has a courtly and literary character, and since defeat is neither appealing nor profitable as a literary topic the bulk of it is concerned with his less successful later years. As well as the works already quoted, written with the benefit of an overall view of Drake's life, there are some topical poems inspired by individual episodes. The early voyages appear to have inspired no literary reaction on the Spanish side. A triumphalist ballad by Alvaro de Flores on the battle of San Juan de Ulúa was published in 1570,[10] but the author's awareness of names extended only to Hawkins (Juan Acle) and the *Minion*. The West Indian voyages of the seventies provided no similar basis for poetic celebration; not even an action sufficiently close-run to be portrayed as a Spanish victory.

The same is true of the great voyage of 1585–6, except for one poem whose very history tells us something about Spanish attitudes to Drake. Pedro de Sarmiento, the great navigator whose advice, if followed, might have put a stop to the circumnavigation when he was aboard one of the ships pursuing Drake after the raid on Callao, returned to Spain around 1590 and became a member of the Council of the Indies. This status gave him the power to examine and censor written material concerning the empire. A work called *Elegías de varones ilustres de Indias* (*Elegies of notable men of the Indies*), by an ex-conquistador called Juan de Castellanos, came under his scrutiny. One book of it, the account of the deeds of the governors of Cartagena, included a passage of 200 pages describing Drake's birth and early career, the circumnavigation, the early part of the 1585–6 voyage, the taking of Santo Domingo, and then in minute detail the attack on Cartagena.

Drake's appearance, efficiency and lively wit are presented in complimentary terms, but his personal campaign against Philip is seen as effrontery, especially in his reaction to finding the royal dispatches in which he is referred to as a pirate:

> ... 'I will go and confront him one day,
> And on him I will be avenged;
> This Philip who sends such a letter.
> Misled by officials and scribes.'
>   All this and much more he declared,
> Frowning and pallid with rage,
> Insane with his triumphs achieved...

Castellanos' poem is by no means a eulogy of Drake, and Governor Fernández de Busto's organisation of the defence is recognised. However, the prominence given to Drake's exploits, especially the circumnavigation, which must have been a very sore point with Sarmiento, were too much for the great Spanish sailor. He wrote angry instructions on the manuscript that the section on Drake should be excised, and Castellanos' poem was published without it. The Drake account was not destroyed, though; it survived to be incorporated into a private library in London during the 1739–48 Anglo-Spanish war. It was sold twice at Sotheby's, and was eventually returned to Spain and published in 1921.[11]

After the raid on Cadiz in 1587, Mira de Amescua produced a piece of never-say-die rhetorical bombast in which Drake's victory is admitted, but is portrayed as the foolish sowing of a wind which will awaken an inevitable Spanish whirlwind. Amescua can be quite a capable poet, but he seems to have written this one in a hurry:

> The galleons of Spain fire their booming guns;
> War on this side! War on that!
> Viva España! Death to the English!
>
> The weak win the day; the strong are defeated;
> But to awaken death is no lasting victory.
> . . .
> This pirate, this heretic, blind in his greed,
> Will be caught like a fish with the hook in its gills,
> Seizing the bait with no thought for the danger.
> This impious glutton for gold and for silver
> Has come to Spain only in search of his death![12]

After the failure of the Armada it was difficult for Spain to find any crumbs of comfort, and her poets mostly left the events of 1588 alone. In the short term, however, some people simply lied about the result. A curious work published in London in 1589 is a piecemeal collection of claims that the Armada had won, and Drake had been captured, each piece with a refutation, and all in Spanish. Some of the claims are in letters written by merchants, etc., from Rouen to Spain; others are in popular ballad form, and are attributed to a Cristóbal Bravo of Córdoba.[13] The ballads refer to Drake as *aquel pestífero inglés*, 'that pestilential Englishman', or *el gran ladrón*, 'the great thief'. One claims that seventeen of his ships had been sunk, dismasted or captured, and the rest put to flight; another describes Drake's defeat in a ship-to-ship encounter. Drake is depicted as having sole charge of the English fleet in these ballad accounts; Bravo does not even mention Howard.

Three years later, the fleet of Admiral Alonso de Bazán, the new Marquis of Santa Cruz, was setting off on a voyage which culminated in the action in the Azores in which Sir Richard Grenville made his celebrated last stand in the *Revenge*. A poet called Andrés Falco de Resende addressed a sonnet to Drake in which he eulogised Santa Cruz's victories and alluded very selectively to the events in the Channel in 1588. Drake's reckless individual pursuit and capture of the *Rosario* is distorted into a flight from Medina Sidonia (here called the Duke of Guzmán), and used as a microcosm of the Armada action. The implication is that Drake is destined for further defeat at the hands of Santa Cruz:

> Famous Drake, and yet most infamous;
> Vile ingrate, unrelenting enemy
> Of all the precepts of our Holy Church;
> No captain you; much better called corsair;
> Upon your own home waters, timidly,
> You fled from the good Duque de Guzmán.
> How do you hope to face, on higher seas,
> The prospect of Alonso de Bazán?
> This, our great General, by the hand of God,
> Ruling the waters, powerful in war,
> Agent and servant of our Spanish King,
> Has many captured banners on his walls;
> His palace in Bazán is full of them,
> Yet he, with God's help, hungers after more.[14]

Spanish satisfaction at the failure by Drake and Norris to take the high town at La Coruña in 1589 was manifested in popular legend rather than poetry, and centred on the heroism of a woman, María Pita. Having seen her husband die at the breach made by Norris's guns, she took up a pike and a position in the front rank of the defenders and killed an English standard-bearer. Her spirit and example so inspired the defenders that the English were repulsed, and she was rewarded by being granted the pay of an ensign for life, and a pension of half the pay was settled on her descendants in perpetuity. The defence of the high town was the cause of huge local pride in La Coruña, and less than a century later the English casualty figures had been inflated to 1,500, in contrast to thirty-five Spanish. The story of María Pita's heroism remained as a focus of local identity.[15]

On occasions when Spain had anything like a victory over Drake to celebrate, her poets really went to town. The failure to take Las

Palmas opened floodgates of self-congratulatory versifying in Gran Canaria. An anonymous letter from the island,[16] by an author who saw through the euphoria and acknowledged that Drake's failure owed more to the islanders' luck than anything else, commented sardonically on the outpouring:

> We have had endless poems on the military theme; poets have sprouted where no seed had been sown. I swear that there have been more poems than on the battle of Roncevaux, which was a good deal bloodier than this bloodless affair. Such a mob of sonneteers emerged that the *Audiencia* ordered (quite rightly) that production should cease and all the epigrams and poems be handed in for approval and suppression. They included a ballad by Argote which, still unfinished, filled five sheets of paper...
>
> Despite the ban they are still being churned out. Francisco de Pineda, whom they call *el cortesano*, said that one could make a whole Montemayor's *Diana* out of this war. [The *Diana* was a long pastoral novel.]

Bartolomé Cairasco was a priest of Las Palmas cathedral. He may well have taken part in the defence of the town; certainly he was close enough to the action to be aware of specific details of what happened. His *Templo militante*, a series of saints' lives in verse,[17] is rather a hotch-potch, but considerably better than doggerel. In the section devoted to St Peter, with doubtful relevance, he includes a long ballad on Drake's attack. Hawkins is mentioned beside Drake in the preliminary organisation of troops:

> El Draque springs into a boat;
> Juanacre into another
> They dispose their finest men
> In squadrons...

but from that point onwards Cairasco is in no doubt about who is really in charge, and it is Drake who makes a stirring speech from the poop of the flagship.

Cairasco's description of the approach of the landing force not only has a vividness and degree of detail which suggest that he watched it, but also has support from eye-witness accounts on both sides:

> The air seems filled
> With banners and ensigns,
> Pennants and streamers,
> ...

With fife and with drum,
With clarion and bugle,
With loud call of trumpet,
The sea is a-thunder
. . .
The galleons are closer;
The launches row nearer;
Now we see weapons;
The faces grow clearer . . .

The details of the shore batteries' technique are also correct, and their effect is not exaggerated:

And every charge fired
Sends thirty musket balls
To rain on the boats,
Where many a man
Has his game ended;
Like a flock of doves
Pursued by a hunter;
Some fall to his small shot,
While others fly on.
Soon the bugles are stilled;
Soon the banners are lowered;
Oars hang idle;
The launches retire . . .

At the end of the poem Drake is forced to acknowledge the bravery of the islanders as he sails away. In another poem, remarkable in the original for extreme contrivance of rhyme and rhythm, Cairasco portrays Drake's departure as the flight of a wolf, crafty but cringing:

. . . So Drake, the untameable, is chased
From Gran Canaria, wounded now and tamed.[18]

Drake's failure and death in 1596 naturally caused some poetic rejoicing in Spain. An anonymous ballad written in Madrid when the news arrived, the *Romance del combate y muerte de Francisco Draque*,[19] is a completely spurious account of a battle between the English and Spanish fleets. The flying bullets, squealing fifes and blood-soaked rigging with which it is filled leave no room for mundane details of geography or names of participants. The Spanish battle-cry, 'Santiago!', rings out over a sea thick with English corpses;

Drake and 1,000 English noblemen die, at the cost of a mere seven Spanish captains.

Fortunately Drake's death also inspired something better. On hearing of it Spain's famously productive playwright, Lope de Vega, wrote the longest and finest Spanish work about him, *La Dragontea*.[20] If one makes allowances for the mannerisms of the times, it is quite exciting in places. What it does very well is reveal the ambivalence in the Spanish view of Drake. In much of the poem, which is about the last voyage, he emerges as a figure of huge stature whose exploits Lope, when he is not keeping a tight rein on his pen, is forced to admire. The religious feeling in the poem is obviously sincere, but when Lope is describing Drake's atrocities and death a slight air of obligation creeps in, a sense of political correctness and concern for the reactions of his patrons. The note of hatred in his climax has a forced ring to it, as if he has read over what has gone before and is worried that he may have sounded too admiring.

The title, which might be translated as *The Drakead* or *The Dragontead*, echoes those of classical epic poems, and the first line is a close imitation of 'Arma virumque cano' in the opening of Virgil's *Aeneid*:

> *Canto las armas, y el varón famoso*
> *Que al atrevido inglés detuvo el paso...*
>
> I sing of arms, and of the famous man
> Who stopped the course of the bold Englishman
> ...

The Drake = dragon association comes handily from the Latin form of Drake's surname, *draco*, meaning 'dragon'. English poets, too, were aware of this; it is good to have a dragon on one's side. Lope makes great play with the fire-breathing possibilities of the association at certain points in the poem. He is surprisingly vague about Drake's origins, calling him *el protestante pirata de Escocia*, 'the Protestant pirate from Scotland', and later he mentions Caledonia (but also England) as his native land. In view of the religious and political factors dividing Britain at the time, this is odd. He evidently had access to detailed Spanish material, but little or none to English information.

In this poem of ambivalent sympathies, the famous man of the first line is not Drake, but Philip; he plays little individual part in the action, whereas Drake has an epic stature from the start. In Virgil's

Aeneid, with which comparison has been invited by the opening, there are two virtually equal and opposed heroes, Aeneas and Turnus, each assisted by a divinity. Here too, Drake is inspired and guided by an allegorical goddess: *Codicia* or Greed. Sleeping, rich and at peace, in a Renaissance allegorical landscape, his sword hanging idle from the tree above him, he has a vision of the goddess. She recalls to him his earlier exploits in the Indies, and the circumnavigation:

> 'The Queen knew well the greatness of your heart,
> Which made the deep sea tremble as you passed,
> When she gave you those three brave little ships
> Which in one voyage saw the Earth's twin poles.'

The Goddess reviews other exploits: the encounter with Zarate; Cartagena, La Coruña, Lisbon. She recalls various dragons of classical mythology with which Drake should equate himself, and finally calls on him to stir himself and take up the sword again. Drake, inspired, asks Elizabeth for ships and men, and says she will be his Pole Star. She makes him Admiral, and puts Hawkins in command of the land forces. When Drake is expounding his plans Lope credits him with a precise geographical knowledge of Panama, and mentions his famous friendship with the cimarrons:

> 'I know the land; I have it measured out,
> Step by step, and yard by certain yard.
> My anchor I will drop off Santiago,
> A town full of my black and secret friends.
> ... Capira's sierra holds no fear for me;
> The dangers of Las Lajas; Capireja;
> The river Pequenil has heard my name;
> I know the plains through which the Chagre flows...'

The action at Las Palmas is dealt with very briefly, and Lope gives more space to the incident while the ships were watering at Arguineguín. Imagination takes over as the heroic shepherds, whirling biblical sling-shots, fall on twenty Englishmen, of whom fourteen are killed and their bodies smashed and dismembered; three are captured and the rest throw themselves off the cliffs.

Admiral Tello's capture of the *Francis* follows. Lope unblushingly justifies the torture of the crew on the grounds of their anti-Catholicism:

He interrogates the eighteen Englishmen,
Skin pressed on sinew, sinew pressed on bone,
And those who hate confession soon confess.

Lope clearly had access to full accounts of the night raid on San Juan. The official reports bear out his details: gun positions, the burning of the frigates, the English withdrawal lit by the fires on the *Magdalena*.

Río de la Hacha and Santa Marta are quickly dealt with. It is only after Drake's arrival at Nombre de Dios that Lope begins to supplement fact with imagination. So far Drake has been to some degree an admired figure, with an acknowledged record of brilliant achievement, going about his naval business but foiled by Spanish heroism. As Drake has barely set foot on land, there have been no atrocities to describe. Lope makes up for this in the episodes following the arrival in Nombre de Dios; ideology now looms larger, and usurps admiration. In a carefully worked sequence of incidents, some just possibly based on local reports brought back to Spain, but more likely created by Lope, the events of the English assault on the town, especially on its women, are made to symbolise the unsuccessful assault by Lutheranism on the virginal purity of the Catholic Church. Some aspects of the incidents may be taken to symbolise the rupture of the long-feared alliance between Drake and the negro population for the overthrow of Spain's empire. Spain's triumph is not only military, but political and ideological. Some of the Protestant English are brought to the truth by miraculous means; brands snatched from the burning. Lope, however, was prepared to concede no such redemption to Drake.

Baskerville (*Basbile*) departs towards Panama. The cimarrons of Santiago del Príncipe defy Drake's attempt to secure an alliance with them, and the chief praises the benevolence of Spanish colonial rule. The battle of La Capirilla is described with much accurate and lively detail. Drake sends boats to the Chagre, but recalls them when the news of Baskerville's defeat arrives. Meanwhile a crucifix saved from the cathedral has been sitting in a hollow tree, waiting to play its miraculous part. It is found by one of Drake's men, William, who is immediately converted by it to Catholicism, and deserts to the Spanish:

'I am determined to return to God.
The pseudo-prophet [Luther] I do here revile...'

The Spanish spare him; he tells them all Drake's movements in the voyage, and is sent to Panama, 'healthy in soul, who once was sick'. Vanquished, Drake and Baskerville re-embark under a sky glorious with the iconography of triumphant Catholicism:

> Above the vessels of the English fleet
> God's true religion soared in victory,
> Surrounded by the spirits of the blessed,
> Wielding her sword of fire and punishment;
> And there, against the holy vault of Heaven,
> There flew a dove, shining and white and fair;
> Her beak of rubies, and her feet of stars...

Drake's natural death from fever was not enough for Lope; deprived of success and health, he now loses the support of his countrymen, who plot his murder. Poison is put in his medicine, and he dies writhing in agony. After his life has passed before his eyes,

> Something he saw beyond, behind these things.
> In faltering voice, and trembling, 'Yes,' he said,
> 'I come, I come; oh fearsome shades, I come.'
> With that he died; his frozen tongue was stilled.
> The staring pupils flickered now no more;
> The livid mouth, cold with the chill of death,
> Spat out the stubborn soul; out from the breast
> Into the deep, eternal mouth of Hell.

All the resentment and frustration accumulated in the Spanish mind during Drake's thirty-year career seems to be vented in this. The closing stanzas read almost as if Lope feels he has gone too far. After an account of Baskerville's battle with Avellaneda and his limping return to Plymouth, and a passage of eulogy addressed to Philip for his victory, Lope ends with a fiery, glittering picture of Drake the dragon in the pomp of his heyday:

> His eyelids, raised, released the light of dawn;
> His snorting breath lit up the heavens with fire;
> His mouth sent tongues of flame into the sky;
> His nostrils poured out black and smoking clouds.
> Armoured in glittering scales of greenish black,
> His steely sides remained impregnable
> To all the darts, and all the spears of Spain,
> While he heaped gold, and gold, on glittering gold.

Drake's reputation in the Hispanic world was, if anything,

LA DRAGONTEA
DE LOPE DE VEGA
CARPIO.

Al Principe nueſtro Señor.

En Valēcia por Pedro Patricio Mev. 1598

The title-page of Lope de Vega's epic poem La Dragontea, *in which he describes Drake's last voyage and miserable end. Drake, the dragon, is succumbing to the eagle of Spain.*

The Cadiz raid of 1587, drawn by William Borough as part of his defence against Drake's charges of mutiny and cowardice. The capital J (top centre) shows the point to which Borough withdrew the *Golden Lion*.

Drake's taking of the *Rosario* in the Armada action. At first light on
1 August the *Rosario*, her bowsprit and foremast destroyed (bottom
left), is about to be captured by the pinnace of the *Revenge*. Howard's
Ark Royal, having looked in vain all night for Drake's stern lantern,
finds herself detached from the English fleet and close to the Armada
with little support.

The 2^d Fight betweene ŷ English and Spanish Fleetes being the 23 of Iune 1588. wherein only Cock an Englishman being wth his litle Vessell in ŷ Midst of ŷ Enemies died valiently. but ŷ Spaniards much worsted.

The Galleon of Don Pedro taken Prisoner by Sr Francis Drake, and sent to Darthmouth.

Two of a set of playing cards commemorating incidents of the Armada actions.

A modern view of the *Rosario* incident: Pedro de Valdés hands his sword to Drake in Seymour Lucas's painting *The Surrender*.

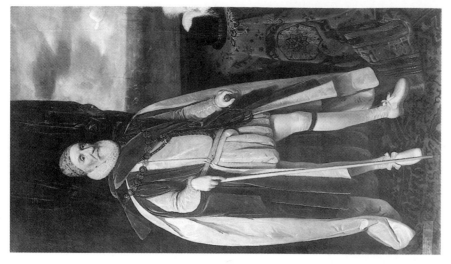

Charles, Lord Howard of Effingham, Lord Admiral.

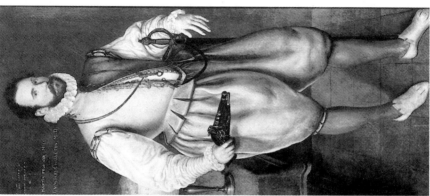

Martin Frobisher in a truculent pose.

John Hawkins, knighted during the Armada action.

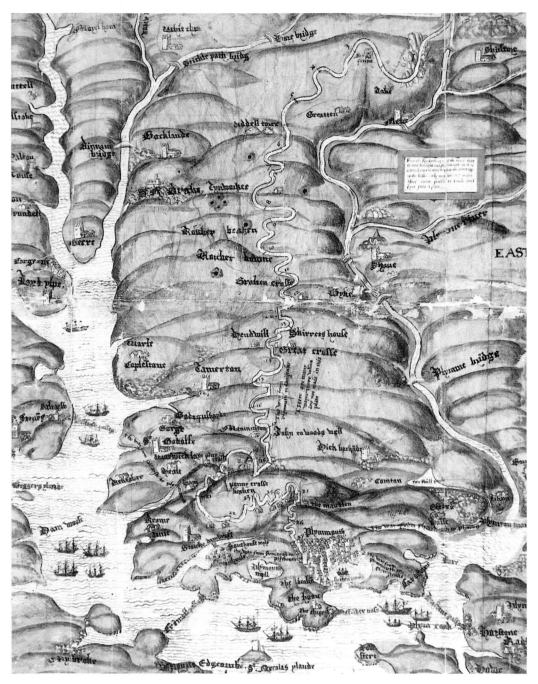

Drake's leat, built to convey the waters of the Meavy from Dartmoor to Plymouth. The 27-mile leat winds along the contours down the centre of the map. To the west, the Tamar estuary. Buckland Church is shown towards the top left, and below it the Abbey, marked 'Sir F Draks'. The leat provided Plymouth with water for three centuries.

To the west of this lande 3 leags of is aloue pointe and from that pointe you haue 5 leags vnto Nombra de Deos

one hill *South* *The other hill*

A rock

Some to of the se

The marche of thes too hilles one maie know by this representacion, This lande is parte of the Terafirma and parte of the neche of the lande by Nombra de Deos, 8 leagues to the westar is Nombra de Deos from this place. and to the eastuardes of this place theare are many Ilandes Longeste the coaste This Rocke is also amarck vnto you to knowe whether ye be yet com to Nombre de Deos or no.

S.S.E. *9 degres 30 m.* *N.N.W.* *Rock* *W.B.N.* *Iland* *Iland* *Iland*

4 Leagues of at see

This head lande heare representid is the Cape which lies to the westuarde of Nombre de Deos som 10 leags or as y saie the westarde Cape of the baie of Nombre de Deos, by the forme of this lande or Cape it is a verisoficent marke to knowe wheare you be y meant for. Nombra de Deos Ilandes Lickwise are a principall marck The fourme of the baie with some of the easterne coaste y heare set doune in platewise.

The toune of Nombrade Deos

Baie of Nombrade Deos

In this place the Compas varieth 22 Degres or wel nighe 2 pointes of the Compas as it is in the heithe of 8 degres

.Tera Firma.

Farlion   Baftimentos   eft   ya de puerto Bello

The coaft lieth E.N.E. and W.S.W.

This lande heare prefentid ftherwith the firme or runinge of parte of the neck and from Nombre de Dios / or ftmeane from the wefte Cape of Nombre de Dios Caulid Baftimentes untill you com to the weftwarde unto the flandes of Laies Minas Viefas de difcribinge the rocks and flandis betwene thes two placis alfo thentranc in to the good harburo calid Puerto Bello, note hou the corauente fetith heare to the N. E. The variation of the Compas 2. pomtes to th weft and all what fomeuer J. haue heare in this place notid J haue notid it plamelie with out englifhe Compas. as it hathe fherwid with refpecte of the variafion /

This Morninge / when the difcription notid or taken of this lande beinge the 28. of Yanuarie 1595. beinge Wedens daie in the morninge. Sr Francis Dracke Died of the bludie flix right of the flande de Buena Ventura fom. 6 Leagues at fea whom nou refteth with the Lorde

The coast near Porto Belo, drawn and described on the day of Drakes's death, which is noted by the navigator in his final paragraph.

The Buckland Abbey window engraved by Simon Whistler to mark the four hundredth anniversary of the Armada. Top right: the Abbey; bottom left: the two fleets; bottom right: Drakes's arms, with the two stars representing the poles separated by the *fesse wavye*, and the divinely-guided *Golden Hinde* on the crest.

increased by time and his elevation to the status of myth. Another two centuries on, in an era of recurring tension between the Hispanic and Anglo-Saxon worlds, Puerto Rico produced a jingoistic biography of Drake equalling in hostility anything produced by the subjects of Philip.[21] Its exclamatory title, 'Que viene el Draque! (Drake is coming!), and a translation of its opening lines will give an idea of its unremitting attitude:

'Que viene el Draque!'
  This was the cry repeated in anguish by women and in anger by men during the last third of the sixteenth century, in both Spain and Spanish America.
  'Que viene el Draque!' The exclamation summed up everything. El Draque, or 'The Dragon', as he was called, meant battle, ruin, mourning and desolation. It was synonymous with the approach of violence, pillage, cruelty and slaughter. This fatal name brought every evil; it was a comet presaging every disaster. This new Attila left pain and sorrow behind him; his ships left a red wake of freshly spilled blood.
  And who was this cruel, inhuman man? . . .

Drake is still a powerful myth, then, for many Spaniards and Latin Americans; they share a folk memory of an elusive and enviable enemy, the mere mention of whose dragon-like name, El Draque, retained the power to frighten misbehaving children, or to infuse vaguely erotic fantasies into the minds of García Márquez's decent South American ladies.

In England the mythification of Drake took a little longer than in Spain. During his lifetime England had a reality to set against the myth, which Spain on the whole did not. There were plenty of people in England who had small cause to worship Drake: the widows and orphans of the men who died in the voyages which enriched him; sailors and soldiers long unpaid, ranging the countryside and the streets of London; more orthodox and less rewarded officers such as Borough; aristocratic adventurers such as Doughty's brother and Francis Knollys; diplomats walking a tightrope during the cold war with Spain; not least the Queen herself, for long periods, and therefore anyone seeking the Queen's favour. Nevertheless, his exploits gave rise to literary eulogies ranging from street ballads to verbose classical outpourings and the chiselled lines of latinists.
  Popular balladeers in the Elizabethan period were fond of nautical themes. Some of their lyrics were cheerful generalities; others narrated

specific incidents of exploration, war or piracy. Most are lost, and survive only as registered titles.[22]

In England, as in Spain, Drake's early voyages appear to have aroused little literary response, though Stow's *Annales*, published in 1615, tell us that his knighthood was the occasion of books, pictures and ballads in his praise. There are various Latin eulogies of Drake, some being in generalised terms which give little clue to the date of composition; some probably followed closely on the return from the circumnavigation.[23] If *The World Encompassed* had been published sooner, it would no doubt have gained wide circulation and furnished the material for a greater number of popular ballads, but for diplomatic reasons the details of the voyage were not trumpeted around. The earliest published work on Drake's achievements, with the possible exception of some of the Latin poems, is Nicholas Breton's *Discourse in commendation of the valiant as vertuous minded Gentleman, Maister Frauncis Drake, with a rejoysing of his happy adventures*, published in 1581.[24] This is extremely rare, and is written in a high-flown style which must have destined it for a restricted public. It is a celebration rather than a narrative. For readers the most intriguing sentence was possibly the statement that Drake had found 'the land where treasure lyes, the way to come to it and honor by the getting of it'.

Cartographers had a pressing and competitive interest in the results of the circumnavigation, but information on Drake's route and findings was hard to come by. The great map-maker Gerard Mercator complained in a 1580 letter to Abraham Ortelius, the Cosmographer Royal in Antwerp, that

> the only reason for concealing the route of the voyage so carefully, or putting out different accounts of the route and the areas visited, must be that they have found wealthy regions never before visited by Europeans ... The huge treasure in silver and jewels which they claim to have gained by plunder supports this idea ... You might probe for information among your friends; if enough of them are asked, they cannot all lie so well as to conceal the truth forever.[25]

Elizabeth's wish to prevent publication of the details of the voyage may well be the reason why Richard Hakluyt's *Divers Voyages* of 1582 failed to mention the circumnavigation. One map-maker succeeded where Mercator had failed. Drake presented a painted map of his route to the Queen, and it was hung in the Palace of Whitehall. Somehow a Dutchman called Nicola van Sype managed to produce an engraving based on it early in the 1580s, with text in French and the title *La Herdike* [*sic*] *enterprinse faict par le signeur Draeck d'avoir cirquit toute la terre.* It shows the whole route accurately, with drawings of Drake's reception in the Moluccas and the grounding of the *Golden Hinde* in the Celebes, and a portrait of Drake aged forty-two. It also claims to have been 'seen and corrected' by Drake. How far this circulated in England is not known, but the detail of the route served as the basis for later representations, including a commemorative medal struck in more than one version by Michael Mercator, a relative of the famous Gerard.[26]

By 1585, and his departure for the great West Indies raid, Drake's celebrity was enough to warrant a poetic send-off. Henry Robarts' *A most friendly farewell, Given by a welwiller to the right worshipful Sir Francis Drake, Knight* claims on its title page to touch briefly on 'his perils passed on his last daungerous voyage, with an Incouragement to all his saylers and souldiers, to be forward in this honourable exploite'. Anyone who paid money for Robarts' pamphlet must have felt seriously deceived. He mentions the previous voyage, but gives no details whatsoever. He appears equally ignorant of the ships and officers of the present voyage, and apart from some fulsome comparisons of Drake to Hannibal, Alexander, David, etc. the piece is taken up with general assertions of Drake's merit and Robarts' own unworthiness. It is, however, interesting in that it corroborates the absence of previous literary praise of Drake:

> Unthankfull Englishmen that can suffer your worthy countreyman to rest in oblivion, and his renowned deeds with unthankfulnesse, so soone to be forgotten; my selfe the unworthyest of the countrey have long expected some thing from the learned in your commendation, but seeing them all to be so unmindfull of so worthy a personage, I have thus rudely adventured ... to let all my good countreymen by publishing the same to understande of your Worships departure to the Seas.

In contrast to Robarts' uninformed vagueness, Thomas Greepe's *True and perfecte Newes of the woorthy and valiaunt exploytes, performed and doone by that valiant Knight Syr Frauncis Drake* is a fully detailed account of the 1585–6 voyage, in naive but lively verse.[27] If Greepe did not take part in the voyage, he had information from one who did. His Prologue sets Drake up as an exemplar for future generations, 'for there is nothing can more profitte ... posteritie heereafter, than the leaving in memory so worthy a thing, for how shoulde we know the woorthy deedes of our Elders, if those learned

Poets ... had not sette them downe in wryting'. Drake is praised as a peerless navigator, but also for his one-man war against Philip: 'God bee praysed for hys good successe, to the great terror and feare of the enemie, he beeing a man of meane calling, to deale with so mightie a Monarke'.

Greepe has few poetic skills, but plenty of facts and a boundless enthusiasm. Here he is justifying Drake's failure to take Las Palmas:

> Then setting sayle from thence in hast,
> To the Canaries swift they flye;
> Three hundred leagues by count were past
> Ere the town of Palme came nie.
>> These proude Townesmen envying theyr fleete,
>> They shot at them in great despite.
>
> Let not these Townesmen be so bolde,
> I wish them not to bragge or vaunt;
> Twas not theyr Gunnes nor force that could
> Once make our English harts to daunt.
>> If wynde and waves had not so wrought,
>> Full derely they theyr pride had bought.

Papism is ridiculed, and sacrilege and pillage justified. At Santiago, for example,

> Fourteen dayes they kept this towne,
> With honour, fame and victory;
> Theyr Idoll gods eche where [sic] puld downe,
> With all theyr fond Idolatry.
>> With brasse Ordenaunce of good weight
>> They ballast their ships which were light.

and in Santo Domingo the inhabitants pray uselessly to the Virgin:

> Then for theyr Ladies helpe they pray,
> *Misericordia*, how chaunceth this;
> Our Fryars said no Masse today,
> For want of leasure they did misse.
>> Their Gods likewise they did desire,
>> But Saint Domingo could not heare.

The attack on Cartagena is narrated with particular liveliness and detail, down to the poisoned spikes set in the sand, and the victory is credited to God as Drake sails trimly away. The final stanzas are a eulogy of Drake as agent of God and servant of Elizabeth:

> Ulisses with his Navie great
> In ten yeeres space great valour wonne;
> Yet all his time did no such feate
> As Drake within one yeere hath done.
>   Both Turke and Pope and all our foes
>   Doo dread this Drake where ere he goes.
>
> ... His valiant minde, his secrete skill,
> By flying Fame eche where is spread.
> His loyall love, his meere good will,
> To Queene and Realme both seene and read.
>   Sith God is dooer of the same,
>   Let us all preys his holy name.

Greepe's poem was not published until after the Cadiz raid in 1587, and bound with it was the text of Drake's letter to John Foxe recounting the victory but stressing the continued Spanish threat. The words of the hero himself, in Drake's elaborately pious phrasing, must have been very effective in impressing a public divorced from current events by a lack of news media, and in stiffening national resolution:

> ... we purpose to sette apart all feare of daunger, and by God's furtheraunce to proceede by all the goode meanes we can devise to prevent theyr comming, wherfore I shall desire you to continue faithfull in remembraunce of us in your prayers, that our purpose may take that good effect, as God may be glorifyed, his Church, our Queene and Country preserved, and these Enemies of the trueth utterly vanquished, that we may have continuall peace in Israel. From aboord her Maiesties good Ship the Elizabeth Bonaventure.
>
> Your loving freende, and faythfull
Sonne in Christ Jesus.
Frauncis Drake.
>
> Our enemies are many, but our protector commaundeth the whole world, let us pray continually, and our Lorde Jesus wyll heere us in good time mercifully.

This is the full extent of the material on the Cadiz raid promised by Greepe's title page. Another work registered around the same time, by the printer Henry Haslop, *The most fortunate and honourable service for England performed by Sir Ffrauncis Drake the 19 of Aprill 1587 with his latest exploictes,* does not survive.

The defeat of the Armada contributed hugely to folklore about Drake, and in England, as in Spain, he was assumed by many to have led the fleet and was credited with the glory. Ballads were written on individual incidents, especially the surrender of the *Nuestra Señora del Rosario.* In the rather primitive *Eighty-eight, or Sir Francis Drake,* Drake's reckless departure from the fleet and defeat of the *Rosario* became fused with the fireship attack organised by Howard, who is given no credit:

> The Spanish train launched forth amain,
> With many a fine bravado,
> Their as they thought, but it proved nought,
> Invincible Armada.
>
> There was a little man of Spain
> That shot well in the gun,
> Don Pedro hight, as good a knight
> As the Knight of the Sun.
>
> ... The Queen was then at Tilbury,
> What could we more desire?
> Sir Francis Drake for her sweet sake
> Did set them all on fire.

A rather better Armada ballad, *The Great Galleazzo,* does not mention Drake by name, but the vessel in the title is certainly the *Rosario,* 'wherein Don Pietro de Valdez was the chiefe'. The capture of the *galleazzo* is the opening incident in the action, and an augury of good success overall:

> This great Galleazzo
>   which was so huge and hye,
> That like a bulwarke on the sea
>   did seeme to each mans eye.
> There was it taken,
>   unto our great reliefe;
> And divers nobles in which traine
>   Don Pietro was the chiefe.
> Strong was she stuft
>   with Cannons great and small,
> And other instruments of warre,

A Spanish argosy, free to use the four winds under the vault of heaven, in Pedro de Medina's influential Regimento de navegación.

which we obtained all.
A certaine signe
of good successe we trust,
That God will overthrow the rest
as he has done the first.

The same prominence given to Drake, at the expense of Howard, is notable in the refutations of Spanish lies in the *Respuesta y desengaño* mentioned earlier.[28] These can have caused little stir in England, being written as English propaganda for Spanish consumption, but they too reveal how popular feelings about the Armada were already centred on Drake. The reply to one ballad lists his triumphs in La Coruña, Cadiz, Santo Domingo, Santiago, San Agustín and Cartagena. The reply to the other is interesting in that it uses the same imagery of the eagle and dragon as was used by Lope de Vega in *La Dragontea*, but fuses the qualities of both creatures in Drake. This ballad gives some importance to Howard, but the battle is presented almost as a single combat between Drake and Medina Sidonia, with Howard looking on in support:

> The Duke flees; Drake follows,
> For Drake has his orders
> From the Admiral, Charles,
> Who sails at his shoulder.
> From his shade and his warmth
> Drake waxed strong in courage;
> The fame of his deeds
> Made all the world wonder.
> Like a ravening eagle
> Which stoops on its quarry
> With both its wings folded
> And talons spread open,
> So Drake folds his wings
> And swoops on his enemy...

With war fever thriving, Drake's next departure, for Portugal in 1589, caused an effusive piece of good cheer: George Peele's *A Farewell Entituled to the famous and fortunate Generalls of our English forces: Sir John Norris and Syr Frauncis Drake Knights, and all theyr brave and resolute followers.*[29] Peele would have made a first-rate recruiting sergeant:

> Have done with care my harts, aborde amaine,
> With stretching sayles to plowe the swelling waves.
> ...
> And let God Mars his consort make you mirth,
> The roring Cannon and the brazen Trumpe,
> The angry sounding Drum, the whistling Fife,
> The shrikes of Men, the princelie coursers ney
> ...
> Adiewe: to Armes, to Armes, to glorious Armes,
> With noble Norris, and victorious Drake,

> Under the sanguine Crosse, brave England's badge,
> To propagate religious pietie...

Peele is a little vague about the destination of the voyage (as indeed was everyone else to some degree, not excepting Drake and Norris): along with 'the Golden Tagus' he mentions 'the westerne Inde' and even Rome,

> There to deface the pryde of Antichrist,
> And pull his Paper Walls and Popery down...

but he is in no doubt about the shared command, carefully giving Drake and Norris equal space:

> You follow Drake by sea, the scourge of Spayne,
> The dreadfull Dragon, terror to your foes,
> Victorious in his return from Inde...
> You follow noble Norrice, whose renowne,
> Wonne in the fertile fields of Belgia,
> Spreades by the gates of Europe...

Drake's celebrity was increased in 1589 by the publication of the first English edition of the *Summarie and True Discourse of Sir Frances Drakes West Indian Voyage*, begun by Walter Bigges and continued after his death by a Lieutenant Croftes.[30] Both this and the 1588 Leyden edition in Latin included the marvellous maps by Baptista Boazio showing the movements of the English ships and troops in the actions of the 1585–6 voyage. With the previous grounds for secrecy now swept away by the openness of the war and the jingoistic atmosphere, Bigges' lively narrative filled out Drake's reputation with hard and inspiring facts. The authentic air of Boazio's maps caused them to be copied in England and abroad, even to the extent that the one of Cartagena was slightly altered and labelled Havana in a biography of Drake published in Amsterdam in 1596.[31] The months of 1589 preceding the news of the unhappy outcome of the Portugal venture were probably the high point of the sixteenth-century fever of interest in Drake. The inclusion of *The Famous Voyage* as a late addition to Volume III of Hakluyt's *Principal Navigations* in that year is further evidence of the demand for information about him.

In 1595 the departure of the fleet for the West Indies inspired Henry Robarts to compose *The Trumpet of Fame*[32] as 'an encouragement to all sailors and soldiers, that are minded to go, in this worthy enterprise'. In Robarts' eyes, this is Drake's expedition; Hawkins is relegated to a secondary position, not far ahead of a string of other officers including Cross, Thomas Drake, Crafton, etc, and neither Baskerville nor Clifford is mentioned. There may be a slightly tactless memory of the Doughty affair in the lines:

> Go with them then, and love him as you ought;
> Let not your minds to mutiny be wrought,
> Lest Justice' sword do cut off vital days,
> Whose power is such, for to command at seas.

Robarts knows the history of some of the ships in the fleet, and his poem is brisk, cheery and readable. The optimism continues in his ending, but if he reread these lines a year later he must have done so ruefully:

> And, for my part, I wish you always health,
> With quick returns, and so much store of wealth
> That Philip's regions may not be more stor'd
> With pearls and jewels, and the purest gold.

It was only after Drake's death that a really ambitious poem was written in his praise. Charles FitzGeffrey's *Sir Francis Drake, His Honorable Life's Commendation, and his Tragical Death's Lamentation*[33] is the closest English counterpart in style and imagery to Lope's *Dragontea*. The first pages of the book are taken up by a series of Latin encomia of Drake by various obscure poets, 'partly to supply the superfluity of vacant paper, partly to upbraid our Englishmen, whose negligence hath left him unremembered'. FitzGeffrey is no popular balladeer; his tribute is full of the ringing phrases of High Poetry:

> The Gods' Pandora, heaven's bright firmament,
> Fair Albion's bulwark, castle of defence,
> The world's rare wonder, th'earth's rich ornament,
> Heart's adamant, mind's sacred excellence,
> Wisdom's grave Delphos, virtue's quintessence,
>   Right perfect workmanship of skilful nature,
>   Some demi-god, more than a mortal creature.
>   . . .
> Where'er it be, where worthy DRAKE doth lie,
> That sacred shrine entombs a Deity.

No pretence of a balanced judgment from FitzGeffrey, then,

although he is well aware that Drake was far from universally popular:

> Some such there are, O shame, too great a sum!
> Who would impeach the work of worthy Drake,
> With wrongful obsequies' sinister doom,
> And eagerly their serpents' tongues they shake;
> And sith they cannot sting, a hissing make.
> But he who made all Spain quake with his fame
> Shall quell such mush-rumps[34] only with his name.

The poem is bursting with grandiose comparisons of Drake to antique gods and heroes ('which when he list could make great Neptune quake'; 'Equal with Hercules in all save vice', etc.), and uses the now familiar image of the dragon:

> Such was our Dragon, when he list to soar,
> And circuit Amphitrite's wat'ry bower;
> The rampant lion, and the tusked boar,
> The ravenous tiger born still to devour
> To bar him passage never has the power.

The individual achievements on which FitzGeffrey dwells include the circumnavigation, the Armada and the Plymouth leat. The ending, like Lope's, repeats the dragon motif, but with an assertion of a durable and effective after-life of fame:

> The sea no more, heaven then shall be his tomb,
> Where he a new-made star eternally
> Shall shine transparent to spectator's eye,
> But shall to us a radiant light remain.
> He who alive to them a dragon was,
> Shall be a dragon unto them again;
> For with his death his terror shall not pass,
> But still amid the air he shall remain
> A dreadful meteor in the eye of Spain;
> And, as a fiery dragon, shall portend
> England's success, and Spain's disastrous end.

XXIV

The Stirring Up of Heroick Spirits

Of late we had within our land
  A noble number of command:
Of gallant leaders brave and bold
  That almost all the world controld:
As Essex, Cumberland and Drake,
  Which made both sea and land to shake,
The Indian silver to obtaine;
  Then let us to the warres againe!

Ballad, *Gallants, to Bohemia*

Even FitzGeffrey might be surprised to learn how far his claims of perpetual future fame for his hero have been fulfilled. The first hundred years after Drake's death saw the publication of accounts of individual voyages withheld during his lifetime, complete biographies, and even an opera. There was a surge of interest in the 1620s; in 1625 Samuel Purchas' *Pilgrimes* provided much fuller information on Drake's exploits than Hakluyt had been able to give.[1] The titles of the seventeenth-century accounts of individual voyages stress the idea of patriotic inspiration. *Sir Francis Drake Reviv'd*, the account of the 1572–3 voyage, was published in 1626, 'Calling upon this Dull or Effeminate Age, to folowe his Noble Steps for Golde and Silver'. Its success was such that another edition came out only two years later. *The World Encompassed*, published in 1628, was 'Offered ... at last to publique view, both for the honour of the actor, but especially for the stirring up of *heroick spirits, to benefit their Countrie, and eternize their names by like noble attempts*'. This too had a second edition (1635).

The nation, especially England, continued to confer this inspirational role on Drake as the Empire grew, until his importance as the great example of adventurous Britain abroad reached its height as the pink areas on the map of the world spread in the late Victorian period.

As is usual with heroes whose mature exploits outlive them, there was interest in Drake's early life. This was partly supplied by Purchas and by William Camden's *Annales*, first published in Latin in 1615, then translated into French (1624) and then into English, by Abraham Darcie in 1625.[2] Later works made much of the details provided by Purchas and Camden of Drake's humble origins and religious upbringing.

William Fuller's *The Holy State* of 1642, which alternates chapters about the ideal characteristics for different callings with short biographies of the best examples of them, uses Drake to exemplify the Good Sea-Captain. Despite his praise of Drake, especially of his religious qualities, it is Fuller who comes closest to mediaeval moralising in his reflections on over-ambition and on the contrast between Drake's dashing early exploits and the long-planned but ill-fated Panama voyage:

> And sicknesse did not so much untie his clothes, as sorrow did rend at once the robe of his mortality asunder. He lived by the sea, died on it, and was buried in it. Thus an extempore performance (scarce heard to be begun before we hear it is ended) comes off with better applause, or miscarries with lesse disgrace than a long studied and openly premeditated action. Besides, we see how great spirits, having mounted to the highest pitch of performance, afterwards strain and break their credits in striving to go beyond it.

Fuller's final words suggest that there was still a lack of unanimity about Drake's merits: 'In a word, should those that speak against him fast till they fetch their bread where he did his, they would have a good stomach to eat it.'[3]

The demand for narratives of the voyages continued. Bigges' *Summarie and True Discourse* was republished in 1653, and again in the following year, this time as part of a compendium of four voyages under the title *Sir Francis Drake Revived*, 'who is or may be a pattern to stirre up all Heroicke and active Spirits of these times ...'. This last publication may have been the inspiration behind Sir William Davenant's lively opera *The History of Sir Francis Drake: Exprest by Instrumentall and Vocall Musick, and by Art of Perspective in Scenes*. This was first performed in the winter of 1658–9 at the Cockpit, Drury Lane, at a time when the country, under Cromwell, was at war with Spain. It is a good example of the resuscitation of Drake at times of national threat or war against foreign powers. The action, and particularly the settings, were governed partly by historical fact and partly by theatrical convenience.

Davenant's subject is the 1572–3 raid on Nombre de Dios and the

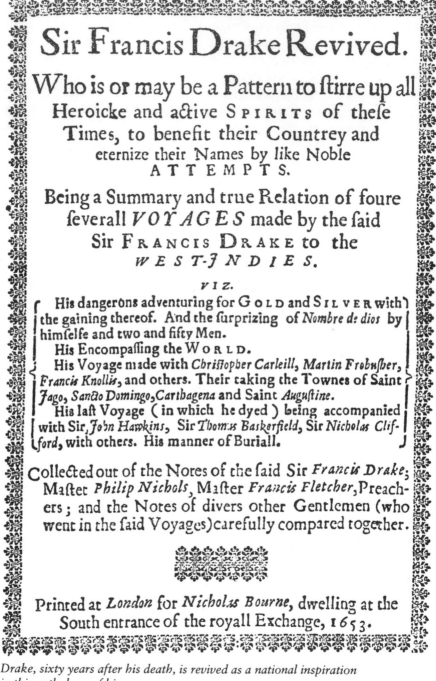

Sir Francis Drake Revived.

Who is or may be a Pattern to ſtirre up all Heroicke and active SPIRITS of theſe Times, to benefit their Countrey and eternize their Names by like Noble ATTEMPTS.

Being a Summary and true Relation of foure ſeverall *VOYAGES* made by the ſaid Sir FRANCIS DRAKE to the *WEST-INDIES*.

VIZ.

His dangerous adventuring for GOLD and SILVER with the gaining thereof. And the ſurprizing of *Nombre de dios* by himſelfe and two and fifty Men.

His Encompaſſing the WORLD.

His Voyage made with *Chriſtopher Carleill, Martin Frobuſher, Francis Knollis*, and others. Their taking the Townes of Saint *Jago, Sancto Domingo, Carthagena* and Saint *Auguſtine*.

His laſt Voyage (in which he dyed) being accompanied with Sir *John Hawkins*, Sir *Thomas Baſkerfield*, Sir *Nicholas Clifford*, with others. His manner of Buriall.

Collected out of the Notes of the ſaid Sir *Francis Drake*; Maſter *Philip Nichols*, Maſter *Francis Fletcher*, Preachers; and the Notes of divers other Gentlemen (who went in the ſaid Voyages)carefully compared together.

Printed at *London* for *Nicholas Bourne*, dwelling at the South entrance of the royall Exchange, 1653.

Drake, sixty years after his death, is revived as a national inspiration in this anthology of his voyages.

mule-trains. Precise geography, though, was of small importance to him and, one hopes, his audiences, Panama being located in Peru to economise on art-work in decorating the proscenium. This bore 'an Antick shield, PERU', flanked by two others, 'the one bearing the figure of the Sun, which was the scutcheon of the Incas ... the other did bear the Spread Eagle, in significance of the Austrian family. This Frontispiece was the same which belong'd to the late representation; and it was convenient to continue it, our Argument being in the same country'.

Another concession to pragmatism was the creation of a visually striking role for a dishevelled lady. At one point Drake's company suddenly come across a bride who has been seized from her wedding by the cimarrons. She is in a distressed state, and is appealing, mute, to Heaven. Drake, in his well-known concern for the welfare of foreign ladies, makes the cimarrons release her, and the real action continues. The opera includes many correct details of the 1572–3 expedition: the building of the pinnaces at Port Pheasant; the alliance with Rance (here called Rouse); the *recuas*, which Davenant calls 'recoes'; and the name of Drake's cimarron ally, Pedro. We see Drake climb the tree from which he obtained his famous view of the Atlantic and Pacific, and we hear a prophesy of the circumnavigation from Pedro, who is implausibly fluent for a Panamanian negro:

DRAKE [*ascending the tree*]:
   When from those lofty branches I
   The South Atlantic spy,
   My vows shall higher fly,
   Till they with highest heav'n prevail
   That, as I see it, I may on it sail.
PEDRO:
   If Prophesie from me may be allow'd,
   Renowned DRAKE, Heav'n does decree
   That happy Enterprize to thee ...

There are several jolly choruses and dances by the Indians, and scenes are introduced by *a martiall saraband, a symphony variously humour'd*, etc. The attack on the mule-trains was an obvious problem in a production constrained by economics, but with a good deal of ringing of bells and clash of arms off-stage, and some fevered entries and exits by commentators, Drake is enabled to make off to the ships in triumph, leaving the stage vacant for a dance symbolic of a triple alliance against colonial Spain:

The Grand Dance begins, consisting of two Land-souldiers, two Sea-men, two Symerons, and a Peruvian; intimating, by their severall interchange of salutations, their mutuall desires of amity. The Dance being ended,

The Curtain falls.

A second part was promised, but does not survive. The first part was revived in 1663, and printed in the author's works ten years later, shortly after the appearance of a new popular biography, *The Life and Death of the Valiant and Renowned Sir Francis Drake, His Voyages and Discoveries in the West Indies, and about the World, with his Noble and Heroick Acts*, by Samuel Clark. Clark is eager to cast Drake in a heroic and empire-building mould. By this time selectivity is burnishing some incidents of Drake's career and dulling others. Questionable events (the Doughty affair) and lack of success (Portugal and the final voyage) are passed over very quickly. The climb from humble birth and upbringing is admired, and the capture of the *Rosario* is dealt with at length, with anecdotal detail taken from *Purchas His Pilgrimes*:

> Valdez, to seem valorous, answered, that himself was Don Pedro, and stood upon his Honour, and therefore propounded certain conditions. Drake replyed, that he had no leasure to Parley. If he would immediately yield, well and good; If not, he should soon find that Drake was no dastard. Pedro, hearing that it was the fiery Drake (whose very name was fearful to the Spaniards) that had him in chase, presently yielded, and ... came aboard ... where he protested that he and all his men were resolved to have died fighting, had they not faln into such Noble hands, whose valour and felicity was so great, that Mars and Neptune seemed to wait on him in all his enterprises ...

Another incident dwelt on by Clark is the claiming of Nova Albion. At a time when the geographical sovereignty of North America was unclear, the crowning of Drake by the local chief is given a grand significance:

> [The King] by signs resigned to him his right and title in that whole land; wherefore in the name and to the use of Her Majesty, he took the Scepter, Crown and Dignity of the said country into his hand ...
>
> This country Captain Drake named Nova Albion, and nailed fast to a tree a Plate of brass whereon was engraven Queen Elizabeth's name; the day and year of their arrival, and of the resignation of that kingdom by the King and People into her Majesties hands ...

Sr. Francis Drake.

Enter Drake *Junior*.

Drak. MOre Pikes! more Pikes ! to reinforce
jun. That Squadron, and repulſe the Horſe.

Enter Rouſe.

Rouſ. THe Foe does make his firſt bold count'-
　　　　nance good.　　　　　　　(ſtood.
OurCharge was bravely made, and well with-

Enter Pedro.

Rouſ. YOur *Sym'rons*, valiant *Pedro*, ſeem to reel.
Pedr. Suſpect your Rocks at Sea. They do bur
　　　　wheel.　　　　　　　　　(Bank,
Haſte! haſte! brave *Sym'rons*, haſte to gain that
And with your Arrowes gall them in the Flank.
　Claſhing of Arms within again.　　　*Exeunt.*

Enter Drake *Senior, Page.*

Drak. HOw warmly was this ſtrife
ſen. Maintain'd 'twixt Death and Life,
Till Blood had quench'd the flame of Valours fire?
　Death ſeeming to advance in haſte,
　Whilſt Life, though weary, yet ſtood faſt ;
For Life is ſtill unwilling to retire.
　My Land-men bravely fought,
　And high renown have got,

Drake as operatic hero: the alliance with Pedro's cimarrons enlivens Sir William Davenant's seventeenth-century piece, Sir Francis Drake.

Demand for biographies of Drake continued to the end of the century: the compendium *Sir Francis Drake Revived* was republished, with additions, in 1687, and had gone through three further printings by 1695.

In the eighteenth century, literary creativity centred on Drake faded away, though versions based on the earlier accounts continued to appear. Dr Johnson's *Life of Drake*, which appeared in serial form in *The Gentleman's Magazine* in 1740 and 1741, is a pot-boiling summary based on seventeenth-century accounts, with some ponderous reflections on the merits of determination.[4] Popular interest still justified the production of souvenir items, particularly snuff-boxes, bearing Drake's portrait, and in some cases a design perhaps based on a sixteenth-century emblem of Drake which shows a globe surmounted by a ship guided by a divine hand.[5] The demand for these may have had to do with the rise of genteel tourism to the West Country, and the tradition of these boxes perhaps originated in the sale of items made from the timbers of the *Golden Hinde* when she was broken up after being preserved for several decades at Deptford.

Daniel Defoe's circumnavigator in his *A New Voyage round the World, by a Course never sailed before* (1725) is to some extent an imaginary imitator of Drake, and he mentions his proverbial fame as the first Englishman to pass through the Strait of Magellan:

> Such a mighty and valuable thing also was the passing this Straight, that Sir Francis Drake's going thro' it gave birth to that famous old Wives saying, viz, that Sir Francis Drake shot [i.e. passed through] the gulph; a saying that was current in England for many years, I believe near a Hundred after Sir Francis Drake was gone his long[est] journey of all; as if there had been but one Gulph in the world, and that passing it had been a Wonder next to that of Hercules cleansing the Egean Stable.

So far we have heard nothing of the best-known Drakean legend of all: the game of bowls. None of the sixteenth-century sources mentions Drake's leisured reaction to the news of the Armada's approach, though Stow's *Annals* of 1600 mentions that 'officers and others kept revels on the shore, dancing, bowling, and making merry ... at the instant of the foe's approach'. This is reinforced by a reference in a political tract published in 1624, but still with no mention of Drake. By the early eighteenth century, however, and possibly continuously since 1588, popular oral tradition ascribed a special role in the incident to Drake. In 1736 William Oldys mentions the game in his *Life of Raleigh*, adding that 'the tradition goes that

THE
English Heroe:
OR,
Sir Francis Drake Revived.

Being a full Account of the Dangerous Voyages, Admirable Adventures, Notable Discoveries, and Magnanimous Atchievements of that Valiant and Renowned Commander. As,

I. His Voyage in 1572. to *Nombre de Dios* in the *West-Indies*, where they saw a Pile of Bars of Silver near seventy foot long, ten foot broad, and 12 foot high.

II. His incompassing the whole World in 1577. which he performed in Two years and Ten months, gaining a vast quantity of Gold and Silver.

III. His Voyage into *America* in 1585. and taking the Towns of St. *Jago*, St. *Domingo*, *Carthagena*, and St. *Augustine*.

IV. His last Voyage into those Countreys in 1595. with the manner of his Death and Burial.

Recommended as an Excellent Example to all Heroick and Active Spirits in these days to endeavour to benefit their Prince and Countrey, and Immortalize their Names by the like worthy Undertakings.

Revised, Corrected, very much Inlarged, reduced into Chapters with Contents, and beautified with Pictures.

By R. B.

Licensed and Entred according to Order, March 30. 1687.

LONDON, Printed for *Nath. Crouch* at the *Bell* in the *Poultry* near *Cheapside*. 1687.

A century after Cadiz, Drake continues to serve as an exemplar of national heroism: one of several editions of The English Heroe.

Drake would needs see the game up, but was soon prevailed on to go and play out the rubbers with the Spaniards'. (Drake's famous words, 'There is plenty of time to win the game and beat the Spaniards too', seem to have been coined only in 1835, in Tytler's biography of Raleigh.[6] In 1995 Drake is still the patron of English bowls players, whose association is called The Francis Drake Society.)

The public awareness of exploration aroused in the eighteenth century by the voyages of Captain Cook revived interest in earlier travellers, and George Anderson included 'A New, Authentic and Complete Account' of Drake's circumnavigation in his edition of Cook's voyages in 1784. This is perhaps the only work in English which heartily condemns aspects of Drake's exploits and character, while acknowledging his achievements as a seaman. Anderson's sympathies in the Doughty affair are all with the victim, probably through an over-reliance on John Cooke's account; he writes of Drake's 'perfidy and self-conceit' which ruined the only two enterprises in which he was employed in a joint command, and his summing-up is very much in sympathy with Drake's Spanish victims:

> If we have withdrawn the veil which has hitherto covered his infirmities, it has been in the pursuit of Truth. In the current of success, even crimes of the deepest dye are sometimes patronised even by the public. The actions which gave rise to Drake's popularity, are such as a courageous leader, with an hundred armed followers, might in these peaceable times easily perform, by entering the cities or towns on the coast of Britain, cutting the throats of the watch, and all who happen to be awake in the streets, breaking open and plundering houses and churches, and ... making their escape with their booty. ... Were such a company masters of an armed vessel, ... what should hinder their sailing from place to place, ... performing like exploits in every town they came to? Or would the man who should undertake and execute an enterprise of such a horrid nature, be justly entitled to the name of Hero? ... To dignify actions, therefore, of the most infamous pirate with the name of great is to exalt vice, and to substitute successful villainy in the place of substantial virtue.

In the force of his criticism, Anderson is a lone voice. One should remember that his main subject is Captain James Cook, beside whose stern Yorkshire probity Drake's gold-hunting exploits and fraught relationships with his subordinates could hardly be compared favourably.[7] It was not, however, a time of general enthusiasm for Drake, and there is no trace of any bicentenary celebrations in the 1780s in either the *Gentleman's Magazine* or the *Annual Register*. In 1800, however, with England again intermittently threatened with invasion, and national pride centred on the Navy, Drake was the subject of another opera, James Cross's *Sir Francis Drake and Iron Arm*, presented at the New Royal Circus in London.

Buckland Abbey was becoming part of the itinerary of the cultured traveller, though George Lipscomb's *A Journey into Cornwall* of 1799 gives a rather depressing picture of the house: 'There are no apartments worth describing, and the grounds exhibit a melancholy appearance of neglect and want of management.' He was impressed, however, by the Drake relics inside: his 1594 portrait, a copy of his patent of arms, and 'the sword of this great man, together with an old Drum, which circuited the world with him.'

It was in the nineteenth century, after the Napoleonic Wars had put British troops on Spanish soil again, that the growth in British imperial power renewed and fed the interest in Drake. The developing overseas interests increased the heroic role of the Navy and required men with Drakean characteristics to voyage abroad and face lands and dangers unknown. Many of them combined the Drakean motives of patriotism and enrichment.

In the early 1800s Robert Southey's *Lives of the British Admirals* testified to a renewed interest in the nation's naval past, and James Burney's *Chronological History of the Discoveries in the South Sea* included a long account of Drake's circumnavigation based on a range of sixteenth century sources.[8] In mid-century a wave of editions made Drake material readily available, notably in the publications of the Hakluyt Society, which were so much in tune with the exploring spirit of the times. John Barrow's biography of Drake, published in 1843,[9] was followed by editions of Maynarde's narrative of the last voyage (1849), *The World Encompassed* (1854), and Leng's account of the Cadiz raid (1863).[10]

On a less scholarly level the enthusiastic chauvinism of Kingsley's *Westward Ho!* set the tone for many naive successors for whom the world's oceans were divinely allotted to Englishmen; other nationalities were destined for defeat and subjugation because of their natural inferiority, misguided religion, pride and cruelty. 'Had [Drake and his companions],' wrote Kingsley, 'not first crippled, by their West India raids, the ill-gotten resources of the Spaniard, and then crushed his last effort in ... the glorious fight of 1588, what had we been now but a Popish appanage of a world tyranny as cruel as heathen Rome itself, and far more devilish?' The *Western Antiquary* quoted these words in 1886, when floating the idea of organising, for 1888, 'such a demonstration as should show Young England of the Victorian era how we regarded the deeds of their forefathers of the Elizabethan age'.[11]

In the heyday of imperial expansion in the reign of another strong-willed Queen, and on into the twentieth century, Drake was for many readers, including the young, a bluff, hearty servant of Elizabeth who pored over charts in London taverns, leapt on horseback and dashed through the night to the West Country, punctured the pride of Spanish Dons and behaved with decent English magnanimity towards the defeated, like the Captain of the First XV calling for three cheers for the losers.

The tercentenary celebrations of the 1880s provoked a serious outbreak of verse, non-verse and anecdote.[12] The Drury Lane Theatre mounted a 'grand spectacular drama', *The Armada*.[13] It is a stage manager's nightmare; the action zig-zags dizzily from Plymouth Hoe, where an English sea-dog sings a ditty as overture, to the Escorial, back to Plymouth, on to outside the Tower of London, and again to Plymouth. We are then taken off to the *Revenge*, then to Medina Sidonia's flagship, and finally to Seville, where after an initial report of Spanish victory the true news arrives. Throughout the play Drake is the hero; Howard is allowed two dozen words; Raleigh only four; Frobisher and Grenville are mere walk-on parts. The main ingredients are the game of bowls, the capture of the *Rosario*, and the fire-ships, in all of which Drake is central. The hallowed phrases of Drakean dialogue are introduced: 'Nay, we will finish our game first. There will be time enough to fight the Spaniards after'; and 'Drake is no dastard'. The effects men worked hard to provide broadsides, trumpet-calls, bells, tumult and leaping flames. The defeat of the Armada was now, in the general consciousness of the nation, a victory by Drake. The lines in which Philip complains about English nautical power must have sounded congratulatory to Victoria's imperialist subjects:

> Their flag has compass'd round the globe, defiled
> Our shore, traversed the broad Pacific...
> Spoiled our possessions, contemned our flag,
> Defied us e'en to the far Indies.

The production was accompanied by an exhibition of Armada material in the theatre. This had been transferred from Plymouth, where it had been supported by a pageant, a banquet and a reconstruction of the game of bowls. It was reported that 'as in the case of the portraits, so in that of the relics, there were more specimens of the personal property of Drake than of all the other Armada heroes put together. This seems like evidence that his popularity long outlived him, and that his personal relics were treasured by those who had the good fortune to own aught that he had once possessed'.

Exhibits included two of Drake's walking-sticks, two swords, a dagger, a silk purse, a spoon, tankard and plate, an astrolabe, tapestries, and a dozen examples of the Drake snuff-box. A number of items were obviously of post-1600 origin, though several of the owners claimed that they were gifts from Drake himself to one of their ancestors. Already in Drake's lifetime, and in the years following, gifts from him were greatly treasured, and mentioned as specific bequests in wills. A Thomas White left his son 'my Ringe which I allwaies weare that Sr. ffraunces Drake gave', and his daughter-in-law was to have 'the double hoope ringe that her Mother allwaies wore which Sir ffraunces Drake gave'. A gold-embroidered silk cap and scarf presented to Drake by the Queen when she knighted him were possibly the ones bequeathed by his brother Thomas to his son Francis.[14]

The Plymouth Museum today has a silver-gilt cup in the form of a globe, supposedly a New Year gift from Elizabeth to Drake in 1582 (though recent cartographic evidence suggests that the engraved globe may be later). In Devonport HMS *Drake* has a pair of silver-mounted coconut cups believed to have been acquired on the circumnavigation, and a sword bearing the royal arms and Drake's own, which was used to knight Sir Francis Chichester after his solo voyage around the world in 1967. A few relics survive which were made from the timbers of the *Golden Hinde*: a chair in the Bodleian Library; a table in the Middle Temple.[15]

Relics were all very well, but the great man's bones were elsewhere. The *Graphic*, on 17 February 1883, reported an interesting project for the British navy as it went about its imperial business:

A search for the body of Sir Francis Drake is to be made by the British Squadron belonging to the West Indian and American Stations, which during its coming cruise will visit Puerto Cabello [sic]. Off this port nearly three centuries ago the gallant explorer was buried at sea in a leaden coffin, and every effort will be made to recover the coffin.

It is to be hoped that the Navy did not spend too long dredging and diving off Puerto Cabello, which is in Venezuela, some hundreds of miles from Porto Belo, where Drake's body was disposed of. The coffin has not resurfaced, though the project shows signs of doing so as I write.

The fact that Drake's body had never returned to England, that it was lying under a sunlit sea in an exotic place, may have contributed to the birth of the myth of Drake as the hero who, like Arthur, is merely asleep and will return in the hour of his country's need. There seems to be no trace of this until the nineteenth century, though the seeds were sown by the presentation of Drake as an inspirational example in the seventeenth century and nurtured by popular legends of his magical powers.

The concept of Drake as wizard was already current in Spain and England in his own lifetime. At the level of folklore, especially in the West Country, this idea persisted in local legends. Robert Southey mentions some of them in a review of a book on Lope de Vega in 1818. One current in Somerset concerned Drake's wife: when he left England in 1577 he told her that if he had not returned after ten years she might marry again. She remained faithful, but after ten years accepted a proposal from a suitor. As they were walking to church, a great round stone fell on the train of her gown, and recognising this as a sign from her husband she turned back. Soon Drake returned in disguise and then revealed himself, and they were re-united. 'The stone still remains where it fell; it is used as a weight upon the harrow of the farm, and if it be removed from the estate, it is always brought back, no person knows how.'

Southey also reports the tradition that the Plymouth leat was created by magic: Drake rode his horse over the route and the water followed him. He also used wizardry to defeat the Armada, chopping a piece of wood into pieces, each of which became a man-of-war when he threw them overboard. 'Thus has the great navigator shared the fate of Virgil, Friar Bacon, and Pope Sylvester, in being converted into a magician.'[16]

Some of these legends are included by Southey in his *Lives of the British Admirals*,[17] along with another one concerning a popular misconception about the Strait of Magellan which made Drake's exploit even more sensational:

> To sail round the world was in the popular belief an adventure of the most formidable kind, and not to be performed by plain sailing, but by reaching the end of this round flat earth, and there shooting the gulf, which is the only way of passing from one side of the world to the other.

Drake shot the gulf, one day; when, on the other side, he asked his men if any of them knew where they were, a boy made answer that they were then just under London Bridge; upon which, stung by jealousy, Drake exclaimed, 'Hast thou too a devil? If I let thee live there will then be one man greater than myself;' and with that he threw him overboard.[18]

Variations on these legends persisted. In Mrs Bray's version of 1836 the magic chips of wood were cut when Drake was at play on the Hoe, and turned into fireships which destroyed the Spanish. The magic stone was Drake's cannonball, fired directly down through the earth when one of his magic spirits told him of his wife's intentions.[19]

The cannonball legend may have originated in a large iron ball kept under the great hall table at Combe Sydenham manor house in Somerset, though of course local legend would have it that this is putting the cart before the horse. If the ball was rolled away from its place, it always rolled back, with a thunderous noise. Mere gravity was not accepted as an explanation. It was believed that the ball rolled up and down in times of national peril. There are various stories relating to Drake's association with the Devil in, for instance, the building of Buckland Abbey,[20] and others concerning his unquiet spirit.[21] Bret Harte mentions a belief in nineteenth-century California that Devil's Point, near the Golden Gate, was haunted by diabolical spirits invoked by Drake to guard a quantity of treasure hidden there.

In the mid-nineteenth century an ex-housekeeper at Buckland told the folklorist Robert Hunt that 'if the old warrior hears the drum which hangs in the hall of the Abbey, and which accompanied him round the world, he rises and has a revel'.[22] This appears to be the oldest extant example of a reference to the awakening power of Drake's drum. The drum preserved at Buckland is a sixteenth-century instrument, decorated with Drake's arms. It may have gone round the world with him, though if it did it was repainted later; it may have been rattling as his boats approached Las Palmas, or while his men fired the *Magdalena*; perhaps it mourned at his funeral. Except for its presence at Buckland, there is no indication that Drake looked on it as in any way more important or personal to him than other items of his panoply of war. In 1799 Lipscomb reported its presence in the abbey, but ascribed to it no legend or power.

Near the end of Victoria's reign a simple poem, short but heroic, transformed the drum and made it suddenly central to the myth of Drake. Despite Sir Henry Newbolt's contrived Devonian dialect; his romanticising of sixteenth-century shipboard life, 'wi' sailor lads a-dancing heel-an'-toe'; his inaccuracies ('Rovin' tho' his death fell, he went wi' heart at ease'); and his now unfashionable chauvinism, *Drake's Drum* had and retains a power to move. By combining a glimpse of distant seas with the English Channel and the West Country, but especially by its image of the dead hero waking to the call of the drum, it created a fresh myth in a nation which saw its navy as its cloak and salvation:

'Take my drum to England, hang et by the shore,
   Strike et when your powder's runnin' low;
If the Dons sight Devon, I'll quit the port o' Heaven,
   An' drum them up the Channel as we drummed them long ago.'

Drake he's in his hammock till the great Armadas come,
   (Capten, art tha sleepin' there below?),
Slung atween the round shot, listenin' for the drum,
   An' dreamin' arl the time o' Plymouth Hoe.
Call him on the deep sea, call him up the Sound,
   Call him when ye sail to meet the foe;
When the old trade's plyin' and the old flag flyin'
   They shall find him ware and wakin', as they found him long ago.[23]

Because the nation wished it so, Newbolt's poem was taken to be a literary embodiment of genuine folklore, and the result was that new manifestations of this supposed legend appeared. The powder ran low more than once in the next fifty years, and Drake's drum was heard, or was widely said to have been heard (which is just as helpful) at times of national danger. At the height of the First World War Alfred Noyes, who shared Newbolt's 'sailor lads a-dancing' view of Elizabethan seafaring, claimed in *The Times* that

There is a tale in Devonshire that Sir Francis Drake has not merely listened for his drum, during the last three hundred years, but has also heard and answered it on more than one naval occasion. It was heard, as the men of the Brixham trawlers can testify, about a hundred years ago, when a little man, under the pseudonym of Nelson (for all Devonshire knows that Nelson was a reincarnation of Sir Francis) went sailing by to Trafalgar.[24]

In a meeting of the Devonian Association in the same year, 1916, the Chairman put forward a less literal view of the survival of Drake's influence:

In the great war that is now being waged be assured that we shall triumphantly emerge, largely because of our navy which has generously adopted Drake's principles of naval war, and also because the spirit of Drake is still with us, and still animates the people of this Empire. That is the true significance of Drake's Drum. Confidence, resolution, bravery and patriotism were Drake's characteristics. Let us follow so great an exemplar.[25]

The Empire's will needed some stiffening in naval matters: Jellicoe's debatable victory at Jutland had been followed by the loss of the *Hampshire* and the drowning of Lord Kitchener. When the German fleet surrendered at Scapa Flow at the end of the war, it was reported that the officers of the *Royal Oak* heard the beating of a drum. Its source could not be found, but the beating continued intermittently until the German surrender was complete.

In the peace, Drake continued to figure in literature as the archetypal man of action, and as an inspiration for 1920s youth in the kind of book with a colourful cover presented at school prize-days to the *victor ludorum*. One short extract of this type of thing is enough (this is from Rupert Sargent Holland's *Drake's Lad*, but perhaps Kingsley should shoulder part of the blame):

Stillness, then a voice, that of Francis Drake, low and vibrant with passion. 'Nay, your Majesty, we have more than this island that is England. There is the ocean-sea, there is that world of the deep stretching from pole to pole, that empire of great waters that may be England's own! Let us but hold that empire, and we may send our argosies to shores of untold wealth, carry the flag of England to lands yet unmapped, dare the might of Spain or any other kingdom! There lies our heritage. Oh, claim it, my queen!'

To Elizabeth's eyes came a glow, as of one looking on a vision wonderful, glorious.

'Do thou claim it for me, for me and England!' she said.[26]

On a more cerebral level, but still as an archetype of action, Drake is one of the four main characters in William Henderson's *The New Argonautica* (1928). The general argument of this is that the spirits of Drake and Raleigh have visited Earth during the Great War. Distressed by the desolation, they enlist Ponce de León and Núñez de Vaca, construct a ship capable of space travel, and set out through the cosmos. Each of the four represents a different aspect of Man: Raleigh is the intellectual; Drake the active part. Raleigh, given the chance, might persist in an effort to read the work; Drake would probably give up after a page or two.

In 1938, when Britain's powder was running low again, and her national moral stature was shrinking with it, Alfred Noyes published his long poem *Drake*. This is a verse biography, completely uncritical of the man, which carries his exaltation as the epitome of the Elizabethan and English spirit as far as it can go. Spaniards are disgusting and cruel, and shout *El Draque!* frenziedly; Devon sailors have brawny brown arms; Drake's scuppers are awash with rubies; the perfidious Doughty is beheaded by Drake himself; the Armada action is a combat between 'the huge sea-castles' of Spain and 'the little boats of England'. The English fleet is led by Drake; he organises the fireships, and he shepherds the Spanish fleet away until England is safe.

Despite Noyes' overweening enthusiasm, there are some impressive and inspirational lines. Read the ending, where Drake is watching the remnants of the Armada flee towards the north of Scotland, and consider the resonance of the lines for a beleaguered island nation in the seven years which followed:

> Drake watched their sails go shrivelling, till the last
> Flicker of spars vanished as a skeleton leaf
> Upon the blasts of winter, and there was nought
> But one wild wilderness of splendour and gloom
> Under the northern clouds.
>   'Not unto us,'
> Cried Drake, 'but unto Him who made the sea
> Belongs our England now! Only to Him
> Belongs this victory, whose ocean fame
> Shall wash the world with thunder till that day
> When there is no more sea, and the strong cliffs
> Pass like a smoke, and the last peal of it
> Sounds through the trumpet.'
>   So, with close-hauled sails,
> Over the rolling triumph of the deep,
> Lifting their hearts to heaven, they turned back home.

Drake's drum was not finished yet. On 16 August, 1940, the Overseas Service of the BBC transmitted a broadcast called *Drake's Drum*, by Isaac Foot. It was later published,[27] and at the end of the war it was adapted for inclusion in the leaflet distributed to Plymouth schoolchildren when Foot became Lord Mayor of the city. If one takes Foot's assertions at face value, the old drum had been beating more frequently than even Noyes had thought:

Here in the West Country, we are never surprised to hear the beating of Drake's Drum. Our fathers heard it when the *Mayflower* made its way out of the Sound. When Drake from his place on the Hoe watched it sail, that ship was to him like another *Golden Hinde*.

As Drake died twenty-four years before the *Mayflower* sailed, and his statue on the Hoe was not erected until 1884, it is not easy to see how Foot imagined him watching the departure, except as a hovering spirit. More remarkably, he includes in his list of people who have heard the drum the citizens of Plymouth during the Civil War; Blake, Nelson and Wellington; Napoleon, captive on the *Bellerophon*; those watching the troopships arrive from the Empire early in the current war, and the crews of the ships and boats which saved the troops from Dunkirk. It takes a little thought to perceive that Foot is using the phrase 'heard the drum' in the sense of 'were touched by the spirit of Drake'. He clarifies this a little in the schoolchildren's leaflet, where he says that the drum has been heard 'everywhere where freedom is counted a special thing'.

In the months following the broadcast, army officers on the Hampshire coast heard a drum beating: '... a distinct call ... a very incessant beat, pause, two sharp beats in succession, one sharp beat ...'. The noise was heard over a wide area; a careful security search revealed nothing.[28]

For a rational person, all the above reports of beating drums and animated stones are based on misinterpretation or invention. The existence of the reports, nevertheless, is factual, as is the persistence and adaptability of the myth which they come to reinforce or modify. A legend is more durable than any drum-roll.

The drum's protective power was reinforced in the year after Foot's broadcast by the inclusion in the Oxford University Press *Daily Prayer*[29] of three prayers adapted from Drake's writings. One of these took particular root in the English mind, embodying the national spirit of determination in the difficult days of 1941:

O Lord God, when thou givest to thy servants to endeavour any great matter, grant us also to know that it is not the beginning, but the continuing of the same to the end, until it be thoroughly finished, which yieldeth the true glory; through him who for the finishing of thy work laid down his life, our Redeemer, Jesus Christ.

The book then quoted Drake's original words: 'There must be a begynning of any great matter, but the continewing unto the end untyll it be thoroughly finished yeldes the true glory'. Drake's sentence probably came to the notice of the editors when it was included in a letter to *The Times* on 20 November 1939, with the heading 'The True Glory'. *Daily Prayer* made it perfectly clear that the prayer was merely an adaptation of Drake, but the official leaflet of the National Day of Prayer, 23 March 1941, seized on it and included it with a firm attribution to him, 'on the day he sailed into Cadiz'. The prayer was a great success, was broadcast by the BBC and included on Christmas cards as *Drake's Prayer*, and was used by General Montgomery as a rallying-cry on the radio.[30]

In our piping times of peace, when Spain is equated in many minds with crowded beaches and friendly waiters, the myth of Drake has less resonance for England, still less for the rest of Britain. He is still at the centre of the West Country's awareness of its own identity, and he still rules Plymouth. An authentic replica of the *Golden Hinde*, built in Appledore in the 1970s using the old skills, still sails the coastal waters of Britain (often, alas, under power) and introduces Drake, however fleetingly, to parties of schoolchildren.

The quatercentenary of the circumnavigation naturally called for celebrations in 1977, when the British Library mounted a magnificent exhibition of Drake-related items. The Armada quatercentenary in 1988 kept interest in the period going, though books published to mark the occasion provided a corrective to the traditional view that the victory was Drake's alone. Drake's claiming of Nova Albion for England is still well-known in California, where his landing was celebrated on a grand scale in 1979. After five years of preparation, a resolution in the State legislature and the creation of a Sir Francis Drake Commission, over half a million dollars was spent from federal, private and local funds. Exhibitions were mounted, books and maps published, university seminars organised, schoolchildren exchanged with England, plaques unveiled, the landing re-enacted, services held, feasts consumed, medallions minted and postage stamps stamped. Lots of people, not least the commissioners, had a very good time, and in California the traditions of Drake, not least his hospitality to foreigners, were revivified for a new generation.[31]

REFLECTIONS

Drake's contemporaries often commented with amazement, sometimes with resentful envy, on the contrast between his lowly origins and his achievements. Yet when one examines his life, personality, obsessions, relationships and successes one comes to see how much they grew naturally from his beginnings. Luck played its part; he was especially lucky at the start of his career in being a kinsman of John Hawkins, and their acrimony in their last days together is the saddest aspect of the ill-fated final voyage. He was lucky in living through times of war or near-war which gave opportunities for men like him. Yet without the wars, Drake would still have made a success out of life. Once launched on his career as a small shipowner, a man of his energy and ambition would certainly have built up a thriving business. And with or without Hawkins, his ambitions would almost inevitably have involved him in the piratical profiteering for which his talents and early maritime education made him so suitable.

In any case, it is difficult to know whether some of his successes were due to luck, or to the almost instinctive awareness which guides the expert seafarer. After the dashing entry into the potential trap of Cadiz harbour, which so appalled the conservative William Borough, he was enabled to sail out in triumph by a change of wind just when he needed it. Luck, or planning based on knowledge? Nor was luck always on his side: the Spanish success at San Juan owed everything to Tello's fortuitous encounter with the *Francis*. It was acknowledged by Drake's contemporaries that luck was not the whole story: the Crispin van de Passe engraving of Drake bears the legend *Audentes fortuna iuvat*, 'Fortune favours the brave'.

The influence of his father's prayers and sermons, and his own reading of Protestant martyrology, pervaded his life. His letters, even brief scribbled notes on pressing matters, are imbued with a crusading piety well beyond the normal religious formalities of the period. His patriotism was great, but it is hard to know how much it had to do with a love of English soil and how much with a hatred of Philip of Spain as leader of the church which threatened Drake's own.

Drake's ambition and naked greed were those of a poor man's son. Even after he became rich, they sometimes relegated patriotism to the back of his mind, as in the taking of the *Rosario* in the Armada action, and the decision not to take the fleet to Santander in 1589. In most of his exploits, fortunately, the national interest and his own ran happily in harness together.

For all his success, it is doubtful whether Drake could have said at any time after his early triumphs that he was a completely happy man. Coming from his lowly origins, he moved into a level of society in which he spoke with aristocrats, ministers and royalty. Such an ascent is commonly a source of pride, but not necessarily of happiness. Insecurity in such a situation can breed over-assertiveness, touchiness and aggression, and this may well have played a part in Drake's prickliness towards men such as Thomas Doughty, Knollys and their friends. There is no evidence that he maintained a single long-term personal friendship, and he certainly alienated capable colleagues such as Borough and Frobisher.

Drake's relationship with Mary not only produced no children, but was interrupted by long periods at sea, and there was gossip, at the least, about her infidelity. His explosions of euphoria after victories, the wining and dining of captives, his garrulousness with some of his prisoners, suggest a man grasping opportunities for relaxation from the grinding loneliness of command. He could be brutal, devious and vindictive, as his persecution of Borough and John Doughty shows.

Yet many loved him, and he maintained an affinity with the class of men from which he had emerged. The willingness of his sailors and shipmasters was fundamental to his success; in the circumnavigation; in the raids on the mule-trains; even in the deceiving of Elizabeth, they backed him, partly from duty, but partly because he remained, in some degree, one of them. Drake's speech to his men after the execution of Doughty has been taken by some as an argument for naval democracy, by others as a prophesy of the future of the officer class in the Navy. One might read it, too, as manifesting a longing in Drake for a reconciliation within himself which he never fully achieved, between the Devon farm-boy turned sailor and the rich man he had become: 'the gentleman to hayle and draw with the mariner, and the maryner with the gentleman'.

These elements are, I think, evident in the two epitaphs which follow. They are by men who knew Drake before the myth replaced the man, and who had occasion to remember different aspects of his humanity. Admiral Sir Robert Mansell, who had served with Drake and Hawkins, was asked by Samuel Purchas for a comparison of the two. He thought hard about it, and replied fully and honestly:

... Sir Francis, after many Discoveries of the West Indies, and other parts, was the first Englishman that did ever compasse the World; wherein, as also in his deepe judgement in Sea causes, he did farre exceed not Sir John Hawkins alone, but all others whomsoever. In their owne natures and disposition they did as much differ; as in the managing matters of the Warres, Sir Francis beeing of a lively spirit, resolute, quicke, and sufficiently valiant: The other slow, jealous, and hardly brought to resolution. In Councell Sir John Hawkins did often differ from the judgement of others, seeming thereby to know more in doubtfull things, then he would utter. Sir Francis was a willing hearer of every mans opinion, but commonly a follower of his owne; he never attempted any action, wherein he was an absolute Commander, but hee performed the same with great reputation, and did easily dispatch great matters; Contrariwise Sir John Hawkins did only give the bare attempt of things, for the most part without any Fortune or good successe therein. Sir John Hawkins did naturally hate the Land-souldier, and though hee were very popular, yet he affected more the common sort, then his equals; Sir Francis contrarily did much love the Land-souldier, and greatly advanced good parts, wheresoever he found them. Hee was also affable to all men and of easie accesse. They were both of many vertues, and agreeing in some. As patience in enduring labours and hardness, Observation and Memory of things past, and great discretion in sudden dangers, in which neither of them was much distempered, and in some other vertues they differed. Sir John Hawkins had in him mercie and aptnesse to forgive, and true of word; Sir Francis hard in reconciliation, and constancie in friendship; he was withall severe and courteous, magnanimous, and liberall. They were both faultie in ambition, but more the one than the other; For in Sir Francis was an insatiable desire of honour indeed beyond reason. He was infinite in promises, and more temperate in adversity, then in better Fortune. He had also other imperfections, as aptnesse to anger, and bitterness in disgracing, and too much pleased with open flattery: Sir John Hawkins had in him malice and dissimulation, rudenesse in behaviour, and passing sparing, indeed miserable. They were both happy alike in being Great Commanders, but not of equall successe, and grew great and famous by one means, rising through their owne Vertues, and the Fortune of the Sea. Their was no comparison to be made betweene their wel-deserving and good parts, for therein Sir Francis Drake did farre exceed. This is all I have observed in the Voyages, wherein I have served with them.

R.M.[1]

A humbler testimony to Drake's greatness, and to a quality not observed by Mansell, came from Robert Hayman, who was five years old when Drake came back from the circumnavigation; a different Drake here, the private man, cheerful in the county of his birth; a childless man who loved children. In his own old age, aware of all Drake's travels, glories and plunder, Hayman looked back and recalled one of those untarnished moments of childhood which never leave us: a brief encounter, and an act of kindness, in the steep street of a Devon town:

> *Of the Great and Famous, ever to be honoured Knight,*
> *Sir* Francis Drake, *and of my little-little Selfe.*

> The *Dragon* that over Seas did raise his Crest
> And brought back heapes of gold unto his nest;
> Unto his Foes more terrible than *Thunder.*
> Glory of his age, After-ages *wonder,*
> Excelling all those that excell'd before,
> It's fear'd we shall have none such any more;
> Effecting all he sole did undertake,
> Valiant, just, wise, milde, honest, godly DRAKE.

> This man when I was little, I did meete
> As he was walking up *Totnes* long street.
> He ask'd me whose I was? I answer'd him.
> He ask'd me if his good friend were within?
> A fair red *Orange* in his hand he had;
> He gave it me, whereof I was right glad.
> Takes and kiste me, and prayes, *God blesse my boy.*
> Which I record *with comfort* to this day.

> Could he on me have breathed with his breath,
> His gifts, Elias-like, after his death,
> Then had I been enabled for to doe
> Many brave things I have a heart unto.
> I have as great desire, as e're had hee
> To joy, annoy, friends, foes; but 'twill not be.[2]

ABBREVIATIONS

In the notes and bibliography the following abbreviations are used:

AI: Archivo General de Indias, Seville.

BL: British Library.

EHR: *English Historical Review.*

FD: Cesáreo Fernández Duro, *La Armada Invencible*, 2 vols., Madrid, 1884–85.

FV: *The Famous Voyage of Sir Francis Drake into the South Sea, and there hence about the whole Globe of the Earth*, in Hakluyt, *Principall Navigations*, facsimile edition, Cambridge, 1963.

Hakluyt, PN: Richard Hakluyt, *The Principall Navigations, Voyages and Discoveries of the English Nation, made by Sea or over Land*, edited in 12 vols., Glasgow, 1903–05 (Hakluyt Society Extra Series, 1–12).

Kraus: Hans P Kraus, *Francis Drake: A Pictorial Biography*, Amsterdam, 1970.

Lady Drake: Lady Elizabeth F Elliott-Drake, *The Family and Heirs of Sir Francis Drake*, 2 vols., London, 1911.

LV: Kenneth R Andrews, *The Last Voyage of Drake and Hawkins*, Cambridge, 1972 (Hakluyt Society Series II, No. 142).

MM: *The Mariner's Mirror.*

Monson, NT: M Oppenheim (ed.), *The Naval Tracts of Sir William Monson*, 5 vols., London, 1902–14 (Publications of the Navy Records Society, Vols. 22, 23, 43, 45, 49).

Nuttall: Zelia Nuttall, *New Light on Drake*, London, 1914 (Hakluyt Society Series II, Vol. XXXIV).

PRO: Public Record Office.

SFDR: *Sir Francis Drake Revived*, in Wright, DEV, pp. 245–326.

SP: State Papers.

Tenison: E M Tenison, *Elizabethan England*, 13 vols., Leamington Spa, 1933–60.

Thrower: Norman J W Thrower (ed.) *Sir Francis Drake and the Famous Voyage, 1577–1580*, Berkeley and Los Angeles, 1984.

WA: *The Western Antiquary* (Plymouth).

WE: *The World Encompassed*, London, 1854 (Hakluyt Society).

Wright, DEV: Irene A Wright, *Documents concerning English Voyages to the Spanish Main 1569–1580*, London, 1932 (Hakluyt Society Series II, Vol. LXXI).

Wright, FEV: Irene A Wright, *Further English Voyages to Spanish America 1583–1594*, London, 1951 (Hakluyt Society Series II, Vol. XCIX).

Wright, SDEV: Irene A Wright, *Spanish Documents concerning English Voyages to the Caribbean 1527–1568*, London, 1929 (Hakluyt Society Series II, Vol. LXII).

NOTES

Introduction

1 Robert Tomson, in Hakluyt, PN, IX, pp. 354–55.
2 These included the control of trade in commodities, which enabled functionaries to establish immensely profitable private monopolies in such things as mules and blankets.
3 See Felipe Guaman Poma de Ayala, *Nueva crónica y buen gobierno*, 3 vols., Madrid, 1987, Vol. 2, pp. 690–99.
4 The original title is *Cien años de soledad*.

Chapter I

1 See *Purchas his Pilgrimes*, 20 vols., Glasgow, 1905–07; XVI, p. 113.
2 John Drake's declaration, in Lady Drake, Appendix II.
3 See Michael Lewis, *The Hawkins Dynasty: Three Generations of a Tudor Family*, London, 1969.
4 On all these dynastic matters, see John Lynch, *Spain under the Habsburgs*, 2nd ed., 2 vols., Oxford, 1981, Vol. I.
5 See G R Elton and others, *The Reformation 1520–1559*, Vol. 2 of *The New Cambridge Modern History*, 2nd ed., Cambridge, 1990.
6 See John Sugden, 'Edmund Drake of Tavistock', MM, 59, 1973, p. 436.
7 Lady Drake, I, pp. 18–19.
8 See Brian Chugg, *Devon*, London, 1980, p. 60.

Chapter II

1 In his *Safeguard of Sailors*, London, 1587, p. 3.
2 On fifteenth- and sixteenth-century navigation, see E G R Taylor, *The Haven-finding Art*, London, 1956, especially pp. 151–212; David W Waters, 'Elizabethan Navigation', in Thrower, pp. 12–32.
3 See Wright, SDEV, pp. 17–19; 98–115.

Chapter III

1   Hakluyt, PN, X, p. 74.
2   See Michael Lewis, 'The Guns of the *Jesus of Lübeck*', MM, 22, 1936, pp. 324–45; and 'Fresh Light on San Juan de Ulúa', MM, 23, 1937, pp. 295–315.
3   Hakluyt, PN, IX, pp. 445–65.
4   Wright, SDEV, Docs. 11–12.
5   Wright, SDEV, Docs. 13–15.
6   Wright, SDEV, Doc. 23.
7   Wright, SDEV, Doc. 22.
8   Wright, SDEV, p. 119.
9   Robert Barrett's deposition, in Wright, SDEV, Doc. 28.
10   Hawkins, in Hakluyt, PN, X, p. 67.
11   Hakluyt, PN, X, p. 67.
12   Wright, SDEV, Doc. 25.
13   Miles Phillips, in Hakluyt, PN, IX, p. 405.
14   Job Hortop, in Hakluyt, PN, IX, p. 452.
15   Bland's ship was not destroyed; in the subsequent auction of the vessels Hawkins left in San Juan she was sold for 200 ducats, a third of the highest bid for the *Jesus*. See Lewis, 'The guns of the *Jesus of Lübeck*' and 'Fresh Light on San Juan de Ulúa'.
16   Phillips' account is in Hakluyt, PN, IX. pp. 393–444; Hortop's follows, pp. 445–65. For another account by David Ingram, see Hakluyt, PN, 1589, pp. 557–62.
17   The text of the letter is in Lewis, *The Hawkins Dynasty*, pp. 59–60.

Chapter IV

1   SFDR, pp. 253–54.
2   SFDR, p. 254.
3   Ashmole MS 830.
4   For details of the trade, cargoes, etc., see E Lorenzo Sanz, *Comercio de España con América en la época de Felipe II*, 2 vols., Valladolid, 1979–80.
5   For a description, see Antoneli in Andrews, LV, p. 199.
6   Wright, DEV, p. 21.
7   AI, Panama, 32.
8   Wright, DEV, pp. 16 and 18.
9   AI, Patrimonio 266, R1.
10   The Cartagena incident may well be a reference to the raid in August

1572, when Drake took a vessel described by SFDR as 'a great ship of Sivell, which had discharged her loding, ... difficult to enter, being of two hundred forty Tunne'. SFDR makes no mention of the abducting of the captain. Farina was a slightly shady character; in 1569 goods which he was shipping from Seville to the Indies without registering them were confiscated (see Lorenzo Sanz, I, p. 356).

11 Wright, DEV, Doc. 8.
12 AI, Patronato 267; Wright, DEV, p. xxxi, note.
13 AI, Patronato 267; Wright, DEV, Doc. 6.
14 AI, Patronato 265; see Wright, DEV, Docs. 5 and 9. Compare the phrasing with Drake's letter to the governor of Puerto Rico (p. 247).
15 Wright, DEV, Docs. 7 and 13.
16 The captain-general of the fleet sailed in the *capitana*, or flagship; the *almiranta* was the second ship in importance, in this case the vessel of Admiral Gerónimo de Narváez.
17 Wright, DEV, Doc. 13.
18 Wright, DEV, Doc. 8.
19 Wright, DEV, Doc. 7.
20 See Wright, DEV, p. xxxi, note 3.
21 AI, Patronato 266, R1. This is not too far from the 40,000 ducats' worth of merchandise, plus velvets, taffetas, etc, mentioned in Ashmole MS 830.
22 Wright, DEV, Doc. 9. These could possibly be the two vessels which a Spanish list mentions as having been seized by Drake and taken to Plymouth: 'He also seized two frigates, one owned by Jaime Rafael and the other by Sebastián de Prohenza. He has refitted them; one is in Plymouth and he is reported to have sent the other to the Indies.' (AI, Patronato, 266, R1). The document was compiled in 1575, but no incident of the 1573 voyage seems to fit the description.
23 AI, Patronato 265, R20.
24 SFDR, pp. 255–56.
25 Wright, DEV, Doc. 14.
26 SFDR, p. 254.

Chapter V

1 SFDR, p. 253.
2 See Wright, DEV, p. 254, note.
3 SFDR, p. 256.
4 AI, Patronato 265, R18.
5 SFDR, p. 259.

6   SFDR, p. 264.

7   See Wright, DEV, p. 264, note.

8   SFDR, p. 272.

9   Wright, DEV, p. 49.

10 SFDR, p. 311.

11 On Le Têtu, see Jules Sottas, 'Guillaume Le Testu and his work', MM, 2, 1912, pp. 65–75.

12 Spanish sources call the river the Francisca; SFDR says the Francisco. Spanish documents also mention the Sardinilla as the landing point. See Wright, DEV, pp. 78, 82.

13 See Wright, DEV, pp. 61, 78.

Chapter VI

1   See Corbett, *Drake and the Tudor Navy*, I, pp. 200–202, 207–209.

2   BL, Cotton MS Vitellius VII, fol. 342r.

3   Sir Humphrey Gilbert, *A Discourse of a Discoverie of a New Passage for China*, London, 1576.

4   George Best, *A True Discourse of the late voyages of discoverie, for the finding of a passage to Cathaya, by the Northwest, under the conduct of Martin Frobisher Generall*, London, 1578.

5   See Nuttall, p. 9, note. This was part of Oxenham's testimony to the Inquisition in Lima. John Butler, also interrogated, said that Oxenham *did* agree to accompany Grenville.

6   Nuttall, p. 10, note.

7   BL, Lansdowne MS 100, item 4.

8   See Wright, DEV, Doc. 41.

9   For the Oxenham voyage, see Wright, DEV, and Nuttall.

10 BL, Cotton MS Otho E VIII, fol. 9.

11 Drake certainly said so later. See John Cooke's version in WE, p. 216.

12 John Cooke, in WE, pp. 215–16.

Chapter VII

1   See a recognisance of 9 July 1577 in which he claims payment of the customary royal bounty for the building of the ship (text in MM, 67, 1981, pp. 185–86).

2   The term 'fly-boat' originally designated a flat-bottomed Dutch coasting craft, but was extended to describe a type of small deep-sea auxiliary vessel, swift and handy enough to be used for despatches etc. Edward Cliffe says that the pinnace was of 12 tons, and was called the *Benedict*.

He may have been confusing her with another pinnace assembled later in the voyage. He gives the tonnage of the *Pelican* as 120. See WE, Appendix V, vi, p. 269.

3   See Zarate in Nuttall, p. 207.

4   WE, p. 187.

5   See Callender in MM, 7, 1921, p. 98.

6   See the *Anonymous Narrative*, WE, pp. 178–79, and Peter Carder's report in Nuttall, p. 42, note.

7   WE, p. 7.

8   John Cooke, in WE, p. 187.

9   Cooke says around 40 tons (WE, p. 189).

10 WE, p. 15.

11 WE, p. 189.

12 'Owr lytle barke called the benedict', in Cooke, WE, p. 189.

13 On the cargo of the ship, see the declaration by John Wynter, made at the time when the Portuguese ambassador sought restitution (Nuttall, pp. 386–91).

14 Cooke, in WE, p. 44.

15 See WE, p. 27, note.

16 WE, p. 191.

17 WE, pp. 61–62, note.

18 WE says that they anchored on the 14th, and the *Christopher* rejoined on the second day after that; Cooke says it was the eleventh day after the separation.

19 WE, p. 195.

20 Drake, as leader, obviously had some rights to punish malefactors. Doughty's demand, however, was to be shown documentary proof that, like some expedition leaders, he held a commission from the Queen entitling him to execute martial law. The letters-patent drafted for a voyage planned by Richard Grenville and others in 1574 specifically state that, in the case of 'persons of the companye rebelliously or obstinatly resisting against there commandements', the leaders shall be entitled 'to slaye execute and put to death or otherwise correct without other Judiciall proceedings but by the lawe martiall according to there discression, and that all paynes and execucions of death so to be done ... shall be accompted ... lawfully done as by our [i.e. Elizabeth's] speciall will and commandement'.

In Drake's case, no such document of commission has survived, and on balance it seems unlikely that he had one. Doughty's brother John was allowed to bring a case against Drake for his brother's murder after their return to England, which would hardly have been allowed if Drake had been given a commission in the same terms as Grenville's. The case was never heard, but only because Elizabeth refused to co-operate in a legal technicality. See Chapter XI; also W. Senior, 'Drake at the suit of John Doughty', MM, 7, 1921, pp. 291–97.

21 Cooke, in WE, p. 203. In BL, Harleian MS 6221 Bright (?) states that this conversation happened on the *Pelican* when Doughty was out of favour with Drake (see WE, p. 172).

22 BL, Harleian MS 6221, fol. 7.

23 WE, always sympathetic to Drake, says that he gave Doughty the choice of being executed there and then, being set ashore, and being taken home for trial, and that Doughty chose execution. It seems unlikely that Drake would offer him the chance of a trial in England, which Doughty had earlier demanded unsuccessfully, and even less likely that Doughty would turn down the offer if it were made.

24 BL, Sloane MS 46A, quoted in MM, 35, 1949, pp. 68–69.

25 John Cooke in WE, p. 213.

Chapter VIII

1 WE, p. 71.

2 WE, p. 85.

3 WE, p. 257.

4 Cliffe, in WE, p. 281.

5 BL, Lansdowne MS 100, item 2; printed in E G R Taylor, 'More light on Drake, 1577–80', MM, 16, 1930, pp. 134–51.

6 Printed in Purchas, 1625, Part IV, and quoted in Nuttall, p. 42, note.

7 Variously named *La Capitana*, which simply means the flagship (Nuttall, p. 92), *Grand Capitayne (Anonymous Narrative)* and *Los Reyes* (Nuttall, p. 163).

8 *Abajo, perro.*

9 See WE, p. 175, and *Anonymous Narrative*, in WE, pp. 180–81.

10 Nuttall, pp. 92 and 163.

11 Nuttall, p. 169.

12 For all these, see Nuttall.

13 In WE, pp. 178–86.

14 On the presence of foreigners on South American ships in the sixteenth century, see James Lockhart, *Spanish Peru*, Chapter VII.

15 WE, p. 103. Da Silva's log (Nuttall, p. 288) gives 250 horsemen and as many on foot; the *Anonymous Narrative* 300 horse and 200 foot.

16 WE, p. 104.

17 WE, Da Silva's log (Nuttall, p. 288) says 22 December.

18 Sarmiento, in Nuttall, p. 67.
19 Sarmiento, in Nuttall, p. 68. See also Nuttall, pp. 78, 113, 153.
20 Da Silva says the 6th; WE the 7th; but see Nuttall p. 135 for an eye-witness account by Nicolas Jorge.
21 Three, according to FV and the *Anonymous Narrative*.
22 Not by Drake's orders, according to John Drake (Nuttall, p. 46), and by 'one Fuller and one Tom Marcks' according to the *Anonymous Narrative*.
23 Sarmiento, in Nuttall, p. 69.
24 Sarmiento, in Nuttall, p. 69.
25 Sarmiento says he kept all the crew; da Silva two of them; John Drake mentions only the one Portuguese (Nuttall, p. 46).
26 In Nuttall, p. 69.
27 See Nuttall, p. 47. For a biography of John Drake, orphan son of Francis Drake's uncle Robert, see Nuttall, pp. 18–23.
28 See the report of the viceroy, Francisco de Toledo, in Nuttall, pp. 89–100.
29 See *Anonymous Narrative*, p. 181, and memoranda from BL, Harleian MS 280, fol. 81, printed in Nuttall, pp. 175–76.
30 Nuttall, pp. 93, 128.
31 Nuttall, p. 71.
32 See Jorge and Rodríguez, Nuttall, pp. 135–44.
33 FV, in WE, p. 241.
34 See his testimony in Nuttall, pp. 146–48.
35 Nuttall, p. 267.
36 See Nunho da Silva's account for a different version of Drake's method and motives.
37 On the Spanish side, Nunho da Silva, the Dutchman Nicolas Jorge, Domingo de Lizarza the ship's clerk; on the English, Francis Fletcher, as reflected in WE, and John Drake. All these are in Nuttall, as is the report of the captain, San Juan de Antón, whose nationality has been debated; on the possibility of his being English, see Taylor, 'More light', p. 144.
38 See Nuttall, p. 165.
39 FD, in WE, p. 242.
40 Text in Nuttall, pp. 15–17.

Chapter IX

1 Nuttall, p. 94.
2 Nuttall, pp. 180 ff.
3 See Nuttall, pp. 185–89 (Parraces) and 190–93 (Mesa).

4 See Sánchez Colchero's description in Nuttall, pp. 193–98.

5 See reports of Sánchez Colchero, Zarate and Juan Pascual in Nuttall, pp. 193–210 and 323–39.

6 *Anonymous Narrative*, in WE, p. 182.

7 *Anonymous Narrative*.

8 Nuttall, pp. 323–27, 332–39.

9 *Anonymous Narrative*, in WE, p. 183.

10 WE, p. 113.

11 Local estimates of the number of men in the boat vary from 30 to 70; see Nuttall, pp. 213, 343, 347.

12 For a list of things stolen and destroyed see Francisco Gómez Rengifo in Nuttall, p. 352.

13 Nuttall, pp. 350–59.

14 Nuttall, pp. 356–57.

15 Nuttall, pp. 213–15.

16 Nuttall, pp. 217–19.

17 Nuttall, pp. 256, 259.

18 BL, Harleian MS 280, fol. 81; see Nuttall, p. 294, note.

19 Nuttall, pp. 245–52.

Chapter X

1 On Spanish moves to fortify the Strait of Magellan, see BL, Sloane MS 46A. After an exploratory voyage by Pedro de Sarmiento, Diego Flores de Valdés set out from Cadiz with twenty-three ships and 3,500 men. After repeated storms and losses, and having wintered in Brazil, he was reduced to ten ships, and never penetrated the strait. Sarmiento took a smaller expedition a year later, landed 400 men and 30 women, and built two forts. When Cavendish passed by on his circumnavigation in 1587 he found nobody alive, and it was assumed that the people had died of starvation.

2 In WE, p. 184.

3 Nuttall, pp. 31, 50.

4 WE, p. 221.

5 WE, p. 118.

6 For an exhaustive examination of the possibilities, see Hanna, *Lost Harbor*. A possible site in Oregon is under archaeological investigation.

7 See WE, p. 125.

8 WE, pp. 128–29.

9 Most sources say the plate was brass; the *Anonymous Narrative* says

it was lead. See Hanna, *Lost Harbor*, pp. 242 ff.; MM, 45, 1959, pp. 346–47; MM, 63, 1977, p. 364.

10 The supporters of the reduced crew theory adduce Nicolas Jorge's report that the *Hinde*'s crew was made up of 71 or 72 men (Nuttall, p. 137), and other captives' estimates of 86, including negroes and boys (Nuttall, pp. 181, 186). These figures are set against a supposed statement by John Drake that when the ship reached the Moluccas she had only 60 men (see Hanna, pp. 55–56). The issue is complicated by a mistake in Nuttall's translation of John Drake (Nuttall, p. 32) which says that Drake reduced his crew to 60 in the Moluccas. The Spanish is perfectly explicit; the number 60 has nothing to do with the crew, but refers to the number of islanders who came to the ship; *allegaron al dicho su Navío sesenta hombres* (text in Lady Drake, II, p. 349). However, John Drake does say that at the Cape of Good Hope there were 59 men aboard, one having died. WE describes the leave-taking in California in emotional terms, but makes no mention of Englishmen remaining in Nova Albion. It does, however, state explicitly that there were only 58 men on the *Hinde* when she left the Moluccas (WE, p. 154).

11 Hanna, pp. 58–62.

12 John Drake says that he killed 20 (Lady Drake, II, p. 348).

13 See William A Lessa, *Drake's Island of Thieves*, Honolulu, 1975. Candidates have included Guam, Palau, Yap, Ngulu, etc.

14 John Drake, in Nuttall, p. 52.

15 John Drake, in Lady Drake, II, p. 348.

16 See Hakluyt, PN 1589, pp. 644–72.

17 John Drake, in Lady Drake, II, p. 349.

18 WE, p. 151.

19 WE, pp. 155–56.

20 BL, Harleian MS 280, fol. 81. See WE, pp. 175–77.

21 On Fletcher's ambivalent attitudes, see Callender, 'Drake and his Detractors', especially pp. 67–70, 73–74.

22 John Drake. WE and the *Anonymous Narrative* make no mention of this.

23 WE, p. 162.

Chapter XI

1 SP Spain, 9 January 1581.

2 SP Spain, 23 October, 1580.

3 SP Spain, 16 October 1580.

4   SP Domestic 12/144, No. 17ii. See British Library exhibition catalogue, *Sir Francis Drake*, items 101–102.

5   Mason's confession is SP Domestic 12/153, No. 49.

6   Mendoza to Philip, SP Spain, 9 January 1581.

7   BL, Stowe MS 555, fols. 147, 149.

8   John Ferne, *Blason of Gentrie*, 1586, pp. 144–45.

9   E G R Taylor (ed.), *The Original Writings and Correspondence of the two Richard Hakluyts*, I, pp. 139–46.

10 See Nuttall, p. 430.

11 See SP Domestic 12/148, Nos. 43–47; Mendoza to Philip, SP Spain, 9 January 1581.

12 Mendoza to Philip, SP Spain, 6 April 1581.

13 Edited by Elizabeth S Donno as *An Elizabethan in 1582*, Hakluyt Society, London, 1976.

14 Donno, pp. 239–40.

15 Donno, p. 184.

16 Donno, p. 23.

17 E G R Taylor (ed.), *The Troublesome Voyage of Captain Edward Fenton*, Hakluyt Society, Cambridge, 1959, p. lv.

18 Hakluyt, DV, p. 16.

19 See the National Trust's *Buckland Abbey*, London, 1991; Lady Eliott-Drake, *The Family and Heirs of Sir Francis Drake*; Joyce Youings, 'Drake, Grenville and Buckland Abbey', *Transactions of the Devon Association*, CXII, 1980.

20 See James Barber, 'Sir Francis Drake's Investment in Plymouth Property', *Transactions of the Devon Association*, CXIII, 1981.

21 See National Trust, *Buckland Abbey*, p. 29.

22 Crispin Gill, 'Drake and Plymouth', in N J W Thrower (ed.), *Sir Francis Drake and the Famous Voyage, 1577–1580*, Berkeley and Los Angeles, 1984, p. 85.

23 Andrews, *Elizabethan Privateering*, pp. 11–15.

24 BL, Lansdowne MS 41, fols. 9–10.

Chapter XII

1   BL, Lansdowne MS 100, fol. 98.

2   See Corbett, *Spanish War*, p. 71, for the conflict between the dates in the text (29 December) and in the marginal note (18 December) for the departure from Río de la Hacha.

3   Greepe mentions a total of fifteen pinnaces.

4 For a list of the ships, see M F Keeler, *Sir Francis Drake's West Indian Voyage*, Hakluyt Society, London, 1981, pp. 46–47.

5 The relevant accounts, journals and maps are handsomely published in Keeler, *Sir Francis Drake's West Indian Voyage*.

6 Keeler, pp. 72–73.

7 STD; Keeler, p. 218.

8 Keeler, p. 77.

9 Newsletter, possibly from Carleill to Walsingham; Keeler, p. 108.

10 *Primrose* log; Keeler, p. 182. *Tiger* mentions only one, a lad from the *George Bonaventure*.

11 *Primrose*, Keeler, p. 183.

12 *Tiger*, Keeler, p. 89. *Primrose* says 9 October.

13 See *Tiger*, Keeler, pp. 89 and note; 90–91.

14 *Leicester*, Keeler, pp. 121–23; *Tiger*, pp. 90–91, 93.

15 *Leicester*, Keeler, p. 127, says that the Frenchman had been with Drake on his previous voyage. This probably means that the two had encountered each other in the West Indies rather than that Montaigne had gone on the circumnavigation.

16 *Leicester*, in Keeler, pp. 129–30.

17 STD, in Keeler, p. 229.

18 Keeler, p. 137.

19 Keeler, p. 110.

20 Keeler, p. 82.

21 Keeler, p. 233.

22 Keeler, p. 139.

23 Keeler, pp. 143–44.

24 *Leicester*, in Keeler, p. 144.

Chapter XIII

1 STD, in Keeler, pp. 235–36.

2 *Primrose*, in Keeler, p. 197.

3 Fray Pedro Simón, quoted in G Jenner, 'A Spanish Account of Drake's Voyages', EHR, XVI, 1901, pp. 46–66.

4 See Wright, FEV, Docs. 12–20, 56.

5 AI, Santo Domingo 51.

6 AI, Santo Domingo 73.

7 See Wright, FEV, p. 28.

8 See Jenner, 'A Spanish Account', p. 54.

9 AI, Santo Domingo 51; full translation in Wright, FEV, Doc. 19.

10 AI, Santo Domingo 80.

11   STD, in Keeler, p. 242.

12   See Keeler, pp. 154, 170.

13   In Keeler, p. 199.

14   Castellanos, summarised in Callender, 'Fresh Light on Drake', p. 22. For other Spanish reports, see Wright, FEV, Docs. 21–24.

15   Castellanos, in Callender, 'Fresh Light'.

16   *Primrose*, in Keeler, pp. 198–99.

17   Wright, FEV, Doc. 22, p. 49. Fray Pedro Simón reported, at second hand, that over 200 English died in the engagement at La Caleta.

18   Wright, FEV, Doc. 23.

19   See Keeler, p. 164, note 5.

20   Kraus, pp. 128–29, 202.

21   Wright, FEV, pp. 45, 52, 56.

22   *Primrose*: 28; Drake himself: 25–30 (as reported in a Spanish letter, Wright, FEV, p. 65).

23   STD, p. 258; Governor's report in Wright, FEV, p. 51.

24   Castellanos; see Callender, 'Fresh Light', p. 27.

25   Wright, FEV, pp. 45, 59.

26   *Tiger*, in Keeler, p. 105.

27   *Leicester*, in Keeler, p. 174.

28   Hakluyt, PN, X, pp. 120–24.

29   *Leicester*, in Keeler, p. 170.

30   Wright, FEV, Doc. 28.

31   STD, pp. 265–68.

32   Wright, FEV, pp. 181–91.

33   *Primrose*, in Keeler, p. 206.

34   See the governor's letter to the Crown, Wright, FEV, Doc. 48.

35   See Lane's account in Hakluyt, PN, VIII, pp. 342–44.

36   For a discussion of the date, see Keeler, pp. 69, note 3; 274, note 7.

37   See the accounts in Corbett, Spanish War, pp. 86–92, 94–96; and Keeler, pp. 60–63 and notes.

Chapter XIV

1   For a list, see Corbett, *Spanish War*, pp. 99–100.

2   SP Domestic 200/2.

3   Robert Leng, *The True Discripcion of the last voiage of that worthy Captayne, Sir Frauncis Drake, knight, with his service done against the Spanyardes* (1587). Camden Miscellany, Vol. V, 1864.

4   BL, Royal MS 14.A.III.

5   Horozco; cf. Drake's statements that there were twelve galleys, e.g. Corbett, *Spanish War*, p. 112.

6   Four in Horozco; seven in other reports. See Corbett, *Spanish War*, p. 113.

7   Leng, p. 15.

8   Horozco.

9   Quoted in Jenner, 'A Spanish Account', p. 63.

10 BL, Harleian MS 167, fol. 104v; printed in Leng, pp. 31–33.

11 SP Domestic 200/46; Corbett, *Spanish War*, pp. 107–109.

12 Corbett, *Spanish War*, pp. 123–30.

13 Horozco, fol. 157.

14 Leng, p. 17.

15 Letter in Kraus, pp. 134–36.

16 Fol. 158.

17 Corbett, *Spanish War*, pp. 140–41.

18 Corbett, *Spanish War*, p. 151.

19 Leng, pp. 21–22.

20 Leng (p. 22) says there were 400 slaves and 240 officers and crew. This seems a serious overloading of a fly-boat.

21 Corbett, *Spanish War*, pp. 146–49.

22 For correspondence showing the state of alarm in Spain, see Leng, pp. 38–42, 46–49.

23 Leng, pp. 50–54.

24 Printed with Robert Norman's *The newe Attractive, containing a short discourse of the Magnes or Lodestone*, London, 1581. Facsimile edition, Amsterdam and Norwood, NJ, 1974.

25 Corbett, *Spanish War*, p. 152.

Chapter XV

1   C Martin and G Parker, *The Spanish Armada*, London, 1988, p. 146. A splendid book, largely because of its copious use of Spanish original documents. Most of the relevant English documents are printed in J N Laughton, *State Papers relating to the Defeat of the Spanish Armada*, 2 vols., London, Navy Records Society, 1894.

2   SP Domestic 12/209 No. 58.

3   Figures from Martin and Parker, pp. 53–54.

4   See Laughton, Vol. I, pp. 224–26.

5   See Laughton, Vol. I, pp. 217–19.

6   SP Domestic 12/212 No. 133.

7   C Fernández Duro, *La Armada Invencible*, 2 vols., Madrid, 1884, II,

Doc. 165. See also Docs. 166–72 for Spanish accounts of the action. Future references use the abbreviation FD.

8 See Martin and Parker, plate 38.
9 Howard to Walsingham; Laughton, Vol. I, p. 288.
10 Laughton, Vol. I, p. 288.
11 SP Domestic 12/212 No. 135.
12 SP Domestic 12/215 No. 66.
13 See Laughton, Vol. II, p. 29.
14 See Martin and Parker, p. 170 and note 8.
15 Laughton, Vol. II, pp. 20–21.
16 Laughton, Vol. I, p. 326.
17 FD, II, Doc. 160.
18 FD, II, p. 237.
19 See Valdés' letter to Philip, Laughton, Vol. II, pp. 133–36.
20 Martin and Parker, pp. 177–78.
21 FD, II, p. 237.
22 See FD, II, pp. 240–41.
23 SP Domestic 12/214 No. 12.
24 SP Domestic 12/216 No. 71.
25 SP Domestic 12/214 No. 99.
26 SP Domestic 12/213 No. 65 (old).
27 SP Domestic 12/213 No. 123.
28 SP Domestic 12/214 No. 110.
29 SP Domestic 12/214 Nos. 139–40.
30 Laughton, Vol. II, pp. 104–108.
31 Laughton, Vol. I, p. 356.
32 SP Domestic 12/213 No. 123.
33 Laughton, Vol. II, p. 136.
34 Laughton, Vol. II, pp. 215–17.
35 Laughton, Vol. II, pp. 374–75.

Chapter XVI

1 SP Domestic 214/54.
2 On Elizabeth's difficulties, see R B Wernham, *The Expedition of Sir John Norris and Sir Francis Drake to Spain and Portugal, 1589*, Navy Records Society, 1988, pp. xii–xiii (henceforth referred to as Wernham); id., 'Queen Elizabeth and the Portugal Expedition of 1589', EHR, LXVI, 1951, pp. 1–26, 194–218 (see pp. 2–7).
3 Wernham, Doc. 4.
4 SP Domestic 216/3.

5   Wernham, Docs. 6–7. See also his p. 8, note.
6   See Wernham, Docs. 8–10.
7   Wernham, Doc. 25.
8   Wernham, Doc. 26.
9   Wernham, Doc. 13.
10 Wernham, Doc. 4.
11 BL, Add. MS 12507, fol. 17; quoted in Thomson, pp. 324–25.
12 Wernham, Docs. 32–37.
13 SP Domestic 222/89.
14 Wernham, Docs. 85, 91, 163.
15 In a letter to Hatton; Wernham, Doc. 103.
16 Wernham, Doc. 105.
17 SP Domestic 223/64.

Chapter XVII

1   For a list, see Wernham, pp. 336–41.
2   By Ralph Lane in a letter to Walsingham; Wernham, Doc. 160.
3   John Evesham, in Wernham, Doc. 163.
4   Monson, NT, Vol. I, p. 190.
5   ibid., p. 191.
6   Wernham, Doc. 163.
7   Anthony Wingfield in Hakluyt, PN, VI, p. 486. John Evesham says
    that only seven or eight guns were saved; Wernham, Doc. 163.
8   Wernham, Doc. 110.
9   Ralph Lane to Walsingham; Wernham, Doc. 160.
10 See my Chapter XXIII, n. 15.
11 Wingfield in Hakluyt, PN, Vol. VI, p. 493.
12 Wernham, Doc. 110.
13 Evesham, in Wernham, Doc. 230.
14 SP Domestic 227/35.
15 Ralph Lane; Wernham, Doc. 160.
16 SP Domestic 224/13.
17 Wernham, Doc. 110.
18 Wernham, Doc. 159.

Chapter XVIII

1   SP Domestic 224/53.
2   SP Domestic 224/50.
3   SP Domestic 224/10.

4   SP Domestic 269/fol. 103.

5   Monson, NT, Vol. I, p. 191.

6   See Tenison, Vol. VIII, pp. 163–64.

7   Wingfield, in Hakluyt, PN, Vol. VI, p. 497.

8   William Fenner, in Wernham, Doc. 164.

9   Wernham, Doc. 164.

10 Monson, NT, Vol. I, p. 179.

11 See Wernham, Doc. 169.

12 Monson, NT, Vol. I, p. 179.

13 See M A S Hume, *The Year After the Armada*, London, 1896, pp. 57, 63.

14 Ralph Lane in Wernham, Doc. 135.

15 See Wernham, Doc. 131.

16 Wernham, Doc. 163.

17 Wingfield, in Hakluyt, PN, Vol. VI, p. 512.

18 Wernham, Doc. 164.

19 Wernham, Doc. 163.

20 Wernham, Doc. 140.

21 Wernham, Doc. 182; see also his p. lx.

22 Wernham, Doc. 140.

23 Wernham, Doc. 154.

24 Wernham, Doc. 142.

25 Monson, NT, Vol. I, p. 178.

26 See Wernham, Docs. 168–69.

27 See Wernham, Docs. 143–44.

28 Wernham, Doc. 159.

29 Wernham, Doc. 167.

Chapter XIX

1   For all this, and a full account of privateering, see K R Andrews, *Elizabethan Privateering*, Cambridge, 1974. See also his *English Privateering Voyages to the West Indies 1588–1595*, Hakluyt Society, Series II, Vol. CXI, 1959.

2   AI, Santo Domingo 81.

3   See WA, X, 1890–91, p. 161.

4   Crispin Gill, in Thrower, p. 87.

5   See WA, I, 1881–82, pp. 70–71.

6   BL, Lansdowne MS lxv, 12, 1590.

7   Gill, pp. 87–89.

8   W Murdin (ed.), *A Collection of State Papers ... left by William Cecil, Lord Burghley,* 1759, p. 800.

9   See A Williamson (ed.), *The Observations of Sir Richard Hawkins,* 1933, p. 10.

10 See K R Andrews, *The Last Voyage of Drake and Hawkins,* Hakluyt Society, Series II, Vol. 142, 1972, pp. 15–16. Henceforth references are abbreviated to LV.

11 For the accounts, see LV, Doc. 14.

12 See LV, pp. 13–14; A Rumeu de Armas, *Piraterías y ataques navales contra las Islas Canarias,* 3 vols., Madrid, 1948, Vol. II, pp. 674–76.

13 Museo Naval, Madrid, Colección Sanz Barutell, Nos. 155, 160–62.

14 AI, Santo Domingo 179, R1, No. 4. A month earlier the Governor of La Margarita had obtained similar information from some of Raleigh's men held prisoner; see LV, Doc. 14.

15 Monson, NT, Vol. I, p. 313; LV, Doc. 18.

16 LV, Doc. 4.

17 LV, Doc. 6.

18 LV, Doc. 7.

19 LV, Doc. 8.

20 LV, Doc. 9.

21 LV, Doc. 10. See also Rumeu de Armas, Vol. II, p. 677.

22 LV, Doc. 12.

Chapter XX

1   See LV, p. 57.

2   LV, Doc. 19.

3   Troughton, in LV, p. 109.

4   For an extensive account of the Las Palmas action, see Rumeu de Armas, Vol. II, pp. 682–723.

5   Rumeu de Armas, Vol. III, pp. 986–89.

6   LV, p. 89.

7   *The voyage truely discoursed, made by sir Francis Drake, and sir John Hawkins,* Hakluyt, PN, Vol. X, pp. 226–45; see p. 227. Subsequent references are abbreviated to VTD.

8   LV, pp. 109–110.

9   LV, p. 125.

10 LV, pp. 132–41.

Chapter XXI

1 Maynarde in LV, p. 90.
2 VTD.
3 On the fortifications, see Baskerville in LV, pp. 114–16.
4 For all this, see the official Spanish report in LV, pp. 161 ff.
5 VTD, p. 230.
6 LV, p. 92.
7 See LV, p. 171.
8 AI, Santo Domingo 169.
9 See LV, p. 174.
10 See LV, pp. 156–59.

Chapter XXII

1 VTD, p. 235.
2 Kraus, p. 154.
3 Baskerville, in LV, p. 119.
4 'A Full Relation of Another Voyage made by Sir Francis Drake and others to the West Indies', published with Bigges, *A Summarie and True Discourse* in 1652.
5 *Hanboros* in the text.
6 Maynarde again.
7 AI, Patronato 265, R57.
8 See Maynarde in LV, p. 100.
9 AI, Patronato 265, R57, 'Around five hundred men had died of sickness'.
10 Quoted in LV, p. 46, from John Bruce (ed.), *Liber Famelicus of Sir James Whitelocke, A Judge of the Queen's Bench in the Reign of James I and Charles I*, Camden Society, 1858.
11 LV, p. 122.
12 *A Full Relation.*
13 See Maynarde, Baskerville and an anonymous document, LV, pp. 104–105, 122–23.
14 See LV, p. 251.
15 See LV, pp. 257–58.

Chapter XXIII

1 Compare, for example, the *romance* in Fernández Duro, *La Armada*, Vol. II, p. 490, which makes no mention of Drake, with the account in

Juan Suárez de Peralta's *Tratado del descubrimiento de las Indias* (1589), ed. F. Gómez de Orozco, Mexico City, 1949.

2   AI, Patronato 265, R20.

3   AI, Patronato 265, R14. This has the date '... de Mdlxx ... años'. The context places it in the winter of 1573–74. The blanks suggest that it was a draft awaiting Philip's signature and exact date of signing.

4   Bartolomé Leonardo de Argensola, *Conquista de las Islas Malucas*, Madrid, 1609. See Kraus, p. 97.

5   Martín del Barco Centenera, *La Argentina*, Lisbon, 1602. See the description in J A Ray, *Drake dans la poésie espagnole*, Paris, 1906, pp. 74 ff.

6   Juan de Miramontes Zuazola, *Armas antárcticas: Hechos de los famosos capitanes españoles que se hallaron en la conquista del Peru*. Madrid, Biblioteca Nacional, MS M. 151. See Ray, pp. 79 ff.

7   Francisco Caro de Torres, *Relación de los servicios que hizo a su Magestad ... Don Alonso de Sotomayor*, Madrid, 1620.

8   From *Mil años ha que no canto*; Biblioteca de Autores Españoles, XXXII, 1903, pp. 503–53, No. CV.

9   *Romancero general*, Madrid, 1602, fol. 35. See G Ticknor, *History of Spanish Literature*, 3 vols., New York, 1849, Vol. III, p. 171.

10   See Fernández Duro, *La Armada*, Vol. II, pp. 490 ff.

11   *Discurso de el capitán Francisco Draque*, Madrid, 1921. See G Callender, 'Fresh Light on Drake', MM, 9, 1923, pp. 16–28.

12   Published in Pedro de Espinosa, *Flores de poetas ilustres*, Madrid, 1605. New edition, Seville, 1896. See also Ray, pp. 140–43.

13   D F R de M, *Respuesta y desengaño contra las falsedades publicadas e impresas en España en bituperio de la Armada Inglesa*, London, 1589.

14   *Archivo dos Açores*, VI, 1885, p. 469; Ray, pp. 146–48.

15   See Felipe de la Gandara, *Armas y triunfos del Reino de Galicia*, 1672, p. 472; Anon, *Relación histórica del sitio puesto por los ingleses a ... La Coruña el 4 de mayo de 1589 y del triunfo alcanzado por los coruñeses en esta jornada, debido al valor de la famosa María Fernández de la Cámara y Pita*, La Coruña, 1850; A Martínez Salazar, *La epopeya de Galicia. Las mujeres coruñesas en el sitio de 1589*, La Coruña, 1887; Id., *El cerco de La Coruña en 1589 y Mayor Fernández Pita. (Apuntes y documentos)*, La Coruña, 1889.

16   Rumeu de Armas, Vol III, pp. 986–89.

17   Bartolomé Cairasco de Figueroa, *Templo militante*, Valladolid, 1603.

18   Text in Ray, p. 196.

19   Text in Ray, pp. 212 ff.

20 Valencia, 1598. Also published in 2 vols., with related documents, Madrid, 1935.

21 E Rodríguez Solis, *¡Que viene el Draque!*, San Juan de Puerto Rico, 1898.

22 They include *Saylors for my money: A new ditty composed in the praise of saylors and sea affaires, breifly shewing the nature of so worthy a calling; The praise of Sailors, ... with their hard fortunes which doe befall them on the Seas, when Land-men sleepe safe in their Beds*; and the well-known *Rowe well, ye mariners*.

23 See, for example, *In laudem ffrancisci Drake militis*, by T N Cicistrensis [i.e. of Chichester], in BL Egerton MS 2642, fol. 244v; a Latin note *In commendacion of Sir Frauncys Drake knyght the renowned*, in BL Egerton MS 2642, fol. 405v; William Gager's *In laudem fortissimi viri D. Francisci Draconis*, BL Additional MS 22583, fol. 84; two brief pieces published in WA, Vol. III, pp. 214–15, and a quatrain in WA, Vol. VIII, p. 17; an anonymous poem beginning *Fortunate Draco ...* in *Triumphalia de victoriis Elizabethae*, 1588; various pieces printed as introduction to Charles FitzGeffreys' *Sir Francis Drake His Honourable Life's Commendation*, pp. xxi–xxiii; Joannes Hercusanus Danus, *Magnifico ac strenuo viro D. Francisco Draco Anglo Equiti aurato*, London, 1587, translated in WA, Vol. VIII, p. 27.

24 See Kraus, p. 82.

25 See Kraus, pp. 86–88.

26 On these and other maps of the voyage, see Helen Wallis, 'The Cartography of Drake's Voyage', in Thrower, pp. 121–63.

27 See the facsimile edition by D W Waters, Hartford, 1955.

28 See above, n. 13.

29 London, 1589.

30 Printed as Document 11 in Keeler, and see also her Appendix III.

31 *Franciscus Dracus Redivivus*, Amsterdam, 1596.

32 *The Trumpet of Fame, or Sir Francis Drakes and Sir John Hawkins Farewell*, London, 1595; reprinted Lee Priory, Kent, 1818.

33 Oxford, 1596; reprinted Lee Priory, Kent, 1819, as *The Life and Death of Sir Francis Drake*.

34 OED gives *mushrump* as a variant of *mushroom*: an upstart; an excrescence; a contemptible person.

Chapter XXIV

1 *Purchas his Pilgrimes*, 5 parts, London, 1625. Reprinted in 20 vols., Glasgow, 1905–07.

2 William Camden, *Annales Rerum Anglicarum, et Hibernicarum, Regnante Elizabeth, ad Annum Salutis M. D. LXXXIX*, Books I–III, London, 1615; Book IV, Leiden, 1627. French translation by Paul de Bellegent, 1624; English translation, entitled *Annales, the True and Royall History of the famous Empress Elizabeth*, by Abraham Darcie, London, 1625.

3 William Fuller, *The Holy State and the Profane State*, London, 1642, pp. 130–31.

4 *The Gentleman's Magazine*, X, 1740, pp. 352, 389–96, 443–47, 509–15, 600–03; XI, 1741, pp. 38–44. For a collected edition, see J R Fleeman (ed.), *The Early Biographical Writings of Dr Johnson*, Farnborough, 1973, pp. 36–66. See also T Wright (ed.), *The famous voyage of Sir Francis Drake with a particular account of his expedition in the West Indies against the Spaniards*, London, 1742; *The World Encompassed*, in *A Collection of Voyages and Travels*, London, 1745, Vol. 2; other versions of *The World Encompassed* in J Callender, *Terra Australis Cognita*, Vol. I, 1766, and in *The World Displayed*, Vol. 5, 1775; D Henry (printer), *Sir Francis Drake's Voyages*, in *An historical Account of all the Voyages round the World, performed by English Navigators*, London, 1774; and a chapbook, *Voyages and Travels of Sir Francis Drake into the West Indies and round the World*, London, [1784?].

5 See WA, III, 1883–84, p. 255; VIII, 1888–89, pp. 37–38.

6 See items in MM, 39, 1953, pp. 144–45; 40, 1954, p. 160; 41, 1955, p. 64; and in WA, I, 1881–82, p. 158; VII, 1887–88, pp. 316–17.

7 G W Anderson, *A New, Authentic, and Complete Collection of Voyages round the World, undertaken and performed by Royal Authority; Containing an Authentic History of Captain Cook's First, Second, Third and Last Voyage*, London, 1784; see also G Robinson, 'A forgotten life of Sir Francis Drake', in MM, 7, 1921, pp. 10–18.

8 Robert Southey, *Lives of the British Admirals*, 5 vols., London, 1833–40; James Burney, *A Chronological History of the Discoveries in the South Sea*, 5 vols., London, 1803–17; Vol. I, pp. 304–69.

9 John Barrow, *The Life, Voyages and Exploits of Admiral Sir Francis Drake, with numerous original letters*, London, 1843.

10 *Sir Francis Drake his Voyage, 1595, by Thomas Maynarde*, London, Hakluyt Society, 1849; W S W Vaux (ed.), *The World Encompassed*, London, Hakluyt Society, 1854; R Leng, *The True Discripcion of the last voiage of the worthy Captayne, sir Fraucis Drake, knight*, London, Camden Miscellany, 1863.

11 WA, V, 1885–86, pp. 191 ff.

12 Especially the Plymouth-based *Western Antiquary*; see e.g. I, 1881–82,

pp. 161–62, 163; II, 1882–83, pp. 42, 181; III, 1883–84, pp. 83–84, 214–15; VII, 1887–88, pp. 242, 315; VIII, 1888–89, p. 27.

13 WA, VIII, 1888–89, pp. 63–66.

14 See MM, 5, 1919, p. 160; 11, 1925, p. 317.

15 For notes on other Drake relics, see WA, I, 1881–82, p. 165; III, 1882–84, p. 255; MM, 67, 1981, p. 214.

16 *Quarterly Review*, XVIII, 1818, pp. 27–28.

17 Southey, *Lives of the British Admirals*, Vol. III, pp. 238–41.

18 ibid., pp. 239–40.

19 Mrs Bray, *A Description of the Parts of Devonshire Bordering on the Tamar and Tavy*, 3 vols., 1836; Vol. II, pp. 170–73.

20 See WA, I, 1881–82, p. 161; Katherine M Briggs, *Dictionary of British Folk-tales*, 4 vols., London, 1970–71, Part B, Vol. I, pp. 138–39. The Bret Harte story is cited in WA, VI, 1886–87, p. 193.

21 WA, I, 1881–82, pp. 156, 161; III, 1883–84, pp. 52–53.

22 Robert Hunt, *Popular Romances of the West of England*, 2nd ed., London, 1871, pp. 230–31.

23 *Palgrave's Golden Treasury*, 4th ed., Oxford, 1940, p. 483.

24 *The Times*, 28 August, 1916.

25 Quoted in E M R Ditmas, *The Legend of Drake's Drum*, St Peter Port, Guernsey, 1973, the source for much of my information on the drum.

26 Rupert Sargent Holland, *Drake's Lad*, New York and London, 1929. Other works of a similar kind include G Henty, *Under Drake's Flag*, London, 1883; Gordon Stables, *Old England on the Sea: The Story of Admiral Drake*, London, [1900?]; E M Bacon, *The Boy's Drake*, London, 1911. Rudyard Kipling naturally idolised Drake; see his poem 'Frankie's Trade' in *Rewards and Fairies* (1910): 'Old Horn to All Atlantic said:/(*A-hay O! To me O!*)/"Now where did Frankie learn his trade?/For he ran me down with a three-reef mains'le."/(*All round the Horn!*) . . . The North Sea answered:– "He's my man,/For he came to me when he began –/Frankie Drake in an open coaster./(*All round the Sands!*) . . . If you can teach him aught that's new,/(*A-hay O! To me O!*)/I'll give you Bruges and Niewport too,/And the ten tall churches that stand between 'em."/*Storm along my gallant Captains!(All round the Horn!)*'. Kipling also included in *A School History of England* (London, 1911), in which he collaborated with C R L Fletcher, the poem 'With Drake in the Tropics', in which Drake's fatherly behaviour is in marked contrast to his actual treatment of the Doughty brothers: 'South and far south beyond the Line/Our Admiral leads us on./Above, undreamed-of planets shine; /The stars we knew are gone./Around, our clustered seamen mark/The silent deep ablaze/With fires, through which the far-down shark/Shoots glimmering

on his ways. ... Kindly, from man to man he [i.e. Drake] goes,/With comfort, praise or jest,/Quick to suspect our childish woes,/Our terror and unrest./It is as though the sun should shine – /Our midnight fears are gone!/South and far south beyond the line/Our Admiral leads us on!'

27 In *London Calling*, No. 53 (1 September, 1940), and in *Prediction*, Vol. 5, No. 9, October 1940, pp. 326–27 (information from Ditmas, *The Legend of Drake's Drum*).

28 Again, my source is Ditmas.

29 E Milner-White and G W Briggs (ed.), *Daily Prayer*, Oxford, 1941. See pp. 183–84.

30 See D Bonner-Smith, 'Drake's Prayer', MM, Vol. 36, pp. 86–87.

31 The National Maritime Museum, Greenwich, has a file of material on the California celebrations.

Reflections

1 Purchas, Vol. VI, p. 1185.

2 Printed in G C Moore Smith, 'Robert Hayman and the Plantation of Newfoundland', EHR, Vol. XXXIII, 1918, pp. 21–36.

BIBLIOGRAPHY

Alsedo y Herrera, Dionisio de, *Piraterías y agresiones de los ingleses y de otros pueblos de Europa en la América Española desde el siglo XVI al XVIII deducidas de las obras de D. Dionisio de Alsedo y Herrera*, ed. Justo Zaragoza, Madrid, 1883.

Anderson, George W, *A New, Authentic and Complete Collection of Voyages round the World, undertaken and performed by Royal authority. Containing an Authentic ... History of Captain Cook's first, second, third and last voyages*, London, 1784. Second edition, 4 vols., London, 1790.

Andrews, Kenneth R, *Drake's Voyages: A Re-assessment of their Place in Elizabethan Maritime Expansion*, London, 1967.

Andrews, Kenneth R, *Elizabethan Privateering*, Cambridge, 1964.

Andrews, Kenneth R, *English Privateering Voyages to the West Indies, 1588–95*, London, 1959 (Hakluyt Society Series II, Vol. CXI).

Andrews, Kenneth R, *The Last Voyage of Drake and Hawkins*, Cambridge, 1972 (Hakluyt Society Series II, No. 142).

Anon, *A Full Relation of Another Voyage made by Sir Francis Drake and others to the West Indies, who set forth from Plimouth the 28 of August, 1595*, published with Bigges, *A Summarie and True Discourse*, London, 1652.

Anon, *Buckland Abbey*, London, 1991 (National Trust Guide).

Anon, *Franciscus Dracus Redivivus*, Amsterdam, 1596.

Anon, *Relación histórica del sitio puesto por los ingleses a ... La Coruña el 4 de mayo de 1589 y del triunfo alcanzado por los coruñeses en esta jornada, debido al valor de la famosa María Fernández de la Cámara y Pita*, La Coruña, 1850.

Anon, *Romancero general*, Madrid, 1602.

Anon, *Sir Francis Drake Revived. Who is or may be a Pattern to stirre up all Heroicke and active Spirits of these times*. London, 1653.

Anon, *Sir Francis Drake: An Exhibition to Commemorate Francis Drake's Voyage around the World, 1577–1580*, London (British Library), 1977.

Anon, *The World Encompassed by Sir Francis Drake, Being his next voyage to that to Nombre de Dios formerly imprinted*, London, 1628.

Anon, *The World Encompassed*, London, Hakluyt Society, 1854.

Anon, *Voyages and Travels of Sir Francis Drake into the West Indies and round the World*, London, 1784.

Bacon, E M, *The Boy's Drake*, London, 1911.

Barber, James, 'Sir Francis Drake's Investment in Plymouth Property', *Transactions of the Devon Association*, CXIII, 1981.

Barco Centenera, Martín del, *La Argentina*, Lisbon, 1602.

Barrow, John, *The Life, Voyages and Exploits of Admiral Sir Francis Drake, with numerous original letters*, London, 1843.

Best, George, *A True Discourse of the late voyages of discoverie, for the finding of a passage to Cathaya, by the Northwest, under the conduct of Martin Frobisher Generall*, London, 1578.

Bigges, Walter, *A Summarie and True Discourse of Sir Francis Drake's West Indian Voyage*, London, 1589. Republished, London, 1652.

Bigges, Walter, *Expeditio Francisci Draki Equitis*, Leiden, 1588.

Bonner-Smith, D, 'Drake's Prayer', MM, 36, 1950, pp. 86–87.

Bray, Mrs, *A Description of the Parts of Devonshire Bordering on the Tamar and Tavy*, 3 vols., 1836.

Breton, Nicholas, *A Discourse in commendation of the valiant as vertuous minded Gentleman, Maister Frauncis Drake, with a rejoysing of his happy adventures*, London, 1581.

Briggs, Katherine, M, *Dictionary of British Folk-tales*, 4 vols., London, 1970–71.

Bruce, John (ed.), *The Liber Famelicus of Sir James Whitelocke, a Judge of the Queen's Bench in the Reign of James I and Charles I*, London, Camden Society, 1858.

Burney, James, *A Chronological History of the Discoveries in the South Sea*, 5 vols., London, 1803–17.

Cairasco de Figueroa, Bartolomé, *Templo militante*, Valladolid, 1889.

Callender, Geoffrey, 'Drake and his Detractors', MM, 7, 1921, pp. 66–74, 98–105, 142–52.

Callender, Geoffrey, 'Fresh Light on Drake', MM, 9, 1923, pp. 16–28.

Camden, William, *Annales rerum Anglicarum, et Hibernicarum, Regnante Elizabeth, ad Annum Salutis MDLXXXIX*, London, 1615. English translation by Abraham Darcie, *Annales, the True and Royall History of the famous Empress Elizabeth*, London, 1625.

Castellanos, Juan de, *Discurso de el capitán Francisco Draque*, Madrid, 1921.

Chugg, Brian, *Devon*, London, 1980.

Corbett, Sir Julian S, *Drake and the Tudor Navy*, 2 vols., London, 1892.

Davenant, Sir William, *The History of Sir Francis Drake: Exprest by Instru-*

mentall and Vocall Musick, and by Art of Perspective in Scenes, &c. The First Part, London, 1659.

Dee, John, *General and Rare Memorials pertayning to the Perfect Arte of Navigation*, London, 1577.

Ditmas, E M R, *The Legend of Drake's Drum*, St Peter Port, Guernsey, 1973.

Donno, Elizabeth S, *An Elizabethan in 1582: The Diary of Richard Madox, Fellow of All Souls*, London, 1976 (Hakluyt Society Series II, No. 147).

Eliott-Drake, Lady Elizabeth F, *The Family and Heirs of Sir Francis Drake*, 2 vols., London, 1911.

Elton, G R, and others, *The Reformation 1520–1559*, Vol. 2 of *The New Cambridge Modern History*, 2nd ed., Cambridge, 1990.

Espinosa, Pedro de, *Flores de poetas ilustres*, Madrid, 1605; new edition, Seville, 1896.

Fernández Duro, Cesáreo, *La Armada Invencible*, 2 vols., Madrid, 1884–85.

Ferne, John, *Blason of Gentrie*, London, 1586.

FitzGeffrey, Charles, *Sir Francis Drake, His Honorable Life's Commendation, and his Tragical Death's Lamentation*, Oxford, 1596. New edition, entitled *The Life and Death of Sir Francis Drake*, Lee Priory, Kent, 1819.

Fuller, William, *The Holy State and the Profane State*, London, 1642.

Gandara, Felipe de la, *Armas y triunfos del Reino de Galicia*, n.p., 1672.

Gilbert, Sir Humphrey, *A Discourse of a Discoverie of a New Passage for China*, London, 1578.

Góngora, Luis de, *Poesías*, in Biblioteca de Autores Españoles, Vol. XXXII, Madrid, 1903, pp. 505–53.

Greepe, Thomas, *The true and perfecte Newes of the woorthy and valiaunt exploytes, performed and doone by that valiant Knight Syr Frauncis Drake: Not onely at Sancto Domingo, and Carthagena, but also nowe at Cales, and uppon the Coast of Spayne*, London, 1589. Facsimile edition by D W Waters, Hartford, 1955.

Guaman Poma de Ayala, Felipe, *Nueva crónica y buen gobierno*, 3 vols., Madrid, 1987.

Hakluyt, Richard, *The Principall Navigations, Voyages and Discoveries of the English Nation, made by Sea or over Land*, London, 1589. Second, enlarged, edition, 3 vols., London, 1598/99–1600; reedited in 12 vols., Glasgow, 1903–05 (Hakluyt Society Extra Series, Vols. 1–12).

Hanna, Warren L, *Lost Harbor: The Controversy over Drake's California Anchorage*, Berkeley and Los Angeles, 1979.

Henty, G, *Under Drake's Flag*, London, 1883.

Hercusanus Danus, Joannes, *Magnifico ac strenuo viro D. Francisco Draco Anglo Equiti aurato*, London, 1587.

Herrera y Tordesillas, Antonio, *Historia del mundo de tiempo del señor Rey don Felipe II el Prudente*, 3 vols., Valladolid, 1606–12.

Holland, Rupert Sargent, *Drake's Lad*, New York and London, 1929.

Howes, Edmund, *The Annales, or Generall Chronicle of England, begun first by maister John Stow and after him continued ... unto the end of this present yeere 1614*, London, 1615.

Hume, M A S, *The Year After the Armada*, London, 1896.

Hunt, Robert, *Popular Romances of the West of England*, second edition, London, 1871.

Jenner, G, 'A Spanish Account of Drake's Voyages', EHR, XVI, 1901, pp. 46–66.

Johnson, Dr Samuel, *Life of Drake*, in *The Gentleman's Magazine*, X, 1740, pp. 352, 389–96, 443–47, 509–15, 600–03; XI, 1741, pp. 38–44. Collected and published in J R Fleeman (ed.), *The Early Biographical Writings of Dr Johnson*, Farnborough, 1973, pp. 36–66.

Keeler, Mary F, *Sir Francis Drake's West Indian Voyage, 1585–86*, London, 1981 (Hakluyt Society Series II, Vol. 148).

Kraus, Hans P, *Francis Drake: A Pictorial Biography*, Amsterdam, 1970.

Laughton, John K, *State Papers relating to the Defeat of the Spanish Armada*, 2 vols., London, 1894 (Publications of the Navy Records Society, Vols. I–II).

Leng, Robert, *The True Discripcion of the last voiage of that worthy Captayne, Sir Frauncis Drake, knight, with his service done against the Spanyardes* (1587), in *Camden Miscellany*, V, London, 1864.

Leonardo de Argensola, Bartolomé, *Conquista de las Islas Malucas*, Madrid, 1609.

Lessa, William A, *Drake's Island of Thieves*, Honolulu, 1975.

Lewis, Michael, 'Fresh Light on San Juan de Ulúa', MM, 23, 1937, pp. 295–315.

Lewis, Michael, 'The Guns of the *Jesus of Lübeck*', MM, 22, 1936, pp. 324–45.

Lewis, Michael, *The Hawkins Dynasty: Three Generations of a Tudor Family*, London, 1969.

Lockhart, James, *Spanish Peru 1532–1560. A Colonial Society*, Madison, 1974.

Lorenzo Sanz, Eufemio, *Comercio de España con América en la época de Felipe II*, 2 vols., Valladolid, 1979–80.

Lynch, John, *Spain under the Habsburgs*, 2nd ed., 2 vols., Oxford, 1981 (1st ed., 1964).

335

M, D F R de, *Respuesta y desengaño contra las falsedades publicadas e impresas en España en bituperio de la Armada Inglesa*, London, 1589.

Manera Reguera, Enrique, *El buque en la Armada Española*, Madrid (?), 1981.

Martin, Colin, and Geoffrey Parker, *The Spanish Armada*, London, 1988.

Martínez Salazar, A, *El cerco de La Coruña en 1589 y Mayor Fernández Pita. Apuntes y documentos*, La Coruña, 1889.

Martínez Salazar, A, *La epopeya de Galicia. Las mujeres coruñesas en el sitio de 1589*, La Coruña, 1887.

Maynarde, Thomas, *Sir Francis Drake his Voyage, 1595, by Thomas Maynarde*, London, Hakluyt Society, 1849.

Milner-White, E, and G W Briggs (ed.), *Daily Prayer*, Oxford, 1941.

Miramontes Zuazola, Juan de, *Armas antárcticas. Hechos de los famosos capitanes españoles que se hallaron en la conquista del Perú*, Biblioteca Nacional, Madrid MS M.151.

Murdin, W (ed.), *A Collection of State Papers ... left by William Cecill, Lord Burghley*, London, 1759.

Nichols, Philip, *Sir Francis Drake Revived*, London, 1626.

Norman, Robert, *The newe Attractive, containing a short discourse of the Magnes or Lodestone*, London, 1581. Facsimile edition, Amsterdam and Norwood, NJ, 1974.

Nuttall, Zelia, *New Light on Drake: A Collection of Documents relating to his Voyage of Circumnavigation, 1577–1580*, London, 1914 (Hakluyt Society Series II, Vol. XXXIV).

Olesa Muñido, Francisco-Felipe, *La organización naval de los estados mediterráneos y en especial de España durante los siglos XVI y XVII*, 2 vols., Madrid, 1968.

Oppenheim, M (ed.), *The Naval Tracts of Sir William Monson*, 5 vols., London, 1902–1914 (Publications of the Navy Records Society, Vols. 22, 23, 43, 45, 49).

Oviedo y Herrera, Luis Antonio de, *La vida de Santa Rosa de Santa María, natural de Lima y patrona del Perú*, Madrid, 1717.

Palgrave, Francis Turner, *The Golden Treasury*, fourth edition, Oxford, 1940.

Peckham, Sir George, *A True Report of the Late Discoveries of Newfoundland, by Sir Humphrey Gilbert*, London, 1583.

Phillips, Carla Rahn, *Six Galleons for the King of Spain: Imperial Defense in the Early Seventeenth Century*, Baltimore and London, 1986.

Purchas, Samuel, *Purchas his Pilgrimes*, 4 vols., London, 1625. Reedited in 20 vols., Glasgow, 1903–07 (Hakluyt Society Extra Series, Vols. 14–33).

Ray, Arthur, *Drake dans la poésie espagnole*, Paris, 1906.

Robarts, Henry, *A most friendly farewell, Given by a wellwiller to the right worshipful Sir Francis Drake, Knight*, London, 1585.

Robarts, Henry, *The Trumpet of Fame, or Sir Francis Drakes and Sir John Hawkins Farewell*, London, 1595. New edition, Lee Priory, Kent, 1818.

Robinson, Geoffrey, 'A forgotten life of Sir Francis Drake', MM, 7, 1921, pp. 10–18.

Rodger, N A M, *The Armada in the Public Records*, London, 1988.

Rodríguez Solis, E, *¡Que viene el Draque!*, San Juan de Puerto Rico, 1898.

Rumeu de Armas, A, *Piraterías y ataques navales contra las Islas Canarias*, 3 vols., Madrid, 1948.

Senior, W, 'Drake at the Suit of John Doughty', MM, 7, 1921, pp. 291–97.

Sottas, Jules, 'Guillaume Le Testu and his work', MM, 2, 1912, pp. 65–75.

Southey, Robert, *Lives of the British Admirals*, 5 vols., London, 1833–40.

Stables, Gordon, *Old England on the Sea: the Story of Admiral Drake*, London [1900?].

Suárez de Peralta, Juan, *Tratado del descubrimiento de las Indias* (1589), ed. F. Gómez de Orozco, Mexico City, 1949.

Sugden, John, 'Edmund Drake of Tavistock', MM, 59, 1973, p. 436.

Sugden, John, *Sir Francis Drake*, London, 1990.

Taylor, E G R, *The Haven-finding Art*, London, 1956.

Taylor, E G R, 'Master John Dee, Drake and the Straits of Anian', MM, 15, 1929, pp. 125–30.

Taylor, E G R, 'More Light on Drake', MM, 16, 1930, pp. 134–51.

Taylor, E G R (ed.), *The Original Writings and Correspondence of the two Richard Hakluyts*, 2 vols., London, 1935 (Hakluyt Society Series II, Nos. LXXVI, LXXVIII).

Taylor, E G R (ed.), *The Troublesome Voyage of Captain Edward Fenton*, Cambridge, 1959 (Hakluyt Society Series II, No. CXIII).

Tenison, E M, *Elizabethan England*, 13 vols., Leamington Spa, 1933–1960.

Thomson, George M T, *Sir Francis Drake*, London, 1972.

Thrower, Norman J W, *Sir Francis Drake and the Famous Voyage, 1577–1580*, Berkeley and Los Angeles, 1984.

Ticknor, George, *History of Spanish Literature*, 3 vols., New York, 1849.

Unwin, Rayner, *The Defeat of John Hawkins: A Biography of his Third Slaving Voyage*, London, 1960.

Vega Carpio, Lope Felix de, *La Dragontea*, Valencia, 1598. New edition, with related documents, 2 vols., Madrid, 1935.

Wernham, R B, 'Queen Elizabeth and the Portugal Expedition of 1589', EHR, LXVI, 1951, pp. 1–26, 194–218.

Wernham, R B, *The Expedition of Sir John Norris and Sir Francis Drake to*

Spain and Portugal, London, 1988 (Publications of the Navy Records Society, Vol. 127).

Williams, Paul, 'The Ownership of Drake's *Golden Hind*', MM, 67, 1981, pp. 185–86.

Williamson, James A, *The Age of Drake*, London, 1938.

Williamson, James A (ed.), *The Observations of Sir Richard Hawkins*, London, 1933.

Wright, Irene A, *Documents concerning English Voyages to the Spanish Main 1569–1580*, London, 1932 (Hakluyt Society Series II, Vol. LXXI).

Wright, Irene A, *Further English Voyages to Spanish America 1583–1594*, London, 1951 (Hakluyt Society Series II, Vol. XCIX).

Wright, Irene A, *Spanish Documents concerning English Voyages to the Caribbean 1527–1568*, London, 1929 (Hakluyt Society Series II, Vol. LXII).

Youings, Joyce, 'Drake, Grenville and Buckland Abbey', *Transactions of the Devon Association*, CXII, 1981.

INDEX

Philip II, King of Spain 11 *et passim*
Philip, Archduke, son of Emperor
    Maximilian I 8
Philippines 107, 119
Phillips, Miles 26, 29
Phoenix, ship 251, 257
Pike, Robert 57
pilchard tax 227
pinnaces 21, 52–3, 55, 59, 61–2, 68–
    9, 106–7, 136, 157, 164, 169, 200,
    235, 251
Pinos Islands 46
Pita, María 207, 265
Plate, River 7, 89
Platt, Captain 143, 150, 255
Plymouth 3, 6, 11–12, 30, 64, 72,
    123–5, 131, 135, 163–4, 176, 183–
    4, 199, 201, 219–22, 224, 226–7,
    256, 301
Plymouth Hoe 6, 132, 227
Polo, Diego 38
Polo, Marco 119
Ponce de León, Diego 21
Poor John 139
Poore, Captain 245, 253
Port Pheasant 42–3, 45–6
Port Plenty 47
Porto Belo 36, 41, 42, 251–2, 256,
    296
Porto Praia 146
Porto Santo 218–19, 221
Portsmouth 159
Powell, Edward 137, 141, 148, 150,
    159
prayer, Drake's 301–2
Primrose, ship 136, 140, 147, 148,
    150, 159
privateering 30, 224–5, 251
Prohenza, Sebastián de 311
Protestantism 8–12, 17, 30, 260–61,
    264–5, 269–71
Prudence, ship 225
Puente de Burgo 207–8, 220
Puerto Cabello 295
Puerto de Santa María 168
Puerto Rico 147, 231, 241, 243–7
Puerto San Julián 7, 81, 91
Pugh, Captain 212–13
Purchas, Samuel 284, 305

quadrant 15–16
Quintero 90

Rafael, Jaime 311
Rainbow, ship 168
Raleigh, Walter 6, 133, 224–5, 229–
    30, 232, 235, 299
Rance, James 46–7, 51–2
Rathlin Island 66
Realejo 108–9
recuas 35, 37, 43, 54–8, 60, 227, 258
Red Dragon, ship 225
Reformation 8–10
relics of Drake 294–5
Revenge, ship 185–92, 202, 208, 217
Ría de Vigo 29, 139–40, 162, 166,
    211, 218–19
rigging of ships 20
Río de la Hacha 4, 21–3, 42, 136, 152,
    248–50, 270
Riohacha: see Río de la Hacha
Roanoke 133, 159, 162
Robarts, Henry 275, 281–2
Rodríguez, Custodio 99
Roebuck, ship 186
Royal Oak, ship 299
Rufford, Francis, later Earl of
    Bedford, godfather to Francis
    Drake 5
Ruiz de Ceco, Lope 41
Rush, Captain 216

Sackville, Captain 202, 208
Sagres 166, 171–4
Sagres, observatory 14
sail plans of ships 20
St Bartholomew's Eve, massacre of 59
St Budeaux Church 33
St Christopher 147
St James Islands 118
St Jean de Luz 139, 197
St Nicholas Island 132, 227
St Verian 89
St Vincent, Cape 14, 166–7, 171–4,
    211
Saltash 33, 176
Salvatierra, shipowner 41
Sampford Spiney 131
Sampson, Captain 204–5
San Agustín 157–9
San Antonio, Cape 157
San Antonio, fort 204
San Bernardo Islands 52
San Felipe, battery 167–8
San Felipe, ship 189
San Francisco Bay 117